A SOURCEBOOK OF AFRICAN-AMERICAN PERFORMANCE

A Sourcebook on African-American Performance: Plays, People, Movements is the first volume to consider African-American performance between and beyond the Black Arts Movement of the 1960s and the New Black Renaissance of the 1990s.

The Sourcebook consists of writings previously published in *The Drama Review* (*TDR*) as well as newly commissioned pieces by notable scholars, writers and performers including Annemarie Bean, Ed Bullins, Barbara Lewis, John O'Neal, Glenda Dicker/sun, James V. Hatch, Warren Burdine, Jr, and Eugene Nesmith. Included are articles, essays, manifestos and interviews on

- theatre on the professional, revolutionary and college stages
- concert dance
- community activism
- step shows
- performance art previously published in *TDR*.

The volume also includes the plays *Sally's Rape* by Robbie McCauley and *The America Play* by Suzan-Lori Parks, and comes complete with an Introduction by Annemarie Bean.

Annemarie Bean is an assistant professor of theatre at Williams College, Williamstown, Massachusetts. She was managing editor of *The Drama Review* for three years, and is the co-editor, with James V. Hatch and Brooks McNamara, of *Inside the Minstrel Mask: Readings in Nineteenth-Century Blackface Minstrelsy* (Wesleyan University Press/University Press of New England, 1996), winner of the 1997 Errol Hill Award given by the American Society for Theatre Research for outstanding scholarship in African-American theatre studies. Her current project is a study of gender impersonation by white and African-American nineteenth-century minstrels.

Worlds of Performance
General Editor: Richard Schechner

WORLDS OF PERFORMANCE

What is a "performance"? Where does it take place? Who are the participants? Not so long ago these were settled questions, but today such orthodox answers are unsatisfactory, misleading, and limiting "Performance" as a theoretical category and as a practice has expanded explosively. It now comprises a panoply of genres ranging from play, to popular entertainments, to theatre, dance, and music, to secular and religious rituals, to "performance in everyday life", to intercultural experiments, and more.

For nearly forty years, *The Drama Review* (*TDR*), the journal of performance studies, has been at the cutting edge of exploring these questions. The Worlds of Performance Series is designed to mine the extraordinary riches and diversity of TDR's decades of excellence, bringing back into print important essays, interviews, artists' notes, and photographs. New materials and introductions bring the volumes up to date. Each World of Performance book is a complete anthology, arranged around a specific theme or topic. Each World of Performance book is an indispensable resource for the scholar, a textbook for the student, and an exciting eye-opener for the general reader.

Richard Schechner
Editor, *TDR*
Series Editor

Other titles in the series:

Acting (Re)Considered edited by Phillip B. Zarrilli
Happenings and other Acts edited by Mariellen R. Sandford
A Sourcebook of Feminist Theatre and Performance: On and Beyond the stage edited by Carol Martin
The Grotowski Sourcebook edited by Richard Schechner and Lisa Wolford

A SOURCEBOOK OF AFRICAN-AMERICAN PERFORMANCE

Plays, People, Movements

Edited by Annemarie Bean

London and New York

First published 1999 by Routledge
11 New Fetter Lane, London EC4P 4EE

Simultaneously published in the USA and Canada
by Routledge
29 West 35th Street, New York, NY 10001

Routledge is an imprint of the Taylor and Francis Group

Typeset in Times by Solidus (Bristol) Limited
Printed and bound in Great Britain by Biddles Ltd, Guildford and King's Lynn

British Library Cataloguing in Publication Data
A catalogue record for this book is available from the British Library

Library of Congress Cataloguing in Publication Data
A catalogue record for this book has been requested

ISBN 0-415-18234-4 (hbk)
ISBN 0-415-18235-2 (pbk)

To
the memories of
dreams deferred

Edward Elton Bean
(1938–1972)

Karl Friedrich Bean
(1966–1993)

CONTENTS

ILLUSTRATIONS

Plates

Figures

ACKNOWLEDGMENTS

Some of the material in this volume was previously published in *The Drama Review* (*TDR*). From 1956 to 1959 this was the *Carleton Drama Review*; then it became the *Tulane Drama Review*; since 1967 it has been simply *The Drama Review*. MIT Press took over publication in 1980. The following articles are used by permission of MIT Press Journals:

Dent, Tom, and Jerry W. Ward, Jr. "After the Free Southern Theater: A Dialog." *TDR* 31, 3 [T115] (1987): 120–25.

Drukman, Steven. "Suzan-Lori Parks and Liz Diamond: Doo-a-diddly-dit-dit." *TDR* 39, 3 [T147] (1995): 56–75.

Fine, Elizabeth C. "Stepping, Saluting, Cracking, and Freaking: The Cultural Politics of African-American Step Shows." *TDR* 35, 2 [T130] (1991) 39–59.

Hammer, Kate. "John O'Neal, Actor and Activist." *TDR* 36, 4 [T136] (1992): 12–27.

Martin, Carol. "Anna Deavere Smith: The Word Becomes You." *TDR* 37, 4 [T140] (1993): 45–62.

Patraka, Vicki. "Robbie McCauley: Obsessing in Public." *TDR* 37, 2 [T138] (1993): 25–55.

Schechner, Richard. "Anna Deavere Smith: Acting as Incorporation." *TDR* 37, 4 [T140] (1993): 63–4.

Some of the material in this volume has been previously published in publications other than *The Drama Review* (*TDR*).

Sally's Rape by Robbie McCauley, copyright 1994 by Robbie McCauley. From *Moon Marked & Touched by Sun: Plays by African-American Women*, edited by Sydné Mahone and published by Theatre Communications Group, 1994. Used by permission of Robbie McCauley.

The America Play by Suzan-Lori Parks, copyright 1992, 1994 by Suzan-Lori Parks. From *The America Play and Other Works*, published by Theatre Communications Group, 1995. Used by permission of Theatre Communications Group.

In the case of other pieces published here that previously appeared in the *Tulane Drama Review* or *The Drama Review*, copyright belongs to *TDR* and thus to the publishers of this volume.

PREFACE

The germination of this project possibly began on a late summer day in 1984 when I was an undergraduate student of Robert O'Meally in his Introduction to African-American Studies class. On that particular day, Professor O'Meally entered the classroom, strode over to the open-air window looking down on the illogically placed football field in the middle of the Wesleyan University campus, and placed a tape recorder on the sill. Music began without an introduction, but I soon realized we were learning this lesson by listening to the music of Bessie Smith. We the students sat and waited for interruption, for a critical application by the professor of Smith's fluid yet strained music to our future course of study. There was none. As I remember it, or at least like to tell the story, Professor O'Meally began, administered, and completed that day's lesson in the study of African-American literary studies by pressing a play button; the rest – connections between Smith's music and the novels we were reading, confusion about the value of music in relation to literature, bliss because we were part of the beautiful experience of listening to art – was up to us.

From Robert O'Meally's teaching I realized one could not and should not consider the works of African-American literature without also immersing oneself in the studies of music, art, and performance. From that point in the beginning of a road (to borrow Glenda Dicker/sun's evocation in her introduction to Part Three of this volume, it was a road for which I had no track), the project of this book has emerged as a melding of my multifaceted studies in African-American performance. Many have cleared the brush ahead. As a mentor, James V. Hatch has served as a teacher with no boundaries to his generosity; I have also benefited greatly from the tutelage of Manthia Diawara and Ngugi wa Thiong'o, as well as the encouragement of the missed James Amankulor. Harry Elam, Jr has always questioned and strengthened my work in African-American performance from our first introduction. In the Department of Performance Studies at New York University, I have obtained the basis for critically thinking about all types of performance. I thank Brooks McNamara, Peggy Phelan, May Joseph, José Esteban Muñoz, Barbara Kirshenblatt-Gimblett, and Fred Moten for their teaching in this regard. As an editor, my indebtedness is to my tenure as managing editor of *TDR*, and to my teacher of the craft, Mariellen R. Sandford, associate editor. Richard Schechner, the editor of the Worlds of Performance series and *The Drama Review* (*TDR*), and all-around bon vivant, has always, consistently, and even happily supported this project from the idea, a luxury for any young editor. I would also like to acknowledge the continued support of Talia Rodgers of Routledge, a thoughtful and thorough editor, her assistants, Jason Arthur and Sophie Powell, and desk editor, Sarah Brown.

In relation to this specific project, the development of the new material in the sourcebook has led to my working with extraordinary participants in African-American performance and performance studies: Ed Bullins, John O'Neal, Glenda Dicker/sun, Eugene Nesmith, Barbara Lewis, Warren B. Burdine, Jr, and James V. Hatch. In addition, Robbie McCauley and Suzan-Lori Parks lent both their permission to reprint their plays as well as their enthusiasm for the project, and I thank them for their accessibility. I would also like to acknowledge the work of the photographers included in this volume, as well as the archives of the Hatch–Billops Collection, without which this book would be rather dull illustratively.

From the professional to the personal, I have had many nurturers during the assembling of the sourcebook. My parents, Mac and Leni McCollor, have provided nothing less than a clean, well-lighted space and good lentil soup for me to work and write; my extended family in Maine has also provided much needed encouragement. My far-flung family – Maria Lúcia Lepecki, César Fernandes, Witold Lepecki, and Regina Lepecki – have given sympathetic long-distance inquiries and support. My dear friends especially have allowed me their criticism and support in equal, balanced portions. The word "acknowledgment" cannot approach my gratitude to these people, or to the person for whom I most fail for words in describing his contribution to this project and to my life, André Torres Lepecki, not the least of whom is our daughter, Elsa Lepecki Bean.

Annemarie Bean

INTRODUCTION

Performing Beyond Pre-formations and Between Movements: Thirty Years of African-American Performance

Annemarie Bean

If art is the harbinger of future possibilities, what does the future of Black America portend?

Larry Neal (1968)

In the summer of 1968, Larry Neal put forth the above challenge at the end of his landmark essay "The Black Arts Movement", published originally in *The Drama Review* (*TDR* 12, 4 [T40]) under the guest editorship of Ed Bullins, and reprinted in this volume. Neal called for the emergence of a "black aesthetic" fueled by writers "confront[ing] the contradictions arising out of the Black man's experience in the racist West", while "re-evaluating western aesthetics, the traditional role of the writer, and the social function of art".[1] *A Sourcebook on African-American Performance: Plays, People, Movements* is an attempt to ask Neal's question again thirty years later with a range of examples in African-American performance from the 1960s to the 1990s by including critical essays, previously published in *TDR*, on theatre on the professional stage, the revolutionary stage and the college stage; concert dance; community activism; step shows; and performance art. These previously published texts have been supplemented by newly commissioned essays by Ed Bullins, Barbara Lewis, Thomas DeFrantz, John O'Neal, Glenda Dicker/sun, James V. Hatch, Warren B. Burdine, Jr, and Eugene Nesmith. In addition, African-American performance is both presented, through the inclusion of the plays *Sally's Rape* by Robbie McCauley and *The America Play* by Suzan-Lori Parks, and critiqued.

African-American performance has had to cope with its marginalization within the hegemonic definitions of "culture" and "performance" throughout US history. One of the predicaments or consequences of this marginalization has been the portrayal of clusters of African-American culture as fragmentary, isolated "events" usually categorized under the rubric of "renaissance". Another predicament is the pre-formation of African-American subjectivity within the context of racism (lawful or otherwise), most often manifested in popular culture from minstrelsy to television situation-comedies. This book embraces the vision that African-American performance has a history based in continuum, not renaissances. Through the interweaving of plays, texts, interviews, and contemporary reevaluations of the original *TDR* material that compose this book, I would like to issue a new challenge in 1998 for those looking at the "harbinger" performances (to borrow Neal's metaphor) that have been generated in the last thirty years by African-Americans: let us move beyond and between the limited vision with which African-American performance has been considered thus far.

An understanding of the performing African-American body must depart from the historical insight that this body is bound by its portrayal in white culture as inherently entertaining in its subjection. As Saidiya V. Hartman points out, "torture and torment both generated enjoyment" in the two arenas in which African-Americans were primarily, though not exclusively, presented and re-presented as public spectacle in the nineteenth-century: as the actual black body in pain on the auction block and the re-presentation of that black body on the popular stage by white performers.[2] Therefore, our American image of the performing African-American has been *pre-formed* through certain expectations ingrained through a history of slavery and oppression, as well as of mimetic containment.

However, the performance history of African-Americans has never been

1.   limited to pre-formation, and
2.   bound by temporary periods of rebirth.

The limits of pre-formation are such that we allow ourselves to see *only* what we have learned, through acculturation, to expect in the performances by African-Americans. Renaissances or rebirthings imply that performance has been figuratively deadened or squelched, with the only hope being a new, nascent stage of growth. In 1926, W.E.B. Du Bois in his magazine *The Crisis* warned that "until art of the black folk compels recognition they will not be rated as human".[3] We can then move forward in time to Larry Neal's call in 1968 for a "cultural revolution in art and ideas".[4] These writers about and of art were integral cultural workers with long careers; however, their work has been contained in American cultural history as extraordinary products of designated African-American "renaissances", Du Bois as part of the Harlem Renaissance and Neal, the Black Arts movement. Obviously and in direct contrast to the limiting notion of "renaissances", there is as long a history of performance by African-Americans as there has been an African diasporic presence in America. One of the first to recognize this continuum was Du Bois himself, who began the chapters of *The Souls of Black Folk* (1903) with lyrics and music popular in the African-American community. Du Bois identified the sounds of the sorrow songs in particular as a continuing presence in the African-American experience, whether they were predated by African chants or contributors to what would later become the blues. Rather than perpetuate a belief in preconceived portrayals or a fragmentary existence by and about African-Americans, Du Bois identifies a continuum in performance by his use of the sorrow songs, "the sifting of centuries".[5]

As part of a whole realm of cultural experience, Du Bois' acknowledgment of a continuum through his discussion of the sorrow songs has a contemporary example in *The America Play* by Suzan-Lori Parks, reprinted here. The characters of Lucy and Brazil begin Act Two "in a great hole. In the middle of nowhere. The hole is an exact replica of The Great Hole of History".[6] In this hole, they dig for their husband and father, the Foundling Father. Hampered by the incomplete but encouraged by potential, Lucy and Brazil dislodge that which has been dug before – the hole – and create their own "inheritance of sorts".[7] It is this creation of a whole from a hole that reflects Parks' awareness of a continuum of history and performance in which African-Americans have continually and constantly noted what has gone on before by recognizing influences *and* by creating their own formulations of art. Larry Neal's above-stated question, "If art is the harbinger of future possibilities, what does the future of Black America portend?", can be approached by considering the performances of recognition and reformulation included in this sourcebook.

I have organized the sourcebook in four parts, each of which is introduced by the first essay of the section. Part One – Theatrical In(ter)ventions of the Black Arts Movement – begins with an assessment by Ed Bullins of black theatre as a "cultural paradigm". Bullins speaks of the "truths" of "this sometimes near-mysterious phenomenon" of black theatre, revolutionary in its manifestations during the Black Arts movement as can be seen in the reprinted work of Bullins, Amiri Baraka, Sonia Sanchez, and Larry Neal as well as in the recent words of the playwright August Wilson, whom Bullins states has "brought the entire Black Theatre into a pantheon of global respect".

Part One presents some of the work of the Black Arts movement, but it is by no means all-encompassing. The inclusion of essays on Barbara Ann Teer and the National Black Theatre by Barbara Lewis, and the Black Arts dance movement by Thomas DeFrantz, allow expansion of the male-dominated and theatre-dominated assessment of the Black Arts movement put forth in the 1968 *TDR* issue, but all the essays suffer from a New York-centered bias. Concurrently in time with the Black Arts movement, Part Two – Free Southern Theater and Community Activism – follows the course of the Free Southern Theater as carefully documented by *TDR* from 1965 through the words of John O'Neal in his introduction to this section. O'Neal titles his essay, "A Road Through the Wilderness", the wilderness being one of a struggle to maintain and sustain the artistic struggle for African-American liberation. O'Neal identifies the critical discourse on the Black Arts movement as being northern- and urban-oriented, often discounting the "rural south [as] the cauldron in which we were forged as a people".

Part Three – Moving Beyond the Center – looks at performance outside the boundaries of what is usually considered as revolutionary performance and/or political theatre. As Glenda Dicker/sun addresses through her own performance history, the work presented in this section complicates previous perceptions of African-American performance because they "reveal a shift, a tension, an uneasy sea change as black performance simultaneously outgrows and reclaims its black folk roots". In black college drama before Black Arts movement, step shows, gospel musicals, and performance art, Part Three seeks to document some examples of African-American performance staged before (in the case of Hatch's essay on theatre in historically black colleges) and beside the revolutionary theatre of the Black Arts movement and the Free Southern Theater.

Part Four – Contemporary Challenges to Representations: African-American Women Playwrights – introduces, to borrow Eugene Nesmith's introduction title, "Four Bad Sisters". The astounding and provocative work of four playwrights – Adrienne Kennedy, Robbie McCauley, Anna Deavere Smith, and Suzan-Lori Parks – is credited by Nesmith as "doing and speaking the unspeakable". A read through the words (through essays and interviews) and work (by the plays of McCauley and Parks) can leave one aware of how good the "badness" of these playwrights is. They are, in the end, the voices and performers who will lead the continuum of African-American performance into the twenty-first century. It is notable that all these playwrights consider freely playing with the historical as integral to their work – personal histories, local history, and American history.

As I stated at the beginning of this general introduction, African-American performance continually interprets the past in order to fill the holes of historical and cultural representations and history; to credit it with anything less is a great disservice. Indeed, in considering African-American performers and performances as pre-form(ulat)ed or only part of temporary movements such as the Harlem Renaissance or the Black Arts Movement, there has been the rather distressing result of ignorance, in the academy and the public sphere, on what has happened *beyond* the familiar and *in between* the movements. By focusing this sourcebook on the thirty years including and between the Black Arts Movement and the new Black Renaissance of the 1990s, I hope to offer a representative history of the rich and polyvalent performances presented by African-Americans during this period.

NOTES

1.   Bean 1998: 55.
2.   Hartman 1997: 26.
3.   Paschal 1971: 96.

4. Bean 1998: 55.
5. Du Bois 1903: 380.
6. Bean 1998: 307.
7. Bean 1998: 332.

BIBLIOGRAPHY

Bean, Annemarie, ed., *A Sourcebook of African-American Performance: Plays, People, Movements*, London, Routledge, 1998.

Du Bois, W.E.B., 'The Souls of Black Folk', in *Three Negro Classics*, New York, Avon Books, 1965 [1903].

Hartman, Saidiya V., *Scenes of Subjection: Terror, Slavery, and Self-Making in Nineteenth-Century America*, New York, Oxford University Press, 1997.

Paschal, Andrew, ed., *W.E.B. Du Bois: A Reader*, New York, Collier Books, 1971.

Part I:
Theatrical In(ter)ventions of the Black Arts Movement

BLACK THEATRE 1998: A THIRTY-YEAR LOOK AT BLACK ARTS THEATRE (1998)

Ed Bullins

It is approaching the thirtieth anniversary of the special Black Theatre edition of *The Drama Review* (*TDR* T40) that I edited in 1968. At the time there was skepticism throughout the United States and the world as to whether an adequate case could be made for such a thing as Black Theatre. Nonetheless, a case was made, and curiosity reigned as to the legitimacy of this emerging "cultural paradigm".

In early August 1997, I attended the National Black Theatre Festival and International Black Theatre Colloquium in Winston-Salem, North Carolina. The theme of this fifth biennial Black Theatre Festival was "An International Celebration and Reunion of Spirit". Founder, executive and artistic director of the NBTF, Larry Leon Hamlin, pointed out that "global theatre practitioners and scholars from South Africa, Brazil, Cuba, Nigeria, Jamaica, Republic of Benin, England, Ghana, Canada and other parts of the world come together" here. The National Black Theatre Festival showcased the new World Black Theatre Movement. One of the prominent features of the festival was the International Colloquia/Workshop, organized by Dr Olasope O. Oyelaran of the International Program at Winston-Salem State University. This year's theme for the colloquia was 'The Black Family on Stage', which looked at how Black theatres around the world deal with family issues. In addition, there were ninety performances by more than twenty-three of the world's Black theatre companies in a six-day period. I was able to attend the Crossroads Theatre Company production of August Wilson's *Jitney*, directed by Walter Dallas; Black Goat Entertainment and Enlightenment's *Ghost Café*, featuring Andre De Shields; Woodie King's National Black Touring Circuit's *Do Lord Remember Me*, by James de Jongh, directed by Regge Life; Jomandi Productions' *Hip II: Birth of the Boom*, by Thomas W. Jones II, directed by Marsha A. Jackson; curator Idris Ackamoor's *New Performance in Black Theatre* series, featuring a stand-in reading/performance for ailing Sekou Sundiata by Amiri Baraka with Craig

Harris; and a standing-room-only visit to a reading of a play by Samuel Hay, *Crack Cream an' Brown Sugar,* at the Festival's 'Readers Theatre' under the direction of Garland Thompson.

To say that Black Theatre has come a long way in the past thirty years is to admit the obvious. In examining some of the material of the original *TDR* and comparing it to a quick survey of today's not so hidden, but actually obscured African-American aesthetic and cultural institution, Black Theatre, some truths about this sometimes near-mysterious phenomenon may be revealed. *Clara's Ole Man*, written by me in 1965, was almost immediately produced. I had written *How Do You Do* and *The Rally; or, Dialect Determinism* several months before. The two plays were scheduled to be produced at The Firehouse Repertory Theater in San Francisco, but it was feared that the evening was too short. A grotesque little skit concerning an absurdist minstrel show was proposed to complete the program. Fearful that this could occur, I set to work and completed *Clara's Ole Man*. I felt that *Clara* gave the bill balance, and my co-producers agreed, so my three plays premiered the same night that Watts first blew up from Black rage, as has been documented in the *TDR* T40 issue.

I imagine that a similar black drama could be produced now for the first time on an American stage. But I have my doubts that it could happen quietly. Why? The times are different. Many factors confront *Clara*'s "degree of honesty" and, yes, "rawness" in this era – political correctness, any one of a number of *isms*, and so on. It seems the Free Speech Movement did have good reason to make speeches. Formally, and pathetically, the new myths suggest that the 1960s impulses and urges toward *freedom* have been sublimated to marketable and exploitable strategies disguised as *critical thinking*, watered down in academic and corporate America.

Plays like Baraka's *Home on the Range* and *Police* were nearly unique in American Theatre when they appeared in the late 1960s. The plays have been given the argot of "agitprop" (agitational propaganda), but this seems oxymoronic in theory; the elements of these creations stem from a modern bohemian sensibility and milieu fused with black/white inner-city conflict, and having little to tie it to early twentieth-century anarchism or nihilism which the term "agitprop" stems from. *Home on the Range*, a concise play of the black/white apocalypse foretold, uses avant-garde techniques of symbolic-sounding language and Albert Ayler improvisational jazz, in a form borrowed from Harlem playwright Ben Caldwell's (brief scenario) dramaturgy. *Police* is a minimyth of inhuman (bestial) black/white police versus victimized black street people, who cause the white cops to turn on the black cop and cannibalize him. Both plays exist very much through the nativistic political and cultural revolutionary ideology of the time. Sonia Sanchez' play *The Bronx Is Next* is more traditional in structure but just as extremely radical in Black Revolutionary sentiments and calls to action.

"The Black Arts Movement" essay, by Lawrence P. (Larry) Neal, was commissioned by me as editor of the special Black Theatre issue of *TDR*. Neal had written a short piece for the initial issue of *Black Theatre Magazine*, published by the New Lafayette Theatre of Harlem. Shortly thereafter, I thought Larry would be ideal to write an essay which turned out to be "The Black Arts Movement". It has proven to be the single most significant piece in the edition, and on its subject, arguably, of the period. Having been reprinted numerous times, usually with no acknowledgement of original source, it has helped give a vocabulary and intellectual structure to an important area of African-American aesthetic ideological studies.

Barbara Lewis' essay "Ritual Reformulations: Barbara Ann Teer and the National Black Theatre of Harlem" is a Black Theatre historical "labor of love" based upon the writer's subjective passion and more objective research. Ms Lewis begins, "In 1972, four years after she relocated to Harlem where she established her ritual-based company, Barbara Ann Teer, founder of the National Black Theatre, looked around and saw death and life vying for supremacy in the faces and lives of the people around her. The community where she had chosen to settle and perform her rituals of liberation . . . ". Lewis does not fail to cite the significance of Robert Macbeth as a visionary pioneer of the 1960s who introduced Barbara Ann Teer to the Black Ritual Theatre form. Yes, the great Barbara Ann Teer has devoted the past twenty-five some years to Black Ritual Theatre, and in so doing, has honored the popularizer of this cultural paradigm, Robert Macbeth, founder/director of the New Lafayette Theatre of Harlem (1967–73). Macbeth perfected the "black ritual form" through improvisational and black aesthetic cultural performance practices in workshops with his company for three years and then produced *A Ritual to Bind Together and Strengthen Black People So That They Can Survive the Long Struggle to Come* (1969), *To Raise the Dead and Foretell the Future* (1970), *The Devil Catchers* (1970), *The Psychic Pretenders* (1971), and *A Black Time for Black Folk* (lost). It is fair to say that the National Black Theatre took off with Black Ritual Theatre where the New Lafayette Theatre retired. Barbara Ann Teer and her NBT are pioneers and supremely accomplished and successful in their longevity.

Today is the time of August Wilson. His voice will carry the American Black Theatre Movement into the twenty-first century. Not only are his plays some of the finer theatrical works of this century, his voice gives a "legitimate" discourse to theatre change. August Wilson's art and identity have become the mainstream, and have brought the entire Black Theatre into a pantheon of global respect. So it is fitting that this piece end with his words, taken from an interview with *Neworld Renaissance: A Multicultural Magazine of the Arts* (Spring 1997):

Somehow people got into their minds . . . that I was talking about a Black theater that would exclude whites. That's not what I said. [. . .] I've been saying we've been fighting to be included. So I'm not talking about theater for Blacks only. [. . .] There's a difference in "for Blacks" and "for Blacks only". You see so that American theater is for whites. It doesn't say "for whites only". It just says "for whites". And I think we should have a theater that says "for Blacks". [. . .] I am an inclusionist. I'm fighting to be included. I don't want to be separate. The American theater is separate. It is separate from the Black community. [. . .] So that out of these 66 white theaters they're separate from Crossroads Theater. . . .

I was fired in the kiln of Black nationalism and the Black Power movement when Blacks were seeking ways to alter their relationship to the society, or to acquire some power. [. . .] In 1984, in my first interview I ever did with the *New York Times* I said I am a Black nationalist so why anything should surprise people. [. . .] I gave a speech at Carnegie Man and Ideas Lecture Series in 1987, I talked about cultural imperialism which I mentioned briefly [. . .] the awareness that there is a cultural war going on and has been since Blacks first came over here. And they said, you guys don't have no culture, no language, no gods, you don't have nothing of any value. Of course people fought hard to affirm their sense of self and their manners and values.

There are literally hundreds of playwrights, let's say there's five hundred Black playwrights. And there's one Black theater of the 66 [members of the] League of Resident Theaters and those are theaters that have certain levels of production values, that have certain financial obligations that they're going to make them pay their actors so much and they're judged important theaters. [. . .] There's literally hundreds of Black community groups, theater groups. There's a lot of Black theaters in the country, but only one League theater. It means that of these five hundreds of playwrights, there's this theater here that has a five-play season. So five playwrights will have an opportunity to develop their talent. Now if you're a white playwright and you have 66 times five or seven, then obviously you have more opportunities. So what I am saying as Black theater artists, we do not have the opportunities, the tools meaning the theaters to develop our talent. We are designers. We are actors. We are playwrights, we are all the things that make up theater. We do not have the opportunity. [. . .] I'm sure that people who fund are not discriminating. They're not saying I'm not going to fund any Black theatre. They're not saying that overtly. Then they must not know that there are these theaters here that need lifting up to the level of the [white theaters]. So there will come a time when they can say, Now there's four Black theaters. Why not, there's 35 million people? What's wrong with four, five, or six? What's wrong with nine? It's difficult to even imagine having nine Black theaters, but yet we have 66 white ones. And one Black one. It's gone up. It used to be 65 white ones, and one Black one. Now it's 66 and it's still only one.

CLARA'S OLE MAN (1968)

Ed Bullins

Clara's Ole Man was first performed at the Firehouse Repertory Theatre in San Francisco on August 5, 1965. It was produced by the San Francisco Drama Circle and directed by Robert Hartman. The sets were designed by Louie Gelwicks and Peter Rounds. Lighting by Verne Shreve. In winter, 1968, it was done, along with two other of Mr Bullins' plays, at the American Place Theatre in New York, and in the spring the production continued running at the Martinique.

THE PEOPLE:

CLARA: *a light brown girl of 18, well-built with long, dark hair. A blond streak runs down the middle of her head, and she affects a pony tail. She is pensive, slow in speech but feline. Her eyes are heavy-lidded and brown; she smiles – rather, blushes – often.*

BIG GIRL: *a stocky woman wearing jeans and tennis shoes and a tight fitting blouse which accents her prominent breasts. She is of an indeterminable age, due partly to her lack of makeup and plain hair style. She is anywhere from 25 to 40, and is loud and jolly, frequently breaking out in laughter from her own jokes.*

JACK: *20 years old, wears a corduroy Ivy League suit and vest. At first, Jack's speech is modulated and too eloquent for the surroundings but as he drinks his words become slurred and mumbled.*

BABY GIRL: *Big Girl's mentally retarded teenaged sister. The girl has the same hair-do as Clara. Her face is made up with mascara, eye shadow, and she has black arching eyebrows penciled darkly, the same as Clara.*

MISS FAMIE: *a drunken neighbor.*

STOOGIE: *a local street-fighter and gang leader. His hair is processed.*

BAMA: *one of Stoogie's boys.*

HOSS: *another of Stoogie's boys.*

C.C .: *a young wino.*

TIME:

Early spring, the mid-1950s.

SCENE:

A slum kitchen on a rainy afternoon in South Philadelphia. The room is very clean, wax glosses the linoleum and old wooden furniture; a cheap but clean red checkered oil cloth covers the table. If the room could speak it would say, "I'm cheap but clean".

A cheap AM radio plays rhythm 'n blues music throughout the play. The furniture is made up of a wide kitchen table where a gallon jug of red wine sits. Also upon the table is an oatmeal box, cups, mugs, plates and spoons, ashtrays and packs of cigarettes. Four chairs circle the table, and two sit against the wall back-stage. An old fashioned wood and coal burning stove takes up a corner of the room and a gas range of 1935 vintage is backstage next to the door to the yard. A large, smoking frying pan is on one of the burners.

Jack and Big Girl are seated at opposite ends of the table; Clara stands at the stove fanning the fumes toward the door. Baby Girl plays upon the floor with a homemade toy.

CLARA: (*fans fumes*) Uummm uummm . . . well, there goes the lunch. I wonder how I was dumb enough to burn the bacon?

BIG GIRL: Just comes natural with you, honey, all looks and no brains . . . now with me and my looks, anybody in South Philly can tell I'm a person that naturally takes care of business . . . hee hee . . . ain't that right, Clara?

CLARA: Awww girl, go on. You's the worst messer-upper I knows. You didn't even go to work this morn'. What kind of business is that?

BIG GIRL: It's all part of my master plan, baby. Don't you worry none . . . Big Girl knows what she's doin'. You better believe that!

CLARA: Yeah, you may know what you're doin' but I'm the one who's got to call in for you and lie that you're sick.

BIG GIRL: Well, it ain't a lie. You know I got this cough and stopped up feeling. (*looking at Jack*) You believe that, don't you, young blood?

JACK: Most certainly. You could very well have a respiratory condition and also have all the appearances of a extremely capable person.

BIG GIRL: (*slapping table*) HEE HEE . . . SEE CLARA? . . . SEE? Listen ta that, Clara. I told you anybody could tell it. Even ole hot lips here can tell.

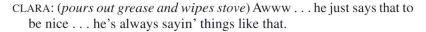

CLARA: (*pours out grease and wipes stove*) Awww . . . he just says that to be nice . . . he's always sayin' things like that.

BIG GIRL: Is that how he talked when he met you the other day out to your aunt's house?

CLARA: (*hesitating*) Nawh . . . nawh he didn't talk like that.

BIG GIRL: Well, how did he talk, huh?

CLARA: Awww . . . Big Girl. I don't know.

BIG GIRL: Well, who else does? You know what kind of line a guy gives ya. You been pitched at enough times, haven't ya? By the looks of him I bet he gave ya the ole smooth college boy approach . . . (*to Jack*) C'mon, man, drink up. We got a whole lot mo' ta kill. Don't you know this is my day off and I'm celebratin'?

JACK: (*takes a drink*) Thanks . . . this is certainly nice of you to go to all this trouble for me. I never expected it.

BIG GIRL: What did you expect, young blood.

JACK: (*takes another sip*) Ohhh, well . . . I . . .

CLARA: (*to Baby Girl on floor*) Don't put that dirty thing in your mouf, gal! (*she walks around the table to Baby Girl and tugs her arm*) Now, keep that out of your mouf!

BABY GIRL: (*holds to toy sullenly*) NO!

CLARA: You keep quiet, you hear, gal!

BABY GIRL: NO!

CLARA: If you keep tellin' me no I'm goin' ta take you upstairs ta Aunt Toohey.

BABY GIRL: (*throws back head and drums feet on floor*) NO! NO! SHIT! DAMN! NO! SHIT!

CLARA: (*disturbed*) NOW STOP THAT! We got company.

BIG GIRL: (*laughs hard and leans elbows upon table*) HAW HAW HAW . . . I guess she told you, Clara. Hee hee . . . that little dirty mouf bitch, (*pointing to Baby Girl and becoming choked*) . . . that little . . . (*cough cough*) . . . hooeee boy!

CLARA: You shouldn't have taught her all them nasty words, Big Girl. Now we can't do anything with her. (*turns to Jack*) What do you think of that?

JACK: Yes, it does seem a problem. But with proper guidance she'll more than likely be conditioned out of it when she gets into a learning situation among her peer group.

BIG GIRL: (*takes a drink and scowls*) BULLSHIT!

CLARA: Aww . . . B.G.

JACK: I beg your pardon, Miss?

BIG GIRL: I said bullshit! Whatta ya mean with proper guidance . . . (*points*) I taught that little bitch myself . . . the best cuss words I know before she ever climbed out of her crib . . . whatta ya mean when she gets among her "peer" group?

JACK: I didn't exactly say that. I said when . . .

BIG GIRL: (*cuts him off*) Don't tell me what you said, boy. I got ears. I know all them big horseshit doctor words . . . tell him, Clara . . . tell him what I do. Where do I work. Clara?

CLARA: Awww . . . B.G., please.

BIG GIRL: Do like I say! Do like Big wants you to!

CLARA: (*surrenders*) She works out at the state nut farm.

BIG GIRL: (*triumphant*) And tell mister smart and proper what I do.

CLARA: (*automatically*) She's a technician.

JACK: Oh, that's nice. I didn't mean to suggest there was anything wrong with how you raised your sister.

BIG GIRL: (*jolly again*) Haw haw haw . . . Nawh, ya didn't. I know you didn't even know what you were sayin', young blood. Do you know why I taught her to cuss?

JACK: Why no, I have no idea. Why did you?

BIG GIRL: Well, it was to give her freedom, ya know?

(*Jack shakes his head*)

Ya see, workin' in the hospital with all the nuts and fruits and crazies and weirdos I get ideas 'bout things. I saw how when they get these kids in who have cracked up and even with older people who come in out of their skulls they all mostly cuss. Mostly all of them, all the time they out of their heads, they cuss all the time and do other wild things, and boy do some of them really get into it and let out all of that filthy shit that's been stored up all them years. But when the docs start shockin' them puttin' them on insulin they quiets down, that's when the docs think they're gettin' better, but really they ain't. They're just learn'n like before to hold it in . . . just like before, that's one reason most of them come back or are always on the verge afterwards of goin' psycho again.

JACK: (*enthusiastic*) Wow, I never thought of that! That ritual action of purging and catharsis can open up new avenues in therapy and in learning theory and conditioning subjects . . .

BIG GIRL: Saaay whaaa . . .? What did you have for breakfast, man?

CLARA: (*struck*) That sounds so wonderful . . .

JACK: (*still excited*) But I agree with you. You have an intuitive grasp of very abstract concepts!

BIG GIRL: (*beaming*) Yeah, yeah . . . I got a lot of it figured out . . . (*to Jack.*) Here, fill up your glass again, man.

JACK: (*to Clara*) Aren't you drinking with us?

CLARA: Later. Big Girl doesn't allow me to start in drinking too early.

JACK: (*confused*) She doesn't?

BIG GIRL: (*cuts in*) Well, in Baby Girl's case I said to myself that I'm teach'n her how in front and lettin' her use what she knows whenever it builds up inside. And it's really good for her, gives her spirit and everything.

CLARA: That's what probably warped her brain.

BIG GIRL: Hush up! You knows it was dat fuckin' disease. All the doctors said so.

CLARA: You don't believe no doctors 'bout nothin' else!

BIG GIRL: (*glares at Clara*) Are you showin' out, Clara? Are you showin' out to your little boy friend?

CLARA: He ain't mah boy friend.

JACK: (*interrupts*) How do you know she might not have spirit if she wasn't allowed to curse?

BIG GIRL: (*sullen*) I don't know anything, young blood. But I can take a look at myself and see the two of us. Look at me! (*stares at Jack*) LOOK AT ME!

JACK: Yes, yes, I'm looking.

BIG GIRL: Well, what do you see?

CLARA: B.G. . . . PLEASE!

BIG GIRL: (*ignores*) Well, what do you see?

JACK: (*worried*) Well, I don't really know . . . I . . .

BIG GIRL: Well, let me tell you what you see. You see a fat bitch who's 20 pounds overweight and looks ten years older than she is. You want to know how I got this way and been this way most of my life and would be worse off if I didn't let off some steam drinkin' this rotgut and speakin' my mind?

JACK: (*to Big Girl who doesn't listen but drinks*) Yes, I would like to hear.

(*Clara finishes the stove and takes seat between the two. Baby Girl goes to the yard door but does not go out into the rain; she sits down and looks out through the door at an angle.*)

BIG GIRL: Ya see, when I was a little runt of a kid my mother found out she couldn't keep me or Baby Girl any longer cause she had T.B., so I got shipped out somewheres and Baby Girl got shipped out somewheres else. People that Baby Girl went to exposed her to the disease. She was lucky, I ended up with some fuckin' Christians . . .

CLARA: Ohhh, B.G., you shouldn't say that!

BIG GIRL: Well, I sho as hell just did! . . . Damned kristers! I spent 12 years with those people, can you imagine? A dozen years in hell. Christians . . . HAAA . . . always preachin' 'bout some heaven over yonder and building a bigger hell here den any devil have imagination for.

CLARA: You shouldn't go round sayin' things like dat.

BIG GIRL: I shouldn't! Well what did you Christian mammy and pot-gutted pappy teach you? When I met you you didn't even know how to take a douche.

CLARA: YOU GOT NO RIGHT!!! (*she momentarily rises as if she's going to launch herself on Big Girl*)

BIG GIRL: (*condescending*) Awww . . . forget it, sweetie . . . don't make no never mind, but you remember how you us'ta smell when you got ready fo bed . . . like a dead hoss or a baby skunk . . . (*to Jack, explaining*) That damned Christian mamma and pappa of hers didn't tell her a thing 'bout herself . . . ha ha ha . . . thought if she ever found out her little thing was used fo anything else 'cept squattin' she'd fall backwards right up in it . . . ZaaaBOOM . . . STRAIGHT TA HELL . . . ha ha . . . didn't know that lil Clara had already found her heaven and on the same trail.

CLARA: (*ashamed*) Sometimes . . . sometimes . . . I just want to die for bein' here.

BIG GIRL: (*enjoying herself*) Ha ha ha . . . that wouldn't do no good. Would it? Just remember what shape you were in when I met you, kid. Ha ha ha. (*to Jack*) Hey, boy, can you imagine this pretty little trick here had her stomach seven months in the wind, waitin' on a dead baby who died from the same disease that Baby Girl had . . .

CLARA: He didn't have any nasty disease like Baby Girl!

BABY GIRL: (*hears her name but looks out door*) NO! NO! SHIT! DAMN! SHIT! SHIT!

BIG GIRL: HAW HAW HAW . . . now we got her started . . .

(*She laughs for over a minute; Jack waits patiently, sipping; Clara is grim. Baby Girl has quieted.*)

BIG GIRL: She . . . she . . . ha ha . . . was walkin' round with a dead baby in her and had no place to go.

CLARA: (*fills a glass*) I just can't understand you, B.G. You know my baby died after he was born. Somedays you just get besides yourself.

BIG GIRL: I'm only helpin' ya entertain your guest.

CLARA: Awww . . . B.G. It wasn't his fault. I invited him.

JACK: (*dismayed*) Well, I asked really. If there's anything wrong I can go.

BIG GIRL: Take it easy, young blood. I'm just havin' a little fun. Now let's get back to the Clara Saga . . . ya hear that word, junior? . . . S-A-G-A, SUCKER! You college boys don't know it all. Yeah, her folks had kicked her out and the little punk she was big for what had tried to put her out on the block and when that didn't work out . . . (*mocking and making pretended blushes . . .*) because our sweet little thing here was soooo modest and sedate . . . the nigger split! . . . HAW HAW HAW . . . HE MADE IT TO NEW YORK!

(*She goes into a laughing, choking and crying fit. Baby Girl rushes over to her and on tip toes pats her back.*)

BABY GIRL: Big Girl! Big Girl! Big Girl!

(*A knocking sounds and Clara exits to answer the door.*)

BIG GIRL: (*catches her beath*) Whatcha want, little sister?

BABY GIRL: The cat. The cat. Cat got kittens. Cat got kittens.

BIG GIRL: (*still coughing and choking*) Awww, go on. You know there ain't no cat under there with no kittens. (*to Jack*) She's been makin' that story up for two months now about how some cat crawls up under the steps and has kittens. She can't fool me none. She just wants a cat but I ain't gonna get none.

JACK: Why not, cats aren't so bad. My mother has one and he's quite a pleasure to her.

BIG GIRL: For your mammy maybe, but all they mean round here . . . (*singsong*) . . . is fleas and mo mouths to feed. With an invalid aunt upstairs we don't need anymo expenses.

JACK: (*gestures toward Baby Girl*) It shows that she has a very vivid imagination to make up that story about the kittens.

BIG GIRL: Yeah, her big sister ain't the biggest liar in the family.

(*Clara returns with Miss Famie staggering behind her, a thin middle-aged woman in long seamen's raincoat, dripping wet, and wearing house slippers that are soaked and squish water about the kitchen floor.*)

BIG GIRL: Hi, Miss Famie. I see you're dressed in your rainy glad rags today.

MISS FAMIE: (*slurred speech of the drunk*) Hello, B.G. Yeah, I couldn't pass up seein' Aunt Toohey, so I put on my weather coat. You know that don't a day pass that I don't stop up to see her.

BIG GIRL: Yeah, I know, Miss Famie. Every day you go up there with that quart of gin under your dress and you two ole lushes put it away.

MISS FAMIE: Why, B.G. You should know better than that.

CLARA: (*re-seated*) B.G., you shouldn't say that . . .

BIG GIRL: Why shouldn't I? I'm payin' for over half of that juice and I don't git to see none of it 'cept the empty bottles.

BABY GIRL: CAT! CAT! CAT!

MISS FAMIE: Oh, the baby still sees them there cats.

CLARA: You should be ashamed to talk to Miss Famie like that.

BIG GIRL: (*to Jack*) Why you so quiet? Can't you speak to folks when they come in?

JACK: I'm sorry. (*to Miss Famie*) Hello, mam.

MISS FAMIE: Why howdie, son.

CLARA: Would you like a glass of wine, Miss Famie?

MISS FAMIE: Don't mind if I do, sister.

BIG GIRL: Better watch it, Miss Famie. Wine and gin will rust your gizzard.

CLARA: Ohh . . . (*pours a glass of wine*) . . . Here, Miss Famie.

BABY GIRL: CAT! CAT!

BIG GIRL: (*singsong, lifting her glass*) Mus' I tell' . . . muscatel . . . jitterbug champagne. (*reminisces*) Remember, Clara, the first time I got you to take a drink? (*to Miss Famie*) You should of seen her. Some of this same cheap rotgut here. She'd never had a drink before but she wanted to show me how game she was. She was a bright little smart thing, just out of high school and didn't know her butt from a door nob.

MISS FAMIE: Yes, indeed, that was Clara all right.

BIG GIRL: She drank three water glasses down and got so damned sick I had to put my finger down her throat and make her heave it up . . . HAW HAW . . . babbled her fool head off all night . . . said she'd be my friend always . . . that we'd always be together . . .

MISS FAMIE: (*gulps down her drink*) Wine will make you do that the first time you get good'n high on it.

JACK: (*takes drink*) I don't know. You know . . . I've never really been wasted and I've been drinkin' for quite some time now.

BIG GIRL: Quite some time, huh? Six months?

JACK: Nawh. My mother used to let me drink at home. I've been drinkin' since 15. And I drank all the time I was in the service.

BIG GIRL: Just because you been slippin' some drinks out of ya mammy's bottle and you slipped a few under ya belt with the punks in the barracks don't make ya a drinker, boy!

CLARA: B.G. . . . do you have to?

(*Miss Famie finishes her second drink as Big Girl and Clara stare at each other.*)

MISS FAMIE: Well, I guess I better get up and see Aunt Toohey. (*she leaves*)

JACK: Nice to have met you, mam.

MISS FAMIE: Well, good-bye, son.

BIG GIRL: (*before Miss Famie reaches top of stairs*) That ole gin-head tracked water all over your floor, Clara.

CLARA: Makes no never mind to me. This place stays so clean I like when someone comes so it gets a little messy so I have somethin' ta do.

BIG GIRL: Is that why Jackie boy is here? So he can so some messin' 'round?

CLARA: Nawh, B.G.

JACK: (*stands*) Well, I'll be going. I see that . . .

BIG GIRL: (*rises and tugs his sleeve*) Sit down an' drink up, young blood. (*pushes him back into his seat*) There's wine here . . . (*slow and suggestive*) . . . there's a pretty girl here . . . you go for that, don't you?

JACK: It's not that . . .

BIG GIRL: You go for fine little Clara, don't you?

JACK: Well, yes, I do . . .

BIG GIRL: HAW HAW HAW . . . (*slams the table and sloshes wine*) . . . HAW HAW HAW . . . (*slow and suggestive*) . . . What I tell ya, Clara? You're a winner. First time I laid eyes on you I said to myself that you's a winner.

CLARA: (*takes a drink*) Drink up, B.G.

BIG GIRL: (*to Jack*) You sho you like what you see, young blood?

JACK: (*becomes bold*) Why sure. Do you think I'd come out on a day like this for anybody?

BIG GIRL: HAW HAW HAW . . . (*peals of laughter and more coughs . . .*)

JACK: (*to Clara*) I was going to ask you to go to the matinee 'round Pep's but I guess it's too late now.

CLARA: (*hesitates*) I never been.

BIG GIRL: (*sobers*) That's right. You never been to Pep's and it's only 'round the corner. What you mean it's too late, young blood? It don't start gettin' good till round four.

JACK: I thought she might have ta start gettin' supper.

BIG GIRL: She'd only burn it the fuck up too if she did. (*to Clara*) I'm goin' ta take you to Pep's this afternoon.

CLARA: You don't have ta, B.G.

BIG GIRL: It's my day off, ain't it?

CLARA: But it costs so much, don't it?

BIG GIRL: Nawh, not much . . . you'll like it. Soon as C.C. comes over ta watch Baby Girl we can go.

CLARA: (*brightens*) O.K.!

JACK: I don't know who's there now, but they always have a good show. Sometimes Ahmad Jamal . . .

BABY GIRL: (*cuts speech*) CAT! CAT! CAT!

BIG GIRL: Let's toast to that . . . (*raising her glass*) . . . to Pep's on a rainy day!

JACK: HEAR! HEAR!

(*He drains his glass. A tumbling sound is heard from the backyard as they drink and Baby Girl claps hands as Stoogie, Bama and Hoss appear in yard doorway. The three boys are no more than 16. They are soaked but wear only thin jackets, caps and pants. Under Stoogie's cap he wears a bandanna to keep his processed hair dry.*)

BIG GIRL: What the hell is this?

STOOGIE: (*goes to Big Girl and pats her shoulder*) The heat, B.G. The man was on our asses so we had to come on in out of the rain, baby, dig?

BIG GIRL: Well tell me somethin' I don't know, baby. Why you got to pick mah back door? I ain't never ready for any more heat than I gets already.

STOOGIE: It just happened that way, B.G. We didn't have any choice.

BAMA: That's right, Big Girl. You know we aint lame 'nuf to be usin' yo pad for no highway.

HOSS: Yeah, baby, you know how it is when the man is there.

BIG GIRL: Well, that makes a difference. (*smiles*) Hey, what'cha standin' there with your faces hangin' out for? Get yourselves a drink.

(*Hoss goes to the sink to get glasses for the trio; Stoogie looks Jack over and nods to Bama, then turns to Clara.*)

STOOGIE: How ya doin', Clara. Ya lookin' fine as ever.

CLARA: I'm okay, Stoogie. I don't have to ask 'bout you none. Bad news sho travels fast.

STOOGIE: (*holds arms apart in innocence*) What'cha mean, baby? What'cha been hearin' 'bout poppa Stoogie?

CLARA: Just the regular. That your gang's fightin' the Peaceful Valley guys up in North Philly.

STOOGIE: Awww . . . dat's old stuff. Sheet . . . you way behind, baby.

BAMA: Yeah sweet cake, dat's over.

CLARA: Already?

HOSS: Yeah, we just finished sign'n a peace treaty with Peaceful Valley.

BAMA: Yeah, we out ta cool the War Lords now from ov'va on Powelton Avenue.

HOSS: Ole Stoogie here is settin' up the war council now; we got a pact with Peaceful Valley and man when we come down on those punk War Lords . . . baby . . . it's just gonna be all ov'va.

BIG GIRL: Yeah, it's always one thing ta another with you punks.

STOOGIE: Hey, B.G., cool it! We can't help it if people always spreadin' rumors 'bout us. Things just happen an' people talk and don' understand and get it all wrong, dat's all.

BIG GIRL: Yeah, all of it just happens, huh? It's just natural . . . you's growin' boys.

STOOGIE: That's what's happen'n baby. Now take for instance Peaceful Valley. Las' week we went up there . . . ya know, only five of us in Crook's Buick.

CLARA: I guess ya was just lookin' at the scenery?

HOSS: Yeah, baby, dat's it. We was lookin' . . . fo' some jive half-ass niggers.

(*The boys laugh and giggle as Stoogie enacts the story.*)

STOOGIE: Yeah, we spot Specs from off'a Jefferson and Gratz walkin' with them bad foots down Master . . . ha ha ha . . .

BAMA: Tell them what happened to Specs, man.

HOSS: Awww, man, ya ain't gonna drag mah man Bama again?

(*They laugh more, slapping and punching each other, taking off their caps and cracking each other with them, gulping their wine and performing for the girls and Jack. Stoogie has his hair exposed.*)

STOOGIE: Bama here . . . ha ha ha . . . Bama burnt dat four-eyed mathafukker in the leg.

HOSS: Baby, you should'a seen it!

CLARA: Yeah, that's what I heard.

STOOGIE: Yeah, but listen, baby. (*points to Bama*) He was holding the only heat we had . . . ha ho ho . . . and dis jive sucker was aimin' at Spec's bad foots . . . ha ha . . . while that blind mathafukker was blastin' from 'round the corner straight through the car window . . .

(*They become nearly hysterical with laughter and stagger and stumble around the table.*)

HOSS: Yeah . . . ha ha . . . mathafukkin' glass was flyin' all over us . . . ha ha . . . we almost got sliced ta death and dis stupid mathafukker was shootin' at the man's bad foots . . . ha ha . . .

BAMA: (*scratching his head*) Well, man. Well, man . . . I didn't know what kind of rumble we was in.

(*Clara and Big Girl laugh as they refill their glasses, nearly emptying the jug. Big Girl gets up and pulls another gallon out of the refrigerator as laughter subsides.*)

BIG GIRL: (*sits down*) What's the heat doin' after ya?

STOOGIE: Nothin'.

CLARA: I bet!

STOOGIE: (*sneer*) That's right, baby. They just singled us out to make examples out of.

(*This gets a laugh from his friends.*)

BIG GIRL: What did you get?

HOSS: Get?

BIG GIRL: (*turns on him*) You tryin' ta get wise, punk?

STOOGIE: (*patronizing*) Awww, B.G. You not goin' ta take us serious, are ya?

(*silence*)

Well ya see. We were walkin' down Broad Street by the State Store, see? And we see this old rumdum come out and stagger down the street carryin' this heavy package . . .

CLARA: And?

STOOGIE: And he's stumblin', see. Like he's gonna fall. So good ole Hoss here says, "Why don't we help that pore man out?" So Bama walks up and helps the man carry his package, and do you know what?

BIG GIRL: Yeah, the mathafukker "slips" down and screams and some cops think you some wrong doin' studs . . . yeah, I know . . . of course you didn't have time to explain.

STOOGIE: That's right, B.G. So to get our breath so we could tell our side of it we just stepped in here, dig?

BIG GIRL: Yeah I dig. (*menacing*) Where is it?

HOSS: Where's what?

(*silence*)

STOOGIE: If you had just give me another minute, B.G. (*pulls out a quart of vodka*) Well, no use savin' it anyway. Who wants some 100 proof tiger piss?

BAMA: (*to Stoogie*) Hey, man, how much was in dat mathafukker's wallet?

STOOGIE: (*nods toward Jack*) Cool it, sucker.

HOSS: (*to Stoogie*) But, man, you holdin' the watch and ring too!

STOOGIE: (*advancing on them*) What's wrong with you jive-ass mathafukkers?

BIG GIRL: Okay, cool it? There's only one person gets out of hand 'round here, ya understand?

STOOGIE: Okay, B.G. Let it slide . . .

BABY GIRL: CAT! CAT! CAT!

BAMA: (*to Hoss*) Hey, man, dis chick's still chasin' dose cats.

STOOGIE: (*to Jack*) Drink up, man. Not everyday ya get dis stuff.

(*Bama picks up the beat of the music and begins a shuffling dance. Baby Girl begins bouncing in time to the music.*)

HOSS: C'mon, Baby Girl; let me see ya do the slide.

BABY GIRL: NO! NO! (*she claps and bounces*)

HOSS: (*demonstrates his steps, trying to out-dance Bama*) C'mon, Baby Girl, shake that thing!

CLARA: No, stop that, Hoss. She don't know what she's doin!

BIG GIRL: That's okay Clara. Go on, Baby Girl, do the thing.

(*Stoogie grabs salt from the table and shakes it upon the floor, under the feet of the dancers.*)

STOOGIE: DO THE SLIDE, MAN! SLIDE!

(*Baby Girl lumbers up and begins a grotesque maneuver while grunting out strained sounds.*)

BABY GIRL: Uuuhhh . . . sheeeee . . . waaa . . . uuhhh . . .

BIG GIRL: (*standing, toasting*) DO THE THING, BABY!!!

CLARA: Awww . . . B.G. Why don't you stop all dat?

STOOGIE: (*to Jack*) C'mon, man, git with it.

(*Jack shakes his head and Stoogie goes over to Clara and holds out his hand.*)

STOOGIE: Let's go, Baby.

CLARA: Nawh . . . I don't dance no mo . . .

STOOGIE: C'mon, pretty mamma . . . watch this step . . . (*he cuts a fancy step*)

BIG GIRL: Go on and dance, sister.

(*Stoogie moves off and the three boys dance.*)

CLARA: Nawh . . . B.G., you know I don't go for that kind of stuff no mo.

BIG GIRL: Go on, baby!

CLARA: No!

BIG GIRL: I want you to dance, Clara.

CLARA: Nawh . . . I just can't.

BIG GIRL: DO LIKE I SAY! DO LIKE BIG WANTS!

(*The dancers stop momentarily but begin again when Clara joins them. Baby Girl halts and resumes her place upon the floor, fondling her toy. The others dance until the record stops.*)

STOOGIE: (*to Jack*) Where you from, man?

JACK: Oh, I live over in West Philly now, but I come from up around Master.

STOOGIE: Oh? Do you know Hector?

JACK: (*trying to capture an old voice and mannerism*) Yeah, man. I know the cat.

STOOGIE: What's your name, man?

JACK: Jack man, maybe you know me by Tookie.

STOOGIE: (*ritually*) Tookie . . . Tookie . . . yeah, man, I think I heard about you. You us'ta be in the ole Jet Cobras!

JACK: Well, I us'ta know some of the guys then. I been away for a while.

BAMA: (*matter-of-factly*) Where you been, man? Jail?

JACK: I was in the Marines for three years.

STOOGIE: Hey, man. That must'a been a gas.

JACK: It was okay. I seen a lot . . . went a lot of places.

BIG GIRL: Yeah, you must'a seen it all.

STOOGIE: Did you get to go anywhere overseas, man?

JACK: Yeah, I was aboard ship most of the time.

HOSS: Wow, man. That sounds cool.

BAMA: You really was overseas, man?

JACK: Yeah, I went to Europe and North Africa and the Caribbean.

STOOGIE: What kind of a boat were you on, man?

JACK: A ship.

BIG GIRL: A boat!

JACK: No, a ship.

STOOGIE: (*rising, Bama and Hoss surrounding Jack*) Yeah, man, dat's what she said . . . a boat!

CLARA: STOP IT!!!

BABY GIRL: NO! NO! NO! SHIT! SHIT! SHIT! DAMN! SHIT!

MISS FAMIE: (*voice comes from upstairs*) Your Aunt don't like all that noise.

BIG GIRL: You and my aunt better mind ya fukkin' ginhead business or I'll come up there and ram those empty bottles up where it counts!

BAMA: (*sniggling*) Oh, baby. We forgot your aunt was up dere sick.

STOOGIE: Yeah, baby. Have another drink.

(*He fills all glasses except Clara's. She pulls hers away.*)

CLARA: Nawh, I don't want any more. Me and Big Girl are goin' out after a while.

BAMA: Can I go too?

BIG GIRL: There's always have to be one wise mathafukker.

BAMA: I didnt mean nuttin', B.G., honest.

STOOGIE: (*to Jack*) What did you do in the Army, man ?

JACK: (*feigns a dialect*) Ohhh, man. I told you already I was in the Marines!

HOSS: (*to Clara*) Where you goin'?

CLARA: B.G.'s takin' me to Pep's.

BAMA: Wow . . . dat's nice, baby.

BIG GIRL: (*gesturing toward Jack*) Ole smoothie here suggesting takin' Clara but it seems he backed out, so I thought we might step around there anyway.

JACK: (*annoyed*) I didn't back out!

STOOGIE: (*to Jack*) Did you screw any of them foreign bitches when you were in Japan, man?

JACK: Yeah, man. I couldn't help it. They was all over, ya know?

BIG GIRL: He couldn't beat them off.

STOOGIE: Yeah, man, I dig.

JACK: Especially in France and Italy. Course, the Spanish girls are the best, but the ones in France and Italy ain't so bad either.

HOSS: You mean those French girls ain't as good as those Spanish girls?

JACK: Nawh, man, the Spanish girls are the best.

BAMA: I never did dig no Mexican nor Rican spic bitches. Too tough, man.

JACK: They ain't Mexican or Puerto Rican. They Spanish . . . from Spain . . . Spanish is different from Mexican. In Spain . . .

STOOGIE: What'cha do now, man?

JACK: Ohhh . . . I'm goin' ta college prep on the G.I. Bill now . . . and workin' a little.

STOOGIE: Is that why you sound like you got a load of shit in your mouth?

JACK: What do you mean!

STOOGIE: I thought you talked like you had shit in your mouth because you had been ta college, man.

JACK: I don't understand what you're tryin' to say, man.

STOOGIE: It's nothin' man. You just talk funny sometimes . . . ya know what I mean. Hey, man, where do you work?

JACK: (*visibly feeling his drinks*) Nawh, man, I don't know what ya mean and I don't go to college, man, it's college prep.

STOOGIE: Thanks, man.

JACK: And I work at the P.O.

BAMA: Pee-who?

JACK: The Post Office, man.

BAMA: No shit, baby.

STOOGIE: Thanks, George. I always like know things I don't know anything about.

(*He turns back on Jack.*)

JACK: (*to Big Girl*) Hey, what time ya goin' round to Pep's?

BIG GIRL: Soon . . . are you in a hurry, young blood? You don't have to wait for us.

JACK: (*now drunk*) That's okay . . . it's just gettin' late, ya know, man . . . and I was wonderin' what time Clara's ole man gets home . . .

BIG GIRL: Clara's ole man? . . . Whad do you mean, man? . . .

(*The trio begins snickering, holding their laughter back; Jack is too drunk to notice.*)

JACK: Well, Clara said for me to come by today in the afternoon when her ole man would be at work . . . and I was wonderin' what time he got home . . .

(*Big Girl stands, tilting over her chair to crash backwards on the floor. Her bust juts out; she is controlled but furious.*)

BIG GIRL: Clara's ole man is home now . . .

(*A noise is heard outside as C.C. comes in the front door. The trio are laughing louder but with restraint; Clara looks stunned.*)

C. C.: It's just Me . . . just ole C.C.

HOSS: Shsss . . . shut up, man.

JACK: (*starts up and feels drunk for the first time*) What . . . you mean he's been upstairs all this time?

BIG GIRL: (*staring*) Nawh, man, I don't mean that!

JACK: (*looks at Big Girl, then at the laughing boys and finally to Clara*) Ohhh . . . jezzus! (*He staggers to the backyard door, past Baby Girl, and becomes sick.*)

BIG GIRL: (*to Clara*) Didn't you tell him? Didn't you tell him a fukkin' thing?

(*C.C. comes in. He is drunk and weaves and says nothing. He sees the wine, searches for a glass, bumps into one of the boys, is shoved into another, and gets booted in the rear before he reaches wine and seat.*)

BIG GIRL: Didn't you tell him?

CLARA: I only wanted to talk, B.G. I only wanted to talk to somebody. I don't have anybody to talk to . . . (*crying*) . . . I don't have anyone . . .

BIG GIRL: It's time for the matinee. (*to Stoogie*) Before you go, escort my friend out, will ya?

CLARA: Ohhh . . . B.G. I'll do anything but please . . . ohhh Big . . . I won't forget my promise.

BIG GIRL: Let's go. We don't want to miss the show, do we?

CLARA: Please, B.G., please. Not that. It's not his fault! Please!

BIG GIRL: DO LIKE I SAY! DO LIKE I WANT YOU TO DO!

(*Clara drops her head and rises and exits stage right followed by Big Girl. Stoogie and his boys finish their drinks, stalk and swagger*) *about. Bama opens the refrigerator and Hoss takes one long last guzzle.*)

BAMA: Hey, Stoogie babe, what about the split?

STOOGIE: (*drunk*) Later, you square-ass, lame-ass mathafukker!

(*Hoss giggles*)

BABY GIRL: CAT! CAT! CAT!

C.C.: (*seated drinking*) Shut up, Baby Girl. Ain't no cats out dere.

MISS FAMIE: (*staggers from upstairs, calls back*) Good night Toohey. See
  ya tomorrow.

(*With a nod from Stoogie, Bama and Hoss take Jack's arms and wrestle
him into the yard. The sound of Jack's beating is heard. Miss Famie
wanders to the yard door, looks out but staggers back from what she sees
and continues sprawling toward the exit, stage right.*)

BABY GIRL: CAT! CAT! CAT!

C.C.: SHUT UP! SHUT ON UP, BABY GIRL! I TOLE YA . . . DERE
  AIN'T NO CATS OUT DERE!!!

BABY GIRL: NO! DAMN! SHIT! SHIT! DAMN! NO! NO!

(*Stoogie looks over the scene and downs his drink, then saunters outside.
Lights dim out until there is a single soft spot on Baby Girl's head, turned
wistfully toward the yard, then blackness. Curtain.*)

HOME ON THE RANGE
AND
POLICE (1968)

Amiri Baraka (LeRoi Jones)

HOME ON THE RANGE
A play to be performed with the music of Albert Ayler improvised in background

> *Home on the Range* was read as part of the 1967 Black Communications Project, produced at Spirit House in Spring '68, taken on tour by the Spirit House Movers and Players in Boston, and performed at a Town Hall rally, New York, March '68.

CHARACTERS

The Father
The Mother
The Son
The Daughter
Black Criminal
A Crowd of Black People
  Black Man 1
  Black Woman 1
  Black Man 2
  Black Man 3
  Black Girl

American front room. Window upstage center. BLACK CRIMINAL *appears, in window.* FAMILY *seated in room watching television, eating popcorn, chattering.*

FATHER: Red hus beat the trim, doing going.

MOTHER: Yah, de 89 red garter shooting.

FATHER: Siboom, das blows.

MOTHER: Coil.

DAUGHTER: Deedee, dodo! Laredgrepe and stooble.

SON: Noik. Dissreal grump!

FATHER: Yak. Yak. (*laughs*)

MOTHER: Dirigible.

FATHER: Dulux cracks. The river. Yips.

MOTHER: And me.

FATHER: Tering. Gollygolly.

DAUGHTER: Ahhhhhhk. Bretzel. Mamarama.

(*Criminal watches, pulls his gun up. He is pulling himself up to look in the window. Family goes on with their "talk".*)

FATHER: Crackywacky. Riprip. Dullong dulux cracks. Dirigible.

SON: Bahl-grepe. Ramona!

DAUGHTER: Dirigible.

(*Criminal disappears, family goes on with affairs. Changes TV channel, etc. There is a sudden, loud knock at the door.*)

FATHER: Gestetner, Criminies.

DAUGHTER: Vout. Resistcool. Dribble.

MOTHER: Achtung Swachtung.

DAUGHTER: (*gets up and goes to the door*) Vatoloop? (*she is frozen at the door at the sight of the black criminal*) Bastoloop, Baspobo.

FATHER: (*more concerned*) Swachtung, dirigible. Vatoloop? (*gets up*)

(*At the door, criminal is forcing daughter back into room.*)

CRIMINAL: Back up dollbaby, don't die in the doorway . . .

FATHER: (*seeing criminal, makes nervous step forward*) Lurch. Crud. Daddoom. Crench!

CRIMINAL: What? (*not understanding*) You see this gun, mumbler. Back up or I burn you.

FATHER: Vataloop. Lurch. Crench. Crench. (*shakes with fear, anger*) Vacuvashtung Schwacuschwactung. Yiip!

CRIMINAL: What the hell's wrong with you? Goddam idiot, back up.

(*Rest of family now up and moving concerned toward door. Are frozen when they see father and daughter under the black criminal's gun.*)

SON: Gash. Lurch. Crud. Daddoon.

FATHER: (*turns to son*) Yiip. Vachtung. Credool. Conchmack. Vouty.

MOTHER: (*screams suddenly at scene*) Ahhhhyyyyyyy . . . Grenchnool crud lurch. (*rushes forward, son restrains her*)

CRIMINAL: What kind of shit is this? What the fuck's wrong with you people?

(*Family now huddles together in a collective whimper. Mother is still being restrained, now collectively. The father strokes her nose.*)

CRIMINAL: Jesus. (*looking around . . . tentatively, cautiously*) All of you, back up in the other room. Take your seats. Do what you was doing.

(*Laughter is coming from the television set. A cold hideous sustaining laughter. That backs the criminal unintentionally into the wallpaper.*)

CRIMINAL: Goddam. (*he waves gun at television*)

(*Laughter goes on, rising. Then broken by explosions, of great dimension. Screams. People in violent turmoil. The laughter rises again above it. Now the family, the mother starting it, passing it to the son, to the daughter, then the father. They all begin to imitate the laughter on the television screen. They are wiggling and shaking, slapping each other and grabbing themselves in a frenzy of wicked merriment.*)

FATHER: HAHAHAHAHAHAHAHA!

CRIMINAL: (*shaken, and pointing his gun now at one of the group, who are falling on the floor, or onto the furniture still laughing*) Goddamit. What the hell's wrong with you folks? Goddamit, shutup, shutup.

SON: (*pointing at criminal*) Vataloop bingo. Vashmash. Cratesy. Ming.

(*The family howls even louder.*)

CRIMINAL: Shutup, shutup. (*He aims and shoots at the television set. And the family stops laughing as suddenly as the bullet shattering the set's tubes.*) Shutup! (*His shout now alone is very loud.*)

(*The family begins to sit down stonily. The criminal, panting, and distressed, stands tensely shaken in the center of the room. The family stares sadly at the television set.*)

MOTHER: (*very sadly*) Vachtung.

CRIMINAL: What? Goddamit, why do you people talk like that? What kind of language is that? I'm no fool. I been places. What kind of language you speaking?

(*No answer from the family. The mother and son turn languidly and look at the criminal with a slothful mixture of despair and hatred. Criminal moves over to the father.*)

CRIMINAL: Hey, you. (*raising gun near his face*) You hear me talking to you. Your ears ain't painted on.

FATHER: (*looks at the criminal steadily, then he mumbles*) Vo eein. Ruggles. And stuff.

CRIMINAL: What? What you mean? (*shakes gun*) Speak up.

MOTHER: (*shouts*) Crindlebindle. Stoopnagel funk.

CRIMINAL: What? (*Moves gun toward her, but father steps forward in front of gun, raises his hand*)

FATHER: Crillilly bagfest. Gobble Gobble. Gooble.

CRIMINAL: What?

FATHER: (*Begins unbuckling his belt, steps out of his trousers. He has huge valentines sewn on his drawers*) Gooble. Crillilly.

MOTHER: (*stands, waving her finger at father*) Yaaash. Passsh.Chameleon.

FATHER: (*turning to her angrily, waving her into her seat*) Gnash. Pash. Flags and Fags.

FATHER: (*begins doing a little step, showing his dancing form to the criminal; he sings a song*) Bubbles. Bubbles. Bubbles. Bubbles. Witchnight creaks. And bang.

CRIMINAL: You almost made sense that time. What the hell's going on? Look you, sit down. I don't have time to look at your boney ass trying to dance. I'm just a working man. And I've come, quite frankly, to commit a crime.

(*Family looks at him startled.*)

You can't sit here, looking as weird as you do, and talking as weird as you do, and look at me weird when I say I came to commit a crime. This is the reign of terror, and I am Robespierre.

(*Family begins to giggle. Father does a dance, threatening to strip off his pants. Daughter in background, starts to loosen her clothes, watching her father cavort. She gets up and begins to cavort. She jiggles around loosely, opening her clothes. Son begins to clap his hands to imaginary unrhythmical beat.*)

SON: Vataloop. Vataloop. Bingo. Stringo. Vataloop jingo.

CRIMINAL: Shutup that shit, moron. If you want to talk, talk. For instance, you should have said, this is not the reign of terror, and Robespierre is dead, and was white, anyway.

(*Father stands holding his legs as if he was cold.*)

Put on your clothes, Moriarti. And you people say something real; in fact from now on if any of you come out with that junglegoop bullshit, I'm gonna blow holes in you. Dig it?

(*Family looks at each other. Father suddenly makes a slight gesture at wall behind criminal. A voice comes over a concealed loudspeaker.*)

LOUDSPEAKER: THIS IS THE VOICE OF GOD, EVERYTHING'S COOL! REPEAT! THIS IS THE VOICE OF GOD. YOUR GOD, WHOEVER YOU ARE, AND IT'S ME SAYING, EVERYTHING'S COOL! REPEAT. EVERYTHING'S COOL!

(*Criminal turns and shoots where the sound is coming from and the voice breaks off. The family jumps up startled.*)

CRIMINAL: (*Jewish accent*) You got the wrong vampire. Sit down.

(*Now all family begins talking at once. In loud dinnish babble.*)

FAMILY: Criminies. Vatloop. Crouch. Bibble. Bibble. Crunch. Jab. Cribble. Awwwk. Awwwk. Crunch. Loop. Question. Bablies. Deaths. Robots. Jobs. (*they end by screaming in unison*) LIGHT LIGHT LIGHT LIGHT LIGHT LIGHT LIGHT LIGHT LIGHT LIGHT LIGHT LIGHT LIGHT LIGHT LIGHT LIGHT.

CRIMINAL: I understand you. You're talking close to right now. Keep it up. Keep it up.

(*They begin jumping up and down in place, screaming at the top of their lungs. Jumping wildly, trying to reach the ceiling. A screaming fear is tearing their faces.*)

FAMILY: LIGHT LIGHT LIGHT LIGHT LIGHT.

CRIMINAL: (*backs away from them*) Light? What kind of place is this? They were more together when they were talking that other jive. Light, what?

(*The family jumps until they are exhausted then they crumple to the floor, or on the furniture, one by one.*)

CRIMINAL: Jesus, what kind of place . . .

(*Starts cautiously to look around for something to steal. Moves gun around in front of him as he moves. Looks in drawers, turning very often to look at the slumping family. Picks up a few small things, throws some back in disgust. Finally turns to family.*)

CRIMINAL: Hey, you people . . . wake the hell up . . . (*still looking, alternating between mumble and loud exasperated talk*) Hey kid . . . (*going over to son*) What the hell's going on in this place? I mean, jesus white christ, you go into some slick looking dump just to do a little business, make a little money . . . goddam, this ain't even my neighborhood. I come down here, to pop these chumps, and look what I run into . . . (*gesturing*) Paddyboy Christ! (*shaking son again*) Hey, hey, boy. Wake the fuck up, willya?

(*Son stirs, looks up dazed and shaking his head. He tries to stand. Criminal helps him upright. When he is standing, now trembling, he makes final effort to stand and then with great difficulty, gets words out.*)

SON: Light! Lightlight light!

CRIMINAL: Aw shit. (*throws son back where he was sprawled*) I heard that before . . . Ya' little . . . (*searches for word*) . . . punk! Damn . . . (*stands looking at them*) Damn. All I did . . . (*throwing up his hands*) . . . was go out and look for a job . . . like all them cats in the newspapers say niggers ought to . . . and what do I run into . . . a goddam funnyfarm!

(*Daughter comes to consciousness for a brief second. She opens her eyes, raises her head.*)

DAUGHTER: Vataloop. Crunch. (*sinks back*)

CRIMINAL: Aw bullshit. She done retrogressed!

(*Hole in the wall where speaker was, starts grinding again, with broken, churning, gurgling sound.*)

LOUDSPEAKER: Awwwwwwkkkk . . . awkkkk . . . (*seems to be gaining momentum, as if it was about to start, does start*) Vataloop, Crunch. Criminies. Swachtung . . .

(*Criminal turns and fires again.*)

CRIMINAL: Oh, nogood, nogood . . . none of that bullshit from you!

(*Speaker gurgles, responding as if wounded by shot . . . cuts off with final statements.*)

LOUDSPEAKER: Light . . . awwk . . . li . . . awwk . . . awwk . . . awwwwkkkkkkk. (*runs out*)

(*Now lights dim, and go down . . . finally off. Black. Lights come up and the entire family is standing up at attention. Criminal is slumping against the bar, sound asleep, but in a few seconds, as the family stands at attention, the mother even, finally, clears her throat.*)

MOTHER: Aruuuuumph.

(*The black criminal comes awake with a start. The gun comes up, but then he seems to sense a different set of vibrations in the place, and he, too, comes to attention. The mother sort of beckons to him to come over to where they are standing with just a slight toss of her head. Criminal comes over. Then he, as if from a pre-signal, jams his gun into his breast pocket, and takes a collapsible baton out of the other pocket.*)

He begins, with great fanfare (tapping on chair as if it is a music stand, calling for attention with his head and now very haughty demeanor, turning to acknowledge an invisible audience) to conduct the family singing: first a version of "America the Beautiful", then a soupy stupid version of the Negro national anthem, "Lift Every Voice and Sing", which comes to a super-dramatic climax, with the criminal having been moved to tears, finally giving a super-military salute. As they reach the highest point of the song, suddenly a whole crowd of black people pushes through the door. The criminal wheels around, at first, startled, then he lets out a yell of recognition, and there is a general yowl from all the black people, and they proceed to run around and once they all take in the family, with second takes, over the shoulder jibes, and stage-whispered insult-inquiries, they race around and begin getting ready for a party.

CRIMINAL: Hey. Hey. What's happening? What the hell you folks doing here?

BLACK MAN 1: Hey, Billy, baby, we heard you was here working out, we figured we'd come down and see what was happening.

BLACK WOMAN 1: Yeh, Tillie figured there might be some grey-chicks down here, so she sent us down here to keep you cool. (*Black people laugh*)

(The family is standing in the middle of the floor, speechless, at first. But when the records go on, most of them 45s taken out of one of the women's bags, the family tries to get involved in the party, mostly dancing with each other. The daughter finally dances with a very light-skinned sissy type negro with a briefcase and snap-brimmed Madison Avenue hat. The negro, when dancing frug-like with the daughter still never lets his briefcase out of his hand. He also holds onto his hat. Two big negroes are also dancing and tossing the mother back and forth between them.)

BLACK MAN 2: Hey, dig this bitch dance!

(A wild nigger party rises to full blast in the house. Dancing, singing, cursing, fighting. The mother is tossed back and forth. The mother is sprawled catatonically on the floor doing a spastic jerk as The Jerk. The son crawls around the floor on his hands and knees following a black red-eyed girl with blonde hair and round sunglasses. The father dances around nude with a young negro in leather jacket who waves his knife in front of him to make the father keep his manly distance. The criminal is absorbed in the party, then backs off to watch. Then he turns smartly toward the audience, holding his gun out at them.)

CRIMINAL: This is the tone of America. My country 'tis of thee. (*he shouts out over the audience*) This is the scene of the Fall. The demise of the ungodly. (*he shoots once, then quickly twice*) This is the cool takeover in the midst of strong rhythms, and grace. Wild procession. Jelly beans.

French poodles. Razor Cuts. Filth. Assassinations of Gods. This is the end. (*he shoots*) Run. Bastards. Run. You grimy motherfuckers who have no place in the new the beautiful the black change of the earth. Who don't belong in the motherfucking world. Faggot Frankensteins of my sick dead holy brother. You betta' get outta here. (*he shoots again three times*) The World!

(*Black.*)

(*The scene is as before with niggers lying all over everything. The house broke up. The weird talking grays piled in the center of a whiskey sleep dope ring of colored people. The criminal squats over the family along with two others, the only people awake in the house.*)

CRIMINAL: O.K. Let's have it again.

FATHER: I was born in Kansas City in 1920. My father was the vice-president of a fertilizer company. Before that we were phantoms . . . (*waving at his family*) Evil ghosts without substance.

(*Criminal looks at his brothers, nodding as if a theory of his has been proven.*)

BLACK MAN 1: (*somewhat sleepily*) Yeh . . . yeh . . . well ast the bastid why they put everybody through all these changes. (*droops*)

(*Black man 2 spots one of the women, the blonde-head black girl, stirring in the corner. He rises quickly, punching the criminal.*)

BLACK MAN 2: Hey . . . the tricky one is still breathin' . . .

CRIMINAL: Beautiful.

BLACK MAN 2: Baby.

BLACK GIRL: Wow. That was some bash, all right.

BLACK MAN 2: You still look good lady. Wish you belonged to me.

BLACK GIRL: Everything'll be O.K. I'm real. And healthy.

BLACK MAN 3: (*comes out of his droop, seeing the girl awake*) We're the only survivors, maybe, maybe . . . I better see if any of them other . . . (*heads for the women, begins shaking them*) Sister, Hey sister. (*slapping them gently on the faces*) Hey, snap out of it. Hey, if you don't open your eyes right now, you gon' miss a beautiful man. (*all laugh*)

CRIMINAL: (*turning to family, who still sit apparently asleep, except for the father, nodding heavily*) Hey . . . (*prods father*) Hey. Now let's begin again. From the top Mr Tooful. (*all laugh*)

FATHER: I was born in Kansas City in 1920. My father was the vice-president of a fertilizer company. Before that we were phantoms . . . (*nodding heavily, head hanging*)

CRIMINAL: Come on, come on.

BLACK GIRL: (*going to look out the window*) Hey look, the sun's coming up. (*turns around, greeting the three brothers*) Good Morning, Men. Good Morning.

THE END

POLICE

CHARACTERS

Black Man
Black Woman
Black Cop
White Cops
Old Street Woman
Young Boy
Young Girl
1
2
3

BLACK MAN: Hello.

BLACK WOMAN: Discovery.

BLACK MAN: Discovery.

BLACK WOMAN: Hello.

BLACK MAN: Discovery.

BLACK WOMAN: Sings

BLACK MAN: We Hurt–ing. We Hurt–ing.

BLACK COP: I'm crazy. I don't know why I hurt people. I hurt people. I don't know why. (*takes out paper penis–pistol*) I don't know why. I'm sick to hurt. Hurt to hurt. It is myself being hurt. I hurt. Please let me stagger. Hurt you. Hurt you. (*rhythm*) Hurt and hurt you. Please. (*staggers against desk*)

WHITE COP: You couldn't take it that's all. You're not fit for justice among the civilized. The great face tooters. That's all.

BLACK COP: I'm a savage? I'm a savage? Savage?

BLACK MAN: Hello.

BLACK WOMAN: Discovery.

BLACK COP: Savage. Define it propine it combine it with a scotch and make a drink. Salute it. Boot it. Cutie! Wake up to yourself. A savage in the world.

BLACK MAN: Tell the world, you don't want to integrate. Don't want to hesitate.

BLACK WOMAN: Evolve. Just evolve, my man!

BLACK COP: As a tree.

BLACK WOMAN: You could use it.

WHITE COP: No justice, Savage.

BLACK WOMAN: Not savage, bloody teeth. Primitive. First. Last. Always.

BLACK MAN: We're religious. We want to help you, evolve. Do you want to go. Meet your maker.

BLACK WOMAN: Us. (*laughs*)

BLACK COP: I don't know what to do where I is. Am. I hear voices crying Herbie, and thass not my name. I been framed.

OLD STREET WOMAN: You a black cop that can't cop.

WHITE COP: You a black cop that won't kill germs.

BLACK MAN: And injure your soul.

WHITE COP: I have not . . . (*goes over behind desk with other cops*)

BLACK WOMAN: Your soul is your business. No more no less. Don't philosophize, just take out that gun.

COPS: What's going on!

ALL: We want to convince this nigger to stop killing us, for you. What do you think?

YOUNG BOY: No we want to report a crime. A murder of sanity.

YOUNG GIRL: A murder.

BLACK COP: Where? I must solve it!

BLACK WOMAN: You did it.

BLACK COP: Y . . . me?

BLACK WOMAN: To you!

ALL: By them. Look at them. Dance with me Henry! Work with me anger. Slop. Bump a chump a lump.

(*Sudden pantomime. Lights dim – come up to shift of players. Black man and black woman take up roles.*)

BLACK WOMAN: You don't have no money. You don't have no life in sun. You just swagger black heaviness. Where's a sweet thing for me? A cool, a hip diamond layout. I want good lovin' in public honey and soft stuff too. You can't get it.

BLACK MAN: Later black bitch. Later. I got terrible life shit to buck. And you always on me 'bout some soft shit. It ain't no soft shit. It just ain't no soft shit around. None. So shut up.

BLACK WOMAN: It is some soft shit. It is. (*snaps on TV*) Look. Soft shit. Look . . . diamond studs and greasy sugar. I want it! They got it!

BLACK MAN: Aw shut up.

(*He makes to hit. She draws ice pick. Freeze in tableau. Lights change.*)

BLACK COP: I'm not a killer but I ain't afraid'a nuthin. I ain't no cold killer. But I ain't afraid'a nuthin. I'll burn your ice ass. But I'm a good guy, kids.

YOUNG BOY: Cop.

ALL: We want to report a murder. We want to report a murder. You're killin us, snot rags.

BLACK MAN: Scabs! (*turns around, starts to stalk imaginary bank–jewelry shop*) OK, throw up your hands. Bastards. Flags. Help eyes. Blonde jewish freaky softee. Gimme what you got.

BLACK COP: I don wanna. (*looking*) I don wanna. (*looking*) I don wanna.

ALL: We want to report a murder. Agg. We want to report a murder. Nigger freak rocket. Bucket a space. Blood. Grope shock jealousy. Dirty collar limp glass. Hurts. Hurts. Hurts.

BLACK COP: I don wanna. But the constitution sez "freak off".

COPS: What's going on? You people are gonna get picked up.

ALL: We wanna report a murder, (*at cop*) you murderin' freak!

BLACK COP: I don wanna. Soap and water. Freak. Quiet. Freak. Lines across the eyes. Water shine sauce. Keep the freak, baby! I *don* wanna, but it's economics.

BLACK MAN: TAKE DOWN YOUR PANTS AND DON'T TRY TO FOLLOW! What fool. 30 cents. Stop it! Stop it! (*they struggle, black cop and black man*) Bang. (*with mouth*) Bang bang . . . Get back . . . what??

BLACK COP: (*running in place*) I don wanna . . . I don wanna!

COPS: Yeh, Yeh, Yeh.

ALL: No, No, No. We wanna report a murder!

BLACK COP: I don' wanna. (*runs over, starts shooting*) Boing Bang Bang Ban – I don' wanna.

BLACK MAN: (*falls dead*) 30 cents and a bent frame. America, you eat shit, for real.

BLACK WOMAN: Soft shit! I want soft shit. His dead ass don't change nuthin. (*jumping up and down, weeping*) I want soft shit!

YOUNG GIRL: Love is a pose if there's no rose money. Liquid balls but rose money is a fuel for animals. If you bees a animal you needs animal fuel!

BLACK COP: I didn' wanna . . . but economics. You got to get around this stuff the easy way. You see. Get around this stuff the easy way.

YOUNG GIRL: Help! Murder! Will you (*to cops*) solve this crime?

BLACK WOMAN: (*from a trance*) But you are the murderers. The killers of men. What are you then? Man killers? Man killers?

YOUNG GIRL: (*running outside or out among the crowd*) Help. Help, murder . . . murder. The cops are murderers. The cops are murderers. A black cop is a murderer. He just shot my man.

(*People appear from audience, or out in the crowd.*)

BLACK WOMAN: What's that bitch sayin? Her man. Bitch. What? That's my man, there dead.

YOUNG GIRL: (*weeping*) You like dead folks for husbands. All you want is soft shit. Not no husband. Just soft shit. Get away. Help people. Black cop shot my man.

BLACK WOMAN: You shut up. It's my man.

YOUNG GIRL: A dead man. Nobody's man. A dead man. And bitch you killed him.

BLACK WOMAN: Don't talk to me like that. My man.

YOUNG GIRL: Soft shit's your man. Help people. Cops. Cop face cracker America killed my man. My . . .

BLACK WOMAN: Was my husband.

YOUNG GIRL: Was my brother! And I was his sister! But was you his wife, woman? Don't lie! PEOPLE, TRAITOR, NIGGERS KILLED MY BROTHER . . . KILLIN YOU!

BLACK WOMAN: (*softer*) I was his wife. I gave him children . . .

YOUNG GIRL: Sof' shit. Your brother is that nigger cop.

BLACK WOMAN: Naw it ain't . . . he ain't no kin to me . . . the lousyass murderer . . . for white folks too.

BLACK COP: I didn' wanna!

YOUNG GIRL: Why don't you use your whip on him?

BLACK WOMAN: Whip?

YOUNG GIRL: Yeh, that whip you used on "your" man. My dead brother.

BLACK WOMAN: Whip?

YOUNG GIRL: Yeh, whip!

BLACK COP: I didn' mean it!!!

BLACK WOMAN: (*searching in her clothes . . . comes up with it . . . an evil yellow "cat-'a-nine" . . . looks at it . . . curls it up . . . snaps it, begins snapping it at cop, first tentatively, then with power*) Whip? . . . You Bastard!

BLACK COP: (*sensing that he's going to resist . . . then he folds*) Oh! Please I didn't mean it. Please . . .

YOUNG BOY: Tell him to kill himself.

BLACK WOMAN: Kill yourself murderer. (*Snaps whip. She snaps it at his gun and his gun shoots*) TAKE YOUR JOINT OUT AGAIN! Big thing shoot it off. Jug yourself with it man!

COPS: OOOOHOOH . . . WHWH, (*sucking breath like fags contemplating joint*) Whhhhh ohh . . . ooh take it out take it out whhhhhhhooooh . . . oooh . . . whhhhhhhhh. . . .

(*They jump up and down in weird comey ecstasy.*)

BLACK WOMAN: (*snapping whip at the penis–pistol*) Take it out!

YOUNG GIRL: (*running in crowd*) Hey people, black white man killed my brother. Please help me!

(*People leap up out of audience crowd.*)

1: What?

2: What?

3: Killer . . . Black cop crazy shit in America.

YOUNG GIRL: Black people. Where's some human beings. Allah be praised Humans.

1: Yeh who? We human.

2: Yes.

YOUNG BOY: 'Swhat we need . . .

BLACK WOMAN: (*whipping black cop*) COPS. TAKE IT OUT.

WHHHHHH OOH OOH OOOH OOOOOOOOOOH!

(*Young girl and young boy "arrive" on scene. Take people to police station under pretense of play plot.*)

BLACK WOMAN: (*whipping black cop*) Dirty Thing!

BLACK COP: Ooooh Please I didn' wanna Please Please!!!!

BLACK WOMAN: Whyn' you shoot yourself with that joint?

1, 2, 3: That's him, huh. Look at him. HaHaHaHaHaHaHaaahahahahahaha.

YOUNG GIRL: Yeh. A Swine Eater and A Swine.

YOUNG BOY: Wig mama poppin him good!

1, 2, 3: Beat him sister. Beat the black off him so his outsides be just like his insides!

BLACK WOMAN: (*to black cop*) Kill yourself.

COPS: Look how big!

BLACK WOMAN: You gon kill yourself or you want all the whities to know how freakish you is. Punk man . . . for real.

BLACK COP: No . . . you kill me. I can't do it . . . to myself.

COPS: Put it up your own ass please!

BLACK COP: Ahyessss.

BLACK WOMAN: Shoot yourself, white man's fool.

BLACK COP: BANG (OOOH) BANG (OOOH) BANG!! (*falls*)

YOUNG GIRL: (*to cops*) You savages keep the body.

BLACK WOMAN: Yes, let these savages keep their crazy freak. Where's a good black man? Now, I'ma find one.

1, 2, 3: You savages keep your own. Come on woman let's get out of here and get our own stuff together.

2: (*to black woman*) A man? What I look like to you?

YOUNG GIRL: Let's go.

ALL: Goodbye Savages.

YOUNG BOY: When we come back . . . it'll be some heavy business being taken care of. (*all laugh*) Some very heavy business.

(*White cops do not even hear, they are all assembled around the dead nigger cop doing pixie steps, or slobbering on his flesh, a few are even eating chunks of flesh they tear off in their weird banquet.*)

(*Black*)

THE BRONX IS NEXT (1968)

Sonia Sanchez

CHARACTERS

Charles
Old Sister
Larry
Roland
Jimmy
White Cop
Black Bitch

The scene is a block in Harlem – a block of tenement houses on either side of a long, narrow, dirty street of full garbage cans. People are moving around in the distance bringing things out of the houses and standing with them in the street. There is activity – but as CHARLES, *a tall, bearded man in his early thirties, and* OLD SISTER *move toward the front, the activity lessens. It is night. The time is now.*

CHARLES: Keep 'em moving Roland. C'mon you mothafuckers. Keep moving. Git you slow asses out of here. We ain't got all night. Into the streets. Oh shit. Look sister. None of that. You can't take those things. Jest important things – things you would grab and carry out in case of a fire. You understand? You wouldn't have time to get all of those things if there was a real fire.

OLD SISTER: Yes son. I knows what you says is true. But you see them things is me. I brought them up with me from Birmingham 40 years ago. I always keeps them right here with me. I jest can't do without them. You know what I mean son? I jest can't leave them you see.

CHARLES: Yes sister. I know what you mean. Look. Someone will help you get back to your apartment. You can stay there. You don't have to come tonight. You can come some other time when we have room for your stuff. OK?

OLD SISTER: Thank you son. Here let me kiss you. Thank the lord there is young men like you who still care about the old people. What is your name son?

CHARLES: My name is Charles, sister. Now I have to get back to work. Hey Roland. Jimmy. Take this one back up to her apartment. Make her comfortable. She ain't coming tonight. She'll come another time.

ROLAND: Another time? Man you flipping out? Why don't you realize . . .

CHARLES: I said, Roland, she'll come another time. Now help her up those fucking stairs. Oh yes. Jimmy, see too that she gets some hot tea. You dig? Ten o'clock is our time. There ain't no time for anyone. There ain't no time for nothing 'cept what we came to do. Understand? Now get your ass stepping.

(*Roland and Jimmy exit.*)

LARRY: Hey Charles, over here fast. Look what I found coming out one of the buildings.

CHARLES: What, man? I told you I ain't got no time for nothing 'cept getting this block cleared out by 10 p.m. What the fuck is it?

LARRY: A white dude. A cop. An almighty fuzz. Look. I thought they were paid enough to stay out of Harlem tonight. (*turns to cop*) Man. Now just what you doing here spying on us, huh?

WHITE COP: Spying? What do you mean spying? You see. Well you know how it is. I have this friend – she lives on this block and when I got off at 4 p.m., I stopped by. Well. I was just leaving but this guy and another one taking someone upstairs saw me – pulled a gun on me and brought me out here.

CHARLES: What building and what apartment were you visiting my man?

WHITE COP: No. 214 – Apt 10 – but why are you interested?

CHARLES: Larry, bring the black bitch out fast. Want to get a good look at her so I'll see jest why we sweating tonight. Yeah. For all the black bitches like her.

WHITE COP: (*has turned around and seen the activity*) Hey. What are all the people doing out in the middle of the street? What's happening here? There's something going on here I don't know about and I have a right to know . . .

CHARLES: Right? Man. You ain't got no rights here. Jest shut your fucking white mouth before you git into something you wish you wasn't in. Man. I've got to call in about this dude. Is there a phone in any of these fire traps?

JIMMY: Yeah. I got one in my place during the year I lived here. It's No. 210 – 1st floor – 1C – back apartment. I'll stay here with this socializing dude while you call.

(*Charles splits.*)

WHITE COP: (*takes out some cigarettes*) Want a cigarette?

JIMMY: Thanks man – in fact I'll take the whole pack. It's going to be a long night.

WHITE COP: What do you mean a long night?

JIMMY: (*smiling*) Jest what I said man – and it might be your longest – (*laughs*) – maybe the longest of your life.

WHITE COP: (*puffing on cigarette – leans against garbage can*) What's your name son?

JIMMY: You don't git nothing out of me 'til Charles returns. You hear me? So stop asking so many damn questions. (*moves to the right, screams*) Goddamn it Roland. Your building is going too slow. We have only two more hours. Get that shit moving. We have to be finished by 10 p.m.

WHITE COP: Look. What are you people doing? Why are all the people moving out into the street – What's going on here? There's something funny going on here and I want to know what it is. You can't keep me from using my eyes and brains – and pretty soon I'll put two and two together – then you just wait . . . you just wait . . .

(*Charles has appeared on stage at this time and has heard what the cop has said. Is watchful for a moment – moves forward.*)

CHARLES: Wait for what my man? Wait for you to find out what's happening? It's not hard to see. We're moving the people out – out into the cool breezes of the street – is that so difficult to understand?

WHITE COP: No. But why? I mean, yeah I know that the apartments are kinda hot and awful . . .

CHARLES: You right man. Kinda awful. Did you hear that description of these shit houses Jimmy? Kinda awful. I knew we weren't describing this scene right and it took this dude here to finally show us the way. From now on when I talk to people about their places I'll say – I know your places are kinda awful . . .

JIMMY: In fact, Charles, how 'bout – I know your places are maybe kinda awful . . .

CHARLES: (*laughing*) Yeah. That's it. Perhaps. Maybe could there be a slight possibility that your place is kinda – now mind you, we ain't saying for sure – but maybe it's kinda awful – (*becomes serious*) Yeah. That's the white man for you man. Always understating things. But since both you and I know that these places are shit-houses that conversation can end now.

JIMMY: What they say 'bout the dude, Charles?

CHARLES: (*turns to white cop*) Oh everything is cool. You can leave man when you want to, but first have a cigarette with us.

WHITE COP: (*relaxing*) I would offer you some of mine but he took them all.

CHARLES: C'mon man. Give them back to the dude. And Jimmy go get Roland. Tell him to come talk a bit. What a night this has been. It's hard working with these people. They like cattle you know. Don't really understand anything. Being a cop, you probably found that too. Right?

WHITE COP: (*lighting a cigarette*) Yeah. I did. A little. But the hardest thing for me to understand was that all you black people would even live in these conditions. Well. You know. Everybody has had ghettos but they built theirs up and there was respect there. Here. There is none of that.

CHARLES: How right you are my man. C'mon in Jimmy and Roland. We just talking to pass some time. Of course, getting back to your statement, I think the reason that the black man hasn't made it – you ain't Irish are you? – is a color thing – I mean even though the Irish were poor they were still white – but as long as white people hate because of a difference in color, then they ain't gonna let the black man do too much. You dig?

WHITE COP: But all this hopelessness. Poverty of the mind and spirit. Why? Things are so much better. All it takes is a little more effort by you people. But these riots. It's making good people have second thoughts about everything.

ROLAND: It's a long time going – man – this hopelessness – and it ain't no better. Shit. All those good thinking people changing their minds never believed in the first fucking place.

JIMMY: (*stands up*) Man. Do you know that jest yesterday I was running down my ghetto street and these two white dudes stopped me and asked what I was doing out so early in the morning – and cuz I was high off some smoke – I said man – it's my street – I can walk on it any time. And they grabbed me and told me where everything was.

CHARLES: That gives me an idea. Let's change places before this dude splits. Let him be a black dude walking down a ghetto street and we'll be three white dudes – white cops on a Harlem street.

WHITE COP: Oh c'mon. That's ridiculous. What good would that do. Why I'd feel silly . . .

CHARLES: You mean you'd feel silly being black?

WHITE COP: Oh no – not that – I mean what would it prove? How would it help – what good would it do?

JIMMY: But what harm could it do?

WHITE COP: None that I could imagine . . . it's just that it's strange . . . it's like playing games.

ROLAND: Oh c'mon. I've always wanted to be a white dude – now's my chance. It'll be exciting – sure is getting boring handling this mob of people.

JIMMY: If you afraid, man, we don't have to.

WHITE COP: Afraid? No. OK. Let's start.

CHARLES: (*jumps up – looks elated*) Then we'll jest be standing on the corner talking and you c'mon by. Oh yeah, maybe you should be running. OK?

(*Charles, Roland and Jimmy move to one side of the stage – the white cop moves to the other side and begins to run toward them.*)

CHARLES: Hey slow down boy. What's your hurry?

WHITE COP: (*stops running*) Yes. What's wrong officer?

JIMMY: Where you running to so fast?

WHITE COP: I just felt like running officer. I was feeling good so I decided to run.

ROLAND: Oh you were feeling good. So you decided to run. Now ain't that a load of shit if I ever heard one.

WHITE COP: It's true, officer. I was just thinking about the day – it was a great day for me so I felt like running – so I ran.

CHARLES: Boy! Who's chasing you? What did you steal?

WHITE COP: Steal? I haven't stolen anything. I haven't stolen anything. I haven't anything in my pockets. (*goes into his pockets*)

JIMMY: (*draws gun*) Get your hands out your pockets boy. Against the wall right now.

WHITE COP: But what have I done? I was just running. This is not legal you know. You have no right to do this . . .

ROLAND: You are perfectly correct. We have no right to do this. Why I even have no right to hit you but I am. (*hits white cop with gun*)

WHITE COP: (*falls down – gets up*) Now wait a minute. That is going just a little too far and . . .

CHARLES: I said why were you running down that street boy?

WHITE COP: Look. Enough is enough. I'm ready to stop – I'm tired.

JIMMY: What's wrong nigger boy – can't you answer simple questions when you're asked them. Oh I know what's wrong. You need me to help you to remember. (*hits white cop with gun*)

WHITE COP: Have you gone crazy? Stop this. You stop it now or there will be consequences.

ROLAND: What did you steal black boy – we can't find it on you but we know you got it hidden someplace. (*hits him again*)

WHITE COP: Oh my god. Stop it . . . This can't be happening to me. Look – I'm still me. It was only make believe.

CHARLES: Let's take him in. He won't cooperate. He won't answer the question. Maybe he needs more help than the three of us are giving him.

JIMMY: I don't know. Looks like he's trying to escape to me. Take out your guns. That nigger is trying to run. Look at him. Boy, don't run. Stop. I say if you don't stop I'll have to shoot.

WHITE COP: Are you all mad? I'm not running. I'm on my knees. Stop it. This can't continue. Why . . .

ROLAND: You ain't shit boy. You black. You a nigger we caught running down the street – running and stealing like all the niggers around him.

CHARLES: Now you trying to escape – and we warned you three times already. You only get three warnings then . . . (*noise from off stage – a woman's voice*)

LARRY: Man. This bitch ain't cooperating Charles. She said she didn't have to come. Finally had to slap her around a bit.

CHARLES: Now is that anyway to act bitch? We just want to talk to you for a minute. Hear you were entertaining this white dude in your place. Is that so?

BLACK BITCH: (*stands defiantly – has a reddish wig on which is slightly disheveled*) Who you? Man. I don't owe no black man no explanations 'bout what I do. The last black man I explained to cleaned me out, so whatever you doing don't concern me 'specially if it has a black man at the head.

JIMMY: Smart–assed bitch.

BLACK BITCH: (*turns to Jimmy – walks over to him*) That's right kid. A smart–assed – black bitch – that's me. Smart enough to stay clear of all black bastard men who jump from black pussy to black pussy like jumping jacks. Yeah, I know all about black men. The toms and revolutionary ones. I could keep you entertained all night long. But I got to get back. My kids will be coming home.

CHARLES: How many kids you got bitch?

BLACK BITCH: Two. Two boys. Two beautiful black boys. Smart boys you hear? They read. They know more than me already, but they still love me. Men. They will know what a woman is for. I'll teach them. I ain't educated, but I'll say – hold them in your arms – love them – love your black woman always. I'll say I am a black woman and I cry in the night. But when you are men you will never make a black woman cry in the night. You hear. And they'll promise.

ROLAND: Oh shit. Another black matriarch on our hands – and with her white boyfriend. How you gonna teach them all this great stuff when you whoring with some white dude who kills black men everyday? How you explain that shit to them? (*black bitch laughs – high piercing laugh – walks over to white cop*) Explain this. (*points to white cop on ground*)

BLACK BITCH: I only explain the important things. He comes once a week. He fucks me. He puts his grayish white dick in me and dreams his dreams. They ain't 'bout me. Explain him to my boys. (*laughs*) Man. I am surviving. This dude has been coming regularly for two years – he stays one evening, leaves and then drives on out to Long Island to his white wife and kids and reality. (*laughs*) Explain. I don't explain cuz there ain't nothing to explain.

CHARLES: Yeah. But you still a bitch. You know. None of this explaining to us keeps you from being a bitch.

BLACK BITCH: Yeah. I know what I am. (*looks around*) But all you revolutionists or nationalists or whatever you call yourselves – do you know where you at? I am a black woman and I've had black men who could not love me or my black boys – where you gonna find black women to love you when all this is over – when you need them? As for me I said no black man would touch me ever again.

CHARLES: (*moving toward the black bitch*) Is that right? You not a bad looking bitch if you take off that fucking wig. (*throws it off*) A good ass. (*touches her face, neck, moves his hands on her body – moves against her until she tries to turn away*) No don't turn away bitch. Kiss me. I said kiss me. (*begins to kiss her face – slowly – sensuously – the black bitch grabs him and kisses him long and hard – moves her body against him*) Yeah. No black man could touch you again, huh? (*laughs and moves away*) I could fuck you right here if I wanted to. You know what a black man is don't you bitch? Is that what happens when you fuck faggoty white men?

(*Black bitch runs across the stage and with that run and cry that comes from her she grabs Charles and hits him and holds on. Charles turns and knocks her down. The white dude turns away. Jimmy moves toward her.*)

BLACK BITCH: No. Watch this boy. You still young. Watch me. Don't touch me. Watch me get up. It hurts. But I'll get up. And when I'm up the tears will stop. I don't cry, when I'm standing up. All right. I'm up again. Who else? Here I am, a black bitch, up for grabs. Anyone here for me. Take your choice – your pick – slap me or fuck me – anyway you get the same charge.

JIMMY: Here black bitch. Let me help you. Your eye is swollen. (*doesn't look at Charles*) Can she go back to her place and get some things out Charles? I'll help her.

CHARLES: You have five minutes to help the black bitch then get you black ass back here. We wasted enough time. (*stoops*) Here don't forget her passport to the white world. (*throws wig at her*) And keep your mouth shut black bitch. You hear?

BLACK BITCH: (*putting on her wig*) I told you I only explain important things. There ain't nothing happening here yet that's important to me. (*exits with Jimmy*)

CHARLES: (*laughs*) That's a woman there. Yeah wig and all. She felt good for awhile. Hey you. Dude. You can get up now. All the unpleasantness is over. Here let me help you get cleaned up. (*begins to brush white cop off*) We just got a little carried away with ourselves.

WHITE COP: Can I go now? I'm tired. It's been a long night. You said I could go.

CHARLES: But don't you want to go and see the bitch – see how she is – make sure she's okay?

WHITE COP: No. I don't think so. It's late. My wife will be worrying by now.

CHARLES: Isn't there anything else you want to see before you go? Can't I fill you in on anything?

WHITE COP: I've seen people moved into the street. That's all. Nothing else. I want to know nothing.

CHARLES: Would you believe that it's happening on every street in Harlem?

WHITE COP: (*nervously*) I'm not interested. I just want to leave and go home. I'm tired.

CHARLES: Yeah man. You look tired. Look. Do me a favor. I want to go to the bitch's place and apologize. You know it wasn't right. Hurting her like that. Come with me. Hey Roland. Shouldn't he come with me?

ROLAND: Yeah man. He should. After all, he knows her better than you. He can tell you what approach to use with her.

WHITE COP: No. I don't want to go. I don't want to see her again. It's all finished now. I'm tired. You tell her. Just let me go on home.

CHARLES: But man. I need you. I need you to help me talk to her. She'll listen to you. Anyway with you there, you'll keep me from getting violent again – c'mon man. Just this one thing then you can go.

LARRY'S: (*voice from off stage*) We ready to light, Charles – should we start now?

CHARLES: Yeah. All 'cept No. 214 – we have some business there. Give us ten minutes then light it up.

(*White cop tries to run – Charles and Roland grab his arm and start walking.*)

WHITE COP: I don't want to go. I must get home. My wife and two boys are waiting for me. I have never hurt or killed a black person in my life. Yes. I heard talk that some cops did – that they hated black people – but not me. I listened. It made me sick but I never participated in it. I didn't ever do anything to negroes. No. I don't want to go. I haven't done anything. (*begins to cry*) Holy Mother – you can't do this to me. (*screams*) But, I'm white! I'm white! No. This can't be happening – I'm white!

(*Tries to break away and Roland knocks him out – they pull him off stage. The stage becomes light – buildings are burning – people are moving around looking at the blaze. Jimmy, Roland and Charles reappear.*)

JIMMY: Well. That's that, man. What a night. Do I still have to write this up tonight Charles?

CHARLES: Were those your orders?

JIMMY: Yes. Okay. I'll do it while we wait. I'll drop it in the mail box tonight. See you soon.

CHARLES: A good job, Jimmy. Stay with them. Talk to them. They need us more than ever now.

ROLAND: We got to split Charles. We got a meeting going tonight. You know what the meeting is about man? (*takes out a cigarette*) You think this is the right strategy burning out the ghettoes? Don't make much sense to me man. But orders is orders. You know what's going down next?

CHARLES: (*lighting a cigarette*) Yeah. I heard tonight when I called about that white dude. The Bronx is next – Let's split.

THE BLACK ARTS MOVEMENT (1968)

Larry Neal

1.

The Black Arts Movement is radically opposed to any concept of the artist that alienates the artist from his/her community. Black Art is the aesthetic and spiritual sister of the Black Power concept. As such, it envisions an art that speaks directly to the needs and aspirations of Black America. In order to perform this task, the Black Arts Movement proposes a radical reordering of the western cultural aesthetic. It proposes a separate symbolism, mythology, critique, and iconology. The Black Arts and the Black Power concept both relate broadly to the Afro-American's desire for self-determination and nationhood. Both concepts are nationalistic. One is concerned with the relationship between art and politics; the other with the art of politics.

Recently, these two movements have begun to merge: the political values inherent in the Black Power concept are now finding concrete expression in the aesthetics of Afro-American dramatists, poets, choreographers, musicians, and novelists. A main tenet of Black Power is the necessity for Black people to define the world in their own terms. The Black artist has made the same point in the context of aesthetics. The two movements postulate that there are in fact and in spirit two Americas – one black, one white. Black artists take this to mean that their primary duty is to speak to the spiritual and cultural needs of Black people. Therefore, the main thrust of this new breed of contemporary writers is to confront the contradictions arising out of Black people's experience in the racist West. Currently, these writers are re-evaluating Western aesthetics, the traditional role of the writer, and the social function of art. Implicit in this re-evaluation is the need to develop a "black aesthetic". It is the opinion of many Black writers, I among them, that the Western aesthetic has run its course: it is impossible to construct anything meaningful within its decaying structure.

We advocate a cultural revolution in art and ideas. The cultural values inherent in Western history must either be radicalized or destroyed, and we will probably find that even radicalization is impossible. In fact, what is needed is a whole new system of ideas. Poet Don L. Lee expresses it:

We must destroy Faulkner, dick, jane, and other perpetuators of evil. It's time for Du Bois, Nat Turner, and Kwame Nkrumah. As Frantz Fanon points out: destroy the culture and you destroy the people. This must not happen. Black artists are culture stabilizers; bringing back old values, and introducing new ones. Black Art will talk to the people and with the will of the people stop impending "protective custody".

The Black Arts Movement eschews "protest" literature. It speaks directly to Black people. Implicit in the concept of "protest" literature, as Brother Knight has made clear, is an appeal to white morality:

> Now any Black man who masters the technique of his particular art form, who adheres to the white aesthetic, and who directs his work toward a white audience is in one sense, protesting. And implicit in the act of protest is the belief that a change will be forthcoming once the masters are aware of the protestor's "grievance" (the very word connotes begging, supplications to the gods). Only when that belief has faded and protestings end, will Black art begin.

Brother Knight also has some interesting statements about the development of a "Black aesthetic":

> Unless the Black artist establishes a "Black aesthetic" he will have no future at all. To accept the white aesthetic is to accept and validate a society that will not allow him to live. The Black artist must create new forms and new values, sing new songs (or purify old ones); and along with other Black authorities, he must create a new history, new symbols, myths and legends (and purify old ones by fire). And the Black artist, in creating his own aesthetic, must be accountable for it only to the Black people. Further, he must hasten his own dissolution as an individual (in the Western sense) – painful though the process may be, having been breast-fed the poison of "individual experience".

When we speak of a "Black aesthetic" several things are meant. First, we assume that there is already in existence the basis for such an aesthetic. Essentially, it consists of an African-American cultural tradition. But this aesthetic is finally, by implication, broader than that tradition. It encompasses most of the usable elements of Third World culture. The motive behind the Black aesthetic is the destruction of the white thing, the destruction of white ideas, and white ways of looking at the world. The new aesthetic is mostly predicated on an Ethics which asks the question: whose vision of the world is finally more meaningful, ours or the white oppressors'? What is truth? Or more precisely, whose truth shall we express, that of the oppressed or of the oppressors? These are basic questions. Black intellectuals of previous decades failed to ask them.

Further, national and international affairs demand that we appraise the world in terms of our own interests. It is clear that the question of human survival is at the core of contemporary experience. The Black artist must address himself to this reality in the strongest terms possible. In a context of world upheaval, ethics and aesthetics must interact positively and be consistent with the demands for a more spiritual world. Consequently, the Black Arts Movement is an ethical movement. Ethical, that is, from the viewpoint of the oppressed. And much of the oppression confronting the Third World and Black America is directly traceable to the Euro-American cultural sensibility. This sensibility, anti-human in nature, has, until recently, dominated the psyches of most Black artists and intellectuals it must be destroyed before the Black creative artist can have a meaningful role in the transformation of society. It is this natural reaction to an alien sensibility that informs the cultural attitudes of the Black Arts and the Black Power movements. It is a profound ethical sense that makes a Black artist question a society in which art is one thing and people's actions another. The Black Arts Movement believes that your ethics and your aesthetics are one. That the contradiction between ethics and aesthetics in Western society is symptomatic of a dying culture.

The term "Black Arts" is of ancient origin, but it was first used in a positive sense by LeRoi Jones:

> We are unfair
> And unfair
> We are black magicians
> Black arts we make
> in black labs of the heart
>
> The fair are fair
> and deathly white
>
> The day will not save them
> And we own the night

There is also a section of the poem "Black Dada Nihilismus" that carries the same motif. But a fuller amplification of the nature of the new aesthetics appears in the poem "Black Art":

> Poems are bullshit unless they are
> teeth or trees or lemons piled
> on a step. Or black ladies dying
> of men leaving nickel hearts
> beating them down. Fuck poems
> and they are useful, would they shoot
> come at you, love what you are,
> breathe like wrestlers, or shudder

> strangely after peeing. We want live
> words of the hip world, live flesh &
> coursing blood. Hearts and Brains
> Souls splintering fire. We want poems
> like fists beating niggers out of Jocks
> or dagger poems in the slimy bellies
> of the owner-jews

Poetry is a concrete function, an action. No more abstractions. Poems are physical entities: fists, daggers, airplane poems, and poems that shoot guns. Poems are transformed from physical objects into personal forces:

> Put it on him poem. Strip him naked
> to the world. Another bad poem cracking
> steel knuckles in a jewlady's mouth
> Poem scream poison gas on breasts in green berets

Then the poem affirms the integral relationship between Black Art and Black people:

> Let Black people understand
> that they are the lovers and the sons
> of lovers and warriors and sons
> of warriors Are poems & poets &
> all the loveliness here in the world

It ends with the following lines, a central assertion in both the Black Arts Movement and the philosophy of Black Power:

> We want a black poem. And a
> Black World.
> Let the world be a Black Poem
> And let All Black People Speak This Poem
> Silently
> Or LOUD

The poem comes to stand for the collective conscious and unconscious of Black America – the real impulse in back of the Black Power Movement, which is the will toward self-determination and nationhood, a radical reordering of the nature and function of both art and the artist.

2.

In the spring of 1964, LeRoi Jones [Amiri Baraka], Charles Patterson, William Patterson, Clarence Reed, Johnny Moore, and a number of other Black artists opened the Black Arts Repertoire Theatre School. They produced a number of plays including Jones' *Experimental Death Unit #*

One, *Black Mass*, *Jello*, and *Dutchman*. They also initiated a series of poetry readings and concerts. These activities represented the most advanced tendencies in the movement and were of excellent artistic quality. The Black Arts School came under immediate attack by the New York power structure. The Establishment, fearing Black creativity, did exactly what it was expected to do – it attacked the theatre and all of its values. In the meantime, the school was granted funds by OEO through HARYOU-ACT. Lacking a cultural program itself, HARYOU turned to the only organization which addressed itself to the needs of the community. In keeping with its "revolutionary" cultural ideas, the Black Arts Theatre took its programs into the streets of Harlem. For three months, the theatre presented plays, concerts, and poetry readings to the people of the community. Plays that shattered the illusions of the American body politic, and awakened Black people to the meaning of their lives.

Then the hawks from the OEO moved in and chopped off the funds. Again, this should have been expected. The Black Arts Theatre stood in radical opposition to the feeble attitudes about culture of the "War On Poverty" bureaucrats. And later, because of internal problems, the theatre was forced to close. But the Black Arts group proved that the community could be served by a valid and dynamic art. It also proved that there was a definite need for a cultural revolution in the Black community.

With the closing of the Black Arts Theatre, the implications of what Brother Jones and his colleagues were trying to do took on even more significance. Black Art groups sprang up on the West Coast and the idea spread to Detroit, Philadelphia, Jersey City, New Orleans, and Washington, D. C. Black Arts movements began on the campuses of San Francisco State College, Fisk University, Lincoln University, Hunter College in the Bronx, Columbia University, and Oberlin College. In Watts, after the rebellion, Maulana Karenga welded the Black Arts Movement into a cohesive cultural ideology which owed much to the work of LeRoi Jones [Amiri Baraka]. Karenga sees culture as the most important element in the struggle for self-determination:

> Culture is the basis of all ideas, images and actions. To move is to move culturally, i.e. by a set of values given to you by your culture.
>
> Without a culture Negroes are only a set of reactions to white people.
>
> The seven criteria for culture are:
>
> 1. Mythology
> 2. History
> 3. Social Organization
> 4. Political Organization
> 5. Economic Organization

6. Creative Motif
7. Ethos

In drama, LeRoi Jones [Amiri Baraka] represents the most advanced aspects of the movement. He is its prime mover and chief designer. In a poetic essay entitled "The Revolutionary Theatre", he outlines the iconology of the movement:

> The Revolutionary Theatre should force change: it should be change. (All their faces turned into the lights and you work on them black nigger magic, and cleanse them at having seen the ugliness. And if the beautiful see themselves, they will love themselves.) We are preaching virtue again, but by that to mean NOW, toward what seems the most constructive use of the word.

The theatre that Jones proposes is inextricably linked to the Afro-American political dynamic. And such a link is perfectly consistent with Black America's contemporary demands. For theatre is potentially the most social of all of the arts. It is an integral part of the socializing process. It exists in direct relationship to the audience it claims to serve. The decadence and inanity of the contemporary American theatre is an accurate reflection of the state of American society. Albee's *Who's Afraid of Virginia Woolf?* is very American: sick white lives in a homosexual hell hole. The theatre of white America is escapist, refusing to confront concrete reality. Into this cultural emptiness come the musicals, an up-tempo version of the same stale lives. And the use of Negroes in such plays as *Hello Dolly* and *Hallelujah Baby* does not alert their nature; it compounds the problem. These plays are simply hipper versions of the minstrel show. They present Negroes acting out the hang-ups of middle-class white America. Consequently, the American theatre is a palliative prescribed to bourgeois patients who refuse to see the world as it is. Or, more crucially, as the world sees them. It is no accident, therefore, that the most "important" plays come from Europe – Brecht, Weiss, and Ghelderode. And even these have begun to run dry.

The Black Arts theatre, the theatre of LeRoi Jones [Amiri Baraka], is a radical alternative to the sterility of the American theatre. It is primarily a theatre of the Spirit, confronting the Black man in his interaction with his brothers and with the white thing.

> Our theatre will show victims so that their brothers in the audience will be better able to understand that they are the brothers of victims, and that they themselves are blood brothers. And what we show must cause the blood to rush, so that pre-revolutionary temperaments will be bathed in this blood, and it will cause their deepest souls to move, and they will find themselves tensed and clenched, even ready to die, at what the soul has been taught. We will scream and cry, murder, run through the streets in

agony, if it means some soul will be moved, moved to actual life understanding of what the world is, and what it ought to be. We are preaching virtue and feeling, and a natural sense of the self in the world. All men live in the world, and the world ought to be a place for them to live.

The victims in the world of Jones' early plays are Clay, murdered by the white bitch-goddess in *Dutchman*, and Walker Vessels, the revolutionary in *The Slave*.

Both of these plays present Black men in transition. Clay, the middle-class Negro trying to get himself a little action from Lula, digs himself and his own truth only to get murdered after telling her like it really is:

> Just let me bleed you, you loud whore, and one poem vanished. A whole people neurotics, struggling to keep from being sane. And the only thing that would cure the neurosis would be your murder. Simple as that. I mean if I murdered you, then other white people would understand me. You understand? No. I guess not. If Bessie Smith had killed some white people she wouldn't need that music. She could have talked very straight and plain about the world. Just straight two and two are four. Money. Power. Luxury. Like that. All of them. Crazy niggers turning their back on sanity. When all it needs is that simple act. Just murder. Would make us all sane.

But Lula understands, and she kills Clay first. In a perverse way it is Clay's nascent knowledge of himself that threatens the existence of Lula's idea of the world. Symbolically, and in fact, the relationship between Clay (Black America) and Lula (white America) is rooted in the historical castration of black manhood. And in the twisted psyche of white America, the Black man is both an object of love and hate. Analogous attitudes exist in most Black Americans, but for decidedly different reasons. Clay is doomed when he allows himself to participate in Lula's "fantasy" in the first place. It is the fantasy to which Frantz Fanon alludes in *The Wretched Of The Earth* and *Black Skins, White Mask*: the native's belief that he can acquire the oppressor's power by acquiring his symbols, one of which is the white woman. When Clay finally digs himself it is too late.

Walker Vessels, in *The Slave*, is Clay reincarnated as the revolutionary confronting problems inherited from his contact with white culture. He returns to the home of his ex-wife, a white woman, and her husband, a literary critic. The play is essentially about Walker's attempt to destroy his white past. For it is the past, with all of its painful memories, that is really the enemy of the revolutionary. It is impossible to move until history is either recreated or comprehended. Unlike Todd, in Ralph Ellison's *Invisible Man*, Walker cannot fall outside history. Instead, Walker demands a confrontation with history, a final shattering of bullshit illusions. His only salvation lies in confronting the physical and psychological forces that have made him and his people powerless. Therefore, he comes to understand that the world must be restructured along spiritual imperatives. But in the interim it is basically a question of *who* has power:

EASLEY: You're so wrong about everything. So terribly, sickeningly wrong. What can you change? What do you hope to change? Do you think Negroes are better people than whites . . . that they can govern a society *better* than whites? That they'll be more judicious or more tolerant? Do you think they'll make fewer mistakes? I mean really, if the Western white man has proved one thing . . . it's the futility of modern society. So the have-not peoples become the haves. Even so, will that change the essential functions of the world? Will there be more love or beauty in the world . . . more knowledge . . . because of it?

WALKER: Probably. Probably there will be more . . . if more people have a chance to understand what it is. But that's not even the point. It comes down to baser human endeavor than any social-political thinking. What does it matter if there's more love or beauty? Who the fuck cares? Is that what the Western ofay thought while he was ruling . . . that his rule somehow brought more love and beauty into the world? Oh, he might have thought that concomitantly, while sipping a gin rickey and scratching his ass . . . but that was not ever the point. Not even on the Crusades. The point is that you had your chance, darling, now these other folks have theirs. *Quietly.* Now they have theirs.

EASLEY: God, what an ugly idea.

This confrontation between the black radical and the white liberal is symbolic of larger confrontations occurring between the Third World and Western society. It is a confrontation between the colonizer and the colonized, the slavemaster and the slave. Implicit in Easley's remarks is the belief that the white man is culturally and politically superior to the Black Man. Even though Western society has been traditionally violent in its relation with the Third World, it sanctimoniously deplores violence or self-assertion on the part of the enslaved. And the Western mind, with clever rationalizations, equates the violence of the oppressed with the violence of the oppressor. So that when the native preaches self-determination, the Western white man cleverly misconstrues it to mean hate of *all* white men. When the Black political radical warns his people not to trust white politicians of the left and the right, but instead to organize separately on the basis of power, the white man cries: "racism in reverse". Or he will say, as many of them do today: "We deplore both white and black racism". As if the two could be equated.

There is a minor element in *The Slave* which assumes great importance in a later play entitled *Jello*. Here I refer to the emblem of

Walker's army: a red-mouthed grinning field slave. The revolutionary army has taken one of the most hated symbols of the Afro-American past and radically altered its meaning.* This is the supreme act of freedom, available only to those who have liberated themselves psychically. Jones amplifies this inversion of emblem and symbol in *Jello* by making Rochester (Ratfester) of the old Jack Benny (Penny) program into a revolutionary nationalist. Ratfester, ordinarily the supreme embodiment of the Uncle Tom Clown, surprises Jack Penny by turning on the other side of the nature of the Black man. He skillfully, and with an evasive black humor, robs Penny of all his money. But Ratfester's actions are "moral": That is to say, Ratfester is getting his back pay: payment of a long over-due debt to the Black man. Ratfester's sensibilities are different from Walker's. He is *blues people* smiling and shuffling while trying to figure out how to destroy the white thing. And like the blues man, he is the master of the understatement. Or in the Afro-American folk transition, he is the Signifying Monkey, Shine, and Stagolee all rolled into one. There are no stereotypes any more. History has killed Uncle Tom. Because even Uncle Tom has a breaking point beyond which he will not be pushed. Cut deeply enough into the most docile Negro, and you will find a conscious murderer. Behind the lyrics of the blues and the shuffling porter loom visions of white throats being cut and cities burning.

Jones' particular power as a playwright does not rest solely on his revolutionary vision, but is instead derived from his deep lyricism and spiritual outlook. In many ways, he is fundamentally more a poet than a playwright. And it is his lyricism that gives body to his plays. Two important plays in this regard are *Black Mass* and *Slave Ship*. *Black Mass* is based on the Muslim myth of Yacub. According to this myth, Yacub, a Black scientist, developed the means of grafting different colors of the Original Black Nation until a White Devil was created. In *Black Mass*, Yacub's experiments produce a raving White Beast who is condemned to the coldest regions of the North. The other magicians implore Yacub to cease his experiments. But he insists on claiming the primacy of scientific knowledge over spiritual knowledge. The sensibility of the White Devil is alien, informed by lust and sensuality. The Beast is the consummate embodiment of evil, the beginning of the

---

*In Jones' study of Afro-American music, *Blues People*, we find the following observation: "Even the adjective *funky*, which once meant to many Negroes merely a stink (usually associated with sex), was used to qualify the music as meaningful (the word became fashionable and is now almost useless). The social implication, then, was that even the old stereotype of a distinctive Negro smell that white America subscribed to could be turned against white America. For this smell now, real or not, was made a valuable characteristic of 'Negro-ness'. And 'Negro-ness', by the fifties, for many Negroes (and whites) was the only strength left to American culture".

historical subjugation of the spiritual world. *Black Mass* takes place in some pre-historical time. In fact, the concept of time, we learn, is the creation of an alien sensibility, that of the Beast. This is a deeply weighted play, a colloquy on the nature of man, and the relationship between legitimate spiritual knowledge and scientific knowledge. It is LeRoi Jones' most important play mainly because it is informed by a mythology that is wholly the creation of the Afro-American sensibility.

Further, Yacub's creation is not merely a scientific exercise. More fundamentally, it is the aesthetic impulse gone astray. The Beast is created merely for the sake of creation. Some artists assert a similar claim about the nature of art. They argue that art need not have a function. It is against this decadent attitude toward art – ramified throughout most of Western society – that the play militates. Yacub's real crime, therefore, is the introduction of a meaningless evil into a harmonious universe. The evil of the Beast is pervasive, corrupting everything and everyone it touches. What was beautiful is twisted into an ugly screaming thing. The play ends with destruction of the holy place of the Black Magicians. Now the Beast and his descendants roam the earth. An off-stage voice chants a call for the Jihad to begin. It is then that myth merges into legitimate history, and we, the audience, come to understand that all history is merely someone's version of mythology.

Slave Ship presents a more immediate confrontation with history. In a series of expressionistic tableaux it depicts the horrors and the madness of the Middle Passage [the ocean journey of slaves in captivity]. It then moves through the period of slavery, early attempts at revolt, tendencies toward Uncle Tom-like reconciliation and betrayal, and the final act of liberation. There is no definite plot (LeRoi calls it a pageant), just a continuous rush of sound, groans, screams, and souls wailing for freedom and relief from suffering. This work has special affinities with the New Music of Sun Ra, John Coltrane, Albert Ayler, and Ornette Coleman. Events are blurred, rising and falling in a stream of sound. Almost cinematically, the images flicker and fade against a heavy back-drop of rhythm. The language is spare, stripped to the essential. It is a play which almost totally eliminates the need for a text. It functions on the basis of movement and energy – the dramatic equivalent of the New Music.

3.

LeRoi Jones [Amiri Baraka] is the best known and the most advanced playwright of the movement, but he is not alone. There are other excellent playwrights who express the general mood of the Black Arts ideology. Among them are Ron Milner, Ed Bullins, Ben Caldwell, Jimmy Stewart, Joe White, Charles Patterson, Charles Fuller, Aisha Hughes, Carol Freeman, and Jimmy Garrett.

Ron Milner's *Who's Got His Own* is of particular importance. It strips bare the clashing attitudes of a contemporary Afro-American family.

Milner's concern is with legitimate manhood and morality. The family in *Who's Got His Own* is in search of its conscience, or more precisely its own definition of life. On the day of his father's death, Tim and his family are forced to examine the inner fabric of their lives: the lies, self-deceits, and sense of powerlessness in a white world. The basic conflict, however, is internal. It is rooted in the historical search for black manhood. Tim's mother is representative of a generation of Christian Black women who have implicitly understood the brooding violence lurking in their men. And with this understanding, they have interposed themselves between their men and the object of that violence – the white man. Thus unable to direct his violence against the oppressor, the Black man becomes more frustrated and the sense of powerlessness deepens. Lacking the strength to be a man in the white world, he turns against his family. So the oppressed, as Fanon explains, constantly dreams violence against his oppressor, while killing his brother on fast weekends.

Tim's sister represents the Negro woman's attempt to acquire what Eldridge Cleaver calls "ultrafemininity". That is, the attributes of her white upper-class counterpart. Involved here is a rejection of the body-oriented life of the working-class Black man, symbolized by the mother's traditional religion. The sister has an affair with a white upper-class liberal, ending in abortion. There are hints of lesbianism, i.e. a further rejection of the body. The sister's life is a pivotal factor in the play. Much of the stripping away of falsehood initiated by Tim is directed at her life, which they have carefully kept hidden from the mother.

Tim is the product of the new Afro-American sensibility, informed by the psychological revolution now operative within Black America. He is a combination ghetto soul brother and militant intellectual, very hip and slightly flawed himself. He would change the world, but without comprehending the particular history that produced his "tyrannical" father. And he cannot be the man his father was – not until he truly understands his father. He must understand why his father allowed himself to be insulted daily by the "honky" types on the job; why he took a demeaning job in the "shit-house"; and why he spent on his family the violence that he should have directed against the white man. In short, Tim must confront the history of his family. And that is exactly what happens. Each character tells his story, exposing his falsehood to the other until a balance is reached. *Who's Got His Own* is not the work of an alienated mind. Milner's main thrust is directed toward unifying the family around basic moral principles, toward bridging the "generation gap". Other Black playwrights, Jimmy Garrett for example, see the gap as unbridgeable.

Garrett's *We Own the Night* (see *TDR* 12, 4 [T40], pp. 62–9) takes place during an armed insurrection. As the play opens we see the central characters defending a section of the city against attacks by white police. Johnny, the protagonist, is wounded. Some of his Brothers intermittently fire at attacking forces, while others look for medical help. A doctor arrives, forced at gun point. The wounded boy's mother also comes. She is a female Uncle Tom who berates the Brothers and their cause. She tries to get Johnny to leave. She is hysterical. The whole idea of Black people fighting white people is totally outside of her orientation. Johnny begins a vicious attack on his mother, accusing her of emasculating his father – a recurring theme in the sociology of the Black community. In Afro-American literature of previous decades the strong Black mother was the object of awe and respect. But in the new literature her status is ambivalent and laced with tension. Historically, Afro-American women have had to be the economic mainstays of the family. The oppressor allowed them to have jobs while at the same time limiting the economic mobility of the Black man. Very often, therefore, the woman's aspirations and values are closely tied to those of the white power structure and not to those of her man. Since he cannot provide for his family the way white men do, she despises his weakness, tearing into him at every opportunity until, very often, there is nothing left but a shell.

The only way out of this dilemma is through revolution. It either must be an actual blood revolution, or one that psychically redirects the energy of the oppressed. Milner is fundamentally concerned with the latter and Garrett with the former. Communication between Johnny and his mother breaks down. The revolutionary imperative demands that men step outside the legal framework. It is a question of erecting *another* morality. The old constructs do not hold up, because adhering to them means consigning oneself to the oppressive reality. Johnny's mother is involved in the old constructs. Manliness is equated with white morality. And even though she claims to love her family (her men), the overall design of her ideas are against black manhood. In Garrett's play the mother's morality manifests itself in a deep-seated hatred of Black men; while in Milner's work the mother understands, but holds her men back.

The mothers that Garrett and Milner see represent the Old Spirituality – the Faith of the Fathers of which Du Bois spoke. Johnny and Tim represent the New Spirituality. They appear to be a type produced by the upheavals of the colonial world of which Black America is a part. Johnny's assertion that he is a criminal is remarkably similar to the rebel's comments in Aimé Césaire's play, *Les Armes Miraculeuses* (*The Miraculous Weapons*). In that play the rebel, speaking to his mother, proclaims: "My name – an offense; my Christian name – humiliation; my status – a rebel; my age – the stone age". To which the mother replies: "My race – the human race. My religion – brotherhood". The Old Spirituality is generalized. It seeks to recognize Universal Humanity. The New Spirituality is specific. It begins by seeing the world from the concise point-of-view of the colonialized. Where the Old Spirituality would live with oppression while ascribing to the oppressors an innate goodness, the New Spirituality demands a radical shift in point-of-view. The colonialized native, the oppressed must, of necessity, subscribe to a *separate* morality. One that will liberate him and his people.

The assault against the Old Spirituality can sometimes be humorous. In Ben Caldwell's play, *The Militant Preacher*, a burglar is seen slipping into the home of a wealthy minister. The preacher comes in and the burglar ducks behind a large chair. The preacher, acting out the role of the supplicant minister begins to moan, praying to De Lawd for understanding. In the context of today's politics, the minister is an Uncle Tom, mouthing platitudes against self-defense. The preacher drones in a self-pitying monologue about the folly of protecting oneself against brutal policeman. Then the burglar begins to speak. The preacher is startled, taking the burglar's voice for the voice of God. The burglar begins to play on the preacher's old time religion. He *becomes* the voice of God insulting and goading the preacher on until the preacher's attitudes about protective violence change. The next day the preacher emerges militant, gun in hand, sounding like Reverend Cleage in Detroit. He now preaches a new gospel – the gospel of the gun, an eye for an eye. The gospel is preached in the rhythmic cadences of the old Black church. But the content is radical. Just as Jones inverted the symbols in *Jello*, Caldwell twists the rhythms of the Uncle Tom preacher into the language of the new militancy.

These plays are directed at problems within Black America. They begin with the premise that there is a well defined Afro-American audience. An audience that must see itself and the world in terms of its own interests. These plays, along with many others, constitute the basis for a viable movement in the theatre – a movement which takes as its task a profound re-evaluation of the Black man's presence in America. The Black Arts Movement represents the flowering of a cultural nationalism that has been suppressed since the 1920s. I mean the "Harlem Renaissance" – which was essentially a failure. It did not address itself to the mythology and the life-styles of the Black community. It failed to take roots, to link itself concretely to the struggles of that community, to become its voice and spirit. Implicit in the Black Arts Movement is the idea that Black people, however dispersed, constitute a *nation* within the belly of white America. This is not a new idea. Garvey said it and the Honorable Elijah Muhammad says it now. And it is on this idea that the concept of Black Power is predicated.

Afro-American life and history is full of creative possibilities, and the movement is just beginning to perceive them. Just beginning to understand that the most meaningful statements about the nature of Western society must come from the Third World of which Black America is a part. The thematic material is broad, ranging from folk heroes like Shine and Stagolee to historical figures like Marcus Garvey and Malcolm X. And then there is the struggle for Black survival, the coming confrontation between white America and Black America. If art is the harbinger of future possibilities, what does the future of Black America portend?

RITUAL REFORMULATIONS

Barbara Ann Teer and the National Black Theatre of Harlem (1998)

Barbara Lewis

In 1972, four years after she relocated to Harlem where she established her ritual-based company, Barbara Ann Teer, founder of the National Black Theatre (NBT), looked around and saw death and life vying for supremacy in the faces and lives of the people around her. The community where she had chosen to settle and perform her rituals of liberation was in flux, divided in its heart, stumbling forward and also regressing in its efforts to discover and unmask its true and characteristic features. This tumultuous tug of war between the firm grip of a servile past and an independent future aborning was fraught with meaning in the most symbolic and famous black community in the world, a virtual Promised Land synonymous with black transcendence since the mass relocation of sun-kissed peoples from all over the nation and globe that occurred during the Harlem Renaissance.

But Teer, very much aware of the history and symbolism of her new home, understood, in true ritual fashion, that her agenda was to move on up to higher ground, not regurgitate the nostra of an earlier era, no matter how stellar. "I always tell people that this is not a Renaissance, it's a Reinvention", Teer said recently in the living room of her Harlem brownstone:

> Now why is it a reinvention? Because we are coming from an alternative reality, not from a victimized three-fifths of a man, low self-esteem, no-dignity mentality. When you come from an outside-in reality, I call it self-conscious art. God-conscious art comes from an inside-out reality. In the Renaissance, the artists were doing work that was basically addressed to white people, which meant that we were entertaining them and not coming from uplifting our people. The Black Arts Movement that Imamu [Amiri Baraka] was the father of took it to another level. What I have done is take that level to another level which is called God-conscious art which is also designed to come from a different place, a cultural historical place that says our ancestors volunteered themselves into a serving position to learn the ways of the West.
>
> We in fact were a divine race of people called into existence to carry out the work of the Most High. Our labor and love have built a super-power nation. It is now time for us as cultural leaders to fuse spirit

with materialism and come up with a totally different paradigm which I think is the vision of artists. I also believe that we brought the fine arts to this planet and that the fine arts have a particular function that will lift people up, elevate them to the highest level of their awareness so that they can celebrate the joy and wonders of being human. We are in the business of human transformation, lifting the thought patterns of our people out of that victim culture and putting them into a heroic, liberated, victorious culture. We've got to be self-empowering or we're not going to be here. So that's my point of view.[1]

When Teer, once married to comedian and actor Godfrey Cambridge, decided to make Harlem the site of her company just before the dawning of the 1970s, she did so with full appreciation of the meaning of her actions. She took note of her audience, a conflicted community at war with itself, too unsure of its inherent worth to work together as one or make a firm commitment to bringing into fruition a more secure future for itself. The community had to be motivated, but in order to do that, Teer had to understand it on its own terms, find out where it was in its heart. Some Harlemites were enmeshed in abuse against themselves and their neighbors and others were asserting their pride of origin and disconnection from Western ideals, affirming their right and desire to be Other, proclaiming their prerogative not to be homogenized into the mix. The community was in a vertiginous and liminal state, poised on the edge of transition, caught equidistant between a past of enslavement to – and manipulation by – outside forces and a present yearning for more than a superficial attachment to a source, a motherland, that could sustain it in autonomy and self-expressiveness.

Mired in chaos without a liberating myth to call its own, but on the point of transforming itself, the community was ripe for change. The 1960s and the gospel of liberation and independence had come and gone, leaving their mark. So had the Harlem Renaissance. The architecture and achievement of that legendary era still stand as testaments and reminders of another time when blacks wanted to sail home on the boats of Garvey and when indigenous, artistic gods of both genders were created. Those were the days when divinities that are now names in books and pictures on posters cavorted along Elysian paths supposed to lead to freedom and equality. But the road to progress ended in political and cultural bankruptcy. Still, that earlier, ground-breaking generation had sown the seeds for a culture of self-veneration.

"Black consciousness is on the rise", Teer said in an interview in *Theater* magazine at the beginning of the 1970s:

> We have seen it rise steadily in the last four years that we've been in Harlem. People are dressing in African motifs, the naturals are now very common, the black, red and green flags and buttons are displayed all over. But these realities exist alongside an increasing crime rate, a

proliferation of drug addicts, dirtier streets, more and more homicide and the organizing of vigilante teams to get people home safely. These latter situations have not decreased, as should be expected, with the increase in Black consciousness. What is the reason for this situation? How come, if everybody is so Black and proud, Harlem, the largest Black community in the United States, is dying?[2]

More than twenty-five years later, thanks to people of commitment and vision like Barbara Ann Teer, and cultural institutions like the National Black Theatre that have invested and stayed in Harlem, the community has been revitalized, restored to a burgeoning and throbbing life. Harlem may not be dancing at the Savoy any more but it is getting back on its feet and making the effort to find and exert the full measure of its height. Not that the drugs, crime, and dangerous streets have disappeared, but the mix has been leavened. More and more members from the spectrum of the black middle classes, artists, artisans, and professionals like painters, performers, and sculptors, photographers and writers, technocrats and lawyers, entrepreneurs and professors have made Harlem their home. Whether by choice or economic exigency, the Harlem community is literally *remembering* itself, putting the body politic back together again after the dismemberment, the disassembly that was desegregation. In the process, what has been engendered is a recollectivized mass whose presence and needs present a potent and more productive front. There is now a sizeable resident community capable and desirous of supporting the arts, especially when those artistic endeavors speak directly to and about them. Consequently, the community's cultural component and the pride that were previously only specters struggling for substance have gotten stronger. There is a definite mood among African Americans to cleave to their own, to see themselves as a special and unique community, distinct from other communities, a social and cultural collective, a family unto itself.

Ritual, as Teer comprehends it, has much to do with this metamorphosis, this social and cultural realignment and reassessment. Teer was not alone in privileging ritual as the form that represented a separation from artistic paradigms imposed from the outside. The New Lafayette Theatre, which was started in Harlem in 1966, two years before Teer moved uptown, also gravitated toward ritual instead of traditional dramatic structure. "[I]t doesn't serve our purpose", Robert Macbeth said in 1969.[3] Macbeth was head of the New Lafayette, whose name recalled and paid homage to the Lafayette Players, a theatrical group based at the Lafayette Theatre and popular during the Harlem Renaissance. Joined by writers Ed Bullins, Richard Wesley, Martie-Evans Charles, Sonia Sanchez, and OyamO, and actors such as Sonny Jim, Roscoe Orman, Rosanna Carter, Yvette Hawkins, and George Miles, the New Lafayette was the leading Harlem theatre in the 1960s.

Macbeth championed the development of a ritualistic theatre that

Plate 1: Class session of Group Theatre Workshop in the 1960s. Standing is Robert Hooks and seated on the high chair is Dr Barbara Ann Teer. Other members include, on the bottom right, Hattie Winston and other students. Photo courtesy of Dr Barbara Ann Teer.

departed from the canonical Aristotelian format and was more in line with the natural tendencies of the indigenous community. Under the rubric of ritual, audiences would be active rather than passive recipients and more involved in improvising on the received texts that represented disabling rather than enabling fictions. This attitude was consistent with the revolutionary thinking of the time that sought to disengage from artistic and social configurations that had served to strangle and contain an agenda of autonomy. Paul Carter Harrison argues in his introduction to *Kuntu Drama* that in order to emerge from under the shadow of past subordination, the theatrical artist subscribing to the African continuum must focus on the living quality of the *event* and not on the static *play*, expressing the philosophy behind the modality of contemporary black ritual form.[4] The ritualistic theatre is the theatre of liberation.

Since it is symbolic behavior that both joins and separates people, ritual, on the very simplest level, means pattern that has become institutionalized as practice. Patterns of behavior that are regular and customary constitute the rituals of our lives, those repeated actions that structure and give meaning to our daily existence, that erect the pillars of our universe and tell the rest of the world who we are and what we believe. Usually, however, ritual is imposed on us by necessity or we settle comfortably into the lethargy that is habit, pursuing a pattern of least resistance, adopting a mode of behavior dictated by those powers and authorities that hold the whip of control poised, ready to crack, over our lives. Rarely do we have the opportunity or foresight to restructure our reality totally, to decide who and what and when we want to be, to refashion ourselves in line with our desire.

But that is what Barbara Ann Teer did when she moved to Harlem. And in so doing, she took an active stance toward ritual, embracing and employing it to reflect and register a seismic shift in her consciousness, a reorientation with major repercussions for herself as well as her company and community:

> Instead of having rites performed on us, we do them to and for ourselves, and immediately we are involved in a form of self-creation that is potentially community-building.[5]

Trained in drama and in dance, which is the most collective and ritualistic of all the art forms,[6] Teer possesses an intimate and full awareness of the synergistic significance of routines and roles, which are forms of ritual, and how they can be readjusted and restructured. The individual is not limited to the roles that are inherited by virtue of membership in a given family or group or nation. We can rewrite those roles, choose to follow another ritual, to remake the self in accord with whatever choices the individual deems desirable and worthwhile.

By making the decision to come to Harlem, to separate herself from the life she had known and pursued before, to change her status from actress to producer and theatrical entrepreneur, to withdraw from what she perceived as an alien climate, Teer was using ritual to her advantage. By taking an active role, forcing a breach, performing her own rite of passage from one life phase to another, Teer was empowering herself and others. By turning her back on the commercial world and endeavoring to situate herself fully in the life of Harlem, Teer was acknowledging the transformative potential of Harlem as well as a need for new patterns and innovative rituals, thereby recreating herself and her company in relation to an ancestral and alternative past. By repudiating a cultural configuration that failed to embody her vision of herself, she was redesigning and expanding the collective panorama of expectation. "I think that a ritual is a reverend rite that marks the passing from one space, one mind set to another more highly evolved space",[7] Teer has said. "It's always something that elevates you. That's how I view it. And so my job was and is to elevate the level of awareness of my people to a higher level of consciousness about who they are".[8]

Ritual is collective and participatory. Contrasted with traditional theatre, ritual is inclusive rather than exclusive. There exists a line, in theatre, between observer and observed, seer and seen, watcher and watched. In ritual, there is no such division. Ritual is not performed for the benefit of the spectator, but rather to engender cohesion and communitas between all who join in the act. Everyone who engages in the ritual is a performer, an initiate in the rite, and the possibility of self and group transformation is enhanced in proportion to the density of adherents. Ritual is not voyeuristic, but pragmatic and purposeful, effecting individual benefit as well as group solidarity. Theatre, an exercise in aesthetics, is designed to pleasure the viewer, providing vicarious experience, sectioning off labor, creating separate cadres of workers and leisured. Ritual abrogates class; theatre reinforces it.

Changing the ritual of her life, either because of physical or psychological pain, is something that Teer has had to do more than once in her career. After studying the Mary Wigman technique in Germany and Switzerland and spending some time in Paris, Teer landed her first job on Broadway in 1961, dancing in *Kwamina*, a musical with an African motif. In that production, she also took charge of the other dancers, running them through their paces for the show's choreographer, Agnes de Mille. After earning a Tony for her performance, Teer went on to dance in a variety of venues, including Las Vegas as a back-up dancer for Pearl Bailey and in the companies of several major African-American choreographers, including Louis Johnson and Alvin Ailey. Because of an injury to her knee, Teer had to stop dancing, so she switched from dance to drama, making her debut as an actress at the Provincetown Playhouse in New York in 1962, playing Bella Belafunky in *Raisin' Hell in the Son*. Two years later, she was back at the Provincetown, performing the role of Violet the maid in *Home Movies*, the first Rosalyn Drexler play to be produced. In *Home Movies,* Teer sang two songs that parodied black spirituals, "Sometimes I Feel like a Chocolate Turkey", and "I'll Tell You What de Lawd Done for Me – Nothin'!" For her role in this show, Teer won an Obie in 1964 and the Vernon Rice Award in 1965.

Just before Thanksgiving in 1965, Teer opened in *Day of Absence* and *Happy Ending*, both by Douglas Turner Ward. In the first of the two shows, Teer appeared in whiteface and was directed by Robert Hooks, with whom she was affiliated at the Group Theatre Workshop, the precursor to the Negro Ensemble Company. "Robert and I were very good friends", Teer recalled:

> [W]e had been friends for years. He was in *Dutchman* at the time and I was studying with Sanford Meisner. I was a perpetual student. [. . .] There were lots of young people who used to come to the theatre in the village to see Robert in this play. He had a loft down on Nineteenth Street and he would invite them to come over. I was born into a family of educators. All my family were teachers on some level. So it was just natural for me to want to teach. What I discovered was that there was no art form to teach

them even though I was studying with the best in the business. I mean between Sandy Meisner and Lee Strasberg you couldn't get any higher as far as teachers or mentors in the theatre. The Stanislavsky Method that I was learning was totally irrelevant to these kids who came out of the streets.

So I began to experiment. No books, just intuition. I took an eight-line poem by Gwendolyn Brooks called *We Real Cool* and expanded it into a whole evening and the Group Theatre Workshop became an entity. We used Robert's space and Robert's magnetism because he was in *Dutchman* to recruit the young people and I did the teaching and the directing and the creative work. Joe Papp was so impressed with what we had done that he put the show on the Mobile Unit. We got a lot of publicity. People like Antonio Fargas and Hattie Winston were teenagers in this particular group. So that's how the Group Theatre Workshop started. We were very intense in our commitment to giving them a creative outlet.

At a certain point, Doug had written *Day of Absence* and he was trying to find a producer. Actually my father was the first person to put up a thousand dollars to produce that show and so most of us went into the production of that first piece down in the Village. As a result of that, Doug wrote an article that appeared in the *New York Times*. That article got a lot of attention and the Ford Foundation gave the grant to start the Negro Ensemble Company. Well, I was opposed to the title, the Negro Ensemble Company. I was opposed to the geography, the location. I was opposed to the whole thing and I didn't win so I left and I came to Harlem. And they stayed downtown. And that's the way it went.[9]

Teer won a second Obie for her performance as Mary, a southern wife and mother who had no conception of the domestic requirements of either role. Mary was absolutely dependent on her maid Lula who, like all the other black servants in *Day of Absence*, has decided to take the day off; hence the title of the play. Mary can't cook or change her baby's diaper and when it cries, she would rather kill than comfort it. *Day of Absence* was double billed with *Happy Ending*, and despite a transportation strike that would have killed off lesser shows, the plays continued to attract an audience intrigued by their novelty. Ward, who became a major power in black theatre for the next two decades, was raising a revolutionary question about where the locus of power existed, with the workers or with the leisured. The answer to the question was not lost on Teer. Because the workers were the ones making the engines churn, they could, with the exertion of courage and will, make their presence or absence felt and thus direct the course of their own productivity rather than be forever at the command of others.

Three years later, Teer staged her own moratorium, turning her back on the downtown commercial theatre. She was tired of playing maids, prostitutes, and exotics, roles that depicted her as menial and fulfilling someone else's fantasy of how she should be, a cipher on someone else's

Plate 2: Esther Pulliam and Conrad Neblett in *The Legacy* by Gordon Nelson, performed during the 1989–90 season of the National Black Theatre. Photo by Leon Pinkney.

book rather than a factor in her own store of assets. The turning point came in a gospel show written by Langston Hughes called *Prodigal Son*. The director of that show made it clear that he wanted her to talk and gesture like Butterfly McQueen and look like Lena Horne. Teer decided to initiate her own disassociation from the past rather than try to fit into rituals devised by others that did not accord with her reality. She cut her hair as both a sign of defiance and rejection of the roles allotted to her and of identification with the political climate of the 1960s, realizing that she was capable of writing her own future through and with her body. Her future was not going to be authored by others. She wasn't going to be what people wanted; she was going to please herself and find a space where her natural image was acceptable. She created an entirely new role for herself, casting herself as primary rather than secondary, a role that no one but she could have written or performed. Writing years later in the *Amsterdam News*, Teer expressed the opinion that "each of us is our own author, director, producer and star. In each moment, we have the power, the unalienable right to alter our actions and reinterpret the circumstances of our lives. In each moment, we have the freedom to speak, write and invent our own scripts. Invent our own beginning, middle and end".[10]

But before going uptown to the freedom to recreate herself that Harlem offered, Teer fired her manager and agent and went home to East St Louis, Illinois for six months. "One of these days people will study East St Louis", Teer said in homage to the city of her birth:

> It's a very fascinating place. It is the home of innovation and it gave us people like Miles Davis, Josephine Baker, Coltrane, Dick Gregory, Donal McHenry, Leon Thomas, Harry Edwards, and Jackie Joyner. When you come from East St Louis, you come from an environment that is black. I didn't see white people until I was fourteen. They were on the other side of the railroad tracks. They lived on one side of town and we lived on the other. We had our own schools and they had their own schools. We didn't mix. So we had some of the finest educators. We had the best education, sports, art, culture, dance, and theatre.
>
> We grew up like that. A lot of us are innovators. That only means that you are already where you are supposed to be. You are clear where you are. You don't have to wade up the hill to try to prove to white people that you are as good as they are. That's not even an issue. That's why I could form a theatre in Harlem and not try to be downtown. I'm not trying to prove to anybody that I can do what they do. So when you come from a paradigm of thinking and being that doesn't have to compete with other standards, being as good as the Joneses and all that, you've got a whole lot of energy to create with.[11]

During her self-enforced break from the commercial New York circuit, Teer was home recharging her batteries and taking time to think and reconceptualize, waiting to make her next move. Then she heard from some friends that Amiri Baraka had been arrested in Newark. She returned to New York to produce a benefit, *We Sing a New Song*, for him. After that, she directed *The Believers*, co-written by Joseph Walker, the author of *The River Niger*, which was a big success for the Negro Ensemble Company in the 1970s. In response to requests for her to teach acting again, Teer found a loft in Harlem and that is how the National Black Theatre began.

When she first moved to Harlem, Teer and the members of her company, who prefer to be called liberators because their perceived role is liberating themselves and their audiences from unproductive thinking, created a questionnaire designed to survey the predispositions of their prospective audience, to find out everything they could about their adopted community on the outer and upper margin of Manhattan. "We learned", Teer wrote in the *Amsterdam News*, "from living our lives [. . .] on the edge, asking questions, seeking answers, being in the heart of life".[12] To get their questions answered, they went to where the people were. First, the liberators attended the churches in Harlem. Ecumenical in their visiting practices, they went to the Holy Roller, Pentecostal, and Baptist churches, speaking to the preachers, deacons, and sisters. After they had visited all the churches, Teer and company went to the bars, another hot spot of secular congress for the Harlem community. After that came the revival meetings, and then they returned to the churches to listen to the singing. The final stop was the Apollo [Theatre] where the group learned the most. "[W]e studied the different performers and we began to understand how they related to an audience", Teer told Charlie Russell during an interview in *Essence* in March 1971:

> We began to discover how they did what they did to the audience. [. . .] In many ways we've patterned ourselves after the Church. There was a time when the Black Church satisfied all the spiritual, social, cultural, economic, and recreational needs of our people. As a matter of fact, we see ourselves as being more in the vein of a church rather than a theatre, and we are attempting to provide an alternative for those people who can no longer go to the Black Church because of its ideology.[13]

Teer's theatre is ritualistic and communal, designed not to maintain divisions and distinctions between people, but to erase them. During intermission, the liberators do not go backstage, separating themselves from the audience. Instead, they seek communion with the crowd, welcoming them, serving them drinks and reinforcing the feelings and ideas that were broached in performance. Ritual is especially effective in Harlem which is essentially an enclave of equals and therefore possesses a greater potential of unison in its population. Hierarchies exist and do foment hostilities but the stratifications are more porous than they are downtown. Uptown, pigment is the great leveler, and everyone belongs to the same rather inchoate but extended family. The external perception of the group identity forces everyone belonging to the group into the same mold. There is little if any differentiation accorded to the constituents of the group. By default, all are members of the same denomination, forced to genuflect at the same altar.

A high point for the National Black Theatre came in 1977 when the company traveled to Nigeria for FESTAC, an international festival of arts and culture. Teer and company performed "Soljourney into Truth", a mosaic of song and dance, music and theatre which Teer wrote and directed. The effect on the audience, drawn from all the black nations of the world, has been described in terms of mass euphoria. Before going to FESTAC, Teer and company decided to test the production on an international black audience and so NBT traveled to Trinidad and Guyana, generating enthusiastic responses. In the 1970s, Teer and company toured to other islands in the Caribbean, expanding NBT's audience base. NBT generally performs about six productions a year. In addition to traditional plays with scripts such as *Revival* which Teer co-authored with Charlie Russell, *Wine in the Wilderness* by Alice Childress, *Seven Comes Up, Seven Come Down* by Lonnie Elder III, Teer and company also regularly perform rituals called *blackenings*, adapted from West Indian and African sources.

NBT grew steadily from its beginnings in The East Wind, a loft on 125th Street that Teer and her acting students shared with Gylain Kain, an actor who had been one of the Last Poets, a performance group popular in the 1960s. About six months after its 1968 inception, NBT moved down the street and leased the top floor in a three-story former jewelry factory on the corner of Fifth Avenue. Everyone in the company helped to convert the dusty space into a rehearsal and performance loft. NBT continued to grow and leased the second floor, converting the third floor into administrative and training facilities. The second floor became home to the children's component. Finally, NBT occupied a berth on the ground floor, establishing a visible presence on the 125th Street business corridor.

"Fifth Avenue is the symbol of opulence all over the world. And 125th Street is a symbol of Black culture", Teer has stated, emphasizing the significance of the location that NBT has occupied and fought hard to maintain for the last thirty years. Teer has refused to budge from there and, further, has revitalized the spot, erecting a multimillion-dollar arts complex where the avenue of affluence runs into the reputed home of poverty. "That is why this location is so important. A lot of people don't know that Fifth Avenue goes through Harlem",[14] but Fifth Avenue intersects the heart of Harlem, and that is the site of the most self-sufficient black theatre in America.

By 1983, when the old building burned out, Teer and her company

> had been all over the African world declaring in huge performances that
> Harlem was now and forever the cultural capital of the world and we

Plate 3: Elmo Terry Morgan's play *Song of Sheba* was performed by NBT in its 1989–90 season. Featured here are, in the top row, from right to left: Brenda Dansby, Michael Lewis, Gloria McNeal; and, in the bottom row, from right to left: Carla Hill, William Breedlove, and Marsha Z. West. Photo by Bruce Williams.

were on the corner of Fifth Avenue and 125th Street, their home away from home. People loved it and began to identify with it. So it was only a natural progression that we would buy that building. The fire happened about two or three days before our option to buy expired. Kentucky Fried Chicken was the anchor tenant and they had a lot of grease in the basement. Anyway, we were vying with them as to who was going to get this building. We did a lot of negotiating and there was a court case. It was a whole big thing with Kentucky Fried Chicken because they wanted to level the building and put in a drive-in. But we had been there for fifteen years and our vibes were there. Of course we won and we bought the building and the rest is history.[15]

Not one to be easily daunted by setbacks of any kind, Teer reached deep into her store of ritual, understanding that she had to climb higher, not fall back. So, almost immediately, she began the process of rebuilding. But that endeavor took much longer than expected. Finally, however, she put together the necessary funding and created a megacomplex of art, business, and theatre in Harlem, the first African-American artistic institution in the country to establish economic emancipation, finding a

Plate 4: Kerry Ruff and Doreen Whitten in *Power Play* by Lorey Hayes, part of NBT's 1989–90 season. Photo by Patricia Thorpe.

way to pay its bills and guarantee its future without being limited to and having to pursue the nonprofit route, which is at best precarious.

Getting the company reestablished and solidly into the black took Teer ten years and many millions of dollars. To do so, she knocked on the doors of more than ten metropolitan banks before one said yes. She had to convince the business community that she was serious and her plans for the future fiscally sound. Her persistence and refusal not to let her dream die have created tangible results. Now, the National Black Theatre is landlord to other artistic institutions as well as an insurance firm, an international chain catering to the comfort and care of the body, a store specializing in dance and sportswear, and a computer facility. Revenue from real estate keeps the company's artistic ball rolling. But more important, the National Black Theatre is no longer dependent on funding sources at a time when funds for art are becoming more and more scarce, and artistic companies are falling left and right like wheat in the path of a raised sickle.

Moving beyond an insistent allegiance to the past that was inscripted in the names of the New Lafayette Theatre and the Negro Ensemble Company (the former defunct and the latter struggling), Barbara Ann Teer believes that separate is superior to being designated equal when someone else owns and controls the house. She has created a citadel of culture in Harlem, built on a foundation that accommodates art and business on a compatible footing. Out of the rhetoric and s(t)and of the 1960s, there emerged, in Harlem, a people's temple of theatre and ritual, connecting past memory to present pulse, a monument finally making manifest in steel and glass what an investment in the uniqueness and genius of the people of Harlem can yield in dividends.

The structure was designed by Geppaul Architects, a Brooklyn-based black firm. "Architecturally, we were always trying to stay consistent with an African modality", Teer said about the design of the theatre:

> It's circular and not linear. It's octagon-shaped and it's got a dome. It's got the largest Yoruba art collection in the western hemisphere. All the twenty-two statues on the inside give off a certain frequency. They tell stories about our ancestors. The relief art in aluminum, copper, and brass tells stories about our journey to the New World. [. . .] African people are empowered by themselves, the self inside. We have a museum in our theatre now, a living museum. It's called the African Museum of the Tradition of Self-Empowerment. We start in 1690 with Prince Hall and we go all the way up to Ron Brown and we demonstrate how over sixty to seventy of our men and women who were cited as leaders were about self-empowering their people. That tradition was broken down at the end of the Civil Rights movement. Integration intervened there.
>
> But the fact of the matter is that the people who stayed downtown did not have vision, in my opinion. You can see that ultimately, things come, things go. Governments change. Parties change. If you are dependent on something outside yourself to take care of you, when that thing no longer exists, you're out of business. What I wanted to do was build an institution that was an alternative learning environment that was also an alternative reality from the victim culture that we were born into in this country. And I made it very clear. When you want to prove to white people that you can do their forms as well as they can, then that's what you do. I have no need to prove to European Americans that I can compete and compare with their art forms. I didn't appreciate the fact that I was limited by that linear art form. And I wanted to break it up, to bust it open – that whole linear Western thought. And it will happen, not just by me but by many, many people.
>
> So because I have been a straight A student all my life – I come from a highly intelligent family, my sister was a declared genius, I graduated from high school when I was fifteen, I graduated from college *summa cum laude* when I was nineteen – I never had a need to prove to white people that I was as good as they are. I just never did. It was never in my consciousness so I had no need to stay downtown although I worked downtown. I had a need to invent my own. And that's what I did.[16]

NOTES

1. Lewis 1997.
2. Jones 1972:18–19.
3. Gant 1972:50.
4. Harrison 1974.
5. Myerhoff 1982:130.
6. Copeland and Cohen 1983:316.
7. Lewis 1997.
8. *Ibid.*
9. *Ibid.*
10. Teer 1997:13.
11. Lewis 1997.
12. Teer 1997:13.
13. Russell 1971:57, 58.
14. Shepard 1995:8.
15. Lewis 1997.
16. *Ibid.*

BIBLIOGRAPHY

Copeland, Roger, and Cohen, Marshall, *What Is Dance?*, New York, Oxford University Press, 1983.

Gant, Lisbeth, "The New Lafayette Theatre: Anatomy of a Community Art Institution", *TDR* 16, 4 (1972), 46–55.

Harrison, Paul Carter, ed., *Kuntu Drama: Plays of the African Continuum*, New York, Grove Press, 1974.

Jones, Martha, "National Black Theater: Temple of Liberation for a Black Nation in Harlem", *Theater*, Summer 1972, 19–23.

Lewis, Barbara, Personal interview with Barbara Ann Teer, New York, 22 August 1997.

Myerhoff, Barbara, "Rites of Passage: Process and Paradox" in *Celebration: Studies in Festivity and Ritual*, Victor Turner, ed., Washington, DC, Smithsonian Institution Press, 1982, 109–35.

Russell, Charlie, "Barbara Ann Teer: We Are Liberators, Not Actors", *Essence*, March 1971, 48–52.

Shepard, Joan, "National Black Theater Survives and Maintains Its Independence", *The City Sun*, 9–15 August 1995, 8–9.

Teer, Barbara Ann, "Reinvention of a People", *The New York Amsterdam News*, 14–20 August 1997, 13, 45.

TO MAKE BLACK BODIES STRANGE

Social Critique in Concert Dance of the Black Arts Movement (1998)

Thomas DeFrantz

BLACK BODIES DESTABILIZED – MANIFESTOS OF BLACK ARTS MOVEMENT

The Black Arts Movement of the late 1960s inspired a heightened critique of American social [dis]order by African American artists. Like their "New Negro" counterparts of a generation earlier, the group of writers and visual artists spearheading this movement denounced the seeming complacency of their immediate elders. "We Shall Overcome", the motto of the 1963 March on Washington led by Reverend Martin Luther King, Jr, was replaced by "Up Against the Wall, Motherfucker!" a slogan popularized by playwright LeRoi Jones [Amiri Baraka], whose play *Dutchman* opened in New York in March of 1964.

In that play, Lula, a white demon–woman, taunts an Ivy-League educated Negroman called, with dripping irony, Clay. Lula leads her changeling into a dance of death which ends, inevitably, when she kills him and prepares to seek out her next victim. The play hinges on an assumption that Clay wears a mask in public. It is a mask which has allowed him to survive and flourish in a hostile atmosphere, but it is a mask nonetheless – and Lula rattles him, prods and pokes, until he lets the mask drop to reveal vast stores of rage. Lula is able to push Clay to the edge and then kill him because she knows him so well. As critic Larry Neal observed, Lula's knowledge of Clay is extensive because in many ways she has created the mask that he wears. She has created him.

The young artists of the Black Arts Movement resisted this presumption of knowledge on the part of their white audiences. They worked, as Neal wrote, towards art which could suggest its own symbolism, mythology, critique, and iconology.[1] As in *Dutchman*, art created in service to the movement attempted to destabilize stereotypical imagery of the Negro. Rendered apparent, the mask of a long-suffering but tolerant black populace crashed to the floor, revealing a vigorous black body barely able to contain its anger in the face of overwhelming social inequity.

The Black Arts Movement held a unique and important relationship to the Black Power Movement. Artists were indeed concerned with the relationship between art and politics, and through their affirmed association with Black Power, they sought to create an essentialized vision which could prescribe artistic products. As Abby Arthur and Ronald Mayberry Johnson point out in their insightful study of 1960s literary magazines,

> As revealed in black little magazines, the theorists and practitioners of the black aesthetic focused on both the appearance and purpose of the new literature. The purpose determined all other aesthetic matters, considered secondary in importance. Stated in general terms, the literature was to be an instrument of separatism, a means of disengaging blacks from Western culture. [. . .] Separatism, emphasized in contemporary literature, was not an end in itself. The larger goal was a new black consciousness and hence a new black community. [. . .] Inspired by their sense of purpose, writers of the black aesthetic presented themselves as missionaries of blackness, talked about art-for-people's sake, and dreamed of a literature exclusively by, about, and for, blacks.[2]

The movement assumed an infrangible connection between politics and art, and espoused a communal model of art production which valued participation of artists and audience as a guiding principle. On some level, the art explicitly confirmed the well-being of the group. Because, as Neal writes, the movement was "opposed to any concept of the artist that alienates him from his community",[3] its artists rejected abstract metaphor in favor of direct expression which could immediately inspire its audience. The purpose of the art, as a tool of community engagement, mattered.

CONCERT DANCE

The task of pushing concert dance toward a politically viable use as both an instrument and expression of black power ideology fell to young dancers weaned on the largely apolitical choreographic standard common by the 1960s. Established modes of concert dance concerned themselves to a large degree with abstractions of, or dramatic narratives describing, everyday political concerns. Following an aesthetic lineage including Katherine Dunham, Martha Graham, Lester Horton, and Pearl Primus, young black artists in the 1950s imagined concert dance as the exploration and expression of the individual self through movement design. For these artists, the dancing body could achieve transcendency through the exploration of intimate personal truths. In this model, the purpose of the art derived from the individual artist's ability to communicate to an audience.

Talley Beatty and Alvin Ailey number among the most prominent choreographers working in this individualistic idiom during the 1950s. Beatty's classic work, *Road of the Phoebe Snow* (1959), described an interracial love affair which ends in tragedy along the Lackawanna Railway in the South. Beatty had been one of Katherine Dunham's earliest company of dancers trained in Chicago, and he later worked with filmmaker Maya Deren in the landmark film *A Study in Choreography for Camera* (1945). He appeared in a revival of the musical *Showboat*, and in a 1946 ballet *Blackface*, created for the Ballet Society (the precursor to the New York City Ballet). Beatty began making dances for his own company in the late 1940s and his work, which was filled with fluid patterns and challenging, spitfire combinations, positioned its audience as a bystander to onstage dramatic events.

Alvin Ailey's *Revelations* (1960) presented an oblique narrative of spiritual uplift through a chronological setting of abstract dance to black religious music. An immediate success, *Revelations* suggested the triumph of black spirit through song and dance, from its opening dances with slavery-era costuming and music, to its enthusiastic promise of deliverance in its final song, "Rocka My Soul in the Bosom of Abraham". *Revelations* established Ailey's company as the pre-eminent interpreter of black experience for a large international audience. But Ailey's choreography, like Beatty's, created an abstract metaphor for survival; dance created in the context of the Black Arts Movement, with its constant exploration of a performative dialectic between performer and audience, was to provide a tool for survival. The Black Arts Movement produced dance works with radical, inflammatory content which, in essence, sought to destabilize the familiar image of black people dancing – to make the dancing black body strange.

Concert dancers who approached the Black Power Movement faced a contradictory dilemma. Many of them had trained in ballet and established modes of American modern dance, two forms which had been created from a Europeanist vantage and for a largely white audience. The separatist demands of the nationalist moment precluded an acknowledgment of Eurocentric dance heritage; still, young black dancers respected the amount of information their bodies contained from intensive studio training. Even as younger dance artists strove to find forms which could be identified as conforming to an emergent black aesthetic, they could not easily dismiss their dance training as "inappropriately white". Black nationalists with no dance background eyed concert dance warily; they suspected work created in a mold favored by already established choreographers like Ailey and Beatty as complicit in maintaining the racist *status quo*.

BLACK ARTS DANCE PRACTICE

To create work, the movement spawned numerous aesthetic salons of black artists. Quoting from the Johnsons again about the concurrent literary movement, we can extrapolate a sense of the dance scene: "These gatherings gave considerable impetus to the Black Arts Movement. They brought writers together, enhanced their sense of community, and provided a setting and forum for the debate over and celebration of the black aesthetic".[4] Dancers were no different in this, and coalition-building throughout the 1960s led to several shared performances and the First Annual Congress on Blacks in Dance held at Indiana University in Bloomington, Indiana.

Artists hoped to grab at an aesthetic momentum for making black art; to make work which spoke to a nationalist identity even as it rejected conventional Eurocentric models of dance composition. Few achieved this goal so completely as Eleo Pomare. Born in Colombia, South America, Pomare attended New York's High School of the Performing Arts, founded a company in 1958, disbanded it to travel to Europe to study and perform with Kurt Joos and Harold Kreutzberg, then returned to the United States in 1964 when he revived and expanded his company. Pomare, thus, began like many other dancers in the Black Arts Movement with a Eurocentric background, but he soon became enmeshed in the momentum of the moment and began making protest work.

Pomare's early landmark work, *Blues for the Jungle* (1966), explored a dysfunctional black community peopled by drug addicts, prostitutes, and various denizens. Like Ailey's earlier work *Blues Suite* (1958), Pomare staged a scene of socially disaffected black people, and implicated his mostly white audience in the construction of familiar black stage stereotypes. But where Ailey's work had offered an entertaining and only slightly critical take on the racial conditions, Pomare's work reached off the stage and into the audience, forcing the issue of social change on his dancers and their audience. In the solo "Junkie", for example, the dancer careers across the stage in search of a fix, finally tumbling off the stage and directly entreating the audience to satisfy his needs. The dance assumes the involvement of its audience in its construction; the dancer approaches and finally rejects his audience when he cannot get what he needs from them. The dance itself is conceived as an act of protest, and the inclusion and subsequent rejection of the audience here is an expression of that protest.

Understandably, the easiest emotion to express in art of protest then, as it is now, was rage. In the work of several choreographers of this moment, the dancing black body was destabilized and marked by its eccentric movements or outlandish costuming. Concert work of this era often had titles which expressed black nationalist ideology: John Parks' 1971 work *Trilogy* had sections titled "It Happens Every Day (in which a

Brother dies)", "A Woman's Way (in which a Sister mourns)", and "the Man's the Klan (in which Brother and Sister come together)". According to a performance review by critic Zita Allen, "[t]he idea was clear: raised fists, the sound of explosions, the angry death of the brother in the first part, the lyrical mourning of the second part and in the third section, the determination and togetherness of both in the face of the enemy".[5] Eleo Pomare's work "Gin Woman Distress" of 1971, danced by Carole Johnson in a lecture demonstration at the National Black Theatre in Harlem, was set to the spiritual "I'm Going Through". According to Arthur Wilson's review of the dance, Johnson created a portrait of a wayward woman: "As the dance ended, Carole stood limp and sorry eyed, her wig thrown on the floor, two large earrings sailing about the room, and her dress torn half off".[6] The rending of her mask – in this case, a whorish identity contained in her hooker apparel – revealed submerged anguish and rage beneath the familiar veneer of the stereotype of black woman as sexually available. In a way, the dance echoed the dropping of the mask, the revelation of an estranged, alternative reality long denied.

In the same performance review, Wilson comments on another Pomare work danced by Johnson, an excerpt from *Black on Black*, also of 1971:

> The piece from Eleo's new *Black on Black* in which Carole dances the role of Cleaver's wife is very strong in its didactic message of "niggers is afraid of revolution" (using the music of The Last Poets. HEAVY!) but needs much more work. A gun, sunglasses, and a black leather coat are used to give the appearance of the transition necessary to slip into revolutionary shoes. At the end of the dance Carole fires her gun several times in the declaration of "a ready to burn yo' ass nigger". This momentum is clearly necessary, but does not follow from the dance. ... Maybe Eleo was concerned with suggestions, you know, THE MESSAGE, and not the MEDIUM. And if so, that's hip, black dance need not be structured or performed in the traditional emotionally contrived mime technique of Graham. We are no longer puppets on white strings.[7]

Part of forming a nationalist black art identity involved claiming a concert environment which valued participation of audience in the creation of the performance. The Black Arts Movement encouraged a vocal, call-and-response model of participatory spectatorship in which audience members answered performers' movements with applause, encouragement, and shouts. This was closely tied to African diasporic spiritual practice, and the black church offered obvious and sustained precedent for participatory performance. In this, the Black Arts Movement held profound implications for concert dance practice. We can track the change in a broad dancegoing public from silent witnesses to the cheering fans familiar by the 1980s to the efforts made by artists working within the Black Arts Movement. An emphasis on the relationship between concert performance and the community meant a reevaluation of the audience's role in the performance as well as that audience's expectations. This also inspired the most important shift among black concert choreographers – the use of contemporary black music for concert dance. Again, this innovation held enormous implications and effected a profound impact upon concert dance practice the world over.

But the subsequent commodification of contemporary black music into an amorphous, unmarked category of "popular music" complicates this argument terribly. I mean to suggest that the artists of the Black Arts Movement ignored Eurocentric categories of high and low art which placed Aretha Franklin or Otis Redding below William Grant Still or Duke Ellington, or the entire body of spirituals, for that matter. Choreographing to black music which could be concurrently heard on radio hit parades or at house parties was not, for them, necessarily an ironic parody of concert dance convention or a gesture towards the articulation of a deracialized American cultural memory (as it might have been for the audience of, say, white American choreographer Twyla Tharp). For the black nationalist audience, as well as for many African Americans who didn't define themselves as nationalists, contemporary black music could rouse the aesthetic efficacy of its predecessors (which included William Grant Still, Duke Ellington, and the spirituals). Dancing to Donny Hathaway or Otis Redding offered an opportunity to confirm, with an audience, where contemporary black expressivity lay. A generation later, I think that African American choreographers still work differently with contemporary black music than their white counterparts do; witness the irony in white choreographer Neil Greenberg's "Disco Project" (1995) compared to the insistent spirituality of African-American Ronald K. Brown's choreography to similar club music selections which he titled "Heaven/Home" (1995).

THE FEET

The reviews I've quoted come from *The Feet,* a monthly dance magazine published occasionally from 1970 to 1973. Carole Johnson, a dancer who worked with Pomare, and also as a soloist, was affiliated with *The Feet* for its entire existence, as contributor, subject, and editor. *The Feet* was created as a project of MODE, the Modern Organization for Dance Evolvement, of which Johnson was founder and president. In the premiere June 1970 issue of *The Feet*, MODE listed a two-part emphasis: to be of service to professionals in dance, and to be an educational and informational organization for the general public and people in other professions interested in dance. A twelve-part list offered the organization's goals as follows:

1. Design programs and projects that will create more work for black companies.
2. Take dance performances into the black communities so that the people will feel and understand the importance of dance in their lives.
3. Provide information about black dancers, choreographers, companies, and schools.
4. Begin a picture file and act as a clearing house so that magazines, especially black ones, can get information and feature dance in their publications.
5. Develop more written material on dance by printing articles and pamphlets.
6. Develop educational programs that make use of audio-visual techniques.
7. Start a newsletter for communication of ideas and activities.
8. Help develop and maintain up-to-date archives on black dancers and choreographers.
9. To develop financial support from a greater portion of the black people.
10. Help create centers in other areas of the nation so that companies can have residencies of at least a week.
11. Help black colleges find teachers.
12. Design programs so the neighborhood dance schools in the various cities can establish relationships with each other as well as with professional dance companies.[8]

This last goal speaks to the black nationalist agenda of MODE and *The Feet* as its publication instrument.

The nationalist moment assumed a commonalty among black people in communities scattered across the country which could be enriched by the creation of black art, art which contained an incontrovertible political component. *The Feet* forwarded black nationalist rhetoric in varying degrees of ferventness throughout its publication, and a page 1 article of vol. 1, no. 3 entitled "It's Nation Time – Labor for a Nation" solicited money to send delegates to the 4th annual Black Power Conference held in Atlanta, Georgia. Nine months later, *The Feet* reported how that festival established The Langston Hughes House of Kuumba as an outgrowth of the Creativity Workshop held at the Black Power Conference, and sponsored by the CAP, the Congress of African People. (This was the 1960s: there were lots of organizations with acronyms to be deciphered.)

In April and May of 1971, The House of Kuumba hosted a dance festival of groups which fit its prescribed statement of black art, as follows:

For Black Art to be of relevance and importance to the struggle for National Liberation, that art must possess three qualities:

1. Collective,
2. Committing, and
3. Functional.

COLLECTIVE – It must come from a whole people showing all the aspects of the people, the community, and the family.
COMMITTING –It should dedicate Black people to change; to struggle against those who struggle against them, and make peace with those who make peace with them.
FUNCTIONAL – It must be a communicating instrument that will speak to and inspire Black people and that will let Black people see themselves in order to better themselves.[9]

The festival program included the Chuck Davis Dance Company; Kawaida Village from Newark, New Jersey; Black Ensemble from Albany, New York State; the Eleo Pomare Dance Company; Black Dance Union (under the direction of Michael Peters, who later became Michael Jackson's choreographer); Larocque Bey Drummers and Dance; Rod Rodgers Dance Company; Morse Donaldson's Armageddon in Babylon; Movements Black Dance Repertory; Olatunji Dancers; and Glenn Brooks' "Interpret A People".

During its existence, *The Feet* ran reviews, poetry, interviews with dancers and choreographers, class listings, dance community news (such as who had changed companies), and touring schedules. As the arts movement gained momentum, MODE began an important initiative to pay tribute to "a person who contributed to the black experience in dance" in a formal ceremony. Its first award was given in May 1971 to Ismay Andrews, the early teacher of many black performing artists including Chief Bey, Commodore Joe, Eartha Kitt, Eleo Pomare, Bea Richards, and Brunilda Ruiz. Andrews taught in New York community centers from 1934 to 1959, leading African dance, music and drama classes within the black community which instilled artists with ideas of black pride. *The Feet* is especially notable in its efforts to fix a definition of "black dance", a maneuver necessitated by its common but vague usage by white journalists throughout the period. *The Feet* followed funding patterns of government agencies, and in February 1971 published a listing of grants from the New York State Council on the Arts given to all dance and Harlem-based organizations. Members of MODE were concerned with critical writing which was inevitably invoked to rank the companies in competition for funding.

Several editorials by Carole Johnson were devoted to the impossible task of defining "black dance":

The term "Black dance" must be thought of from the broadest point that must be used to include any form of dance and any style that a black person chooses to work within. It includes the concept that all Black dance artists will use their talents to explore all known, as well as to invent new forms, styles, and ways of expression through movement. [. . .]

Since the expression "Black dance" must be all-inclusive, it includes those dancers that work in:

1. the very traditional forms (the more nearly authentic African styles);
2. the social dance forms that are indigenous to this country, which include tap and jazz dance;
3. the various contemporary and more abstract forms that are seen on the concert stage; and
4. the ballet (which must not be considered as solely European).[10]

The breadth of this definition renders it pointless, and the debate over terminology continues to this day.

The Feet published a final anniversary issue in June 1973. In this final issue, Carole Johnson offered a column titled "Reflections on 'Organization' in the Dance World" which contained a history of MODE and its predecessor, the Association of Black Choreographers; and a list of summary of projects executed by MODE, which included *The Feet*, the dance service award, a television panel discussion, a community dance series, and the First National Congress on Blacks in Dance held at Indiana University in Bloomington, Indiana, from 26 June to 1 July 1973. In this essay, Johnson offers a candid assessment of the organizational, structural and functional problems she encountered in administering MODE:

> One is that the goals have been too broad for the small group of people committed to executing them; two is that services have not been clear to dancers and often have not been realized because of a lack of funds, and three is that MODE came into existence before the dance companies were physically prepared to lend the support necessary [to make the organization work].[11]

Here, black nationalism is all but replaced by a softer dance-nation rhetoric as Johnson concludes:

> because the dance community black and white is so small, everyone is needed to change the status of dance. The majority of black people do not feel welcome or that they have the power to make changes in the larger or more established dance institutions. Black people are part of the nation and must also share a part in helping solve the problems peculiar to the dance. For black people, the work necessary for the recognition of dance in the structures of this country can be best coordinated in conjunction

with the attempt to assure the rightful place of black people in the dance history of this country. If this is revolutionary or militant, then, indeed, MODE is just that.[12]

CONCLUSIONS

According to the Johnsons, the Black Arts Movement dissipated because its participants "could not achieve a consensus on the meaning of separatism, nationalism, and revolution, all expressions central to the movement. As a result, the political implications of art-for-people's sake, a slogan used as a partial definition of the black aesthetic, never became sufficiently clear".[13] In terms of concert dance, the 1973 congress marked the end of the era, although I'm not sure why that happened. Maybe the large gathering of dancers and companies working in an Africanist mode confirmed a healthy, *sub rosa* constellation of performance which revived confidence in diasporic regeneration. The dance boom continued, and companies which grew from dance schools in regional locations – such as Dayton Contemporary Dance Company, Philadanco, Dallas Black Dance, and Denver's Cleo Parker Robinson – followed the models of Alvin Ailey and Arthur Mitchell in integrating their companies and nurturing an integrated, though predominantly black, audience base. Each of these groups turned to the emergent black middle class as their ideal audience members; that middle class had less interest in blatant social protest ideology.

Still, artists of the Black Arts Movement profoundly helped toward the alteration of the dance world *status quo*. Like their literary kin, these artists drew attention to unresolved questions of cultural aesthetics and mythologies surrounding black bodies in concert dance. Their dances, filled with inflammatory content which spilled off the stage, sought to destabilize the familiar image of black people dancing. They replaced the smiling, feel-good dances to blues and jazz music, which were common on the popular stage of the 1950s, with angular and unpredictable imagery of protest to make the dancing black body strange. Their work demands sustained investigation and interpretation.

NOTES

1. Neal 1968:29.
2. Johnson 1979:172.
3. Neal 1968:29.
4. Johnson 1979:171
5. Allen 1971:3.
6. Wilson 1971:3.
7. Wilson 1971:6.

8. Johnson 1970:7.
9. "First Dance":4.
10. Johnson 1971:2.
11. Johnson 1973:27.
12. *Ibid*:32.
13. Johnson 1979:198.

BIBLIOGRAPHY

Allen, Zita, "Commentary: Gus Solomons, John Parks, and Elina Mooney", *The Feet*, May–June 1971:3.

"First Dance Festival in Harlem at House of Kuumba", *The Feet*, September 1971:4.

Johnson, Abby Arthur and Ronald Maberry Johnson, *Propaganda and Aesthetics: The Literary Politics of Afro-American Magazines in the Twentieth Century*, Amherst, The University of Massachusetts Press, 1979.

Johnson, Carole, "Modern Organization for Dance Evolvement", *The Feet*, June 1970:2, 7.

——, "Reflections on 'Organization' in the Dance World", *The Feet*, June 1973:26, 27, 30, 32.

——, "What Is Black Dance", *The Feet*, July 1971:2.

Neal, Larry, "The Black Arts Movement", *TDR* 40, Summer, 1968:29–39.

Wilson, Arthur T., "Carole Johnson Dance Theatre in Black 'Love, Technique, and Teaching with Love'", *The Feet*, May–June 1971:3, 6.

Part II:
Free Southern Theater and Community Activism

A ROAD THROUGH THE WILDERNESS (1998)

John O'Neal

so many ways love has
that none may seem the bitter best
nor none the sweetest worse
Countee Cullen

Summer '97. Hot. Mid-August morning. I'm visiting with my daughter in Atlanta. She's just done with an undergraduate degree in painting at Spelman University. We'd needed her transcript.

"Let's go see the show in the new museum", she says.

"Why," I smile, "do you have something in it?"

Wendi giggles in her special way, "No. But it's a good show anyway".

The museum is in the new Camille Cosby Building. You can see where every one of the twenty million dollars went. Unfortunately, the museum was closed. It had been under construction for much of Wendi's career at Spelman so I was anxious to see it finished.

"I'd like to take a look at the building".

"Sure", said Wendi. "I need to visit my friend in the dean's office anyway".

As we made our way about the ornate yet functional work of art, I found myself reflecting, not quite idly, on the difference between The Cos and me. "Sometimes", I found myself saying to the woman, my child, who is wise beyond her years, "Sometimes I wonder if I made the right choices with my life".

"What do you mean?"

"Given my values and goals, might it have been better for me to have tried to do what Cosby has done rather than to have tried to [. . .] cut a road through the wilderness".

Wendi thoughtfully took in my remark and said, "This way may have been too expensive".

"Maybe. Maybe not. There're no guarantees either way".

The Free Southern Theater (FST) was indeed a result of the effort that a group of us undertook to carve through a certain wilderness.

The articles and interviews that follow are like photo albums from different portions of that journey. They show how the writers and editors represented here saw what was going on at one time or another. You'll see something of the dynamics between us as we struggled along the way. I'm not surprised by the progression in thought reflected here, but I am still surprised by what people heard me say and how it differs from what I remember. Of course, there's more to be said about the Free Southern Theater, and the movement of which it was a part, than space allows but there's no need for apology. These articles provide valuable insights into the FST, which played a key role in the black arts movement.

I'm glad to participate in a sourcebook on African-American performance. It is greatly needed. The black arts movement was not well understood when it occurred. The passage of time, I fear, has compounded that confusion. Much of the scholarship on this very significant passage in our history has had the effect of raising the initial confusion to the level of principle. The discussion of the black arts movement is corrupted by three erroneous tendencies that have dominating roles in the Western cultural mainstream:

1. We ignore or devalue history;
2. We overvalue money and fame; and
3. We invert the relationship between politics and art.

HISTORY

The black arts movement developed as a subset of the African-American people's liberation struggle. That struggle has always been focused in the Black-belt South and is fed by southern culture. During the middle of the twentieth century, that struggle was led, for the first time, by a mass movement of black, southern, rural workers. Culture played a major role in the movement of the 1960s but the Freedom Singers and the Free Southern Theater were the only cultural organizations that developed into programs of the Student Nonviolent Coordinating Committee (SNCC). As such, our efforts informed what was later to emerge as the black arts movement. Yet, much of the critical discourse on that phase of the movement has focused on events that occurred *later* in the urban north.

In addition to its racism, modern American culture is biased against things domestic, southern and rural. These biases have often obscured the study of African-American life. The rural south is the cauldron in which we were forged as a people. It's "down home" for us. It is the base from which our unrequited efforts were expropriated to create the wealth that became the foundation upon which the American empire has been erected. Black culture was forged and tempered in the struggle to overcome slavery* and is still based in the Black-belt South.

---

*The horror of the crime of slavery is rivaled only by the unprincipled extermination of the indigenous people whose progeny still hold legitimate claim to two continents.

African-American culture is a direct expression of this history. That's why the Free Southern Theater and its successor, Junebug Productions, are rooted in the rural culture of the Black-belt South and its proud traditions of resistance.

MONEY AND FAME

Another typical American error laced through the discussion of the black arts movement is the idea that the value of art can be measured by how much money and fame it produces. It simply is not so. Money and fame are important but only as instrumentalities. The value of art depends on its ability to illuminate the important political and aesthetic concerns of life. Confusion on this point leads the most popular scholars and critics to focus on things that happen in and around major commercial distribution centers. This approach distorts history, cuts away the basis of African-American culture in the Black Belt South, and forces us to affirm our own oppression by requiring us to imitate those who oppress us.

INVERSION OF POLITICS AND ART

The tendency to invert the relationship between politics and art reflects a decadent trend inside modern Western culture. I was watching an MTV special recently about the history of rhythm and blues music. I was washing dishes and couldn't see the screen so I couldn't tell whether it was Curtis Mayfield or someone talking about him. Whoever it was made the outrageous claim that Mayfield's "message" music *made the movement* happen. A stronger case could be made for the SNCC Freedom Singers, the Georgia Sea Island Singers, Guy Carawan, Pete Seeger, Bernice Reagon, the Free Southern Theater, or even Bob Dylan. All of these were among those involved in and committed to the movement. There's no question that Mayfield is an important figure in American popular music but this assertion is upside down! The movement compelled its artists to remarkable accomplishments just as it drafted its leaders to their roles. Not only did the movement provide the creative impulse that was celebrated in these "message songs", but the movement created the market that the recording industry sought to exploit and to gain a measure of control over.

The same confusion shows up in the theater. I remember my excitement about the Negro Ensemble Company's production of *The River Niger* in the early 1970s. Some years later at a conference of the National Association of Speech and Dramatic Arts, the segregated alternative to the American Educational Theatre Association, I was happy to tell Joe Walker how important I thought his play was because of the way he was able to ennoble the "Negro kitchen drama" and show

how politics and personal life are integral. Before I could fully express my appreciation, Joe declared that "politics is nothing more than the projection of the artist's imagination". I was shocked. Maybe that's why Joe called his theater company "The Demi-Gods".

Artists do make startling predictions sometimes, but our ruminations are still reflections on our experiences. The aesthetic process and its products are inseparable from history, economics, and politics, politics being the process by which we make decisions about our collective life. Along with the greater consideration of the nature and challenges of our spiritual life, politics, history and economics provide the content that art celebrates or cautions us about.

Life is a constant process of change and development. Sometimes things move along in small, hardly perceptible steps. Then sudden, dramatic leaps occur. The temperature of the water over a flame changes slowly in barely noticeable degrees before it suddenly bursts into steam. When society goes through extreme states like this, extraordinary art is one result. The movement of the 1960s was just such a time. In the broad sweep of history I expect that other things like the civil war, reconstruction, and the great migration will surely prove to be more important. The coming struggle to bring down racism and injustice will be more important still. Yet the movement of the 1960s marked a critical period of transition. Much of what happened is reflected in the art from that era. This sourcebook will aid those who seek to sharpen their sense of history. In more particular ways it will be useful to those artists who are preparing themselves for the important battles that lie ahead.

There is cruel irony in the fact that despite the transformative impact of the civil rights movement, racism, like a wolf in sheep's clothing, continues its deadly rampage. By comparative measures, the vast majority of African Americans are worse off in 1997 than we were in 1957. We are more uneducated, more underemployed, more unemployed and more incarcerated. We are less healthy, die younger, and have more inadequate housing. We are more confused, frustrated and hopeless and nobody seems to care. To borrow from the blues standard, "nobody loves me but my mother and she could be jiving too".

To make matters worse, many of the "Black Bourgeoisie", as the class of professionals and small business owners was called by the noted black scholar E. Franklin Frazier, have retreated from the struggle in order to give priority to efforts at personal advancement. Since the end of "official" segregation, the Black Bourgeoisie have been prevented by racism from fully realizing the dubious goal of integrating the new suburbs created by white flight from urban centers. Many of the black intelligentsia, lost in academic and bureaucratic rat races, have subjugated their critical intelligence to the pursuit of the ever more tantalizing carrots of academe. Too many of our youth, if not lost in the fog of clever but pointless metaphysical sophistry, have become victims of self-indulgent, drug-induced delirium that leaves them useless to the effort to mount meaningful struggle for change. It's social dynamite. Primed. Waiting for the right spark.

Bill Cosby chose to gamble on the main roads of American popular culture. He has worked with dedication, diligence and discipline. His efforts have been richly rewarded. He and his wife, early supporters of the FST, have been generous and conscientious with their gifts. Their way differs from mine: *so many ways love has/that none may seem the bitter best/nor none the sweetest worse.* My rewards are rich in different ways. I look back with no regret. I look forward with confidence and hope.

I'm working on a new play right now. Recently I came to the conclusion that this play will be about the movement and will be addressed to my daughter, Wendi, my son, William, and others of their age group. Some of them have claimed the term "hip-hop" to describe themselves. Some of them are among the most energetic who affirm the bond between the culture of oppressed people and resistance. I hope the play will help to strengthen the quality of their contribution to the ongoing liberation struggle. If the play is to be effective, those to whom it is addressed must identify with people and themes in the play. So I asked my son to help me to gather stories from his peers and to lead me in conversation with them. I was pleased that he was willing to do so and seemed to be proud that I asked. If this first foray into the culture of the "Hip Hop Nation" is mutually beneficial, I will continue on the path. The working title for the play is *yours in the struggle*.

I don't know who started it but somebody in SNCC started closing their letters with "yours in the struggle". The phrase became the epistolary equivalent of a clenched fist raised high in defiance or pressed to the heart with reverence and resolution – *yours in the struggle* – it seems to fit the idea for the play. I proceed in the faith that the play will be useful to the hip hop generation. I hope this book is useful to them too.

yours in the struggle,
john

DIALOG:

The Free Southern Theatre (1965)

**Gilbert Moses, John O'Neal, Denise Nicholas,
Murray Levy and Richard Schechner**

This dialog was tape-recorded [in 1965] in the TDR [Tulane Drama Review] office in New Orleans. Participating were Gilbert Moses and John O'Neal, Executive Producers of the Free Southern Theater, Denise Nicholas and Murray Levy, actors, and Richard Schechner, Chairman of the Board of Directors. However, the FST, like all fledgling theatres, demands a variety of skills from its participants: Miss Nicholas is also the company's play reader and one of its secretaries, Levy is the business manager. The FST completed its second tour of Mississippi this winter. The company has performed In White America, Waiting for Godot, *and* Purlie Victorious *in more than thirty Mississippi towns. The FST also played in New Orleans, Memphis, and Atlanta, Moses and O'Neal are its founders. The company is now preparing a new set of plays for summer and fall presentation, including works by Brecht and O'Casey; its headquarters are in New Orleans.*

O'NEAL: The Free Southern Theater started in September, 1963, when Gil Moses and I met. Each of us had come south to work with the civil rights movement, Gil with the *Mississippi Free Press* and I with SNCC. We thought that if theatre means anything anywhere it should mean something here in the south too.

MOSES: Our first production was in the summer of 1964, when we did *In White America*. We toured that in sixteen cities and towns ranging in size from New Orleans to Mileston in Holmes County, Mississippi. The Holmes County people came in from the farms to see us. We had to play in the afternoon because they wanted to get back home by dark.

NICHOLAS: We added a section to *In White America* dealing with the murder of Chaney, Schwerner, and Goodman. The whole play had quite an impact.

MOSES: In New Orleans we had integrated audiences. In Mississippi less: COFO workers, a very few local whites.

NICHOLAS: In Indianola twenty-five members of the White Citizens' Council came to the play. Along with them – I suppose to protect them – were forty-two patrolmen in riot uniforms, helmets and all. People crowded around the Council men, behind them, looking at their reactions, watching us. The whole house was joyous, as well as a little scared.

MOSES: A few of the Council men laughed, but mostly – what I could see from stage – they sat back in a grim block. After the play one of them told Erika Munk: "Some good actors, good acting". And that's communication of a kind. Although we found out later that they'd come to check whether the Movement was "Communist agitation" and decided that it was.

SCHECHNER: Would you like to repeat that experience?

MOSES: Yes. If we did it again with those same people something would happen: either they would have to break or become totally fanatic.

SCHECHNER: What kind of audiences do you have?

NICHOLAS: They vary from city to city. Most of Mississippi is rural, even the medium-sized towns like Clarksdale are rural. In New Orleans, Memphis, Atlanta – there you have a different kind of audience.

MOSES: In Sunflower County, for instance – the home of Senator Eastland – we got no middle-class people, but the only class which exists there: the share-cropping class. They aren't so militant; they aren't so much involved in the Movement. But they individually stand up, or think they are standing up, for what they want. The church we played in had been shot into the week before we came with *Purlie Victorious* and *Waiting for Godot*. There were bullet holes above the door. Yet when we played they all came out.

SCHECHNER: In Reverend Hausey's church in New Orleans the women put on their furs and made a social event of it. Did they do that in Mississippi?

MOSES: They try to – the women don't dress up, but they put on a clean dress.

NICHOLAS: One of the beautiful things about the audience is that preconceptions are different – and where theatre is concerned there are no preconceptions: they've never been to a theatre. So the idea "social event" is vague. People came in farm clothes, overalls, women in house dresses, kids in school clothes.

SCHECHNER: What's the connection between the FST and the Movement?

O'NEAL: By *free* we mean more than the fact that the theatre doesn't charge anything. We mean we are seeking a new kind of liberation – a liberation from old forms of theatre, old techniques and ideas. A freedom to find new forms of theatrical expression and to find expression in people who have never expressed themselves in theatre before. The connection between the FST and the Movement? The Movement, with its political manifestations, is one thing – people are acting together for something and through their actions letting their wishes and the way they'd like to live be known. The *other* thing is that in order for these actions to take on form and be subject to internal control there have to be things that come, logically at least, before action: thought, reflection, criticism.

MOSES: I think John means that the theatre was started because of the Movement's lack of clarity – the fact that the revolt has no time for art. We found, when we lived in Jackson, that the thinking there was circumscribed; newspapers omitted news, radio stations played only rock-and-roll, churches were medieval, schools were state-controlled. But there must be more than emotions behind actions, more than the impetuous call to order. To go beyond that first beautiful movement when the slave says "No", there must be a clarity, a subtlety which the revolt is at no time able to give, simply because it is a collective call to immediate action. People begin to revolt by singing "We Shall Overcome", not knowing, though certainly feeling profoundly, *what* they should overcome.

SCHECHNER: But if we want to stimulate critical thought, or whatever the motto may be, we can do that through education. There are, at least for me, other reasons for getting involved in the FST: a personal commitment to theatre, a belief that the theatre is the most universal of the arts. It is the only thing that can make *this* individual aware of himself while *that* individual, next to him, is becoming aware of himself in another way. The theatre is not a great leveller, but a great distinguisher, and, of course, one of the contradictions of a political movement is that people want an entire group, or society, to have equivalent opportunities while allowing each individual to go as far as he can. The theatre is also at the intersection between political and artistic forces. Its forms, from the Greeks on, have been concerned with the community in conflict. And here we had a situation which suited those old forms.

O'NEAL: I don't think the Movement is fundamentally political. And we didn't pick theatre because of the Movement. We selected theatre because that's what we want to do, that's what we want to be. Theatre is our vocation. If the Movement were political, if the changes being wrought were political, then how could something as non-political as the theatre fit into what's happening?

SCHECHNER: I understand "political" as a pyramid: its real meaning is in that very broad base, the polis, of things that involve the community.

It focuses itself at the apex of that pyramid which is what we normally call "political action" and which seeks to restructure the very base from which it emerges. And the non-political is man's relationship to himself or to his God, if he believes in one.

O'NEAL: The Movement is concerned with man's relationship to himself and his God.

SCHECHNER: Well, what is the relationship between the FST and the community?

MOSES: Frankly, I don't know. The community doesn't need the FST, very few of them know anything about theatre. The need must be shown. We're grafting an idea onto a community. The graft will heal and slowly the FST will become one with the community. Finally the community will change and create its own type of theatre.

O'NEAL: A bunch of fallacies operate in present-day thinking about theatre. People think that meaning comes from somewhere out there, pre-established, predetermined. I don't think that's so. Meaning comes from involvement, you create the truth of your situation. Look at American theatre! People are involved in an art that only has abstract meaning now, predetermined by a Dionysus who said, "This is what theatre is". But no one can hear the oracle any more and theatre has become a diversion for people who can afford the time not to be involved in doing something. Theatre has taken the tone of the rest of our lives: meaninglessness, otherness, outsideness. The last *Dolce Vita*. Gil calls it the "ice-cream parlor theatre" – a place you go to not even for dessert, just to do *something*. But the FST has to be bread – a bakery which makes something vitally needed. Theatre doesn't have to be entertainment. I don't know what it can be. We're young, naïve, probably stupid, but we're also arrogant and pretentious. So we're going to insist on doing something. Maybe we'll fall on our asses. But out of our involvement with these audiences – the audience *we have chosen* – meaning will come. It's that kind of involvement that theatre denied itself in this country. But meaning doesn't come from oracles; you forge it on the anvil of your own experience with each other.

SCHECHNER: Well, in the bakery, then: how many people are in the company?

MOSES: There were eight of us on the last tour. We left New Orleans on November 17 1964, took a break for Christmas, and finished touring at the end of January. Then we did some fund-raising performances in New York. We traveled in a station wagon and a Dodge Econoline truck. We carried everything with us: lights, costumes, flats; the bus had a two-way radio so that if we got in trouble we could radio COFO. But there were no incidents. The company had three whites and five Negroes. In New Orleans, which is home base, we have an office, a mailing address, and a board of directors. The company has twenty-three now.

O'NEAL: The tour is back-breaking. You get to one town, set up, play, strike, and drive on to the next town. We did two plays in most towns: *Purlie* and *Godot*.

NICHOLAS: It wears people down. Next time we're going to stay longer in each town. The way we've been going we hardly get a chance to contact our audience. After each performance we had a discussion of the play. We wanted people to talk about the experience.

O'NEAL: In McComb, after finishing *Godot*, a man got up and started to say something. But he couldn't say anything. He just mumbled, "slave . . . whupped him . . . no! . . ." He *felt* something; but he couldn't get the words to say it. That's our job: to help this man find the vocabulary to say what he wants to say. Another man in McComb said that he thought Pozzo and Lucky were figments of Gogo and Didi's imagination. That started us thinking. This thing between audience and performer – it's not one way. They give us images to think with too.

SCHECHNER: Let's go through the repertory. Why did you pick *In White America*?

MOSES: It was a funny choice. We picked it because its theme essentially stated that the Negro revolt was like the American Revolution. And it shows the Negro a history, his history here, from the beginning to now. It doesn't show Negroes as maids or shoe-shine boys or as people with white faces; it shows people brutally treated, still brutally treated, who have suffered for recognition for three hundred years, still seeking recognition, who have never lost their humanity.

NICHOLAS: *In White America*, at a very special time – last summer – was such a profound experience for everyone in the audience, and for us. The amazing thing was that this play gave people a frame of reference they'd never had before. They saw today's struggle as an *old* fight, and they recognized that people had been fighting much the same way, all over the country, for a long time: for *all the time*. They found the history they had always been denied.

SCHECHNER: What about *Godot*?

MOSES: What about *Godot*?

SCHECHNER: I remember our discussions last fall. We decided to do *Purlie* – which I now think was a mistake – and we tried to find the other play: *Blues for Mister Charlie*, *Godot*, *Antigone*, *The Mother*. And we picked *Godot* . . .

MOSES: We wanted to see what would happen. We chose it because it's a great play, and we thought *Godot* would act as a barometer of the limits, the ceiling of this audience. It didn't operate that way. All we learned was that our audience can take *Godot*.

SCHECHNER: How did people react?

MOSES: Let's talk about the kids. They were fascinated. In Ruleville, the morning before *Godot*, we held a drama workshop and did improvisations with about thirty kids. They enjoyed it tremendously. In this group was a kid named Jerry Johnson who had remarkable sensitivity. After the play that night he and a friend went back-stage and put on the costumes of Pozzo and Lucky. Jerry picked up the whip, put the hat on his head, attached the rope to his friend's neck and shouted, "On! Back! Dance!" *Godot* achieved our purpose: it gave Jerry Johnson a theatrical image, offered him an experience that wouldn't have been there but for us. This kid had something he could use, play with, think with, live with.

SCHECHNER: This raises a question. I've seen the FST *Godot* in New Orleans, McComb, and New York. The FST isn't one theatre, it's three. The audiences don't come together. At the New School in New York people came to do their Movement duty; we helped them cope with their hangups and they gave us money. In New Orleans people had alternative choices those nights and they chose to come to the FST. Speaking to them afterwards, I knew they'd enjoyed the shows and wanted to see more. In McComb the audience was fascinated by a new experience. It wasn't a "meeting", and it wasn't a movie: it was something else. Someone opened the window. But these audiences contradict each other. Can you play for them all the same way? What about the risk of patronizing?

LEVY: If you are legitimately trying to open avenues of communication – regardless of motives – you are not patronizing. As an actor in *Godot* I was not trying to open up communication in New York, I was trying to shock an audience I disliked – I already disliked it when I worked there before joining the FST – and that I feel comes to every theatre with the wrong attitude; they're as dead as the theatre they see. But in the south the experience isn't sterile.

O'NEAL: Which is to say that the contradictions exist. The audiences demand different things.

MOSES: Within the framework of the play all the audience asks for is good acting . . .

O'NEAL: No. Murray [Levy] is right: the way he feels demands certain things of him as an actor – he plays Gogo differently. He never blew his nose at an audience anywhere but in New York, he never kicked his clothes at them. But these things become contradictions only when you're not certain of your stand or where you stand; then you're subject to the mirror an audience brings you. You oscillate more when you're uncertain of what assertions you want to make.

SCHECHNER: I was struck by something else watching the three audiences. The New York audience looked for meanings; they saw the play in the context of a hundred critics. In New Orleans and in McComb they looked at Beckett's play – right in the face – and they laughed at the characters. "We're *not* waiting!" they said, during and after the play. These audiences weren't waiting for Godot like Gogo and Didi; built right into the text of the play was an alienation and the audiences stood back and looked at these silly characters. Maybe it was all a delusion: maybe they really were waiting but didn't realize it. Still, it was not a play of despair in Mississippi. But New York is a rich enough city for despair to become an occupation.

MOSES: The problems are the same in McComb and New York: neither audience accepts itself as waiting. But the New York audience is intellectually better able to deal with the meaning of the play; they scratch their heads and ask, "What's the meaning of this despair"? Because of the academic approach, they usually miss the play. But in McComb they don't miss seeing and enjoying the play because of preconceived notions. They come to the play with ideas only about what amuses them, but theatre can expand that idea.

SCHECHNER: The McComb audience doesn't have the kind of despair which depends upon the separation of thought and act. *Godot* was really a comedy in New Orleans and Mississippi. They laughed at Lucky; in New York they were embarrassed by a Negro at the end of a white man's rope.

MOSES: OK. In Mississippi they sat *outside* of the play, maybe not following the verbal gymnastics but getting the theatrical images which burn in their brains.

SCHECHNER: But why did you put on whiteface half-way through the tour? For me that destroyed the reality of the play.

MOSES: James Cromwell, who directed it, could answer that better than I. The reason was, I think, that the audience couldn't go beyond the Pozzo and Lucky situation: the image of the white man holding the rope around a Negro's neck shocked them out of comprehension.

NICHOLAS: Whiteface immediately stopped that first black-white reaction and forced the audience to deal with something else. Maybe they don't know what this "something else" is until the end of the play or until they get home. But in the discussions – after we began using whiteface – it was clear that the change worked with the audience. It brought them closer to the human heart of the play.

SCHECHNER: The problem for me was that the whiteface robbed *Godot* of reality; we no longer were on a country road. It made the production phony.

O'NEAL: Finally we rejected the idea of whiteface, but kept it anyway because there was no other way to deal with the problem of racial hangups. My feeling is that we should accept these hangups and deal with them – with whatever is implicit in the play – and try to manipulate it from that point of view. No matter how you handle it there are going to be connotations. We had a white Gogo and a Negro Didi; two Negroes doing the roles would have been different, etc. But that's implicit in our milieu. Cromwell didn't agree with that because he couldn't accept the milieu. If we keep *Godot* in the repertory – and we will – we'll have to work these things out.

SCHECHNER: The FST is integrated. But outside New Orleans, Memphis, and Atlanta (let's not count New York), you played almost exclusively to Negro audiences. From what John said earlier, it's out of the specific Negro experience that he wants to create the theatre. Is the FST to be a Negro theatre then?

O'NEAL: There's no such thing as a Negro. You can't make your thinking contingent on that category.

MOSES: John's right. What he says doesn't erase the fact that internally and with our audience we have to grapple with black and white. But behind that are our own subjective needs.

O'NEAL: Why do we *have to be* hung up with the same problem for three hundred years? Negroes won't accept that they're Negroes and whites won't accept that they're whites. We're all trying to say that there's really no problem and we can integrate without changing anything. But there'll have to be some drastic changes. These changes have to be controlled and come from something real about people. There's something real about that cat in McComb who can't talk; or those twenty-five Citizens' Council men in Indianola. Let me give you an analogy. You and your wife can't touch each other. Alternatives? You can go to a whorehouse, try to pick up a piece on the side, or avoid the whole thing by saying "we'll just do something else". These alternatives don't face the problem. You can turn to each other and really go into that relationship and try to understand what's happening. All the pain and suffering that's involved. What we've been doing with race in this country is going to the whorehouse. Look at James Baldwin and LeRoi Jones and William Faulkner and Tennessee Williams. All four end up not dealing with the problems.

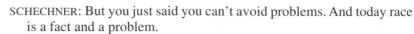

SCHECHNER: But you just said you can't avoid problems. And today race is a fact and a problem.

O'NEAL: True, but those terms lead us into a dead-end. They don't really explain the thing. What we have to do is have a company with Negroes and whites in it because we want to do things that require both. The problem – and I don't know how to make this clear except by talking about what's wrong with the word "integration" – is that to limit the theatre to black, white, or black and white is to avoid the situation. The word "integration" assumes the *status quo* – white on top, black at the bottom – and it means that we should get the black and white together by moving the Negroes up since the whites don't want to be pulled down and the "poor colored folks" don't want to stay down and out either. But the point is that nobody wants to be benevolently "lifted up". The Movement – the Negro revolt – is of people who have recognized that society as it stands has no place for them and so that society must be transformed. The FST is neither black nor white nor mixed up. It's *us* trying to do something, and it will have to be put in those terms. To talk of "integrated" is to put us in a bag we're not really in; like the whole racial thing – nothing but a labyrinth that always turns back on itself. If you start with black and white as premises you always come back to them as conclusions and you can't establish a dialectic that creates a new situation.

SCHECHNER: What were the aesthetic challenges?

LEVY: I found that I was working at top capacity for the first time in my life. I was looking for absolute clarity and pure notes in my work. The internal problems of the company were no different, I guess, than any group of people with egos working together. But we were doing something bigger than ourselves and though we were not legally tied with contracts, we were morally tied and no one from our company ever even entertained the idea of not performing or quitting on tour no matter how difficult things became.

SCHECHNER: But four of the eight company members aren't coming back. Some of that was due to personal conflicts within the company. Cromwell told me he wasn't sure whether the FST wanted to be a theatre or part of the Movement.

MOSES: We want to be a theatre.

O'NEAL: We are part of the Movement, in our own way.

MOSES: We're expanding the company – if we find the money – to include eleven actors and five apprentices from Mississippi and Louisiana, an administrator, some office staff, tech. people.

NICHOLAS: We're very limited, aesthetically as well as financially. I found out during *Purlie* how much training we need. I think we know the problems.

MOSES: From April 1 until July 1 we will be training and rehearsing in New Orleans. After that and until December 31 we'll be performing either in New Orleans or on the road. We're going to keep *Godot* in the repertory, and, if we can find the proper staging for it, *Purlie*. We don't know about *In White America* yet. It would mean a new production because only three of us are left from that cast. The company is very much larger now. During the last tour there were eight of us – now we hope to have twenty-three, including the administrative staff.

O'NEAL: The budget for our nine-month season is $98,000 if we pay Equity scale. If we stay at $35 per week then the budget is $59,000.

SCHECHNER: There's about $5,000 in the till now. Will you be able to raise the rest?

O'NEAL: That's up to the foundations, those who are going to give us benefits, individuals. We don't charge admission. There's no way in the world for the FST to break even.

SCHECHNER: Deficit financing is something the foundations have avoided.

O'NEAL: They'll have to change their minds. A box-office theatre in Mississippi – and other places, too, I'm sure – sidesteps the theatre's essential obligation: to play to a broad spectrum of society. We don't want only the guy with a dollar in his pocket.

MOSES: Oliver Rea of the Guthrie Theatre . . .

SCHECHNER: And Chairman of the Theatre Communications Group . . .

MOSES: Is heading a committee in the regional theatre to have benefits for us. Some universities are giving us benefits too. We'll find a way to survive and to develop our own organic style.

SCHECHNER: You mentioned training . . .

MOSES: During the spring, Scott Cunningham, the FST artistic director, will be running acting classes for us, Sally Roberson Sommer will give us dance and movement, and Betty Greenhoe, voice and speech. Our top salary is $35.00 a week – the apprentices get $25.00.

SCHECHNER: Can you live on those salaries?

O'NEAL: We have been.

MOSES: On tour we lived in the homes of the Negro community.

SCHECHNER: Did those contacts affect your performances?

MOSES: Sure. We usually did *Purlie* first and when we came home the lady would have dinner waiting for us. She'd talk about how glorious the play was. And we'd be happy and then immediately apprehension would set in because the next day we would be doing *Godot*, and we didn't know . . . Each town was a new set of realities. We didn't know how this landlady would take it. When we stayed with Fannie Lou Hamer she loved *Godot*. We came home to sleep and sat up three hours talking about it. In other homes we found no dinner waiting, and we'd go to bed and wake up the next morning and the people wouldn't say anything. They'd say, "Yeah, that was a fine play, but I liked the first one best".

SCHECHNER: How will this condition future plays?

O'NEAL: We know now that we need a *repertory*: a series of experiences for people to sound off against.

MOSES: The communities remembered us from the summer. In Hattiesburg one of the signs they made for us said, "The Free Southern Theater, the Theater of Our Own Coming Back". In Gulfport, during *In White America*, I stopped the show because the audience was making so much noise. We played in an old movie house and they were used to shouting there. Someone asked John before *In White America* if we were going to use real bullets – because this was "live theatre" and not movies. The kids were rolling pop bottles down the aisles and eating popcorn. I was furious. I told them that if they didn't quiet down we couldn't continue. When we came back in the winter everyone was very quiet. They knew we were giving a performance.

LEVY: I've gotten quite a few letters from people we stayed with and who saw the plays. Like this one: "Just a few lines to thank you for coming to Meridian to perform for me. Say thanks to the rest of the cast for me. Are you sure that you are coming back this summer? (You better.) How old do I have to be to join your group? I want to be an actress too. I am seventeen years old and I can act pretty good . . ."

SCHECHNER: If I had to pinpoint the real distinction of the FST it would be that it goes out and seeks its audience rather than waiting for an audience to come to it – truly popular theatre whose audience is coming to the theatre for the first time. I don't think we've earned any other distinctions yet. We haven't done new plays; the productions haven't been shattering.

MOSES: We're still defining the theatre for ourselves. Only four of the eight came back. I would have been happy if it had only been two; four out of eight is a good percentage. We want plays written especially for us, out of our experience, for our audiences. Both John and I are writers. You are too. And George Tabori is writing a play for us. We should do classic plays – not only Shakespeare or Molière or the Greeks, but modern plays too. We're doing Brecht's *Carrar*, O'Casey's *Shadow of a Gunman*, and Molière's *George Dandin* this summer and fall.

O'NEAL: We lean toward modern plays because it's much easier for us and our audiences to relate to them.

LEVY: It's one of the symptoms of the sickness of our country that artists don't go to the people. I remember about a year ago I saw a spread in the *New York Times* about the arts in Cuba. There was a picture of a ballet company playing on a dock in some obscure fishing village. I thought: Wow, here at last is the artist extending himself to the people who can't conveniently get to the metropolis to see him. This is what we're trying to do. We're going to all the docks – all the nooks and crannies. To say: we're here not out of any benevolence or social work, but because we care and because we are artists.

MOTION IN THE OCEAN

Some Political Dimensions of the
Free Southern Theater (1968)

John O'Neal

> It's not the size of the ship
> that makes the waves
> It's the motion of the Ocean
>
> **Charlie Cobb***

1.

I remember thinking it strange, when I first started working in the Southern Student Movement in 1962, that there were so many people who, like me, thought of themselves as poets. I wrote a letter (to someone) describing them as poets who had come to the conclusion that the most profound poetry is the poetry of action and movement. When the problem becomes unspeakable then there is simply nothing to say – something must be done.

I was in the third wave of "students" who swept through the South with a dream in the early 1960s. Sit-ins in '60, Freedom Rides in '61, and in '62 the forces gathered around the right to vote. After each wave there was a period of uncertainty while the new motion was in the making. That was a time to survey the damage and chaos which often seem to follow in the wake of dreams.

It was crisp October in Mississippi, that quiet shifting time after the summer of '62 on the campus of Tougaloo College near Jackson. I'd heard a great deal about Gilbert from others who knew of my interest in theatre. They talked about "the Black guy who works for the *Mississippi Free Press* and was in a Broadway show!" (From Mississippi, New York is New York and an Off-Broadway is no less than a Broadway show.) But here at last I had found him, camera in hand, gold-rimmed glasses perpetually sliding off the end of his nose, Gilbert Moses III on his way to the Tougaloo theatre to take pictures for the *Free Press* of the

---

*From a prose poem by Charlie Cobb, who credits an Atlanta DeeJay. Ain't no telling where he got it from.

rehearsal of the current student production of *Inherit the Wind*.

After perfunctory introductions he indicated his haste to get to his business so I promptly invited myself along. Before long we were talking about theatre. Almost immediately the conflict began. The tragic drama, I said, in response to some question or comment, is the highest and most noble of all art forms. Absurd, was his curt reply, anyone who could say that seriously must be both presumptuous and ignorant: comedy is the most perfect form. We talked on. Later that week I moved into Gilbert's apartment, as I was just returning to Jackson and needed a place to live. That was the beginning of the dialogue that led to the birth of the Free Southern Theater.

Each of us had come to the South with the naive thought that it would take a few years to do what we had come to do there, before going on with our lives. Each of us came to realize after a short time that it was not a matter of a few years' work by a few people. We would have to spend lifetimes in the faith that a few keys might be found if enough people worked long enough and hard enough.

We both felt bound by the apparent contradiction between the poet and the person. We claimed to be playwrights and poets; yet the political facts of life presented by the situation we first learned of in the South called for a life of useful (political or economic) engagement. How could we remain true to ourselves and our own concerns as artists and at the same time remain true to our developing recognition of political responsibility?

There was another person, Doris Derby, a young painter from New York. She pointed the way to resolution in a conversation one day: "If theatre means anything anywhere, it certainly ought to mean something here!" That was the magic chord.

Since then, the FST has been more about struggle than realization. Work, people, time, money and incessant philosophy! Where to find good people who could stand the pressures of time, of working in a hostile environment. Always feeling the need to do more, be in more places, do more plays, talk to more of "the people". Never knowing whether there would be enough money for the next week's payroll or to repair the truck the next time it breaks down or some damn fool agent sends in a bill for royalties on a script, threatening legal action if we don't pay. Arriving in Clarksdale to find all our posters and publicity material never got off somebody's desk and no arrangements were made for us to have a place to stay or food and the minister expects rent for the three or four days we'll be using his church. Actors on the streets with handbills, going from door to door. "A real live play – tomorrow night! . . ."

The disappointment of the discovery that the big benefit only made $2,000, not enough to get us to the end of the month. The hassles that grew from the barrier isolating the whites in the company from the Blacks, and the difficulty of making connection with the audience. Perhaps the most dreadful struggle: to keep up the energy required to go on in the drab fashion afforded by the *real* situation, while still being tortured by the vast almost overwhelming potential implicit to the idea. The constant struggle against the confusion engendered by racism in the theatre and out of it, within the Black community and out of it. And finally, as if we didn't have enough problems, the constant struggle with those who felt that our theatre was either too political or not political enough. That question – the relationship between what we were doing and our peers in the "movement" were doing – consumed the largest part of the philosophical struggle.

These conflicts in and around the FST have brought me to some working conclusions, keys to my own perspective, which summarize the effect of that continuing dialogue on me.

There is a popular separation between politics and art, much like the separation of church and state, which strikes me as being improperly conceived. We learn in schools that politics is one thing and art is another and that it is not valid to be both at the same time. But that is false. We talked a lot about the relationship between them, and found ourselves saying the same thing over and over again. It is, finally, a relationship in the abstract. A man simply cannot be divided like that. As a matter of essential form, the theatre (all art, in fact) is political. The question is whose political interests a particular theatre or a particular production will serve.

The artist, to grow, must be nurtured by those who love him. If he loves not wisely, then his love devours him. If his love is wise, then all love's the better for it. It seems simple then to make a place for Black artists to be with people who love and can nurture them. When the Black artist speaks to a critical audience not also Black, he speaks from one set of cultural and political interests and experience to an audience with different, sometimes hostile, priorities and contradicting experience. The Black artist, in order to communicate across that gap, becomes an *explainer*. He must interpret how his own experience relates to the "human experience" of white people so they can understand it. His time is spent in pursuit of more effective explanations of characters or images. That process takes him away from his legitimate work as an artist. He may be eversogood a poet (in his heart) but to explain a rose rather than to sing, is not to make a poem, but an explanation of a rose, in verse perhaps, but an explanation nonetheless. It is the poet's task to sing.

The Black artist suffers from the white audience because he must speak from a divided consciousness to a mentality that refuses to acknowledge the most essential part of that consciousness. He is further limited by cultural, political and economic institutions that incorporate the premises of racism. He is bound by a series of contradictions at the outset if his *intended* audience is white. Few have found the means to transcend those contradictions while remaining vital as artists and "successful" in established terms.

The more seriously the Black artist tries to affect the white consciousness, the more explicative he must become. The more explicative he becomes, the less attention he gives to the essentials of his art. A kind of negative value field is established. Racism systematically verifies itself when the slave can only break free by imitating the master: by contradicting his own reality.

As long as the victims of racism accept the judgments of their oppressors and rely on the approbation of that society, they are locked in. If they do not recognize the presence of positive standards and values in the Black community then they love unwisely and will be devoured in their own flames. When the positive connection is made the world opens up and creativity blooms. The question is not whether the Black community has standards and values of artistic import but whether the Black artist will accept the responsibility of speaking from the context of, and to, those values and needs.

The presumed antipathy between politics and economics on the one hand and art and culture on the other, could better be described as antipathy between politicians and artists. Because of the strength of the Western political establishment, the schism between artists and politicians has been institutionalized as a defense against contradictions in Western culture that have developed out of the efforts of that culture to survive as king of the volcano – when the time for playing that game is gone.

2.

The real question, how to be relevant to the lives of our audience, was one that couldn't be handled abstractly. The theatre, as a discrete form, is largely foreign to the cultural experience and heritage of the Black audience.

Some generalities seem pretty clear:

- The lack of money should not keep people away from the theatre. Most of the people we were most concerned about have very little if any money. We therefore concluded that the Theater was to be free.
- The plays, to be relevant, had to connect with the life. In a real sense, those plays have not been written yet. Those who live the life must write the particular truth of that experience.
- Another objective became clear: to make theatre available to the Black people in the South with the expectation of making the form integral to their cultural experience.

It would not be enough simply to perform. We felt the need for a way to really get involved with, and to involve, the residents of local communities. The Community Workshop Program, an ongoing, year-round program geared specifically to the participation of local people, was developed to meet this need. (Lack of funds for this program made it impossible to extend it outside New Orleans at the time of writing. Lack of money is a continual threat to the whole operation.) The touring company, no matter how relevant, stimulating or exciting in a given repertoire, could not speak to the continuing need of people wanting deeper involvement. This becomes the task of the Community Workshop Program. Since a theatre of the Black people of the South must ultimately be made of those people, the job of the touring company, which is largely "imported", is to catalyze the involvement of local people in the workshop program.

The forms, techniques and even the aspirations of the people we spirit off to the South are by and large defined by the established theatre, movies, and television. The culture that produces those forms has only an abstract relationship to the culture and environment of southern Blacks. That culture produces its own definition of relevance; in the theatre this finally depends on the plays. While there is a sense in which all good plays/art are relevant to universal human experience, each of us finds reflections of our own experience most useful. There is a dreadful scarcity of plays that grow out of the experience of Black people in this country. The reason, I think, lies in the absence of a theatre in which Black writers can develop. That theatre will remain more potential than real until the form itself is seen in the Black community as a meaningful vehicle. There are some plays by and about Negroes. But of those that were not written by whites the majority were written presupposing of a white audience and from that base in values. The process of making forms useful to the Black Community cannot bypass the kind of involvement we seek in the Community Workshop Program.

Our search for relevant scripts has led into all kinds of political problems. One fellow who was in our company for a time was refused his petition for conscientious objector status by the draft board because he was working for FST during the 1965 season, which we called "The Year of Revolt". That bill included *Shadow of a Gunman* by Sean O'Casey, *The Rifles of Señora Carrar* by Brecht and *In White America* by Martin Duberman. The fact that we would produce such a bill was taken as evidence of our "support of violence" and therefore invalidated his claim. The plays chosen for the "Year of Revolt" did not aggravate our cohorts in the South. Those connections seemed clear.

Our production of *Waiting for Godot* on the other hand irritated the hell out of people. Time and time again, the question was raised, "What possible relevance do you imagine *Godot* to have to the lives of Black people in the South?" One of the most common arguments against the play was that it was too "complicated and intellectual" for the "ignorant rural mind". Not only is this a condescending and patronizing argument, it illustrates misplaced Western values, presuming education as a prerequisite for intelligence. The uneducated may lack certain specific skills but they are no less intelligent. Often the very absence of those skills forces people to greater application of creative facilities simply in order to survive competitively in a system loaded against their specific deficiencies.

Moreover, theatre is a living art. While the script is important, the immediate communication takes place between the actors on stage and the audience. The audience is confronted with a theatrical not a literary experience. Our production of the play was very good and did, therefore, communicate forcefully.

Some saw it as a political allegory. Mrs Fannie Lou Hamer in Ruleville, Mississippi, best typified that approach when she said in the discussion after the play, "Every day we see men dressed just like these, sitting around the bars, pool halls and on the street corners waiting for something! They must be waiting for Godot. But you can't sit around waiting. Ain't nobody going to bring you nothing. You got to get up and fight for what you want. Some people are sitting around waiting for somebody to bring in Freedom just like these men are sitting here. Waiting for Godot. . . ." Others read it as a religious allegory making Godot God and the central image the fall of man in the second act. Yet ultimately, I think it must be agreed that Godot, although a brilliant theatre piece, is not the most appropriate kind of material.

It surprised me to notice, after the theatre moved from Jackson to New Orleans, in 1964, how much we were dependent on Movement activity. The theatre depends on its relationship to the activists for relevance and perspective. The awareness of that activity is extremely important for the orientation of new people who had not previously been engaged, and the dialogue is important to all. On our arrival in New Orleans, we felt less relevant because there was very little Movement activity going on in the city. Since that time things have begun to change; several programs and organizations have emerged. I think the presence and activity of the FST has been a little bit responsible for that.

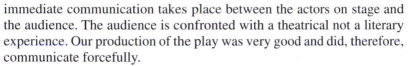

3.

The relationship between the FST and Movement people is important also because it opens up the question of arts as propaganda. It is important to distinguish between the inevitable political function of the arts and propaganda. Propaganda is legitimate, a necessary function of political partisans. The artist has license not available to the propagandist, however. A given work of art may have the qualities of propaganda, if a given partisan position is made clear or illuminated by the artist's work. But the propagandist has the additional responsibility for shaping information to meet political priorities.

It is possible to have good propaganda and not have art at all. At the same time, the artist can speak quite sharply to a specific political situation without sacrificing to propaganda. The artist operates at the vanguard of man's cultural consciousness. In that role his responsibility becomes to inform men's judgments; from this principle he derives aesthetic license. Dereliction of the duty to inform judgment deprives the artist of relevance and leaves him defenseless against history's indictment. The commercial entertainment theatre business is not relevant to Black theatre; but most Black artists have been taken away from the cultural basis of their own development by the lure of "success". Only recently, since the shift in political circumstances has pulled the Blacks into center-stage, has it become possible for the commercial Black artist to retain a bit of integrity without jeopardizing his commercial option too seriously. Even so, most of the commercial markets include Blacks to no significant degree.

In the creation of a relevant theatre the development of an active and critical rather than a passive audience is the most important task. It is not enough that a particular theatre group be composed of Black people or even that it be physically located where Black people live, if the theatre is not addressed to the needs of Black people and grounded in their experience. "Exposure" is not only a patronizing concept – it does not develop an audience. Being in Ireland is not what made the Irish theatre Irish – it was the positive search for the theatrical forms which comprehend and speak to that ineluctably Irish soul. When one finds the essence of an Irishman one finds the same truth that binds all men. Yet the statement remains distinctively Irish. And so with any man or culture.

If the "Irish" theatre could have been distinguished from an English theatre only because it had Irishmen and was in Ireland, then it would have been an English theatre in Ireland. The distinction is largely political. A theatre run and operated by Negroes that can be distinguished from other theatre in this country only by the complexion of the cast is not a Black theatre, it is a white theatre with Negroes.

The inescapable fact remains. There is no truth that speaks so clearly to me as the truth of my own experience. If I cut to the essence of my own truth there will lie a truth for all men. One can only achieve that kind of statement, however, in the context of specific historical, cultural, political, economic circumstances. The work, regardless of whether it deals directly with them, must comprehend such problems. As the truth of Black people finds expression in theatrical forms, new forms will be created. As that truth finds expression, it will be political. It will be opposed to the ruling powers because history (and the ruling powers) makes it so. The Free Southern Theater is one part of the process in the larger context of that struggle.

AFTER THE FREE SOUTHERN THEATER

A Dialog (1987)

Tom Dent and Jerry W. Ward, Jr

WARD: Although John O'Neal didn't have the funeral for the Free Southern Theater until November 1985, the institution seems to have died in the middle of the 1970s.[1]

DENT: It did. It died at the same time that so many black community theatres did. I see the death of the FST as a part of the national backlash against black cultural activity which took a separatist, Black Pride direction and identified strongly with black political and economic gains.

WARD: The concept of national backlash is interesting but debatable. The whole point of black community theatre was independence.

DENT: Independence?

WARD: Yes, independent development. What was never resolved for many community theatres was the fact that they could not depend on foundations and other people to sustain them. Community people had to fund community theatre.

DENT: None of the black community theatres which began in the 1960s and prospered for a while in the early 1970s were funded through communities. Almost all of them had some foundation or National Endowment for the Arts support. We wished that the communities would support theatre, but the black communities were poor. Communities gave funding priority to churches and other organizations that had longer service histories than the new theatres. We were in a catch-22 situation. For instance, if we tried to support a theatre like the Free Southern Theater solely by charging admission, we would have had to charge something like 20 dollars a ticket. Once you begin to do that, of course, you've cut off the community.

WARD: Very much so, the same way Broadway is killing itself with ticket prices.

DENT: But Broadway is not community theatre.

WARD: Right. But the death by cost is similar. When we think of the demise of community theatres in the mid-'70s, we also have to remember the beginning of the Southern network, The Southern Black Cultural Alliance (1974), which tried to address some of the problems facing these theatres.

DENT: Between 1970 and 1974, almost every substantial black community in the South had a theatre crop up. These theatres attempted to add a cultural dimension to other community organizations and to community activities, generally revolving around the ideology of Black Pride. Theatre is an artistic activity that brings together artists from different genres – writers, actors, musicians, visual artists – and that in performance can provide an audience with a unified experience in a particular space. In that space other valuable things can happen which heighten community awareness: exhibits of visual art, photographs, book and newspaper sales, and, in the case of the Free Southern Theater, group discussions that often had not so much to do with the performance itself but current community issues – which in some way the performance might have spurred. It was that coming together, the ensemble quality of theatre, the interaction of performers with audience, that made community theatre a very fine medium for carrying forth cultural questions and ideas.

WARD: I agree that community theatre was an excellent medium for the reasons you specify. Aside from the crucial matter of money, what I find troublesome is the audience the theatre addressed. The theatre was community-oriented, dealing with community problems and politics. Then the audience got carried away. Community theatre began competing with blaxploitation film. Piggy-backing on the serious effort to create black drama was a rush of musicals and spectacles. I think audiences decided Superfly spectacle provided a thrill the community theatre could not. I suspect the loss of audience was connected with a certain loss or co-opting of social consciousness.

DENT: I'm not sure. By 1975 or 1976, the money had shifted and it was not black money. It became apparent that certain kinds of musicals providing work for black performers in New York could get funding and commercial backing. These musicals had no social commentary. There were a lot of them, including one from New Orleans, *One Mo' Time*. With all these musicals – and there were about ten – from *Bubbling Brown Sugar* to *One Mo' Time*, the majority of the audience was white, not black. For example, *One Mo' Time* did not develop out of black community theatre in New Orleans. It never played in the black community. There was sort of a gentleman's agreement, or unstated principle, that if your theatre had an ideological bite, if the play or performance had a sting, you were not going to get funded. Eventually, this was even true, I believe, for the good material coming out of the Negro Ensemble Company in New York. Since 1975, NEC has not received the foundation support it once received. Yet, NEC, at the very least, lived up to the mandate of what high-quality, serious theatre was supposed to be. They maintained a schedule and good budgeting. They went out of their way to increase their black audiences, even in New York. Despite all this, they were losing foundation support. The foundations were saying, "We can't continue to support your theatre. You have to support yourself through your constituents". They don't say that to the symphony or to the opera or to ballet companies. It is accepted that these art forms cannot be entirely supported by subscribers or box office and need to be subsidized. But black theatre groups have to go out and support themselves.

WARD: That goes back to what I wrote in "Unfunding the Arts in the Black Community" (1979). There is a conspiracy to subtract support in favor of so-called mainstream efforts. Money is certainly withheld for ideological reasons. It comes down to a hard question that the Southern Black Cultural Alliance has addressed over and over: What are black communities willing to do once they have been alerted to particular problems in the arts, especially to the death of black community theatre? Is the community willing to be an audience? The problem of building audiences is with us everywhere.

DENT: It was certainly a problem FST faced, especially when we decided to focus on New Orleans. One of the things that made black community theatres distinctive – especially those in the South – was that we *were* consciously directing our performances to black audiences. It did not mean whites were excluded, but we were really trying to create a black receptivity to theatre. This placed a new responsibility on us as artists. It meant the form and substance of our material had to change. We had to address black audiences in terms they could understand. This does not mean our material was less complex. In many cases, it was more complex, but it certainly was different from Shakespeare or Brecht. FST started out doing Brecht and Beckett but by 1969 or '70, we were writing our own material. Black theatre is more than the static existence of black performers before a black audience. It should be a literature and style of theatre that utilizes the genius of Afro-American culture. This does not mean shunning solid principles of drama, but we were forced to begin to draw on the substance of Afro-American culture in ways we had not previously imagined. However, as we became more innovative in our attempts to communicate with black audiences, the foundations became less interested. They didn't really care about the communication developing between black audiences and black theatre. Theatre *does* have an ideological dimension and that can be dangerous.

WARD: Now let me throw you a curve ball. When the black audiences began to notice there were fewer plays, fewer productions, what did they do?

DENT: In New Orleans, in many instances, the most interested of the young people who began as audience members became participants and tried to find some way to keep going, even when there was no money left. Other groups developed from the FST initiative, either as descendants or ancillary groups. In New Orleans over the last 15 years we have seen the blossoming of Dashiki Theater, Nat Turner Theater, Ethiopian Theater, Congo Square Theater, Act I Theater – even without much money. Dashiki has performed with admirable regularity. Performances by the other groups have been sporadic, but the interest continues.

There would be no Act I Theater Festival (a festival for local black theatre companies now in its fourth year in New Orleans) had there been no Free Southern Theater. The people in Act I may not realize that, but it's true. FST introduced the idea of black community theatre in the South. As far as I know, it was the first nonacademic theatre in New Orleans to sustain itself. When we moved the FST out of the Desire Street Housing Project area in 1966, we were really moving into uncharted territory.[2] Twenty years later, when I see people who lived in that neighborhood, especially the children, I still receive a very special greeting. A couple of years ago, John O'Neal and I went out to Louisa Street, where the FST was located, for a TV interview on FST history. Our old building had been dismantled. Someone who lived on the block saw us being filmed and came out to greet us. We asked him to join the interview; it was a really good feeling. I see kids who used to hang around FST when they were 13 or 14. Now they're 33 or 34. They always stop to talk. In purely artistic terms, that may not mean much. But in terms of introducing something positive, it is very meaningful. I hope that when someone else comes along 20 years from now and wants to start another black theatre, these people will say to their children, "Maybe you should tune into that, because we learned about that back in the old days".

WARD: You have that glimmer of hope in New Orleans. There is still a lot of groundwork to do in Mississippi. FST began in Mississippi and did quite a bit of useful work in conjunction with the Civil Rights Movement, but its impact here has been slight. Jackson, Mississippi is not a place where black theatre has been overly successful. We have had many groups in the last ten years – Sunrise Theater, Potpourri Artistic Repertory Theater which still hangs on, a repertory company that Tommie Stewart of Jackson State tried to develop, I.D. Thompson's Showcase Productions Theater Company. Mahogany Performing Arts and the more recent Colored Performing Arts Institute (SunRise Cabaret Theatre) struggle in Meridian. Unless Charles Chiplin produces his own work or David Brian Williams mounts a play by Charlie Braxton, we don't have groups doing original material derived from Mississippi experiences. We have not developed a cadre of people who are committed to theatre whether times are bad or good.

I am just not optimistic about black community theatre in Mississippi. There may be too many options with film, video, television, and rap concerts. I don't have a sense that people want or need theatre. People may find a theatre that focuses on immediate community problems somewhat attractive; The Youth Theatre Troupe of the Black Belt Arts and Cultural Center (Selma, Alabama) doing *Baby Cakes* (1985 or '86), a play about teenage pregnancy conceived by Rose Sanders, was successful in Moss Point, Mississippi and in New York at Papa Charles Dinner Theater in Harlem.

DENT: Hard economic times coupled with the withdrawal of foundation money is what we face. Now is the time for another touring black theatre like the FST. The FST spurred the development of local community theatres in the South, but almost all these have died. If I had $100, 000 to put into black theatre in the South now, I wouldn't divide it up among eight towns. I'd put it into one company that would once again go out on tour.

The question of funding needs to be looked at differently now. If I were trying to make a touring theatre work again, I would hit the black fraternities and sororities and similar organizations that have national budgets and an alleged commitment to cultural activities. I know that the Delta Sigma Thetas have $100,000, though that may be their entire cultural budget for a year. I would try to convince them that even if the "New" Free Southern Theater becomes the only project the Deltas take on, it would be worthwhile and they could be proud of it.

WARD: I'd like to see how such a touring group would fare. There is one thing in the name I would delete – free. It should be called the New Southern Theater. "Free" encourages the assumption that you can have something for nothing. That is no longer the way the game is played.

DENT: No, it isn't. But when FST began, this was very important. It opened up theatre to people who had never seen it before, making possible a radical leap forward in audience participation. Any prior theatre experience had been with a college drama group, a performance for which one had to pay at least a dollar. Besides, the unwritten understanding was that only the educated elite and students went to such performances. One of the aims of the FST was to counteract that elitist image.

The FST was always closely aligned with the ideas and image of the Civil Rights Movement. In fact, the first FST audiences were Movement activists. For the early Mississippi tours, performances were held at Movement meeting places and Movement churches in Movement towns. The FST on tour was housed in the homes of people who were sympathetic to the Movement. They were fed by these people. You go into the community. They house you and feed you. You share an experience with people who are making great sacrifices to support the Movement. After all that, to ask them to pay to see your performance would have violated the spirit of the very experience you were bringing and sharing. Now we can do it, because we don't have the same situation. But it's very important to remember the FST was free because it was part of that larger Movement experience.

WARD: That's true. Some people still can't afford theatre – the unemployed. Yet, if a new touring theatre is to be subsidized by a fraternity or a sorority, shouldn't audiences make a token payment?

DENT: Not necessarily. If you require people to pay, you can be throwing up a barrier, unless you have done a lot of prior work to make people feel a part of your effort, in the hope they would want to support it. By the way, in the early days, although the FST was free, we asked audiences to contribute after performances. Many people put a dollar in our basket. Some people wrote checks. Now, the productions of Congo Square Theater, productions like my *Ritual Murder*, are usually for black professional groups such as the ones working in the Desire area with drug addicts.[3] We ask these groups to pay a small fee to the company; the performances are therefore subsidized by interested community organizations.

If there were a New Southern Theater, it might do four performances – Thursday through Sunday – in Jackson. An organization in Jackson might subsidize all four performances, which could then be free. If a town has a repertory company, then an admission fee makes sense. The important thing is to always make people feel they want to come, that they are a part of the cultural experience you are offering through your art. You do this as much through how you relate to your potential audiences as through the quality of your artistic work.

WARD: I don't doubt black theatre in the South will survive, but *how* it will survive is a question for the future.

1 August 1986

NOTES

1. Free Southern Theater was founded in Mississippi in 1963 by John O'Neal and Gilbert Moses. Tom Dent took over the New Orleans directorship of the theatre in 1966. See "Dialogue: The Free Southern Theater", *The Drama Review* 9, no. 4 (T28, Summer 1965): 63–76 [*reprinted as Chapter 9 of this book*] and TDR's Black Theatre issue, vol. 12, no. 4 (T40, Summer 1968).

2. The Desire Street Housing Project represents a high concentration of poverty, joblessness, and social pathology in New Orleans. We chose to locate the FST there in 1966 so as to make the theatre more directly available to those who "had no theatre". We were warmly received by the community. Desire Street, now virtually all black, is the same street in the title of Tennessee Williams' famous play. In the 1920s and 1930s when Williams knew it, Desire was the hub of a Polish community. The streetcar is now also only a memory.

3. *Ritual Murder* was first performed at Ethiopian Theater in Summer 1976, directed by Chakula Cha Jua. It has been performed almost continuously by various New Orleans and some non-New Orleans groups since then. Two groups who sponsored productions of *Ritual Murder* are the Association of Black Social Workers and the Desire Drug Treatment and Rehabilitation Center at the Desire Street Housing Project.

REFERENCES

Ward, Jerry W., "Unfunding the Arts in the Black Community", *First World* 1979 2, vol. 3:21–3.

JOHN O'NEAL, ACTOR AND ACTIVIST

The Praxis of Storytelling (1992)

Kate Hammer

Without our stories, how will we know it is us?
William Faulkner as quoted by Dudley Cocke, Roadside Theater (1991)

Multiculturalism is one of the hot topics of the 1990s. Cultural brokers, politicians, and academics debating multiculturalism risk diminishing it to the "affirmative action" of artistic expression; representatives from the cultures and communities determined by the power structure to be "other" are invited into cultural arenas as tokens, icons, or ambassadors. The power of art to signify becomes restricted to the extent that art is read as a sociological or anthropological document about "That Other Place/People". Multicultural events may communicate more about their sponsors (whose invitations have earned them the badge of political correctness or have diplomatically appeased systematically disen-franchised communities) than about self-determined cultural expressions emanating from communities of oppressed and exploited people. Effective multicultural action in the arts requires the equitable par-ticipation on all levels of organization, administration, and pro-duction of the marginalized and the privileged.

The Caribbean Cultural Center of New York City sponsored a conference in October 1991 entitled ". . . And Then Columbus: Cultural Diversity Based on Cultural Grounding II".[1] The conference drew together artists, activists, intellectuals, and cultural workers from many communities around the world to begin to formulate a new paradigm for cultural equity. The majority of attendees were people of color. While English was the language used in presentations, it was not a universally shared tongue. One aim of the conference was to begin the arduous task of assembling a lexicon for discussing the quest for cultural equity.

According to Hilda Guiterrez Baldoquin, consultant for VISIONS, Inc., and doctoral candidate at Stanford University's School of Education:

> Power and politics are fundamental factors of a cultural paradigm for equity. Power has been defined as "the ability to influence and/or control people and/or objects in one's immediate environment". Power does not operate isolated from politics. And "politics", then, is the understanding of power and influence. It is the learned skills of generating and exercising power within the context of a relationship – be it social, political, or economic. (Guiterrez Baldoquin 1991)[2]

Empowerment of each community represented at the conference (notably, gay and physically challenged communities were not heard as such among the African, Afro-Caribbean, African American, Native American, Appalachian, Asian, and Latino voices) depends on access to modes of cultural production, recognition of the validity of the modes already in use, and networking. Morenga Bambata, Cultural Director of the NIA Centre for African and Caribbean Culture in Manchester, England, stated: "Within every culture, there is that which is specific and that which is also universal, common to all culture. If we can identify those universal threads, they can serve to link us in a common mission". Such linkage depends on the transcendance by art of geopolitical boundaries, that is, on multicultural exchange and interchange. Bambata continued by urging that unlike the agents of the dominant oppressive system who evacuate content from artistic expressions, "We must be advocates for both content and form" (Bambata 1991). Providing a platform for artistic expression of members of a disenfranchised group is not satisfactory if that expression is emptied of its substance and appropriated for its form as an "event" or an object of study.

In terms of specific artists undertaking creative expression, several issues were addressed at the conference. Dudley Cocke, of Roadside Theater/Appalshop, a grassroots cultural center in Whitesburg, Kentucky, suggested that the dialectic between the paradigms of power and of equity or sharing can be reflected in the artist asking, "Is the work we're making engendering self-reliance in our audience? Is it about exclusion or inclusion?" (Cocke 1991). One aspect of inclusion is the expansion and extension of the traditions by an artist grounded in a specific cultural practice.[3] Validity, recognition of, and respect for artistic expression have replaced "authenticity" as key concepts. In this way, art becomes "a creative struggle to become visible even to ourselves", says Cocke (in Aufderheide 1990:34). Observing the historical tendency among people of African descent to be geographically mobile, Dr Ruth Simms Hamilton, professor of sociology and urban studies and director of the African Diaspora Research Project at Michigan State University, stated that, "When people are displaced, or whether they migrate for whatever reason, one should also understand that they become conduits of ideas, knowledge, cultural forms, and expressions". She called for the inclusion of "the day-to-day reality and epistemology, as a part of that larger cultural form and experience" in the emerging paradigm for "cultural equity" (Simms Hamilton 1991). What kind of art contributes to that quotidian knowledge of a people whose history has been obscured and obliterated over centuries of violent racism and colonization?

John O'Neal's career in theatre predates "multiculturalism" by 25 years at least. In the early 1960s O'Neal was a founding member of the Free Southern Theater which grew from the grassroots organizing of the Student Non-Violent Coordinating Committee (SNCC). The FST began as an integrated ensemble of young amateur and professional artists based first at Tougaloo College, Mississippi, and then in New Orleans, who toured the South presenting plays to predominantly black but usually integrated audiences. Although the FST aimed at exploring "black power in its widest and deepest sense", manifesting it in "myth, allegory, and public performance" (Dent *et al.* 1969:xii), its first seasons included plays not only by African American playwrights but also by Brecht and Beckett. Like other activists in the Freedom Movement, FST members faced discrimination, persecution, and threats of violence as they toured rural communities that had never known theatre. In terms of company, canon, and community, FST invented as it went along.

From its inception in 1963, FST sought the support of influential middle-class white people. Richard Schechner, then at Tulane University, was invited by O'Neal and his partners, Gilbert Moses and Denise Nicholas, to join them as a coproducing director of the young group. A network of white and black supporters in New York and New Orleans worked on fund-raising. Less than a year after FST began its work, the company went to New York to present *Waiting for Godot* (directed by Moses) and *Purlie Victorious* (directed by Schechner) to rally support from major arts funders. The company did receive positive notices in the New York press and eventually foundation support. For many members, however, the showcase was viewed as premature; the work wasn't ready for a New York audience and the audiences in the rural South which the company aimed at reaching had not yet been established. Conflict surrounded the organization's strategy in pursuing its political and aesthetic goals. Only over time, with many changes in leadership, would a clearer vision of constructive political action on the cultural front evolve – a vision addressing the need for nurturing black talent and educating black minds about a history and a future that were both being uncovered.

In the late 1960s the FST settled into Desire, an impoverished black community in New Orleans. New Orleans remains home to Junebug Productions, the successor to the disbanded (in 1985) Free Southern Theater. Nearly three decades of on-the-job training have equipped O'Neal with the skills and charm of a master storyteller. Humanism and Marxism continue to blend in O'Neal's work, along with an intuitive recognition of the cultural constructions of subjectivity and the imperative for oppressed people to gain access to modes of cultural production in order to exercise greater determination in the constitution of that subjectivity. The practice of storytelling that O'Neal has remained committed to interpolates audience members into a dialog that asks them to take responsibility for addressing the racism and exploitation in their own lives.[4] "You are the actors", O'Neal announced to the young audience of a 1964 backyard performance in Ruleville, Mississippi (in Dent *et al.* 1969:24). He continually weaves references to historical and cultural events into his stories, never letting audiences lose sight of the larger sociopolitical arena.

Integration as an early aim of the FST has evolved into a unique practice of *collaboration*. This process of collaborating evolved into An American Festival Project, a nationwide network of community sponsors and nine performance companies. The first coalition began when FST and Roadside Theater exchanged audiences, in effect, by touring to each other's communities as a means of addressing the fear and ignorance that made them see each other as enemies. In 1982, Bob Martin invited both companies to join Teatro Campesino and A Traveling Jewish Theatre at the People's Theatre Festival in San Francisco. A series of festivals followed, produced on an *ad hoc* basis.

Appalshop became the host for the American Festival Project. Appalshop's development director, Caron Atlas, helped to initiate a review of the early collaborations and to generate funding support. While grounding the project in a shared philosophy and providing the nourishment of regular critical review, Appalshop does not steer the course of each festival. Rather, Appalshop provides the nonprofit base. Policy is set by a board comprised of representatives of each participating group. It is staffed by two part-time employees shared with Appalshop and a series of contract workers who provide specific services for each festival. This structure indicates an alternative model of organization which is developing to meet the needs and missions of the participating companies and of the communities which mount festivals. The American Festival Project has developed a subsidy process which allows the flexibility for thorough negotiation between participating artists and community groups. For each festival, the American Festival Project hires a site liaison who speaks on behalf of the artists throughout the planning and residency in order to facilitate this process. The planning itself becomes a crucial and invigorating part of the festival. Festivals include workshops, residencies, performances, and the involvement of local artists. The "art" then is not bound by "a performance", rather it embraces the relationships formed through the context of the performance. This practice gives primacy to the process over the product.

One such "process festival" began in September 1991 and continued through April 1992. Using the theme "Stories into Art", events were presented at different sites throughout Mississippi. The work included a community celebration of an oral history assembled by local youth,

where performance artist Robbie McCauley and actor/director Linda Parris-Bailey participated as respondents rather than as presenters. The Mississippi festival provides a strong model for increasing the involvement of – and focus on – host communities. The festival residencies in host communities allow

- festival artists to attend local events;
- interface with organizations already at work in host communities;
- collaborative creation of a mission statement; and
- the opportunity for follow-up.

A fruitful collaboration may help create the resources for self-sustaining cultural practices once the festival has concluded.

Not surprisingly, some of the most successful festivals have been initiated in affiliated artists' home communities. Caron Atlas states:

> One of the things that the Project is trying to address for the companies is that the economic system basically pulls them away from their missions, because they're not able to be in communities for long periods of time. It's very hard to survive as a professional theatre company in the communities most of these theatres are allied with and grow out of. So they have to tour. (Atlas 1991)

The American Festival Project redefines touring as intercultural exchange by bringing together artists whose work is grounded in a specific cultural community with an empowered host community. "One of the basic premises of the project", according to Atlas, "is that you need to know who you are before you can enter into exchange or collaboration. You have to be coming from a position of strength and identity". The companies in this coalition share the practice of articulating alternative histories. American culture becomes, in O'Neal's words, a "gumbo", a spicy stew of unique and distinct elements that retain their own flavors.

Atlas observes a tendency in the current language of "multiculturalism" to "become diffused of any kind of politics". By contrast, she recognizes that in policy discussions, "John is good at keeping rooted in what our overall mission is, that politics are involved, that it's about power relationships, that it's about oppression and people dealing with it. The other thing that gets me is when people talk about multiculturalism as if it's a new thing", she continues, "when people like John have been involved with these issues for a long time. Denying people's history this way is a way to disempower them" (Atlas 1991).

One of O'Neal's skills is the truthful historicization of existing relations. The Junebug stories are organized to that end. When negotiating a mission statement for a festival in a community, Atlas states, "You need to understand the history of a whole bunch of different kinds of relationships between people that led you to the point where you're having a meeting. People like John can supply you with that information because he's either lived through it or he's studied it or he knows how to ask the questions that can give us that history if we don't know it. That's what makes him really effective". As a founding member of FST, Alternate Roots (a regional organization of southern theatre artists), Junebug Productions, and the American Festival Project, "John has been very instrumental in helping conceive and move forward a lot of alternative models. Organizing is part of his artistic mission. He's artful in the way he organizes".

I talked with O'Neal in New York City on 18 October 1991.

HAMMER: You were raised in southern Illinois and studied philosophy at Southern Illinois State.

O'NEAL: The little town I grew up in is like 50 per cent black. I went through segregated schools all the way until I went to college. I didn't know any white people really until I went to college.

HAMMER: In the 1960s, your work in the Civil Rights Movement with SNCC carried you to Mississippi. Since the earliest days of the Free Southern Theater, your artistic life has been centered in the southern United States. Did you experience a period of acculturation going from southern Illinois to the South?

O'NEAL: Yes, and no. It's important to note that the southern part of Illinois that I come from, the "southern" is more important than the "Illinois!" I think it's probably the case that in terms of African Americans from North America, or from the United States, black culture is still primarily a Southern phenomenon. Most of us are no more than four generations removed from plantation economy. Black people often refer to the South as "down home". It was a very Southern environment where I grew up, the culture, the lifestyle, so in that way I felt at home when I went South. On the other hand, each place that you go has its own particularity that you do have to learn. In most places in the South, for example, when you ask somebody where they're from, they might say, "Well, I've been here for the last 40, 45 years but I'm *from* out by Gees Bend". Now you might be 25 miles from the place that they're talking about, but the importance of *that* place as opposed to *this* place, and *those* people who live *there* as opposed to *these* people who live *here* is recognized and honored.

HAMMER: How does such a recognition filter into your work?

O'NEAL: The work becomes a way of helping to establish the mutual understanding of people between places and respect for those people and places. I try to collect stories as I go along, as well as take stories.

When I get a story from someplace, and tell it again somewhere else, I try to tell who the people were I got the story from, so that one gains insight into the life of the people and the place where the story comes from. Then we take that kind of work and integrate it into the actual performance work that we do.

HAMMER: In addition to touring original plays to communities across the country, Junebug Productions has established collaborative relationships with a number of arts and theatre organizations. Why?

O'NEAL: We develop these pieces; we find that, given the nature of our work and given the nature of the economy of the work, it costs a lot more to create the work than we have to create it with. So we find ourselves seeking out collaborative relationships with other institutions who are interested in seeing the thematic of a given piece accomplished.

HAMMER: What have you learned about multi-institutional, multi-organizational partnerships and collaborations?

O'NEAL: Oh, not enough . . . (*laughter*).

HAMMER: How do they work?

O'NEAL: It's an important device for those of us without the money to do otherwise. I think that probably the most important thing about it is trying to keep the channels of communication clear and open and make sure that everyone who's participating understands what the objective is and what each person's role is in regard to that objective. The problems that come almost invariably come as a result of poor communication and a lack of clarity along these lines.

HAMMER: Junebug Productions is currently collaborating with Roadside Theater of Whitesburg, Kentucky, on *Junebug Jack*, which blends songs and stories from Appalachian and rural Southern black cultures. Are you the primary artistic initiator of that process, as you have been in previous Junebug productions?

O'NEAL: Dudley Cocke [*of Roadside Theatre, director of* Junebug Jack] has the key function there. Although Roadside has a collaborative style within their organization, a cooperative style –

HAMMER: – collective –

O'NEAL: – collective style within their organization that qualifies the process significantly.

HAMMER: Right.

O'NEAL: Because that's the way they work. You gotta work with who you're working with.

HAMMER: Did Junebug ever go through a time when it functioned as a collective?

O'NEAL: Junebug was never a collective. But the Free Southern Theater, which Junebug is the successor to, tried to be collective at one point. My opinion is it's a less effective way to work – for an artistic organization.

HAMMER: Why is that?

O'NEAL: Because there are too many subjective factors involved. Unless you are an intense and long-term ensemble. Even then, my sense is, what tends to emerge is someone ends up with the responsibility for shepherding the vision, someone else tends to get the responsibility for taking care of the administrative and managerial functions, and so forth.

HAMMER: So that people tend to find their niche in the collective.

O'NEAL: I think that's what happens in point of fact.

HAMMER: Does that diminish the notion of collectivity? To find that kind of partitioning?

O'NEAL: Not necessarily. Clearly, you can develop to the point where roles are interchangeable. I've not seen a group where that kind of interchange has been accomplished, to my experience. I do think ensemble is the strongest way to work. And I do think that with the life of a group you can develop a really strong ensemble and that people hold on and hold in. But even there, it's important to credit the distinction in roles. In a way that facilitates more effectively the achievement of the democratic ideal implied by the collective, than if decisions get pushed through this collective forum when everybody knows that this one has the strongest, clearest view about visual stuff and this one has the strongest, clearest view about the management stuff, and this one has the strongest overall; the tendency will be to rely on those people for their strengths anyway. In that context, you facilitate the group's input into that process by saying, "OK Joe, you take care of that. That's your responsibility to make decisions about. And like any good leader, we expect you to solicit our opinions and listen to them when you get them and to integrate them in your process. If we're not satisfied with the results of the decisions you make, Joe, we'll take you out of that role and put Lucille in". (*laughter*)

HAMMER:So it's not requiring a fixedness – it's never letting the fact that someone is occupying a particular role mean that they therefore have the right to a monolog. It sounds to me like a way of structuring the dialog.

O'NEAL: Yeah. Leadership is the function of a group. The influence of a leader on a group, though significant, is secondary. The group holds authority and responsibility ultimately. When we make a common purpose and make a group of ourselves, what's good for the group exceeds what's good for either one of us. If either of us ever forget that and start to operate as if that were not so, then to that extent we distort the group in its effort to achieve its purpose. That is not to say that we should be sheepish and uncritical followers. Each one of us shares the responsibility for the whole thing. I'm as responsible for it as you are. I, as a follower in a given situation, you as the leader. It doesn't mean that because you're the leader you have more responsibility for the overall outcome of the thing that preempts my obligation to make judgments about what should become of it too.

HAMMER: It sounds like one of the things you're kind of pushing towards is a sense of self, an autonomous responsible self in the context of a larger group, in which interests of both the separate selves and the group are functioning and are seeking fulfillment simultaneously.

O'NEAL: That's what I think; it's a dialectic. You state it so well. (*laughter*)

HAMMER: Well, I'm getting it from you. What lessons for political organization and political organizing do you find doing work in theatre? Because it sounds like we're talking about any group trying to achieve a goal.

O'NEAL: Yeah, I think that's true. I think artistic groups bring special problems that require special consideration. There's the history of artistic practice and training that people bring to it and their view about the role of art. Particularly in our society, there are those who view art as the exclusive province of the individual and that it's all about giving that individual – or maybe a collection of individuals – the prerogative to express their feelings and views. There are others who see art as a part of the process of the individual – in the context of community – and the community coming to consciousness of itself. In the first case, the artist is seen as a symbol of the antagonistic relationship betwen the individual and society. In the second case, the artist symbolizes the individual within the context of a dynamic relationship with a community. One role of art is to expose those things which threaten our well-being and to identify those things which reinforce our well-being and to celebrate them and encourage their growth and development.

Obviously the latter view is the one that I identify with. This is the ground that gives basis to the notion that the artist is a vehicle for a force greater than him or herself, you know. I think it includes the whole spirit life that we participate in, as well as the whole political, social, and economic life that we participate in. As it includes the relations we have at a more intimate level, including finally the interrelationship we have within and inside of ourselves. You got all these layers and layers of interaction and interpenetration. Which is exciting. Our job as artists is to be vehicles for these forces at work in the universe and in human social interaction and in nature.

HAMMER: Would you go so far as to say that for you being an artist is a role of service?

O'NEAL: Absolutely. Absolutely. It's a service that we provide, to ourselves and to others.

HAMMER: I mean "serving" in a religious sense, not in the sense of "service economy".

O'NEAL: Yes, I agree with your statement very much. But I want to add that it's also in the economic sense. One of the things that we overlooked both in our artistic movement and in our political movement was the role of economics in the work. Like most everything else that people make, a work of art is a commodity. It has use value and exchange value. That's a part of its life. If artists don't get a fair return for the "products" that they create, then what happens is, we don't do it again. We're unable to make a living from our work. If we can't get the living from the work, we have to making a living out of something else, which means you don't do the work. Or you do it as a completely avocational pursuit, which tends to limit the level of accomplishment that you can expect to achieve with the work.

HAMMER: Have you gone through periods where you've had to seek a living elsewhere? Outside the arts?

O'NEAL: Oh yes. Definitely. (*laughs*) Yeah. I'm fortunate, actually, in that for most of the time since 1963, it has been my primary mode of living. Now sometimes I was making 10, 15 dollars a week, you know, for long periods of time, but when I was younger and my expenses were a lot less. And we lived cooperatively, so it was less difficult to survive. And in the context of the social movement that I got started in, there was a lot of support coming from family, friends, just being "in the Movement" made things happen and opened up possibilities for new things.

HAMMER: That raises an interesting issue. I would think that starting an art collective or an art ensemble in an era like the Freedom Movement provided validation for that work, even before there was necessarily anything to show for the work. Furthermore, it seems like one of the consequences of the hostile economic situation now is that the room for certainly the tangible support, but also, I think the intangible support for the work of artists is –

O'NEAL: Eroded.

HAMMER: Yeah.

O'NEAL: That's true. That's absolutely true. And both in the negative in the current situation and in the positive in the "Movement" situation. The presence of a strong social and political movement augments and amplifies the power of all its elements. The whole is always greater than the sum of its parts. It's true even in the simplest of things. If an organized group walks into the room in rhythm and in step, they make a bigger impact in the room than someone who's not organized. It's an aesthetic principle that structure magnifies the strength of those things which are structured . . . or magnifies the weakness, whatever. (*laughter*)

HAMMER: Right.

O'NEAL: It works both ways.

HAMMER: On that issue of weakness: I've understood that during the intense period of political activism in the '60s and early '70s there was a frustration that the performances or happenings were presented for a group that was already converted to the position that the performers or artists held, and that the function of art of mobilizing new people who didn't already hold those views or positions was not always fulfilled. What is your sense about that?

O'NEAL: Bernice Reagon talks about this more effectively than anyone else I've heard. She says, "There's absolutely nothing wrong with speaking to your family and friends. Talking to the converted is like talking to your family, your friends, those who share your purposes. In order for us to achieve our cause or purpose, I need the benefit of your best thinking to help me strengthen, sharpen, and clarify my thinking about what *we* are trying to do together. It's essential that we who share common purposes and common beliefs come together to build and strengthen ourselves. Black preachers talk about the metaphor of a coal in the fireplace, saying, "If you take the coal out of the fire, it cools off out there by itself, but if you put it in here, in the fire, along with all the other coals, it helps heat and doesn't cool off so quickly".

That's an important thing for us, it's really important. Otherwise not only do we cool off, our beliefs become static, and start becoming unrelated to the growing and creative edge that we need to have if we're going to move forward in any way. Especially if we're talking about social and political change. Because you better believe that those whose interests we oppose get together often and they meet us as an organized force. Those of us who are talking about social change are by definition talking about a weaker group opposing a stronger group. So we have to get together in order to organize and mobilize our strengths.

We *also* have to win the allegiance and support of new people whose interests correspond with ours. It's a "both and" rather than an "either or", and so to set up the opposition between these two things is to miss the point. That's a major concern; it's not just a concern for the arts and the artists, it's a concern for social and political movements as well.

HAMMER: So there is a necessity for both an expansion and extension outward and for consolidation.

O'NEAL: Yeah, you got to do both. It's a "both and".

HAMMER: Dudley Cocke says that in the Bantu tradition, instead of the word "teach" they talk about "sharpening ourselves".

O'NEAL: Ah, yes. Sharpening and deepening ourselves, sharpening—

HAMMER: And "building ourselves".

O'NEAL: Building! Yeah. "Sharpening and building ourselves". Yeah.

HAMMER: I think that's really good language. When you and I were talking earlier and I mentioned the term "outreach", you said that was not a term that you wanted to own. I realize that the term "outreach" comes from an assumption that there is a given—

O'NEAL: – that we got it and you need it—

HAMMER: That "we got it and you need it" or that the art or service that we as artists or producers are creating is available to this certain audience and now we want to *take* it somewhere else. But again, that we already have the art as a finished thing rather than as a dialog.

O'NEAL: Yeah, yeah, and the same guy that Dudley was quoting about sharpening and building talks about how knowledge is not a given thing to begin with that I can bring to you as a teacher or as an artist. [*see Rahman 1990*] Knowledge is the product of what we do together. Until we take action together, to understand, to deal with the given problem that we share in common, neither of us has the knowledge that's required to solve that problem. The knowledge itself is the product of our action.

HAMMER: How can we translate that to the audience–performer relationship?

O'NEAL: Same thing. It's the same thing.

HAMMER: That the performance does not exist in an empty house?

O'NEAL: That's right. A rehearsal exists, and so there's a knowledge which gets developed as I become my own audience, which is a valid thing. But when you become involved as a collaborator in this event, either as another artist or as part of the audience, a new thing is then happening in this moment. If we're not meeting in a place of common interest then no new change will occur, because the occasion of our coming together is an occasion that will only result in our recognition that we ain't got nothin' to do together. (*laughter*) It's a very bold thing, to presume that one has the right to occupy somebody else's time and space, you know. It only becomes do-able, it seems to me, to the extent that you can submit to that role of lens, of instrument to the force that exceeds yourself. If it's just yourself that you're bringing to the thing, then you got no right. But if you can release yourself and let yourself be of service to the force that you don't even create or call into being but that calls each of us into being in that moment, then you can say, "Maybe there's something here worth . . ."

HAMMER: Worth transmitting?

O'NEAL: Yeah, worth the effort. It's about finding ways to get yourself out of the way.

HAMMER: Right.

O'NEAL: It's like a lens. A lens is a good metaphor. You don't see the lens at all. If I do a good job as an artist, what is remembered is not what I did but what came through me.

HAMMER: (*laughing*) My father has a phrase. He says that being told he's done a good performance feels like hearing that he's wearing a nice toupée. That if it were really working, no one would say anything at all about "a performance" as such.

O'NEAL: Yeah, they'd go on and start talking about what was done.

HAMMER: About the events.

O'NEAL: I'm going to borrow that from your father. (*laughs*) Let me just add that I think this is where the power of art comes from. What is true of the artistic expression is also true in this exchange here between you and me, and any other "you and me" that is engaged: to the extent that you come seeking only for yourself, or I come seeking only for myself, then we don't end up together. But if we come seeking that which is greater than you or I, that we share, then we get somewhere, and in some interesting and ironic way we are enhanced, each of us individually.

HAMMER: It sounds like you're talking about the authenticity of self coming through a kind of release and surrender to greater forces and to greater, perhaps unthought of possibilities.

O'NEAL: Yeah.

HAMMER: How do those notions of selflessness and selfhood and of autonomy and surrender translate onto the political level? Being in

my generation, it's hard to have an image of what successful political action is. What is successful resistance, and when is overt resistance not constructive? When should we give over and when should we stand up?

O'NEAL: I think it's all the time on both sides. Now, of course I don't know the answers to these questions—

HAMMER: (*laughing*) – Oh shucks!—

O'NEAL: But I don't think that the answers come from outside the effort to do it. It's like I was saying a moment ago in quoting Rahman: Knowledge is itself the product of the people who are engaged in the effort to solve the problem. The knowledge does not exist *a priori*. It's not like there's a blueprint waiting to tell us what the revolution is and how it's gonna be done. It will be the product of what we create. It's just like being able to see this green napkin in my hand here. The vision, the image of this green napkin is not existing outside of what we're doing in our heads. All these stimuli are not organized into the green napkin until *we do it.*

HAMMER: Insofar as art challenges our minds to organize stimuli, is one of the functions of art to enlarge the possibility of useful recognitions?

O'NEAL: Enlarging is certainly one of the functions. But maybe it is sometimes to reduce too. To be able to narrow in and focus on as well as to enlarge. I'm having so many wonderful teachers right now. Probably the central teacher I have, as I try to grasp all this stuff, is Jowole Willa Jo Zollar, who is the head of Urban Bush Women. She's getting me to appreciate the way in which these things we identify as spiritual phenomena stand as complementary to physical phenomena rather than in some opposition to physical phenomena. You understand what I'm trying to say?

HAMMER: A "both-and" and instead of an "either-or".

O'NEAL: In Western training this tendency is to want to segregate these phenomena from each other rather than to see them in their integrated relationships to each other. Their dynamic relationships to each other. It's always a pulsing, dynamic process of change and transition. In constant creative development – or it may be a degenerative development, which is also an aspect of things.

HAMMER: That notion of integration isn't a dominant theme in our culture but it does get sounded in a lot of different discourses right now. My image of such integration is a three- or possibly four-dimensional dialectic. I see spindles of energy between two points moving and twisting and spiralling in space. People in different places, doing different work are coming to the same outlook. Do you think that this perspective has revolutionary import, in terms of relations of power to material and cultural resources?

O'NEAL: Uh-hmm. Yeah. I agree with you. Very much.

HAMMER: Is there anything that you want to add about your work and your thoughts?

O'NEAL: It's just a very exciting time to be working and living and having a chance here to participate in the creation, to contribute to the development of a new movement.

HAMMER: I'm starting to dis-believe in the feeling of disintegration that I get when I look at what's going on, like on the economic or legislative level. Do you think that it's realistic to stay optimistic in this time?

O'NEAL: I think that if people have no hope, they don't struggle, and if they don't struggle, they die. So not only is it realistic to be optimistic, it's essential. I think it's also essential not to be Polyannaish about it. The reality is that we face serious and terrible problems. We probably have more oppressed and exploited people now than there've ever been before! Oppressed more terribly than they've ever been oppressed and exploited before. *However*, the optimism that you hear in this kind of context, you hear because you're talking with people who are engaged themselves in a process of struggle to change that, to reverse those processes, to reverse those trends and tendencies. What you hear is a product of their belief in the value of the small victories that they accomplish and the recognition that there are others who are engaged similarly in the commitment that the force of life that – what's the word?

HAMMER: Springs forth?

O'NEAL: – that infuses each of us, and all different things, is greater than the force of death. I guess it comes down to the great struggle between good and evil. (*laughter*) And the faith that the good guys will carry the day ultimately. Maybe not in short term, but we're in a period of great transition now, you know, when we oppose probably the most powerful social and political and economic instrument that's ever been created in the world.

NOTES

1. The convention was sponsored by the Caribbean Cultural Center "in cooperation with Con Edison, the Association of Hispanic Arts, the Association of Performing Arts Presenters, and the National Assembly of Local Arts Agencies".
2. Ms Guiterrez Baldoquin acknowledges the pioneering contributions of

Erica Sherover-Marcuse and Dr Price Cobb, and also her grandmother Maria Margarite Vasquez.

3. Appalshop has "been criticized for not collecting and preserving enough of the real traditional music – that they recorded all their young friends. And that is true, too. [. . .] They've looked at culture as moving and changing, and been part of that moving and changing", according to Helen Lewis, founder of Appalachian Studies (in Aufderheide 1990:35).

4. This interpolation is not radical enough to disrupt the formal conventions of storytelling. O'Neal remains the sole performer in the first two Junebug plays, functioning as narrator and embodying the various characters. More radical strategies of audience interpolation are used by choreographer Donald Byrd and performing artist Robbie McCauley. In *The Minstrel Show*, Byrd calls audience members to the stage to recite racist jokes in an improvised send-up of the Mistah Johnson and Bones dialogs of the 19th-century minstrel shows. McCauley and her coperformer Jeannie Hutchins teach hand signals and vocal responses to their audiences in McCauley's work-in-progress *Sally's Rape: The Whole Story*. They regularly call for audience interjections as they explore their heritage of and struggles against racism through a performance that is composed of honed moments loosely linked by casual conversation.

REFERENCES

Atlas, Caron (1991) Interview with author, New York, 23 November.

Aufderheide, Pat (1990) "Talk of the Mountain; An Appalachian Arts Center Comes of Age". *The Progressive*, April: 34–6.

Bambata, Morenga (1991) "International Network of Color: Linking Missions, Linking Resources". Discussion at ". . . And Then Columbus", The Caribbean Cultural Center, New York, 17 October.

Cocke, Dudley (1991) "Cultural Paradigms for Equity: Defining the Philosophical Framework and Steps of Implementation". Discussion at ". . . And Then Columbus", The Caribbean Cultural Center, New York, 17 October.

Dent, Thomas C., Richard Schechner, and Gilbert Moses (1969) *The Free Southern Theater By The Free Southern Theater*. Indianapolis, Indiana: The Bobbs Merrill Company.

Guiterrez Baldoquin, Hilda (1991) "Cultural Paradigms for Equity: Defining the Philosophical Framework and Steps of Implementation". Discussion at ". . . And Then Columbus", The Caribbean Cultural Center, New York, 17 October.

Rahman, Md. Anisur (1990) "Towards an Alternative Development Paradigm". Inaugural address at the biennial conference of the Bangladesh Economic Association. Dhaka, 23 November.

Simms Hamilton, Ruth (1991) "From the Dominance of the Few to the Liberation of the Many: New Definitions". Discussion at ". . . And Then Columbus", The Caribbean Cultural Center, New York, 17 October.

Part III:
Moving Beyond the
Center

RODE A RAILROAD THAT HAD NO TRACK (1998)

Glenda Dicker/sun

> I rode a railroad that had no track.
> **Traditional**
> So we started talking and have been talking quite a bit since that time.
> **Septima Clark**

When I was a high school student, I performed dramatic readings of James Weldon Johnson's *The Creation* and entered a scene from *Raisin in the Sun* in oratory contests. Noting this interest, my father gave me an article from the Sunday *New York Times*, announcing Ellen Stewart's new theatrical idea, La Mama Experimental Theatre Club. This article changed my life. It showed me that a black woman theatre artist in America could break new ground, chart a new course, ride her own railroad. As a Howard Player I studied, with Owen Dodson and James Butcher, the plays of Sophocles and Shakespeare. Later, when I joined the Howard University faculty, I was the "young lion" James V. Hatch mentions (see Chapter 14) who staged N.R. Davidson's *El Hajj Malik*. In 1972, I conceived and directed the gospel musical *Jesus Christ Lawd Today* at the Black American Theater in Washington, DC. Later still I had a brief directorial connection to the Hecksher production of Vy Higgensen's *Mama, I Want To Sing*. More recently, I spent five years chairing the drama department at Spelman College, heir to Baldwin Burrough's crystalline vision and keeper of Anne Cooke's flame. It is out of this swirling cauldron of influences and images that I approach the task of introducing this section.

Moving Beyond the Center examines four modes of African American performance which move beyond more commonly acknowledged forms. They are different from each other; but each, in its own way, celebrates the spirit of survival, the ability to make a way out of no way, which brought African Americans through and beyond slavery. Taken separately, they encompass reclamation, reaching back and resistance. Taken together, they reveal something more complicated. Taken together, these four works reveal a shift, a tension, an uneasy sea change as black performance simultaneously outgrows and reclaims its black folk roots.

In "Theatre in Historically Black Colleges: A Survey of 100 Years", theatre history veteran James V. Hatch traces the development of black academic theatre from its post-civil war missionary roots through the upsurge of black protest dramas on college campuses during the Civil Rights era and finally to its decline in the present day. This is a rich history of theatre rooted in the black folk truism, "Each one teach one". Hatch provides an invaluable record of the pioneers who labored to uplift the race through theatre. Beginning with dramatic readings of Shakespeare and the Greeks, they defined a tradition that burgeoned to embrace the advent of folk drama inspired by the Irish Abbey Theatre. The Negro Intercollegiate Dramatic Association was founded in 1930 by representatives of four black schools to "quicken faculty and student interest in drama". The Association popularized tournaments of one-act plays which were held at different campuses each year. In describing the transformation of these regional drama tournaments into festivals, Hatch could be foreshadowing the plight of fraternities and sororities described in Elizabeth Fine's article. Said transformation occurred because "some felt that competition for prizes did not promote good will and friendship between the colleges".

In Fine's "Stepping, Saluting, Cracking, and Freaking: The Cultural Politics of African-American Step Shows" the women of Delta Sigma Theta, storming down the aisle flaunting their white tuxedos and red masks, resist the good-girl image fostered by the Cult of True Womanhood during Reconstruction. In claiming their space, these stepping, cracking, "uppity" black women move from margin to stage center: subjects of their own drama rather than objects in someone else's. Fine celebrates the vibrant young people who exalt themselves and folk tradition in their dramatic verbal dueling, but who must balance their vitality with the demands of their new found "respectability". Fine offers here perhaps the first codified accounting of the step shows so popular on the same campuses which once hosted one-act play tournaments. She accomplishes something else as well. She shows how the present state of step mirrors the shift from folk to popular culture in the larger society: "Prior to 1983 stepping was largely spontaneous and all but invisible to whites". With the bourgeoisification of the step shows comes a parallel removal of "some of the danger, tension, and political impact of stepping". As one student told the author, "Once you can't crack, it will have to be more of a show with dancing and singing. Otherwise it will be too boring".

More of a show with dancing and singing could be a description of the contemporary gospel musical about which Warren B. Burdine, Jr writes. These plotless songfests sometimes strike the same emotional chords first struck in 1871 by the Fisk Jubilee Singers. In "The Gospel Musical and Its Place in the Black American Theatre", Burdine carefully explores two forms of theatre at which purists "would look askance" – the gospel musicals and their low-brow comedy cousins. While looking at the commercially successful hallelujah chorus musicals, Warren Burdine cannot help but glance back at the withered dreams of black theatre legends who were stymied in their efforts to control their own history by Reaganomics and other factors. According to Burdine, the gospel musical has led black theatre through a new transformation. As black theatre legends of two decades ago "grey" and spend their time remembering, they are being replaced with a new generation of amateurs with little formal training who, nonetheless, have somehow stumbled onto the pulse of the historically elusive black audience. Producers of the new gospel musicals recognized that, for many black people, church was the only theatre that would consistently get us out of our homes and into our pocketbooks. Burdine gathers together the dozens-playing nouveau coon shows along with their marginally more respectable cousins, such as *Mama, I Want to Sing*. He traces their climb to dubious glory, acknowledging that both forms "have etched their indelible marks on the black theatre".

In Lucy Lippard's interview with Adrian Piper, a performance artist who wears clothes saturated with vinegar, eggs, milk, and cod-liver oil as she goes through the rituals of daily life, we find a woman at the opposite end of the spectrum of the "race dramas". Far from appealing to the lowest common denominator among black audiences, far from concerns of racial uplift, Piper riffs out her own call and response, trying to "incorporate them [the people on the street who become her audience] into my own consciousness". She is uppity and self-centered like the Deltas and a self-defined "paradigm of what the society is". At the same time that Adrian Piper inspires through her radical resistance to being other-defined, she troubles when (in response to a question from interviewer Lippard), she claims "woman" but not "black". She might be called granddaughter to Pecola in *Imitation of Life*, isolated in an all-white world where she behaves "inappropriately". But she might also be called granddaughter to Adrienne Kennedy, tapping into our fears as she invokes her own unique voice to elucidate the complex notion of being a woman in our society.

Reading these four articles takes us on a trackless railroad journey from European dramas to African roots; from the ritual killing of Sapphire in the protest dramas of the 1960s to her resurrection in the *Beauty Shops* of the 1990s; from singing our stories to talking quite a bit to singing our stories again.

> Hambone, Hambone, where you been?
> Around the world and back again.

THEATRE IN HISTORICALLY BLACK COLLEGES

A Survey of 100 Years (1998)

James V. Hatch

To speak of Black Performance is to speak of African roots, of popular Black entertainments; to speak of Black academic theatre is to speak of European roots, of Shakespeare and the Greeks. For the most part, African American Performance History and Academic Theatre History have lived discrete lives, separated by the high wall of class discrimination. Black performers, whether amateurs dancing on shingles for pennies or professionals singing on stages for salaries, rarely obtained venues at universities, at least not until the 1930s and 1940s, and even then, the performer was not Redd Foxx or Ethel Waters, but concert artists Roland Hayes or Marian Anderson singing German *lieder*. This tradition changed very little until the Civil Rights Movement of the 1960s.

The Missionary tradition favored denominational colleges. By 1861, America's churches had founded 150 colleges (seminaries), as compared to only eighteen state-supported institutions. With the ink of capitulation hardly dry at Appomatox, the Protestants' American Missionary Association flew into the conquered South and built a series of denominational schools – Tillotson College, Tougaloo College, Livingston College, Fisk University, Spelman Seminary, Straight University and Talladega Institute.[1] There were exceptions – Lincoln University of Jefferson City, Missouri, was founded by Black Civil War veterans, and the Catholics established Xavier in Louisiana – however, New English Protestantism dominated the historically Black college stages for nearly a hundred years.

Labeled "the nursery of ministers", most of the early graduates from the new Black colleges became preachers or teachers or both. The schools, often designated as "institutes", "colleges", or "universities", began instruction on the elementary level, for the vast majority of the former slave population could neither read nor write. A high-school diploma came with completion of the eighth grade, which entitled one to become a teacher: "Each one, teach one". An all-consuming passion for the long-denied education gripped the former slaves. Those who submitted themselves to the discipline of the process internalized the New England values of their teachers, who initially were nearly all white. The boards of trustees, the presidents and the deans of these colleges remained white until after World War II.[2] They controlled curricula, and faculty, and student life with rigid discipline. Florence Read, John D. Rockefeller's appointed President of Spelman College in Atlanta for twenty-seven years, read and censored every play produced on campus. She permitted no drinking of alcohol, sexual innuendoes, or profanity onstage. When Blacks gradually assumed administrative power, they were often as authoritarian as the whites, and in many cases more so.[3]

The dispute between W.E.B. Du Bois, who was a product of New England schools (excepting his BA from Fisk), and Booker T. Washington, who was a graduate of Hampton Institute, Virginia, embodied two diverse approaches to the education of former slaves. The missionary New England school teachers had brought with them the only schooling they knew – the classical study of Greek, Latin, the Bible, and mathematics. Washington, who had come up from slavery, knew that the majority of freedmen needed skills to earn a living:

> What deeds have sprung from plow and pick!
> What bank-rolls from tomatoes.
> No dainty crop of rhetoric
> Can match one of potatoes.[4]

Neither New England Puritanism nor southern pragmatism embraced the theatre. The carpenters, bricklayers, and potato planters of Hampton Institute had little leisure or motive to study drama. The northern Baptists had small tolerance for the stage, unless it was disguised as a moral lecture; nonetheless, their future ministers and teachers studied rhetoric and elocution, which included the Greek and Roman orators. The art of declamation with its rhetorical flourishes led to the recitation of the Bible and Shakespeare aloud.

By the turn of the twentieth century, dramatic readings had become acceptable to both the public and denominational schools. Tuskegee Institute hired Shakespearean Charles Winter Woods to teach English, drama, public speaking, and to direct the Tuskegee Players. In the same years, Atlanta University hired Adrienne McNeil Herndon to head its Department of Elocution, where she produced Shakespeare and Sheridan. Her Atlanta Players, along with Professor Woods' Tuskegee Players, shared the honors of being the first dramatic clubs in southern Black schools, but for many decades their dramatic societies, like their counterparts in New England, would not enjoy curriculum status. Even Howard University, where Professor Ernest Just of the English Department organized the Howard Players in 1911, did not include

Plate 5: Scene from *Mary Rose*, performed at the Atlanta Theatre Company in May 1940. Hatch–Billops Collection. Photographer unknown.

theatre in its curriculum until the 1920s. Richard B. Harrison, whose Broadway performance of the role of de Lawd in *The Green Pastures* (1930) made him famous, made his living by performing his one-man versions of *Macbeth* and *Julius Caesar* in Black colleges.[5] His friend, poet Paul Laurence Dunbar, in 1899 wrote a play, *Robert Herrick*, based on the life of the English poet, for Harrison to perform in the style of Richard Brinsley Sheridan.[6]

By 1900, because of poor facilities and few teachers with college degrees, none of the southern missionary or state schools had earned national accreditation. To remedy the situation, a half-dozen northern philanthropists began to funnel money into scholarships, buildings and stipends for teachers.[7] The major fund to promote theatre and speech was the General Education Board, established by John D. Rockefeller in 1902. Its purpose was to work for accreditation by awarding scholarships to Blacks who would study in northern colleges and then teach in southern schools.

At the same time, three important movements helped change the face of Black college theatre: Little Theatre, Folk Drama, and Pageant. To commemorate the fiftieth anniversary of the Emancipation Proclamation, Du Bois wrote a pageant that would put into dramatic form, for the benefit of large masses of people, a history of the Negro race. On 22 October 1913, at the Twelfth Regiment Armory on Columbus Avenue in New York City, *The Star of Ethiopia* made its debut. Negro colleges followed Du Bois' lead and throughout the 1920s presented dozens of pageants, *The Masque of Colored America*, *Pageant of Progress in Chicago*, *Culture of Color*, and *The Milestones of the Race*. Some schools, like Virginia State College, presented pageants (*The Teachers' Pledge*) annually. Typically, the pageants were written by civic leaders or faculty to celebrate race progress, women's contributions to art and learning, or the history of their college. Pageants clearly embraced civic pride, moral uplift, and respect for education. These spectacles enhanced the status of dramatics.

In 1911, the Irish Abbey Theatre toured America and inspired respect for folk theatre. Frederick Koch and his Carolina Playmakers at Chapel Hill promoted southern folk plays, white and Black. Ridgley Torrence's *Three Plays for a Negro Theatre* (1917) received raves when they opened in New York. Willis Richardson's Broadway debut of his short play *The Chip Woman's Fortune* (1921) set a standard for Black achievement. African Americans and whites saw onstage for the first time rural families speaking in regional dialects, struggling with poverty and race. As the passion for folk theatre spread across the nation, in 1922 philosophy professor Alain Locke designated Howard University as a center where "race drama becomes peculiarly the ward of our college, as new drama, as art-drama, and as folk-drama".[8] However, the university's white president, J. Stanley Durkee, rejected Willis Richardson's folk plays as inappropriate for Howard's stage.

The conflict was classic – a white administrator rejecting Black folk art as inferior. As a response to the prodding by an African-American historian, Carter Woodson, two playwrights – Willis Richardson and May Miller, an English teacher in Baltimore – published *Negro History in Thirteen Plays* (1935), based on the lives of great Black leaders (including six women), aimed at elementary and high-school audiences. Some protagonists spoke in a modified dialect (how could Sojourner Truth and Harriet Tubman not?). Black playwrights had begun to control their own history.

The third boon to college drama was the Little Theatre Movement which swept America in the second decade of the century. By 1925, it was estimated that over 3,000 amateur groups – schools, women's clubs, men's lodges, churches, YMCAs/YWCAs, and settlement houses – had built raised platforms for stages, and "put on plays", one-acts which seldom required more than a single set. Since experienced actors were not available for amateur productions, characters were broadly conceived and generally few in number, ideal for college presentation. The Little Theatres had given a face-lift to the sometimes scurrilous reputation of the American stage by comparing itself to the art theatres of Europe – Théâtre Libre in Paris or the Moscow Art Theatre. Drama became more respectable and acceptable to college trustees.

By the 1930s there was a general recognition that the arts should play an important role in teacher education. The General Education Board awarded scholarships to artists in music, dance, theatre, and painting to allow them to obtain advanced college degrees with the agreement that they would teach in southern colleges. Some did teach.[9] The Julius Rosenwald Foundation sent S. Randolph Edmonds on a fellowship to make an observational study of amateur drama organizations in England, Ireland, Scotland, and Wales. In March 1930, Edmonds, then on the faculty at Morgan College, called together representatives from four schools – Howard, Hampton, Virginia Union, and Virginia State College – to found the Negro Intercollegiate Dramatic Association (NIDA); they elected Edmonds president. Their charter listed six purposes:

1. To increase the interest in intercollegiate dramatics
2. To use dramatic clubs as laboratories for teaching and studying drama
3. To develop Negro folk materials
4. To develop aesthetic and artistic appreciation for the dramatic art
5. To train persons for cultural service in the community
6. To establish a bond of good will and friendship between the colleges.

Their first major project was to quicken faculty and student interest in drama by holding an annual tournament of one-act plays at a different campus each year. In two years, the Association's membership grew to ten. Some felt that the competition for prizes did not promote "good will and friendship between the colleges", and eventually the tournament was changed to a festival. The creation of NIDA achieved immediate results. Morgan College initiated courses which treated every phase of drama, including the first complete dramatic laboratory.

In 1936, Professor Edmonds moved to Dillard University in New Orleans, a distance too great for participation in NIDA. He then assembled another cadre of Black colleges to form the Southern Association of Dramatic and Speech Arts (SADSA).[10] However, the Association's production of Negro plays was frustrated by the scarcity of scripts. To inspire playwrights to write "twenty- to forty-minute plays", which should have a "strong moral or religious point, or deal with a social problem or folk materials", the Association offered students a production at the next festival. After six years, SADSA's objectives had changed from those of the 1930 NIDA charter. The new goals addressed class and race in a different manner:

1. Negro playwrights could write about middle-class life, not always Negro folk drama
2. Negroes might write about white life as they see it
3. More experimentation was needed
4. More plays needed to be written and more needed to go into the wastebasket
5. A desirable attitude should be created among Negroes toward plays of Negro life.

The Association was clearly tired of seeing the "same ol' thing", for the craft of playwriting proved too time-consuming and too demanding for inexperienced students to master. To fill the void, Professor Edmonds produced his own original scripts, which he published in three volumes: *Six Plays for a Negro Theatre*, *Shades and Shadows*, and *The Land of Cotton and Other Plays*. At least three of his one-act plays had already become standards at Black college festivals: "Yellow Death", concerning the malaria experiments on colored soldiers during the Spanish–American War; "Gangsters over Harlem", a contemporary melodrama; and "Nat Turner", an historical presentation of the 1831 slave insurrection. The nineteen member colleges of SADSA, scattered over a distance of 2, 000 miles, found that if they spent two days in travel, and two days watching plays, no time was left for scholarship and Association business. They divided the colleges into three regions.[11] Each school was to send a play to the regional contest where three judges would select the best three plays and have them sent to the central SADSA conference.

The Association's promotion of plays of Negro life raised an issue – the "Purity of Southern Speech". The Association faced a choice: either insist their students adopt the pronunciation of the mainstream and speak standard American English, or embrace regional speech and dialect as a worthy second language. Regionalism never had a chance against the New England perspective of how to speak the Queen's English properly. Some colleges initiated "Better Speech Week". In the 1950s, the drama department of Howard University hired special teachers, in the words of

Owen Dodson, to cleanse the "mushy-mouths" of southern students. This was the same decade that Howard staged fourteen European classics and four African-American plays. Dialect in folk plays was tolerated, but the student actors – like the poet Paul Laurence Dunbar – imposed art upon nature. It was a classic struggle of the oppressed to join or reject the mainstream, a struggle that surfaced again in 1996 in the Ebonics debate of the Oakland schools in California.

Make-up, too, was put on trial. In 1941 at Tuskegee, the Association watched Professor Voorhees conduct a demonstration entitled "Makeup in Sepia". Various shades of Thespian, a greaseless paint, were used to even up complexions for characters in the same play, that is, to bring a dark complexion up and a light complexion down. This was the period when both Broadway and Hollywood refused to cast Negro actors because they were "too white to be Black, or too Black to be white", and Max Factor had not yet manufactured grease paint for amateurs in hues useful to nonwhite actors, who were faced with using mixtures of minstrel black, Chinese yellow, Indian red, and Mexican brown.

White plays, British and American, dominated the college stages during the 1940s through the 1950s. Very few Black plays had been written and most would not appear until late in the 1960s. In addition, the faculty increasingly obtained their advanced degrees from northern and midwestern universities and traveled abroad, and their familiarity with world drama encouraged them to mount European plays. And why not? Professor Anne Cooke of Howard stated frankly that she was preparing her students professionally to play all roles, even though in the late 1940s there were no parts offered to Black actors except maids and butlers. When the actress Roxie Roker (Howard B.A., 1952) became a regular on television's *The Jeffersons* in the 1970s, she expressed her gratitude to Professor Cooke for insisting on world-class theatre.[12] Because Howard University was funded by the U.S. Congress, it offered security in tenure and budget that attracted talented faculty. Designer/ actor/James Butcher, writer/director Owen Dodson, and director/ administrator Anne Cooke led Howard's Department of Theatre from the mid-1940s into the 1960s, and typically produced Maeterlinck, Shakespeare, O'Neill, Sophocles, Tagore, *et al.* – programs more classically oriented than many white colleges of those decades.

On 31 August 1949 in New York harbor, Mrs Eleanor Roosevelt, as a trustee of Howard University, boarded the *S.S. Stavangerfjord* to bid the Howard troupe *bon voyage*. The three faculty members with twenty Black students sailed to Norway, Denmark, Sweden and Germany to perform Ibsen's *The Wild Duck* and the Heywards' *Mamba's Daughters*. The Howard Players received wide international publicity. So enthusiastically were they received that the U.S. State Department began to send artists abroad routinely as a part of its foreign policy, including the Florida A&M Playmakers who toured seven African countries.

Three colleges – Spelman, Morehouse, and Atlanta University –

Plate 6: Hazel Washington and Dorothy Ateca in *Mamba's Daughters* by Dorothy and DuBose Heyward, directed by Owen Dodson for the Atlanta Theatre Company, 17–19 July 1940. Hatch–Billops Collection. Photographer unknown.

merged in 1929 into a single cooperative university. In 1934, Anne Cooke founded the university's Summer Theatre which lasted into the 1970s, making it American's longest running summer theatre. They produced four shows in six weeks; one of them, if available, was a Black play. Most were Broadway hand-me-downs or classic European (Capek's *R.U.R.*, Wilder's *Our Town*, *School for Scandal* by Sheridan). Atlanta's Summer Theatre became the important training center for many talents: Sterling Brown; Marion Douglas; Baldwin Burroughs; Dorothy Ateca; Raphael McIver; John M. Ross and Owen Dodson (both graduates of the Yale Drama School), and Thomas Pawley, who, after receiving his M.A. in theatre from Iowa, took a position at Lincoln University in Jefferson City, Missouri.[13]

Pawley's situation was typical. He taught English and speech, and directed plays. In 1952, to create greater campus interest in drama, he initiated a summer theatre where students would produce three or four plays and take related academic work. To assist him, Pawley brought in John M. Ross as technical director along with two talented women – Lillian Voorhees, a white director, who had served as secretary for SADSA since its founding, and Winona Fletcher, who had recently graduated from Iowa with a M.A. in costuming. The out-of-doors staging made production costly: a stage had to be built, lights brought in, and admission could not be charged. After the summer of 1953, the program ran out of money and was discontinued until 1959 when the new air-conditioned Richardson Auditorium opened and admissions could be charged. However, the summer theatre's box-office never met expenses. Lincoln's summer theatre closed in 1961.

As membership in SADSA grew in numbers, the Association turned their attention to placing theatre in the college curricula by removing it from departments of English, where untrained faculty were often designated to direct the annual class play. SADSA recommended that drama be wed to the other speech arts – debate, oratorical contests, public address, and verse reading. They hoped to create separate departments of Speech and Theatre with their own budget and faculty. In 1947, Grambling State University in Louisiana did just that. Fifteen years later, after they had opened a 212-seat theatre, they offered liberal arts degrees in speech and theatre. Grambling's drama programs remained tied to speech education and speech pathology, and the programs thrived. In 1962 Dr Floyd L. Sandle toured with Noel Coward's *Blithe Spirit* for the USO, taking the play to Newfoundland, Iceland, Greenland, and Labrador for five weeks. Nonetheless, theatre in most schools remained in the English department and play production continued as an extracurricular activity like football or track athletics. A major obstacle to departmental autonomy was a reluctance to commit to a major in theatre; the students did not see any possibility for earning a living. Finally, there was a feeling that the professional theatre was not made up of the "best people".

Following President Truman's 1948 order to integrate the U.S. Army, hope grew that segregation was ending. In 1949, SADSA sought affiliation with the American Educational Theatre Association (AETA) and discovered that to be represented on its advisory council, they must be a national organization. SADSA voted to change its name to NADSA, substituting the word "national" for "southern". In the spirit of the Supreme Court's 1954 decision to end school segregation, mainstream theatre organizations emphasized that they would welcome African Americans. Tom Pawley, then president of NADSA, asked the membership if, after twenty-two years, their original objective – to aid in the development of educational theatre by popularizing the dramatic arts among their students and by impressing college administrators with the values of the speech and theatre profession – had been achieved? The

Plate 7: A scene from J.B. Priestley's *Time and the Conways*, performed by Howard University's University Players on 7 and 8 February 1941. Designed and directed by Owen Dodson with costumes by Anne Cooke. Hatch–Billops Collection. Photographer unknown.

answers might have been a yes, drama has thrived, but we need more – and better trained – teachers; we need our own departments.

The college sit-ins of 1961 spurred young Blacks to demand their full civil rights; and when that access was slow in coming, many joined the Black Power Movement led by the rhetoric of Stokely Carmichael and Rapp Brown. Offstage, they demanded Black autonomy and the establishment of Black Studies Departments to accentuate African–American culture. Onstage, they demanded new plays to teach pride in Blackness. The Free Southern Theater (FST), growing out of a Tougaloo College drama workshop in Jackson, Mississippi, was one such group. Gilbert Moses, Doris Derby, and John O'Neal wrote a *Perspectus of a Free Southern Theater* setting forth the principle of a legitimate theatre in the deep South which would stimulate creative, reflective thought, and relate to the problems within the Black community, many of whom would see a live stage performance for the first time. The urban-based scripts of Amiri Baraka or Ben Caldwell were not appropriate for their conservatively religious audiences, so FST wrote their own didactic message skits of self-pride and liberation.[14]

Conservative Blacks, who included many on the college faculties, felt that the Black Arts Movement, with its rhetoric charged with profanity and race, was a denigration of the humanities, a kind of reverse racism. The militants responded, "If you're not part of the solution, you're part of the problem". Ron Milner revealed the complicity of the bourgeoisie in *Monster* (1969) where the dean of a college is assassinated by the Black students. The concept of class war was again demonstrated in Carlton and Barbara Molette's *Rosalee Pritchett* (1970), performed at Atlanta University and later by the Negro Ensemble Company (1971). Rosalee is raped by the white National Guard which she had insisted was in town to protect her against Black and white trash.

Engaged in a similar generational struggle, students at Howard demanded new faculty, young lions who would no longer produce Thornton Wilder's *Happy Journey* and *Summer and Smoke* by Tennessee Williams, but who did stage *El Hajj Malik* (by N.R. Davidson, on the life of Malcolm X); *Niggers*, a musical by Louis Johnson; and Paul Carter Harrison's *Tabernacle* (1969), in which "no punches are pulled with the language and four-letter words as well as 12-letter more pungent words, are sprinkled through the performance".[15] Yet, in spite of student activism, most small college drama programs retained their same faculty with their same budget problems.

Then, President Johnson's War on Poverty offered a fresh strategy. Professor William R. Reardon of the University of California at Santa Barbara used federal funding to bring Black drama teachers together for a summer institute, where they not only learned but were presented with information and scholarships to enable them to obtain advanced degrees. Reardon had held one institute for teachers of drama in 1967 and no Blacks registered. So, in 1968, he invited only Blacks. With the aid of a federal grant, he assembled a staff of professionals – Ted Shine, Owen Dodson, Frank Silvera, Bill and Alfredine Brown – to produce three plays: Ted Shine's *Morning Noon and Night*, Loften Mitchell's *Tell Pharaoh*, and the Civil Rights musical *Fly Blackbird* by C. Bernard Jackson and James V. Hatch. From the experience, Pawley and Reardon published *The Black Teacher and the Dramatic Arts* (1970), a seminal work of play scripts, essays, and African-American theatre bibliography which led directly to Black theatre's first comprehensive anthology, *Black Theatre USA* (1974) by Ted Shine and James V. Hatch.

At the end of the programs, a seminar on the state of drama in Black colleges was held. Agreement was nearly unanimous that

1. the situation in drama is abysmal
2. the traditional Negro college is woefully understaffed on its administrative levels
3. an over-emphasis is placed on music at the expense of the other arts
4. the Negro college is incredibly divorced from a concern with the community or ghetto which surrounds it.

Nonetheless, the overall results of this institute far exceeded the Director's most optimistic expectations.[16]

Reardon's institute was so successful that the following summer Professor Juanita Oubre of Winston-Salem State University saw an opportunity to upgrade the "inferior" conditions which existed in NADSA institutions. With Joan Lewis of Fayetteville State University and Tom Pawley of Lincoln, they obtained funding from the Office of Education, the Office of Economic Opportunity, and the Southern Education Foundation in the amount of $100, 000 for an institute at Lincoln University. A company of 32 students (all on scholarship) and 16 staff members met for eight weeks, attending workshops and producing two original plays: *Come Back After the Fire* by Ted Shine, and *The Tumult and the Shouting* by Tom Pawley. The institute's program was funded a second summer at Winston-Salem. A number of participants later received doctorates in theatre, but there were still few colleges which offered a theatre major.

Working to create more Black playwrights, in 1976 Robert Nemiroff – with sponsorship from the McDonald's Corporation – established the Lorraine Hansberry Playwriting Award, to be given to the best play on the Black experience produced at the Kennedy Center's annual American College Theatre Festival (ACTF). The first prize was $2, 500 for the playwright and $750 for the producing college. The good news was that many African Americans had learned the craft of playwriting. Over the next two decades, twenty-five of the twenty-nine college winners of the Hansberry contest were Black. The productions, according to Dr Winona Fletcher, President of the University and College Theatre Association, revealed that the acting, directing, and writing in Black colleges had achieved a much higher standard than the technical aspects of lighting, design and costume. Although professors like Carlton Molette, William Brown, and Bob West continued to provide sound technical training in their schools, most college presidents simply did not allocate money to hire faculty trained in technical theatre, preferring the less expensive route of relying on teachers of art, home economics and industrial education.[17]

Fifty years after the Negro Intercollegiate Dramatics Association first issued its six objectives, some had been achieved, others superseded because the militant theatre of the 1960s and 1970s had opened the college repertory to a wider range of performances, ones which eighty years ago would have been considered low-class or vulgar. It had freed the college repertory from the dominance of European-Broadway shows. Another important factor was that the southern Black drama teachers found it convenient and productive to belong to the national associations. NADSA had to compete with the Black Theatre Association, the National Conference on African–American Theatre, the Black Theatre Network, and the National Black Theatre Festival held bi-annually in Winston-Salem, North Carolina. Black theatre scholars – Margaret Wilkerson, Winona Fletcher, Errol Hill, Samuel A. Hay, Tom Pawley, Ted Shine, and others – were receiving national recognition.

The final but not fatal blow to Black regional college drama came in the 1990s when the budgets of the arts and humanities were cut. Howard

University, which once set the standard for quality theatre, considered eliminating its division of fine arts. Talent, which once might have enrolled in small colleges, now chose a university with its better equipped facilities. Talented Black actors often chose professional schools. Over the decades, the colleges did graduate generations of qualified drama teachers who entered the public and private schools. Some graduates – the actors Moses Gunn and Roxie Roker, the writers Joe Walker, Ted Shine and Judy Mason, and the directors Shauneille Perry and Gilbert Moses – became professionals. All in all, the colleges gave their students an appreciation of theatre.

NOTES

1. The American Baptist Home Mission Society supported Virginia Union University, Shaw University, Benedict College, Arkansas A&M, and Normal College at Pine Bluff, Arkansas. The Methodist Episcopal Church established the Centenary Biblical Institute (Morgan College), Shaw University in Holly Springs, Mississippi, and Rust College. The United Methodist Church established Bennett College. The Presbyterians established the Scotia Seminary [Barber–Scotia College, Biddle University, Stillman Seminary, Johnson C. Smith University]. The Episcopal Church established St Paul's Normal and Industrial Institute and St Augustine's College, among others.
2. For a personal account of the freedman's passion for education, read Booker T. Washington's autobiography *Up from Slavery* (1901). To appreciate the conflict generated by the internalization of English literary values over Black folk values, read Adrienne Kennedy's *Funnyhouse of a Negro* (1964) and *The Owl Answers* (1964).
3. For an authentic rendering of Black college life in the early part of the century, read Thomas D. Pawley's play, *The Tumult and the Shouting* (1969), in *Black Theatre U.S.A.* (1974). The classic portrait of a Black college administrator is found in Ralph Ellison's *Invisible Man* (1952).
4. See Cotter 1909.
5. Harrison founded his own Dramatic School at A&T [*Agricultural & Technical*] State University, Greensboro, North Carolina (1922–9).
6. Many African Americans did not want dialect recognized as acceptable speech. After William Dean Howell, the literary lion of New England, had blessed Dunbar's use of dialect in poems, they became quaint and acceptable for reading on college stages.
7. As late as 1916, there were only 67 Negro public high schools and these had fewer than 20,000 students in total; and 85 per cent of southern Negro students were enrolled in the first four grades (normally for ages 6–10). To remedy the problem, major philanthropy came from the George Peabody Fund (1867) which gave the first million dollars; the John F. Slater Fund (1882) gave another million dollars to church and private institutions; the Anna T. Jeanes Fund (1905) provided teachers and supervisors of teachers with salaries; the General Education Board (Rockefeller, 1902) gave $315 million, much of it scholarships for Blacks who would go south to teach; and the Julius Rosenwald Foundation built over 5,000 rural schools and gave teachers advanced training.
8. Locke 1922.

9. Among the recipients of General Education Board scholarships were Warner Lawson (music); Katherine Dunham (dance); Lois Mailou Jones (painting); and Anne Margaret Cooke, Owen Dodson, and James W. Butcher (theatre).

10. The members of SADSA included Florida A&M [*Agricultural and Mechanical*], Alabama State, Alcorn A&M, Lane College, LeMoyne–Owen College, Morehouse College, Morris Brown College, Prairie View A&M, Shorter, Spelman College, Talladega College, Tougaloo College, Southern University, Wiley College, Dillard University, Winston-Salem State Teachers, Atlanta University, Fisk University, and Tuskegee. These were later joined by Bethune-Cookman, Leland, Paine, Texas College, Bennett, Grambling, Tennessee A&I [*Agricultural and Industrial*], Lincoln University of Missouri, Langston University, Kentucky State College, Arkansas AM&N [*Agricultural, Mechanical and Normal*], and Xavier University. In 1997, there were 37 schools which listed themselves on the Internet as "Historically Black Colleges".

11. The three regional divisions of SADSA were the Southwestern, the South, and the Southeastern.

12. "Roker, Roxie interview with James V. Hatch, 10/18/85". Hatch–Billops Collection, Inc. New York City.

13. Other theatre people were important to SADSA and NADSA, but space does not permit the inclusion of their stories: Barbara and Carlton Molette, Thomas E. Poag, Gladys D. Maddox, Francis Perkins, M.B. Tolson, Richard Barksdale, Elizabeth Gordon, Beatrice Walcott, Lillian Voorhees, Winona Fletcher, A. Clifton Lamb, John Lovell, Jr, L.C. Archer, J.P. Cochran, Gladys Forde, Alfonso Sherman, Floyd Sandle, Joseph Adkins, Allen Williams, W. Drury Cox, and many more.

14. John O'Neal, Gilbert Moses, Tom Dent, Sharon Stockard Martin, and Kalamu ya Salaam wrote the skits for FST.

15. See "Afro-American Form Sought" 1969.

16. See Reardon 1968.

17. Among the increasing cadre of highly qualified and gifted teachers of stage lighting and design are James Butcher, William Brown, Robert West, Vantile Whitfield, John M. Ross, Carlton Molette, Barbara Molette, Whitney LeBlanc, Winona Fletcher, Kathy Perkins, and others.

BIBLIOGRAPHY

"Afro-American Form Sought: Howard U. to Unveil 'Black Theater'", Washington, DC, *The Evening Star*, 3 March 1969.

Cotter, Joseph Seamon, Sr, "Dr Booker T. Washington to the National Negro Business League", *A White Song and a Black One*, Louisville, Kentucky, Bradley & Gilbert, 1909.

Ellison, Ralph, *Invisible Man*, New York, Random House, 1952.

Fletcher, Winona, Interview with author, *Artist and Influence* 14, 1995.

———, "Introduction", *The Lorraine Hansberry Playwriting Award: An Anthology of Prize-Winning Plays*, edited by Winona Fletcher, Washington, DC, John F. Kennedy Center for the Performing Arts, 1996.

Kennedy, Adrienne, *Funnyhouse of a Negro* (1964), in *Adrienne Kennedy in One Act*, Minneapolis, University of Minnesota Press, 1988.

————, *The Owl Answers* (1964), in *Adrienne Kennedy in One Act*, Minneapolis, University of Minnesota Press, 1988.

Locke, Alain, "Steps Toward the Negro Theatre", *The Crisis*, December 1922.

Pawley, Thomas D., "Drama and Theatre at Historically Black Colleges and Universities", unpublished paper delivered at the 'Mind on Freedom: Celebrating the History of America's Black Colleges and Universities' conference, Smithsonian Institution, 2 February 1996.

————, Interview with author, *Artist and Influence* 15, 1997.

————, *The Tumult and the Shouting*, in *Black Theater, USA: Forty-five Plays by Black Americans 1847–1974*, James V. Hatch, editor, and Ted Shine, consultant, New York, Free Press, 1974.

Reardon, William R., *Final Technical Report for the Institute for Black Repertory Theatre at the University of California at Santa Barbara*, 1 June–2 August 1968.

Sandle, Floyd Leslie, 'A History of the Development of the Educational Theatre in Negro Colleges and Universities from 1911 to 1959', Dissertation, The Louisiana State University and Agricultural and Mechanical College, 1959.

Washington, Booker T., *Up From Slavery*, William L. Andrews, editor, New York, Oxford University Press, 1995 [1901].

Williams, Allen, *Sheppard Randolph Edmonds: His Contributions to Black Educational Theatre*, Dissertation, University of Indiana, 1972.

STEPPING, SALUTING, CRACKING, AND FREAKING

The Cultural Politics of African-American Step Shows (1991)

Elizabeth C. Fine

Spotlights rake over the dark auditorium as the opening music of *2001 (A Space Odyssey)* blares through the loudspeakers. The audience searches for the performers as the music suddenly shifts to a hard, driving beat and a recorded voice repeats, "Ladies and Gentlemen". Now the spotlights illuminate the white tuxedos of the Delta sisters as they dance down the aisles toward the stage. In their white suits and gloves, their red cummerbunds, boutonnieres, bow ties, and high-heel shoes, and with red masks over their eyes, the 13 performers make a dramatic and well-rehearsed entrance to the Overton Johnson Step Show Competition.

Stepping, or blocking, is a dynamic and popular performance tradition among African-American fraternities and sororities. Approximately 5,000 individual chapters with half a million members throughout the USA participate in stepping. This complex performance event and ritual involves various combinations of dancing, singing, chanting, and speaking, and draws on African-American folk traditions and communication patterns as well as material from popular culture, such as advertising jingles, television theme songs, and top-40 hits.

Few people outside of black Greek-letter societies and black college students have seen step shows.[1] No doubt the widest national exposure to stepping has come from Spike Lee's 1988 film *School Daze*, which contains a step show that embodies interfraternity tensions similar to those described in this article.[2] Despite the prevalence of stepping throughout American universities and colleges, it has received little formal study. Yet stepping deserves attention because it is a rich tradition that involves great creativity, intelligence, wit, and physical skill. While the term stepping suggests only physical movement, many step routines incorporate chanting and singing as well.

This article explores the cultural politics of step shows as they have developed at Virginia Polytechnic Institute and State University

(VPI&SU) in Blacksburg from 1984 through 1989. The term "cultural politics" refers to the social and political forces that influence what elements of a culture are featured or suppressed, promoted or ignored, sanctioned or censored.[3] Since 1984, when I first began videotaping and studying step shows at VPI&SU, I have noticed a real shift in the types of step performed before a large, broad-based audience, such as at the annual step show competition which is held to raise scholarship money for black students. This paper examines the ramifications of a new institutionalized setting for stepping, the Overton Johnson Step Show Competition, on the style and cultural politics of stepping at VPI&SU.

WHAT IS STEPPING OR BLOCKING?

Students at VPI&SU use the terms "blocking" and "stepping" to describe this activity, but stepping appears to be the more widespread name. The term "blocking" originates from the block or yard where

Plate 8: Delta Sigma Theta of Virginia Polytechnic Institute and State University (1990) in a stance typical of the step shows of many African-American sororities and fraternities. Photo by Robert Walker.

members of a fraternity or sorority might gather to talk, sing, or put on a show, according to Calvin Jamison.[4] In 1940, according to an alumnus of Kappa Alpha Psi at West Virginia State College, the fraternities participated in group singing, often while they were holding hands or moving in a circle, but they did not step.[5] Another Kappa said, in a 1987 newspaper article interview, that his fraternity began stepping in the 1940s, and developed stepping from marching in line while pledging to the group: " Through the years brothers added singing and dancing, and in recent years we started using canes when we step" (in Payne 1987:A8). This information corroborates that of a *Wall Street Journal* article which claims stepping's "synchronized and syncopated moves date back to the 1940s, when lines of fraternity pledges marched in lockstep around campus in a rite of initiation' (Nomani 1989:A4). Julian Bond reports that he could remember stepping contests when he was a student at Morehouse in the late 1950s (Freeman and Witcher 1988:148). In the 1950s, according to informants at VPI&SU, blocking or stepping was mainly a singing event, with some movement, usually in a circle.[6] But stepping has changed rapidly in the last

Plate 9: Delta Sigma Theta sisters show their unity and their icon, the pyramid, through their delta-shaped formation and hand gestures (1990). Photo by Robert Walker.

30 years to become a complex performance event involving various combinations of singing, speaking, chanting, and synchronized movement. Fundamentally, stepping is a ritual performance of group identity. It expresses an organization's spirit, style, icons, and unity.

One can't hope to comprehend the complexity and richness of the stepping tradition by surveying only a few groups or routines. The fraternity Kappa Alpha Psi, for example, is noted for their dexterous use of canes, while the brothers of Alpha Phi Alpha pride themselves on the vigor of their stepping. All of the eight organizations[7] draw on such African-American folk traditions and communication patterns as call–response, rapping, the dozens, signifying, marking, spirituals, handclap games, and military jodies. The following excerpts from step shows in front of a student dining hall show four different steps which are based on some of these folk traditions. The first is based on a military jody, the second uses rapping, the third utilizes call–response, and the fourth is based on children's handclap games.

Due to space considerations, as well as the difficulty of completely notating both the verbal and nonverbal dimensions of each routine, in most cases I have chosen to transcribe the words and

Plate 10: Noted for their dexterous use of canes and priding themselves on a suave, debonair image, the Kappa Alpha Psi fraternity at East Tennessee State University steps at the 1990 Southern Dance Traditions Conference. Photo by Elizabeth C. Fine.

some paralinguistic features only, and provide general descriptions of the movement. But in order to provide at least one full example of a step routine, I have attempted to transcribe both the words and movement to the synchronized handclap routine. Bold type indicates a louder, more emphatic voice, and underlined words represent shouting. A blank line represents unintelligible words that were drowned out by audience response.

In the first example, "Do It On Two", performed in 1984, a group of eight Alpha brothers lines up in a file, one behind the other, and begins an iambic step and clap, punctuated by a loud, grunted "Huah". The leader in the front calls out "Do it – huah!" and moves to one side of the group, like a drill sergeant. He then yells out calls, accompanied by a step, which the group in the file imitates. This routine looks and sounds like a military jody, or marching chant, as the following excerpt illustrates:

LEADER: We're gonna roll it on out!

GROUP: We're gonna roll it on out!

LEADER: We're gonna roll it on out!

GROUP: We're gonna roll it on out!

LEADER: We're gonna do it on two!

GROUP: We're gonna do it on two!

LEADER: We're gonna do it on two!

GROUP: We're gonna do it on two!

LEADER: I say one!

GROUP: One!

LEADER: I say two!

GROUP: Two!

The second example, "Clutch Me, Baby", from the same step show, extols the sexual virtuosity of the Alphas through rapping (see Kochman 1972:243). The group again stands in a single file and, after the opening refrain, each member takes a turn standing to one side of the group and rapping out a boast:

ALL: Oh clutch me baby
       You doing okay
       For A Phi A
       You're doing alright
       You do it all night

LEADER: (*standing to one side*)

       Clutch me Baby
       Marcus is my name
       Sex is my fame
       Cause when my luck is right
       I do it every night

Plate 11: Step shows sometimes include dramatic acrobatics, as demonstrated here by the brothers of Alpha Phi Alpha (VPI&SU, 1990) who pride themselves on the vigor of their stepping. Photo by Robert Walker.

> Cause it's a smooth roman rocket
> That always hits your pocket

ALL: (*refrain as above*)

SECOND IN LINE:
> Double clutch me baby
> My name is Rodney P
> Just bear with me a moment
> I got a story, you see

You said I like my women sweet
And I like them plump
Cause all I want to do is the A Phi Hump

(The step continues until each of the eight brothers has performed a rap.)

A very common type of step routine is built on the call–response pattern, which is a prevalent African-American communication pattern (Daniel and Smitherman 1976:26–39). In this show, performed in 1986 in front of a dining hall, the AKA sisters stand in two rows facing the audience, with the stepmaster in the center of the front row. The stepmaster begins a sultry hip-swinging step and calls out a series of questions, to which the sisters respond. This step is called the "Marcita" step, after the woman who created it:

LEADER:	Sorors
ALL:	Ye-ah
LEADER:	I said my sorors
ALL:	Ye-ah
LEADER:	Can we break it
ALL:	Ye-ah
LEADER:	On down now
ALL:	Yeah

At the end of this last response, the group breaks into a fast and complex step with intricate footwork, which contrasts with the slow, sultry hip-swinging step. They then return to the slow hip-swing for another call–response verse.

Still another type of step imitates children's handclap games. Here, the 10 AKA sisters begin facing the audience, then face each other in two rows, and advance toward each other doing a handclap routine. When the two rows meet, they clap with an exaggerated African-American hand slap greeting known as "giving skin" (see Cooke 1972:33–43). As they give skin, they call out greetings in unison, such as, "How you doing!" and "Sorors!" To demonstrate unity, each member rotates down the row and around to the other side, in a circle, so that each has clapped with and greeted everyone. This routine was performed in front of a dining hall in 1986. In order to illustrate the intricate foot and hand work, a detailed text follows on p. 173, with musical notation representing the rhythm of the hands and feet.

The basic rhythm for all three steps is a 4/4 measure: This routine begins with the 11 sisters facing the audience in a row, their hands clasped in front of their chests. Every other woman performs Step I twice, while the others perform Step II, twice. Then the women switch steps – those that performed Step I now perform Step II twice, and vice versa. The entire group then performs Step I nine times while moving backward and splitting into two parallel lines, which then move close together, facing each other, with the leader in the back of and between the two rows, facing the audience. When they are in this position, the

Plate 12: The sisters of Alpha Kappa Alpha sorority "giving skin" in a synchronized handclap routine (VPI&SU, 1986). Photo and video by Robert Walker.

entire group performs Step III twelve times, rotating with each repetition so that each sister has given skin to each other and the leader has moved to the front of, and between, the two rows. The routine ends with the sisters facing the audience, frozen in the stance in which they began the number, hands clasped in front of their chests.

The black Greek-letter organizations step for a number of reasons. The president of AKA sorority says, "It gives good publicity for the organization. It shows unity because there are usually more than three or four people who are blocking together". Groups also step to raise money. The success of the annual Overton Johnson Endowed Scholarship Fund Step Competition at VPI&SU attests to the ability of blocking to draw a crowd. But one of the most important functions of blocking is to express the competitive spirit among the various fraternities and sororities. This competition greatly influences the content and style of blocking, and its influence is evident in the kinds of black folklore that students draw upon to create routines.

Like any other kind of folklore, step routines are transmitted orally. They are also transmitted by videotape and copied texts. Chapters of Greek-letter organizations from nearby schools frequently visit each other and exchange steps, and national meetings provide the opportunity for steps to circulate widely. Since each fraternity and sorority has the

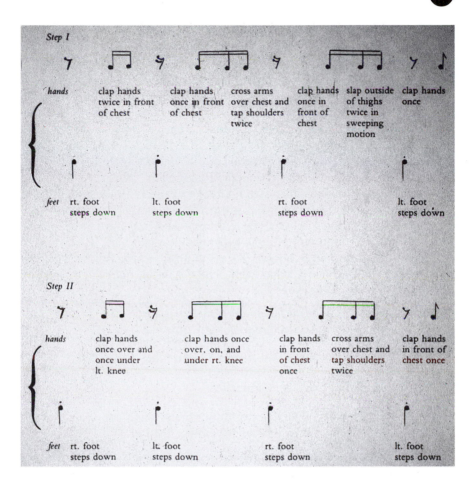

Figure 1: AKA sorority synchronized handclap routine, Step I.
Figure 2: AKA sorority synchronized handclap routine, Step II.

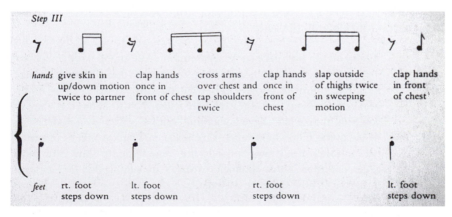

Figure 3: AKA sorority synchronized handclap routine, Step III.

same national organizational history and symbols, each group has a core of common material. For example, each fraternity and sorority has "trade steps", by which they are known. Kappa Alpha Psi performs a trade step called "Yo Baby Yo". The oldest black fraternity, Alpha Phi Alpha, founded in 1906, has a trade step called "The Grand-daddy Step". And the oldest black sorority, Alpha Kappa Alpha, founded in 1908, performs a trade step known as "It's a Serious Matter". Each of these trade steps has a recognizable rhythm, set phrases, and set movements that remain fairly constant, yet each can also be varied in innovative ways.

The following text of "The Grand-daddy Step" (Jackson 1984), with drawings by Milton Jordan (see figure 4 on page 175), illustrates one of the earliest steps, and one that is still performed today. The circular form of the step is typical of early step routines, which may have some roots in the African-American traditions of ring-shouts and juba, dances which were performed in a circle.[8] To symbolize the fraternity's age, the brothers mime an old man's walk, leaning on an imaginary cane and moving with shaking knees:

> We're the Alpha brothers, for heaven's sake
> We're the grand-daddies making no mistake
>
> We're the first, the first and we're never late
>
> From us all the others originate
>
> We're gonna break it down for our grandsons' Que
> We're gonna break it down for Omega Psi Phi

(Depending on the chapter, the group would continue to "break it down" for selected organizations. By "breaking it down", they imitate them.)

While steps such as "The Grand-daddy" are clearly traditional, some students believe that stepping itself is directly linked to African dance traditions. When I asked the president of AKA at VPI&SU about the history of stepping, she said:

> It goes all the way back to African culture. And in the African cultures they had tribes and you know they were just small little centralized, localized groups of people. And what they would do to show rivalry between the kings and different tribes and then to show that they do compete, they would have something similar – they would step, they would block, they would dance. I mean except that it would be of a tribal type of affair. But it was basically the same thing, to show how much better one tribe is than another. So that's something that may have an influence on how come we do it here.

Apparently this belief about African roots is widespread; students at the University of Southern Florida also spoke proudly about stepping

SHAKING KNEES

Figure 4: Alpha Phi Alpha fraternity trade step, "The Grand-daddy".

originating in African dance traditions.[9] While much more comparative research on African dance is necessary, at least one example of a striking similarity to stepping occurs in the West African country of Benin, formerly Dahomey. There, people participate in a monthly dance called *avogan* in which young men and women from different quarters of a city take turns satirizing those of another. As Melville and Frances Herskovits wrote in *Dahomean Narrative:*

> Since each quarter gets its turn, this is an effective device to develop new talent. Much prestige goes to those who live in the same quarter as the composers whose songs bite deepest into the shortcomings of their rivals, and thereby become the popular hits of the city at large. (Herskovits 1958:61)

CRACKING, FREAKING, AND SALUTING

Stepping is a form of ritual communication that employs at least three distinct types of act: cracking or cutting, freaking, and saluting. In the crack or cut, one group makes fun of another group, either verbally, nonverbally, or both. "Freaking" refers to a member who breaks the norm of synchronization and unity, in an attempt to get greater audience response. The freaker, or "show dog",[10] as he or she is sometimes called, is a crowd pleaser. Saluting is a ritualized greeting in which a fraternity or sorority greets another Greek-letter organization by imitating the steps, style, or symbols of that organization.

Like other Greek-letter organizations, black fraternities and sororities

Plate 13: An Alpha Phi Alpha brother "freaks" or "show dogs" by breaking from the group formation in the crack step "We're Laughing at You" (VPI&SU, 1984). Photo and video by Robert Walker.

are intensely competitive and this competitive spirit comes to the fore in the crack or cut. Many cracks are based on the very strong African-American tradition of verbal dueling, expressed in such well-known folklore genres as the dozens (or sounding), rapping, and signifying and marking. Cracking can be done nonverbally as well by parodying the steps or style of another group. Students at VPI&SU call such nonverbal cracks or marking "mocking" and "breaking it down" (see Mitchell-Kernan 1972:332–5).

The first example of cracking, performed by Alpha Phi Alpha, was presented outside a student dining hall in the spring of 1984. This is a popular crack theme called "We're Laughing at You". This step employs the folk tradition of signifying (see Gates 1988), which criticizes through indirection and innuendo. It also uses nonverbal marking, or mocking, to make fun of the Kappas. One student steps forward from the group and says:

> I once (*points index finger*)
> Knew some Kappas
> that went to this school
> They were sloooow walking (*exaggerated slow walk, as in slow motion*),
> Sweeeeet talking (*rubs hand over his hair*)
> Oh, oh
> so very very cool (*closes eye and clinches fists in front of chest on the word "cool"*)

As if to underscore the message, another brother doubles over in an exaggerated belly laugh – "ho-ho-ho". The success of this crack depends not only on the audience knowing that Kappa Alpha Psi cultivates a cool, playboy image, but on the performer's ability to imitate this style in a comic way.

The next example of a crack step also draws on marking, or a nonverbal parody of a group. In addition, however, the step – called "Yo' Mama Didn't Tell You 'Bout A Phi A" – echoes the dozens, or sounding (see Labov 1972:265–314), a verbal dueling game in which one person knocks the other person's mother (as in, "Your mama so ugly that when she cry, the tears run down her back"). In the following example, A Phi A members crack on the style of the Sigmas and salute their own step by first performing their own step, "Yo' Mama Didn't Tell You 'Bout A Phi A", in a lame, uncoordinated fashion (which they say is the way the Sigmas block) and then performing the same step again with the hard-stepping vigor that is a nationally recognized hallmark of A Phi A blocking. This routine was performed outside of a student dining hall.

(One of the brothers goes to the audience and brings a white, blond coed [a friend] back to the center of the performing area. The other brothers form a large circle around her.)

Plate 14: An Alpha Phi Alpha brother cracks on the Kappas' sweet-talking image through marking, or mocking, a nonverbal imitation (VPI&SU, 1984). Photo and video by Robert Walker.

BROTHER: Who was the first person to tell you about A Phi A?

(*The coed smiles, shakes her head, and holds her palms up, empty handed, as if to say, "I don't know".*)

BROTHER: You mean to tell me, your

ALL: Mama didn't tell you 'bout A Phi A
She didn't tell you 'bout the brothers and their sexy ways
She didn't tell you how they slide to the side so sweet

Plate 15: Alpha Phi Alpha mocks the Sigmas with "Yo' Mama Didn't Tell You 'Bout A Phi A," circling a white blond coed friend. Photo and video by Robert Walker.

(The group performs the above verse with faint voices and uncoordinated, weak movements, circling around the girl.)

STEPMASTER: *(interrupting verse)* Hold on, stop, stop

BROTHER: What's wrong, man?

STEPMASTER: Cats, if we're gonna **do** this step,
We can't look like a bunch of **Sigmas**
If you're gonna **do** this step,
You have to put your heart in it, like this: *(loudly)*
I said, Your

ALL: **Mama didn't tell you 'bout A Phi A**
She didn't tell you 'bout the brothers and their sexy ways
She didn't tell you how they slide to the side so sweet
She didn't tell you 'bout the first of all black Greeks
She didn't put you on her knee and break it on down
Uh! Uh! Uh! Uh! A Phi A!

(The group performs this verse loudly while skipping in a counterclockwise circle, with exaggerated and emphatic swinging of arms and hard-hitting feet. The step continues with a series of cracks on other fraternities, repeating the verse above, and ending with two brothers escorting the white coed back to the audience.)

Here we see a remarkable example of performance criticism embodied in a performance. Step shows are full of metaperformances that focus attention and comment on either themselves or on other performances.[11] While the saluting steps imitate other performances in a positive way, the cracking steps imitate in a more critical way. Both steps exhibit what anthropologist Victor Turner terms "performative reflexivity", a condition in which "a sociocultural group, or its most perceptive members acting representatively, turn, bend or reflect back upon themselves, upon the relations, actions, symbols, meanings, codes, roles, statuses, social structures, ethical and legal rules, and other sociocultural components which make up their public 'selves' " (Turner 1986:24).

What are the functions of cracking, and what impact does it have politically, among the competing Greek-letter organizations? First and foremost, cracking creates what Richard Bauman calls "differential identity" (Bauman 1972:31–41). That is, cracking defines a group's identity by contrasting it with other groups. Second, cracking is entertaining – it elicits laughter and howls of appreciation from the audience. If there is little competition between groups, cracking is taken lightly. But if there is intense competition for members, then cracking can create great tensions. Since the mid-1980s, there has been enormous rivalry at VPI&SU between two sororities, Alpha Kappa Alpha and Delta Sigma Theta. In 1986, the president of AKA sorority explained that because of the political atmosphere, her sorority could no longer crack freely:

> I mean you know it's funny; people like to listen to those [cracks] and everything, but again, back to the political atmosphere, like our sorority you can't do it without being cut up left and right. [. . .] It wouldn't be to our benefit to do it. For example, if you wanted to sponsor parties or sponsor other events with other fraternities and sororities, they're less apt to do it if we have – I don't know – splattered blood on another fraternity's or sorority's face, they're less apt to do things with us. So I mean, you know, it's all important to keep good relations with other fraternities and sororities without, you know, hurting somebody's feelings. So, you know, its best for the time being that we don't say anything. But others, like the fraternities, oh they just have a good time cutting up.

CRACKING AND THE INSTITUTIONALIZED STEP SHOW

In 1983, a step competition in honor of a popular black professor, Overton R. Johnson, was inaugurated to raise scholarship funds. This new arena for block shows marked the first institutionalized setting for stepping on the campus. Prior to 1983 stepping was largely spontaneous and all but invisible to whites. The black Greek-letter organizations would perform outside dorms and dining halls, or in small auditoriums, but publicity was mostly by word-of-mouth. With the Overton R. Johnson Step Competition, new forces began to influence the form of stepping, including:

1. A change of place, from the yard, block, or small auditorium to the largest public auditorium on campus
2. A change in audience to include members of all the black Greek-letter organizations, black professors, visiting members of black Greek-letter organizations from other schools, judges (both black and white), members of the general public, and university administrators
3. Formalized standards for judging the stepping competition – these standards emphasize appearance, crowd appeal, precision and synchronization, level of difficulty, vocalization, originality, and personality.

In the new setting of the institutionalized step show, the free-spirited and sometimes ragged and offensive crack steps seemed to be magnified in the intensity of their impact. The first serious problem with cracking occurred in the 1985 Overton Johnson Step Competition with a series of hard-hitting cracks by AKA on their chief rival, Delta Sigma Theta sorority:

I was walking cross the yard just as happy as can be
When a confused little pyramid approached me
I said, "Are you all right can I give you a hand?"
She said, "Stop DST", I said, "Don't understand"
I said, "Let me tell you something 'bout my sorority"
She said, "Is it anything like DST?"
I said, "Me, a D a S a T?"

_____

_____

She even had the nerve to call us names
"We're all kind of animals is what they claim".
"The Sacred pyramid and elephant too"
_____ or to the Zoo.

I said you steal too much
Oh Sigma Gamma Alpha
You know it's hard for you to do that
Because you're nothing but a copy cat
But what can we expect from D.S. Thieves.

The Delta story has now been told
That your new colors are red and gold

They even had to go and change their name

I said we're laughing at you
This is a serious matter.

As in many cracks, the sisters of AKA play off the icons of the Deltas: the pyramid and their colors, red and gold. The lines about the colors and name refer to an event in the history of DST in which they had to change their name and colors because they had already been claimed by a white fraternity. But the crack which was most offensive to the Deltas, and which elicited the biggest audience reaction, was the following: "I said you steal too much [. . .]/Because you're nothing but a copy cat/But what can we expect from D.S. Thieves". As the president of AKA explained, the reference to stealing refers to the Deltas copying other sororities' routines. But the Deltas took the crack more literally to refer to an embarrassing incident a few days prior to the competition in which a couple of the Delta sisters had been arrested in a local store for alleged shoplifting.

These hard-hitting cracks had a tremendous impact on the Deltas and created tensions between the two sororities that continue today. In the weeks following the 1985 competition, the president of the Deltas complained at a presidents' meeting of the black fraternities and sororities that AKA didn't show them any respect. In response to this complaint, AKA picked up the respect issue and turned it into a crack performed in a block show outside a dining hall in the spring of 1986. The crack was performed to their trade step, "It's a Serious Matter":

> Oh Delta Sigma Theta
> (Oh DST)
> You want respect
> (You want respect)
> But it has to be earned
> (But it has to be earned)
> Or you're gonna get burned.
> So don't flick my Bic
> A ha ha ha ha ha
> This is a serious matter
> This is a serious matter

This crack only intensified the tensions between the two largest sororities, and the bad feelings between the groups were felt by many in the relatively small number of black students (about 800) at the university. So the delegates from the eight Greek-letter organizations charged with planning the 1986 Overton Johnson Step Competition drew up rules which prohibited cracking that year. Any fraternity or sorority that cracked would be eliminated from the competition.

In the following excerpt from the 1986 show, one can see the adaptive form of trade steps, as AKA performs a non-crack version of "It's A Serious Matter". This routine recounts the history of the sorority, as well as some of their favorite steps. The leader stands in the middle of the stage, with a group of sisters standing to the left and right of her:

LEADER: Question

STAGE RIGHT GROUP: Question, we have a question for you

STAGE LEFT GROUP: Question, we have a question for you

LEADER: I said, what, what, it's a serious matter

ALL: What, what it's a serious matter

ALL: What, what it's a serious matter

ALL: In 1908 was our founding date

ALL: In '74 we did it once more

LEADER: Tell me

ALL: What, what, it's a serious matter

LEADER: Tell me

ALL: What, what, it's a serious matter

(Group does a nonverbal step and clap routine and repeats the serious matter refrain)

ALL: Nine fine founders at Howard's Miner Hall
       Twelve charter members and that's not all

(*Refrain*)

When it was the Deltas' turn to perform, they showed every sign of winning the competition until they came out with a non-too-subtly disguised crack that responded to the respect crack AKA had launched in front of the dining hall. During the crack an AKA audience member shouted in a high-pitched voice, "Skee Wee", right after the word "Respect". According to an AKA informant, this cry, which is the identifying call of AKA, was used to signal the judges that the caller had interpreted the step as a crack.

    Oh Delta Sigma Theta Incorporated
    From VPI
    We're here to march and we're here to step, I said S.O.I.
    Because you know that we know that you know who you are
    Because you're walking round the yard just a thinking you're a star
    Respect?
    (*Audience member: Skee wee!*)
    And we're laughing at you and you know why
    You wanted the best but you settled for less
    I said we're laughing at you and you know why
    Cause Delta's gonna run it till the day we die.

Plate 16: Delta Sigma Theta cracks on AKA, undercutting their "Respect?" with a contemptuous pose (VPI&SU, 1986). Photo and video by Robert Walker.

CONCLUSION

Each year the Overton Johnson Step Competition grows in popularity. In 1983 it raised $400, and in 1989 it raised over $2,500. The originator of the competition, Calvin Jamison, refers to it as "the superbowl of block shows" and compares it to a "fine art" and a "Broadway musical". Judges, drawn from faculty and staff, utilize criteria for judging which do not include skillful cracking; the rule against cracking in the competition still holds. The spontaneity and freaking found outside on the block is disappearing.

How has this institutionalization affected the style of stepping? First, students say there is a greater emphasis on nonverbal steps, or what some term "hard stepping". In hard stepping, groups strive for intricate, rhythmical steps. Second, since cracking is forbidden, students have changed their traditional crack steps to express non-cracks, as when AKA recited sorority history rather than cracks to their trade step, "It's A Serious Matter". Third, the groups use nonverbal and non-derogatory mocking as salutations. Finally, the groups include more skits and singing, which make their performances look more like variety shows than straight stepping. As one student told me, "Once you can't crack, it will have to be more of a show with dancing and singing. Otherwise it will be too boring".

Clearly, some of the danger, tension and political impact has been taken out of stepping in its institutional setting. These changes parallel the changes David Chaney has found in his study of the shift from folk to popular culture. In his book, *Fictions and Ceremonies*, Chaney discusses four modes of incorporation or types of pressure that structure cultural politics in the transition from folk to popular culture:

1. commercialization – supplanting amateur production of performance by commercially inspired professionals
2. suppression – deliberate attempts to stamp out or control what were felt to be illegitimate performances
3. bourgeoisification – a process in which a concern for respectability came to supplant the value of vitality
4. alienation – transforming of work so for the majority it becomes alienating with consequential implications for leisure (Chaney 1979:42)

Of these four pressures, suppression and bourgeoisification seem to be most evident in the institutionalized step competition at VPI&SU. Chaney's term "bourgeoisification" is not only an awkward sounding word, but is objectionable to many African-Americans who are sensitive to charges of becoming bourgeois.[12] We might replace it with the term "respectability".

Fortunately for the vitality of stepping at the university, the institutional pressures of suppression and respectability are resisted by breaking rules, as the Deltas did with their cracks in the 1986 show, and by continuing to perform in traditional arenas, where such rules are not imposed. The African-American tradition of verbal dueling is so strong that it is hard to leave a verbal attack unanswered. The AKAs refused to let the Deltas have the last word with their respect crack in the 1986 step compettiton. At the Black Alumni Weekend, held the following fall, AKA answered the Delta crack with a new crack sung to the theme of "The Beverly Hillbillies" and performed in their trade step, "It's A Serious Matter". The crack went like this:

> The first thing you know there's DST
> The white man said this is my fraternity
> He said I'm going to sue you and that's the way it be
> He took them to court and what do we see –
> Red-gold, Red-white,
> Why the heck can't you get it right.

This analysis of the cultural politics of step shows at VPI&SU provides a microcosmic view of the phenomenon of step shows in general. Although more case studies are needed, this analysis leads us to some tentative conclusions about the performative genre of step shows within the subculture of black Greek-letter organizations. First, step shows provide an excellent example of Victor Turner's thesis about the interaction of cultural performances with the social drama. Turner argues that: "The major genres of cultural performance not only originate in the social drama, but continue to draw meaning and force from the social drama. [. . .] Such genres partly 'imitate' (by mimesis) the processual form of the social drama, and they partly, through reflection, assign 'meaning' to it" (Turner 1986:94–5). For Turner, a social drama is a "disharmonic social process, arising in a conflict situation" (Turner 1986:74). Richard Schechner explains the crisis situations of social dramas: "These situations – arguments, combats, rites of passage – are inherently dramatic because participants not only do things, they try *to show others what they are doing or have done*; actions take on a 'performed for an audience' aspect" (Schechner 1977:120).

In the social drama provided by black Greek-letter organizations, individuals who pledge a fraternity or sorority participate in a major ritual of status transformation and elevation. Membership represents access to a network of fellow brothers or sisters which can play a vital social role not only in the college years but throughout one's life. To establish and maintain a unique Greek identity, each fraternity and sorority must define itself with symbols and styles that distinguish it from any other group. Indeed, members first learn to step as part of their initiation process, and are expected to perform publicly as a sign of their new status. Stepping performances have become a key venue for displaying and asserting group identity, as well as for negotiating the status of each group within the social order.

The two basic types of steps, saluting and cracking, imitate two fundamental poles within the social drama of black Greek-letter organizations. The first pole is a tendency toward identification and unity with all black Greek-letter members, as certain fraternities and sororities date members from each other's groups, and as all such fraternal organizations share common experiences. The act of saluting by imitating the steps or style of another group embodies this friendly impulse toward unity. The second pole is a tendency toward competition and difference, since organizations must compete against one other for membership. The act of cracking, or making fun of another group, dramatizes the competitive tendency. A well-executed crack simultaneously elevates the status of the performers and lowers the status of the target group.

The third type of step, freaking or show dogging, exercises the need for individual identity within the group. While the main emphasis of stepping is to illustrate group solidarity and unity, the occasional deviations from group synchronization assert the freedom and power of the individual to vary, in creative ways, from the group norm.

As stepping moves from the esoteric arena of intergroup shows to public displays at institutionalized stepping competitions and conferences with heterogeneous audiences, we can expect that groups will tend to suppress the competitive tendency embodied in cracking. For example, when the Kappa Alpha Psi fraternity at East Tennessee State University did a step show for the 1990 Southern Dance Traditions Conference at ETSU, they chose not to perform any crack steps. When I asked the fraternity president why they would not do crack steps, he told me that it would be inappropriate for a non-Greek-letter audience. He said that such a diverse audience would not appreciate the meaning of the cracks, and that they might foster the wrong impression. In the public discussion following the step show, after a few members of rival black Greek-letter organizations in the audience had hooted at some of the Kappa steps, one of the Kappa brothers said, "I want to make it clear that while we do step and while we talk about other fraternities and they talk about us, I want to make it clear that we do get along with the other black Greeks, that there is unity on this campus".

While the suppression of cracking may blunt the potential for stepping to create or redress a breach or crisis in the social drama of black Greek-letter life,[13] even without cracking, stepping remains a fundamentally competitive performance tradition. As one Kappa brother from East Tennessee State University said at the 1990 Southern Dance Tradition Conference, "We mainly step to show the other fraternities that we are the best [. . .]". This agonistic nature of step shows makes them a performance tradition charged with high energy and life.

NOTES

1. As a white folklorist who has never been affiliated with either black or white fraternities or sororities, I could only begin to understand stepping through the cooperation and help of the members of the black Greek-letter organizations who agreed to be interviewed and who took time to explain the many codes in stepping. While there are many nuances of this tradition that only a group member could fully appreciate, I have tried to bring the insights of an outside observer who has recorded step shows and participants for several years. This paper is dedicated to those students who have so generously shared their insights with me.

2. In Spike Lee's *School Daze* (Columbia Pictures, 1988), the step show replicates in a performative genre the major tensions between black students that are the subject of Lee's film. Significantly, cracking precipitates and escalates the rivalry between the Gamma fraternity and the non-Greek-letter faction led by Dap, and their corresponding female counterparts, the Gamma Rays, and the Jigaboos. The Gamma Rays, or little sisters of the Gammas, are light skinned, and espouse "white" standards of judging beauty, while the Jigaboos reject Greek-letter organizations, are dark skinned, and espouse African-American standards of beauty. The women begin the cracking from the audience, and the non-Greek-letter male group, "Da Fellas", escalates the tensions by performing a step routine centered on insulting the Gammas. After calling them poor, and fags, the crack concludes with, "Get back, or we'll kick your Gamma ass". As Da Fellas exit from the stage, a fight breaks out between them and the insulted Gammas. The conflict between the dark-skinned and light-skinned women is similar to the perceived conflict between Alpha Kappa Alpha and Delta Sigma Theta at Virginia Polytechnic Institute and State University, which some students believe involves skin color. One aspiring member of AKA said that some people believe that one has to have skin the color of a brown paper bag to be a member of AKA, while the women of DST are darker. While this stereotype has a slight national consensus, women of all shades of complexions are found in both sororities. For more on the rivalry between sororities see Jenkins (1988).

3. My definition of cultural politics has been influenced by Whisnant (1983).

4. Interview with Calvin Jamison, assistant to the president, VPI&SU, 1986. Jamison is a graduate of VPI&SU and an alumnus of the black fraternity Groove Phi Groove. He participated in stepping as a student and, in 1983, organized the Overton Johnson Endowed Scholarship Stepping Competition at the university. Unless otherwise noted, all interviews are from fieldwork conducted at Virginia Polytechnic Institute and State University during the years 1984–1990. I have omitted names of some informants to protect their privacy.

5. Interview with Thomas Harville, a former member of Kappa Alpha Psi fraternity who now lives in Johnson City, Tennessee. He joined the Kappas in 1940 at West Virginia State College in Institute, West Virginia.

6. This information was gathered in an unpublished student research paper (Jackson 1984) by a member of Alpha Kappa Alpha who interviewed several former fraternity members at VPI&SU familiar with stepping in the 1950s. More research from other campuses is necessary to extend this claim to stepping nationally.

7. The four national black Greek-letter fraternities include Alpha Phi Alpha, Omega Psi Phi, Phi Beta Sigma, and Kappa Alpha Psi. The four national

black Greek-letter sororities include Alpha Kappa Alpha, Delta Sigma Theta, Zeta Phi Beta, and Sigma Gamma Rho. Each of these groups has "sweetheart" organizations of the opposite sex which also engage in stepping.

8. Coburn (1990) cites descriptions of juba dances from Eileen Southern (1983:179) and Solomon Northup (1971:100) that are remarkably similar to some of the hand and feet movements found in stepping.

9. Interview with members of AKA sorority, 9 February 1990, University of South Florida, Tampa.

10. Members of black sororities at the University of South Florida in Tampa were not familiar with the term freaking. They use the term "show dog" instead.

11. For more on metacommunication see Babcock (1977:61–80), Bateson (1972:177–93), Jackobson (1960:350–77), and Turner (1986:102–3).

12. Frazier (1962:83–4) is critical of black Greek-letter societies, holding that they "foster all the middle-class values" and "tend to divert the students from a serious interest in education" (83).

13. Turner identifies four phases to social dramas: breach, crisis, redressive action, and reintegration. The dueling sequence of cracks between DST and AKA described in this paper can be understood as redressive action that "furnishes a distanced replication and critique of the events leading up to and composing the 'crisis.' This replication may be in the rational idiom of the judicial process, or in the metaphorical and symbolic idiom of a ritual process" (1986:74–5).

REFERENCES

Babcock, Barbara A. (1977) "The Story in the Story: Metanarration in Folk Narrative". In *Verbal Art as Performance*, edited by Richard Bauman , 61–80. Rowley, Massachusetts: Newbury House.

Bateson, Gregory (1972) "A Theory of Play and Fantasy". In *Steps to an Ecology of Mind*, 177–93. New York: Ballantine.

Bauman, Richard (1972) "Differential Identity and the Social Base of Folklore". In *Toward New Perspectives in Folklore*, ed. Americo Paredes and Richard Bauman, 31–41. Austin: University of Texas Press.

Chaney, David (1979) *Fictions and Ceremonies: Representations of Popular Experience*. London: Edward Arnold.

Coburn, Letitia (1990) "Juba and Ring Shout: African-American Dances of the Antebellum South". Unpublished paper presented at the Southern Dance Traditions Conference, East Tennessee State University.

Cooke, Benjamin G. (1972) "Nonverbal Communication among Afro-Americans: An Initial Classification". In *Rappin' and Stylin' Out: Communication in Urban Black America*, ed. Thomas Kochman, 33–43. Urbana: University of Illinois Press.

Daniel, Jack L., and Geneva Smitherman (1976) "How I Got Over: Communication Dynamics in the Black Community". *Quarterly Journal of Speech* 62:26–39.

Frazier, E. Franklin (1962) *Black Bourgeoisie: The Rise of a New Middle Class in the United States*. New York: The Free Press.

Freeman, Marilyn, and Tina Witcher (1988) "Stepping into Black Power". *Rolling Stone*, 24 March:143–8.

Gates, Henry Louis, Jr. (1988) *The Signifying Monkey: A Theory of Afro-American Literary Criticism*. New York: Oxford University Press.

Herskovits, Melville and Frances (1958) *Dahomean Narrative: A Cross-Cultural Approach*. Evanston, Illinois: Northwestern University Press.

Jackson, Florence M. (1984) "Blocking: A General Overview". Unpublished manuscript.

Jakobson, Roman (1960) "Closing Statement: Linguistics and Poetics". In *Style in Language*, ed. T.A. Sebeok, 350–77. New York: John Wiley and Sons.

Jenkins, Yvette (1988) "Greek and Elite". *Essence* (August):124.

Kochman, Thomas (1972) "Toward an Ethnography of Black American Speech Behavior". In *Rappin' and Stylin' Out: Communication in Urban Black America*, ed. Thomas Kochan, 241–64. Urbana: University of Illinois Press.

Labov, William (1972) "Rules for Ritual Insults". In *Rappin' and Stylin' Out: Communication in Urban Black America*, ed. Thomas Kochman, 265–314. Urbana: University of Illinois Press.

Mitchell-Kernan, Claudia (1972) "Signifying, Loudtalking, and Marking". In *Rappin' and Stylin' Out: Communication in Urban Black America*, ed. Thomas Kochman, 315–35. Urbana: University of Illinois Press.

Nomani, Asra Q. (1989) "Steeped in Tradition, 'Step Dance' Unites Blacks on Campus". *Wall Street Journal*, 10 July: A1, A4.

Northup, Solomon (1971) *Twelve Years a Slave* [1853]. In *Readings in Black American Music*, ed. Eileen Southern, 94–102. New York: W.W. Norton.

Payne, Melinda J. (1987) "Stepping Out on Campus". *Roanoke Times & World News*, 15 October: A1, A8.

Schechner, Richard (1977) Towards a Poetics of Performance". In *Essays on Performance Theory, 1970–1976*, 108–39. New York: Drama Book Specialists.

Southern, Eileen (1983) *The Music of Black Americans: A History*. New York: W.W. Norton.

Turner, Victor (1986) "The Anthropology of Performance". In *The Anthropology of Performance*, ed. Victor Turner, 72–98. New York: PAJ Publications.

Whisnant, David E. (1983) *All That Is Native and Fine: The Politics of Culture in an American Region*. Chapel Hill: University of North Carolina Press.

THE GOSPEL MUSICAL AND ITS PLACE IN THE BLACK AMERICAN THEATRE (1998)

Warren B. Burdine, Jr

From 1898 to the early 1960s, the commercially produced musicals and plays featuring predominantly black casts were, however inaccurately, thought to comprise what is known as the black theatre. The 1960s saw the birth of a network of institutional, not-for-profit black theatres in New York and other major cities. This network changed the face of what was considered to be the black theatre. Recently, however, a new force has arisen that has led the black theatre through yet another transformation. Gospel musicals, once viewed by theatre purists as song concerts palmed off as theatre onto a nondiscriminating audience, have surpassed the more venerated institutional theatres, if not in terms of aesthetic excellence, then surely in popular appeal with contemporary African-American audiences.

Generally speaking, the primary – if not sole – objective of the independently produced musicals has always been to turn a huge profit. Any consciousness-raising along the way is lagniappe, a bonus. Still speaking generally, the institutional theatres have stressed thought-provoking dramas about the human condition, and many have had a political bent. Regardless of generalities, based on its seniority and historically much higher profile, the black musical has always been the sector of the black theatre most readily identifiable by – and accessible to – mainstream audiences.

Throughout the nearly century-long history of the black musical in America, two aspects have remained constant. With but a few exceptions, notably in the black awareness era of the 1960s and 1970s, most black musical shows have been created to appeal primarily to white audiences. Furthermore, the black musical, notoriously non-innovative, has displayed a penchant for trendiness; one commercially successful show inevitably spawns a slew of imitators. The gospel musical, a phenomenon born in the early 1960s, contradicts the first constant in that its targeted audience is African-American. Moreover, as we shall see, much of the cloying redundancy that plagued the five recognizable trends in the black musical's history before the gospel shows gained popularity has compromised the aesthetic qualities of the newer movement.

The first trend occurred between 1898 and 1911, when a wave of black musicals washed onto Broadway, enjoyed profitable national tours, and even played before full houses in some parts of Europe. Led by the Williams & Walker and Cole & Johnson companies, numerous ragtime musicals – hybrids of the nineteenth-century blackface minstrel shows and Gilbert & Sullivan operettas – helped to define the structure of the Broadway musical as we now know it.

After a ten-year absence from the Broadway arena, the black musical returned in 1921 with *Shuffle Along*. Over the next 16 years, nearly three dozen black musicals played on Broadway. About half the shows were song-and-dance revues modeled after *Shuffle Along*, while the other half were book musicals patterned after the Williams & Walker and Cole & Johnson operettas. Between the mid-1930s and the mid-1940s, numerous black musicals were adapted from European classics such as *The Mikado* and *Carmen*. From the mid-1940s to the late 1950s several Caribbean-flavored musicals were produced on Broadway. All the shows in the aforementioned trends were written strictly to entertain white audiences. With but a few exceptions, the black characters in them were uneducated, dirt-poor-but-happy, dialect-spouting Negroes not far removed from their minstrel show "coon" origins. It was not until the 1960s that the overtly "Sambo"-like character was banished from the commercial stage.

It was also around this time that the gospel musical began to impose a toehold in the commercial theatre. Although gospel music had been a major part of two Depression-era plays-with-music, Marc Connelly's *Green Pastures* (1930) and Hall Johnson's *Run, Little Chillun* (1933), it was first used as full-fledged score for a book musical in the early 1960s, in a trio of musical dramas by Langston Hughes (1902–1967). It is ironic that Hughes, whose agnosticism is well-documented, would help to start the trend of the gospel musical.[1] However, as the self-appointed literary voice of the black American proletariat, he recognized the popularity of gospel music, and saw its dramatic potential. *Black Nativity*, "a Christmas song play" with a self-explanatory title, ran for 57 performances in the weeks before and after Christmas 1961 at the off-Broadway 41st Street Theater. The show elicited an enthusiastic response from the critics, which was rare for a Hughes stage work. His 1935 play *Mulatto*, the 1950 opera *The Barrier* (which was based on *Mulatto*), and his 1957 musical comedy *Simply Heavenly* all received excoriating reviews from the New York press.

The first full-length gospel musical to play Broadway proper was the Langston Hughes–Jobe Huntley collaboration *Tambourines to Glory*, which ran for three weeks in November 1963 at the Little Theater. This time the critics reverted to their standard negative reactions to Hughes' theatrical work. Most of the reviewers complained of what they perceived to be his weak plotting and shallow characterizations. *Jerico-Jim Crow*, also by Hughes, featured numerous traditional gospel tunes. A joint production of the Congress of Racial Equality, the National Association for the Advancement of Colored People, and the Student Nonviolent Coordinating Committee, *Jerico-Jim Crow* earned good reviews, but lasted only 31 performances in early 1964. Perhaps symbolically, it played at the Sanctuary, an off-Broadway church-cum-theatre.

Trumpets of the Lord, an adaptation of James Weldon Johnson's collection of "down-home" sermons, opened in late 1963 at the Astor Place Theater in Greenwich Village. Cicely Tyson, Lex Monson, and Al Freeman, Jr, delivered the fire-and-brimstone orations. Theresa Merritt headed the gospel chorus. Vinnette Carroll, who as a director/librettist/ adapter would become a dominant figure in the black theatre scene of the 1970s, wedged traditional gospel songs among her adaptations of Johnson's sermons. The show enjoyed a relatively long 160-performance stand in its initial run; however, an April 1969 Broadway presentation failed to find an audience, closing after seven showings.

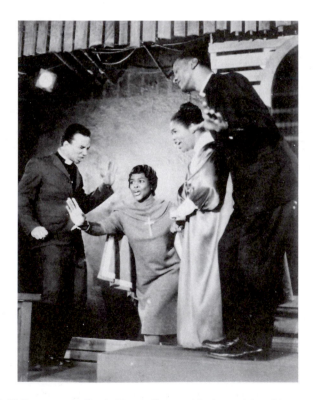

Plate 17: Al Freeman, Jr, Cicely Tyson, Theresa Merritt, and Lex Monson at a dress rehearsal for *Trumpets of the Lord* (1963). This production of the gospel musical was adapted by Vinnette Carroll from James Weldon Johnson's *God's Trombone*, and directed by Donald McKayle. Photograph by Bert Andrews.

Plate 18: Cicely Tyson in a dress rehearsal for the gospel musical *Trumpets of the Lord* (1963). Photgraph by Bert Andrews.

The typical Broadway book musical strives to tell its story via a clear-cut (if sometimes silly) plot, fueled by the proper blend of dialogue, songs, and dance numbers. The more intelligently wrought shows feature an array of interesting, well-drawn characters with whom the audience can identify. Of the four aforementioned gospel musicals of the 1960s, only the creators of *Tambourines to Glory* sought to follow the standard structure of the Broadway book musical, and if the critics are to be believed, with woeful results. The characters in Hughes' *Black Nativity* and *Jerico-Jim Crow* are archetypes designed as sounding boards for the author's didactic messages; the plots are beyond simplistic. *Trumpets of the Lord* has no plot at all; the actors merely deliver their sermons. These plays established a pattern for some of the popular gospel shows that would follow.

The creators of the later musicals did not bother with crafting tightly-structured, cause-and-effect plots. In lieu of original scores, gospel tunes were yanked from the store-house of traditional songs. Characterizations ran from the shallow to the stereotypic to the nonexistent. To theatre purists, this artistically arid brand of entertainment was not so much a dramatic event as a song concert masquerading as a musical play. Gospel music played a major role in *Purlie*, a hit 1970 Broadway musical based on Ossie Davis' popular 1961 comedy *Purlie Victorious*. Davis' play chalked up 261 performances, a splendid run for a rare, black-authored play on Broadway in the 1960s. Davis also supplied the libretto for the musical, with Peter Udell writing the lyrics, and Gary Geld composing the music. *Purlie*, which starred Cleavon Little in the title role, and introduced Melba Moore to Broadway, enjoyed a run of 688 performances, had a successful national tour, and because of its modest production requirements, has been a staple in community and university theatres.

Like *Purlie*, the Micki Grant/Vinnette Carroll collaboration, *Don't Bother Me, I Can't Cope* attracted an unusually high percentage of black patrons during its 1,065-performance Broadway run. Grant's eclectic score featured several rousing, original gospel tunes. This Vinnette Carroll-directed musical pointed toward Broadway's next full-fledged gospel musical, *Your Arms Too Short to Box with God*. *Arms* was developed at Carroll's Urban Arts Corps. Carroll conceived and directed the show, which she based on the Book of Matthew from the Bible. Most of the songs were written by Alex Bradford, with additional compositions by Micki Grant. Arguably the most innovative of the gospel musicals to date, its original score and non-traditional story line separated it from its predecessors. Described by Clive Barnes in 1976 as "the Christ story, from Palm Sunday, through the Passion in the Garden, the Betrayal, the Trial, to the Crucifixion and the Resurrection",[2] Jesus was portrayed by the black actor/dancer Stanley Perryman. Jesus never speaks; rather, he communicates through dance.

Carroll united a pair of seemingly incompatible philosophies in *Arms*: a profound faith in Christianity, and uncompromising black pride. Many militant African Americans of the late 1960s and early 1970s rejected Christianity, scorning it as the slave-master's tool to create a more ignorant bondsperson. Old-fashioned fire-and-brimstone preaching, losing one's emotions in gospel music, and "getting happy" in church were now viewed by many as plantation tomfoolery. The "belief of choice" for those militants who did subscribe to an organized faith had become Islam. However, by the mere act of presenting a black Christ in a Broadway show, Carroll was making a pronouncement of black pride. Taking this idea further, the performers wore standard church choir robes in the earlier scenes of the play, but changed later to garments that combined "a Biblical look with dashikis".[3]

Arms received fine critical reviews, and especial praise from Jack

Kroll of *Newsweek* on 10 January 1977. He castigated the "all-singing, all-dancing, all-jiving presence" of blacks in mid-1970s shows of little substance, and cited Carroll as being a concerned and original talent.[4] The show played 429 performances after its 22 December 1976 opening at the Lyceum Theater. A September 1982 revival starring the rhythm-and-blues icons Patty LaBelle and Al Green netted another 70 showings, and enjoyed a successful national tour.

Gospel music was central to Stephen Lemberg's short-lived *Jazzbo Brown*, which played 44 performances off-Broadway at the City Lights Theater in the summer of 1980, but never opened officially. The musical is a revamping of *The Jazz Singer*, and starred the Broadway musical veteran Andre De Shields as Billy "Jazzbo" Brown. The titular character is torn between following his father's pre-determined path to the ministry and trying to accomplish his true goal to become a ragtime jazz entertainer.

Perhaps the most interesting cult phenomenon in the history of the black theatre has been the one centered around *Mama, I Want to Sing*. Since its second incarnation in March 1983, *Mama* has entertained more than a million patrons. The creators/producers of the show, the husband-and-wife team of Ken Wydro and Vy Higgensen, have boasted that *Mama* is the longest-running black musical in off-Broadway history – a claim that many theatre purists would vehemently challenge. The storybook saga of *Mama* has not been without controversy. *Mama* first appeared as an Equity-approved off-off-Broadway showcase in December 1980 at Rosetta Lenoire's AMAS Repertory Company. In response to the proverbial popular demand, the standard 12-performance run was to be extended for a dozen more, as per Equity regulations.

However, after the thirteenth performance, the show's musical director, Frederic Gripper, bolted with the music for the show – the written orchestrations and the dance arrangements. Along with the rest of the company, he was protesting Higgensen and Wydro's proposed recasting of the show for a planned move to Broadway. Gripper believed this was totally unfair. He maintained that "the highly qualified and professional cast", each of whom was being paid only carfare for the production, had brought their own costumes, created their characters, and improvised lines.[5] In short, the producers had merely supplied the blueprint for the "book", while the performers actually quilted it together.[6] The remainder of the cast followed Gripper's lead, and the rest of the run had to be canceled.

Undaunted by the late-1980 fiasco of *Mama*, Higgensen and Wydro invested $30,000 of their own money for a March 1983 presentation. They staged the show, ironically, in the East Harlem Cultural Arts Center – the same building which housed the AMAS Repertory Company. *Mama* set up business in the 667-seat Hecksher Theatre, while AMAS operated out of a 112-seat room. In view of the structure of the musical – or, more appropriately, the lack of structure – *Mama*'s monumental success appears all the more amazing. Using nonunion performers who were essentially amateurs, a story-line beyond trite, a potpourri of songs from the canon of traditional gospel tunes, 1950s and 1960s rock 'n' roll hits, and original compositions by the show's musical director, Grenoldo Frazier, *Mama*, by the standards of the well-crafted book musical, was, on paper, a mess. Several songs popped up with no relationship to what came before or after them. The main conflict, such as it is, concerns the all-too-familiar tale of the preacher's child whose secular ambitions clash with the religion-centered moral universe of the parents. (This is *The Jazz Singer* story in yet another retelling.) The producers' claim that *Mama*'s story-line is true, purportedly that of Higgensen's sister, Doris Troy (better known for her 1963 song "Just One Look"), does not make it any less hackneyed.

What Higgensen and Wydro lacked – in knowing how to create an insightful, innovative theatrical piece – they made up for with their grasp of audience psychology. Their targeted audience was not the sophisticated theatregoer, but the masses of African Americans. They made the show as dramatically simplistic as possible, knowing that the main lure for their audience would be the rousing gospel music itself. Surely the creators/producers foresaw the problems critics would have with the amateurish acting, and, as Stephen Holden of *The New York Times* wrote, the show's "theatrically primitive" libretto.[7] Certainly Wydro and Higgensen realized the theatre purists would concentrate on the flimsy excuse for a story and most likely pan the show. Hence, no official opening night was declared; *Mama* was heavily advertised in the black media, but not at all in mainstream venues, until the show had established itself as a hit.

Had the producers gone the standard route – signing union performers, musicians and technicians, paying them the much higher standard scale, then inviting the critics and taking a chance on a barrage of negative reviews – the show might not have survived long enough to attract its targeted audience via word of mouth. *Mama* would not have been the first show, black or white, to succumb to this fate. However, with lessened financial pressure due to the contrived cut-rate overhead, and no negative reviews to discourage potential patrons, the show developed onto an audience. Furthermore, for whatever their collective reasons, the New York critics did *Mama* a huge favor. Whenever the producers of a show refuse to designate an opening night, largely because they assume the critics will tear their show apart, the reviewers agree among themselves on the night when they will descend, *en masse* and uninvited, to review the show. *Mama* is one of the few shows in that situation which the critics allowed to remain unreviewed.

Church-related clubs and social organizations comprised the first wave of *Mama* devotees that packed the Hecksher Theatre. Soon bands of students, scout troops, entire church congregations and other groups from along the Eastern Seaboard arrived in busloads at the East Harlem theatre. Simply put, *Mama* became an "event". Being part of the experience became as important as the actual viewing of the play itself. Higgensen and Wydro spurned numerous offers to move the show to Broadway. They felt that the largely black and Hispanic neighborhood and the community center which housed the Hecksher Theatre lent a certain ambience to the show. The producers did, however, launch a national tour in 1985.

In 1986, after the show had been packing in audiences for three years, troubleshooters employed by the City of New York realized that *Mama* was being presented as a profit-making, private-industry venture. This was a violation of a law stating that municipally owned spaces, such as the East Harlem Cultural Center, could be leased only to not-for-profit agencies. A nasty series of suits and countersuits between *Mama*'s producers and the City of New York followed; the final agreement was that *Mama* could stay, with the producers paying $96,000 a year in rent, with an increase of 15 per cent at the end of each ensuing year.[8] On 25 March 1988, *Mama*'s fifth anniversary, it had racked up its 1,608th performance at the Hecksher, according to Higgensen.[9] In 1988 a production was mounted in Japan; later that year *Mama, I Want to Sing, Part II* made its debut. The original *Mama* continued to tour well into the early 1990s. As of this writing, a national tour of *Mama, I Want to Sing, Part III* is making the rounds of US cities.

Amen Corner, a gospel-flavored musical based on James Baldwin's play *The Amen Corner*, opened 10 November 1983 at the Nederlander Theater on Broadway. The show failed to find an audience, closing after just four weeks. The same creative team, minus Ossie Davis, that crafted *Purlie* was responsible for *Amen Corner*. The reviews were horrendous, with most of the critics bemoaning what they felt was sedentary staging, and the poor integration of the "talky" book and its score. A consensus critical complaint was against the "imitation gospel music".[10]

Don't Get God Started had its libretto and direction by the accomplished playwright Ron Milner, and songs by the Grammy Award-winning singer and composer Marvin Winans. A "gospel musical with skits emphasizing moral and religious values, interspersed with gospel songs",[11] the show was interpreted by Clive Barnes as a warning against the possibly increasing "decadence of [. . .] the rising black middle class",[12] the musical's targeted audience. The reviews were mixed, leaning slightly toward the negative. The most common complaint was that the libretto, which many likened to the medieval morality plays, was simplistically trite, and that the show was shamelessly ethnocentric and "designed to appeal only to the converted".[13] Obviously seeking the same middle-income, church-going audience that had made *Mama* such a smash, *Don't Get God Started* stopped eleven weeks after its late October 1987 premiere.

Like Vinnette Carroll's *Your Arms Too Short to Box with God*, Bob Telson and Lee Breuer's *Gospel at Colonus* aspired to something greater than to be the standard-issue gospel musical. Telson and Breuer based *Colonus* on the second play in Sophocles' *Oedipus Rex* trilogy. One must give them degree-of-difficulty points for trying to meld classic Greek tragedy and African-American religious music. The show featured Clarence Fountain and the Five Blind Boys of Alabama as a collective Oedipus. Morgan Freeman, one of America's finest actors, earned rave reviews as The Messenger. Telson was the show's composer, and Breuer, the lyricist, librettist, and director, was a co-founder of Mabou Mines, an offbeat, off-off-Broadway troupe. Mines and its creators have earned numerous off- and off-off-Broadway awards.

Colonus had a long run at the Brooklyn Academy of Music, beginning on 18 November 1983. The production was awarded the 1984 Obie Award for best off-Broadway musical, and a long national tour followed, along with a critically acclaimed cast album, a presentation on the Public Broadcasting System's series *Great Performances*, and an engagement in Paris. However, in the Broadway arena, where formulaic slickness counts for more than true innovation, Telson and Breuer could not sustain an audience for *Colonus*. The critical consensus was that, while Breuer and Telson had made a noble attempt to bridge the two cultures, the black church and Greek tragedy were simply too incompatible to be fused into a satisfying and entertaining theatre piece. Although *Colonus* developed a cult following during its previous manifestation, it closed just 61 performances after its 24 March 1988 Broadway debut at the Lunt-Fontane Theater.

From the beginning of the black theatre as we know it in 1898, through the 1960s, black-themed plays and musicals were mostly produced by independent entities. The major exception is the twentieth century's first black institutional theatre of any note and duration, the American Negro Theatre, founded in 1940, and the training ground for a generation of African-American stage and film luminaries. However, on the heels of the civil rights and black pride movements, several influential non-profit companies propelled themselves to the vanguard of the 1960s black theatre movement. The Negro Ensemble Company, the New Federal Theatre, the Richard Allen Center, the AMAS Theater Company, and Brooklyn's Billie Holiday Theatre, to name arguably the most prolific, all presented award-winning plays to full houses for the latter part of the 1960s and most of the 1970s. Supplementing this activity were frequent productions of plays by black authors at Joseph Papp's otherwise "white" New York Shakespeare Festival/Public Theatre.

This windfall of activity was not confined to America's theatre capital. Institutional and community theatres abounded in cities across the country. The metropolitan areas with large black populations often had several thriving black theatrical companies from which to choose. Many productions by these companies were as aptly presented as anything one could find on the professional Manhattan scene. Simply stated, the black theatre – or more precisely, the umbrella of activity in black theatres – established a large and loyal following. A formidable segment of culturally aware black Americans viewed regular theatregoing as merely part of experiencing a well-rounded intellectual life. That they often had a variety of productions from which to choose made people more receptive to going to plays. Furthermore, it was not about people electing to see either Play A or Play B, but in which order they would see them.

Ironically, the 1980 election to the presidency of a former actor, Ronald Reagan, tolled the death knell for many institutional theatres. A major aspect of "Reaganomics" was for the federal – and by extension, state – government to make severe cuts in funding to the arts. As not-for-profit ventures, every institutional theatre was largely dependent on state- and federally-funded grants. Some theatres had to close their doors immediately; others hung on for a few years before expiring. Those institutional theatres that did survive were forced to reduce the number of presentations over a given season, and to scale down the production values of the shows they did stage. This resulted in a major change in the type of plays producers chose to mount. Better wrought plays that called for larger casts and more opulent set, light, and costume designs were now routinely bypassed for plays deemed more "do-able"; that is, featuring small casts, and little in the way of sets and costumes.

Less working capital resulted in fewer risks that the artistic directors were willing to take. Nepotism – a given in the theatre since the first cast trod the boards – became even more pronounced. Producers stayed with known quantities, recycling a small cadre of writers, directors, technicians, and to a lesser extent, performers. In short, the years following Reaganomics saw a lack of infusion of the proverbial new blood. This was especially true in the umbrella of production companies known as the black theatre in America. Arguably more prone to cronyism than their counterparts in the theatre at large, many of the major black producers/artistic directors in the New York professional theatre developed reputations for running closed shops. Those theatre artists who had not been on board before Reaganomics need not apply.

This exclusionary mentality generated many consequences. The quality of the work presented itself suffered. The producers relied on voices that had already had their say. Once-fresh techniques had become hackneyed. Audiences began giving these companies votes of no-confidence by staying away. The live theatre, which for decades had run a distant third to films and television in terms of earning power for its artists, became even less attractive in that aspect. Clichés aside, to embark on theatrical ventures was to undertake a labor of love in the truest sense. During the 1980s, countless artists aspiring to flourish in the live theatre were discouraged partly by the slimmer chances of economic gain, and partly by what many complained were the exclusionary tactics of a handful of holdovers from the black theatre's halcyon days. Thus, the black theatre underwent a decided "graying". All one has to do is to attend one of the black theatre conferences to confirm this. (That these conferences invariably, and often immediately, dissolve into a class reunion of sorts, replete with much backslapping about past glories, is another subject entirely.)

The loyal audience that had been cultivated in the 1960s and 1970s had found better things to do with its entertainment dollar. The natural regeneration of talent was not happening. By the end of the 1980s attendance in the theatre was reserved for special occasions. This fading of popularity by the institutional theatres opened the gates for less structured forms of entertainment. Most notable were what will be termed the "low-brow comedies", and, of course, the gospel musicals. Some theatre purists would argue that comedies such as *Beauty Shop*, *Barber Shop*, and the like are the first cousins to *Mama, I Want to Sing,* to *Mama, Don't* and *My Grandmother Prayed for Me.*

The two types of show do share some striking and undeniable similarities. Hardly anyone connected with these shows – be it as a writer, director, performer, or backstage talent – has served an apprenticeship of any appreciable length in the professional theatre. The writing is often devoid of true craft; the "characters" have been pulled from the shelf; a linear, cause-to-effect through-line is seldom presented; the dialog is broad, obvious, and designed to play to the lowest common denominator. The acting, mostly by a no-name cast of amateurs, is broad to the point of making one wonder what all the hoopla was against Amos 'n' Andy in past decades. Furthermore, the low-brow comedies and gospel shows use similar marketing and packaging ploys. Rather than risk an open-ended run at a smaller house, these shows travel from city to city, making one-night stands, or staying but a few days at the most. The producers rent cavernous houses of a thousand-plus seats, then fill them up by means of an inundation of advertisement in the local black media that is relentless, featuring blurbs that are as subtle as a knife in the neck, and perversely ingenious.

The creators of the gospel musicals and low-brow comedies, unlike those who write "black" musicals and plays for the mainstream theatre, could care less if white audiences understand or "like" the material. This is strictly black theatre for black people. Hence the topical references and the use of popular songs, secular and religious, that have never "crossed over". The creators of these shows firmly believe, to quote a line from *Purlie Victorious*, that "bein' colored can be a lot of fun when [no outsiders] are watchin' ".

As for the low-brow comedies, nothing is sacred. Toilet and anatomical humor abound. These shows generally feature a parade of ghetto stereotypes: flamboyant gays; razor-totin', grossly-overweight, loud-mouthed "big-mama" caricatures; gold-digging party girls, scantily-clad in the loudest, cheapest of outfits and wigs; aspiring "mack-daddies" and popcorn pimps. Popular recordings somehow find their way into the "action"; in the case of the shows written and produced by – and starring – the 1970s diva of raunch, Millie Jackson, sometimes the stars break into song at less than dramatically appropriate moments. Gratuitous dance sequences, the better to show some flesh, are often incorporated. For the low-brow comedies the sole objective, pure and simple, is to entertain, by means of an idiom on which the targeted audience will have to exert a minimal amount of intellectual energy.

The gospel musicals, of course, eschew the vulgarity that seems to be the backbone of the low-brow comedies. Both genres, however, share a decided avoidance of the high road in terms of theatrical craft. To repeat, the doctrines of the "well-made play" have seldom sullied the minds of the creators of the comedies and gospel shows. Similarly, the gospel musicals generally depend upon their own lowest common denominator: the familiar music that will cause a large segment of the audience to "get happy" and "feel the spirit". As is the inevitable result of amateur writing, the gospel tuners promote their own set of stereotypes. The preachers line up at two extremes: the sincere, hard-working man of God, and the pimp-cum-charlatan. The congregations are composed of barb-tongued, busybody sisters (often, like their low-brow counterparts, buffoonishly obese); former "hot mamas" who have not fully reformed from their good-timin' ways; virginal ingénues and saintly preachers' wives; and adolescent males torn between urban contemporary evils and the more Godly life offered in the morality tale at hand. Seldom is there subtlety in the writing. The acting is broad to fit the shallow "characterizations". The dialog, such as it is, is merely a pause between songs. As with the low-brow comedies, the numbingly familiar is delivered in lieu of something more creative on the part of the writers. Like the comedies, the gospel shows are not mounted to inspire speculative thought on the human condition, but merely to reinforce what the audience already knows – and feels. However you cut it, a certain cynicism toward their audiences informs the content and structure of both the comedies and gospel musicals.

Gone is the time when the productions from the institutional theatres (and their community theatre counterparts across the country) set the standard for what can be collectively called the black theatre in America. What was a cultural force during its heyday has been reduced to something that many in the black proletariat deem as "elitist". As an educator who has taught courses in the African-American theatre at various colleges in New York City, no one knows this more than this writer. At the beginning of every semester, I take a survey among the students in my black theatre class. Sadly, few have seen a live black theatre production in the past year. Those who have usually report partaking of a "special event" night out to see the latest black Broadway musical (most likely created and packaged by whites), or a gospel musical, or one of the low-brow comedies. This writer finds it particularly distressing that many of the twentysomething and younger age bracket are under the assumption that shows like *Beauty Shop* and *Older Woman, Younger Man* actually represent the "black theatre". Conversely, when I ask if anyone has seen a play at one of the surviving non-commercial theatres, a response is rare.

For better or for worse from an aesthetic sense, the two forms at which theatre purists would look askance, the gospel musicals and low-brow comedies, have etched their indelible marks on the black theatre in the last two decades of this century. The former will surely be with us for a while; though the comedies, as of this writing, appear to have peaked in their popularity, one can never count them out. Let it be noted that, in the 1991 original version of this article, yours truly wrote that the gospel musicals had run their course.

How wrong I was.

Any argument that the comedies and gospel musicals cynically play toward people who are unsophisticated in terms of theatrical tastes is immediately rendered moot by the inability of the champions of more substantive theatre fare, the artistic directors of the institutional theatres, as the O'Jays used to sing, to "give the people what they want". The Shelley Garretts, Millie Jacksons, Vy Higgensens, and Kenneth Wydros are doing something right; the so-called "living legends of the black theatre" who are two decades removed from their salad days would do well to see how their less venerated counterparts have put their fingers on the public's pulse. That the holdovers from past decades use their contacts and name recognition to continue to receive what relatively little grant money is being bequeathed, while fledging theatre creators are shut out from any real funding does not help the situation in that area. With apologies to another soul-era song, "you just can't win making those same mistakes".

In an interview this writer was privileged to have a few years ago with Rosetta Lenoire, a true "living legend" of the theatre, the great artist, when asked what she thought was the future of the black theatre, replied, "Black folks will always find a way to put on theatre, somehow, some place. Others may not consider it to be theatre, but that will be beside the point for the performers and the audience".[14] Whatever some may see as the theatrical "purity" of the gospel musical (in terms, of course, of Eurocentric dictates on the drama), that genre's popularity resides in the universal truths upon which it touches. Those truths will never change, and the impact of the gospel musical on the overall scene in the black theatre, though it may ebb and reach a crest, will never disappear.

NOTES

1. See Rampersad 1986–8. Hughes' nonbelief in any form of organized religion is mentioned throughout both volumes of this definitive biography.

2. Barnes 1976:20.
3. See Gottfried 1976:30.
4. Kroll 1977:66.
5. See Fraser 1980:C23.
6. *Ibid.*
7. Holden 1984:C22.
8. See Stanton 1986:27.
9. See Nemy 1988:C2.
10. See Sharp 1983:20.
11. See Guernsey 1988:350.
12. Barnes 1987:41.
13. See Holden 1987:12.
14. Burdine 1992.

BIBLIOGRAPHY

Barnes, Clive, "Your Arm's Too Short To Box with God", *The New York Times*, 23 December 1976:20.

——, "Gospel Fills 'Don't Get God Started'", *New York Post*, 20 October 1987:41.

Burdine, Warren B., Jr, Interview with Rosetta Lenoire, April 1992, New York City.

Fraser, Gerald C., "Rights Dispute Closes Musical", *The New York Times*, 22 December 1980:C23.

Gottfried, Martin, "'Arms' Short of Good Theater", *The New York Times*, 23 December 1976:30.

Guernsey, Otis L., Jr, and Sweet, Jeffrey, eds, *The Best Plays of 1987–88*, New York, Applause Theatre Book Publishers, 1988.

Holden, Stephen, "'I Want to Sing': Gospel Find of 5th Avenue", *New York Times*, 13 April 1984:C22.

——, "'Don't Get God Started': A Gospel Musical", *The New York Times*, 31 October 1987:12.

Kroll, Jack, "Gospel Truth", *Newsweek*, 10 January 1977:66.

Nemy, Enid, "An Anniversary", *The New York Times*, 25 March 1988:C2.

Rampersad, Arnold, *The Life of Langston Hughes*, 2 vols, New York, Oxford University Press, 1986–8.

Sharp, Christopher, "Amen Corner", *Women's Wear Daily*, 11 November 1983:20.

Stanton, Ali, "'I Want to Sing' . . . or Cry?", *New York Amsterdam News*, 27 September 1986:27.

CATALYSIS

An Interview with Adrian Piper (1972)

Lucy Lippard

Last year, Adrian Piper did a series of pieces called "Catalysis". They included: **Catalysis I**, *"in which I saturated a set of clothing in a mixture of vinegar, eggs, milk and cod liver oil for a week, then wore them on the D train during evening rush hour, then while browsing in the Marboro bookstore on Saturday night";* **Catalysis VIII**, *a recorded talk inducing hypnosis;* **Catalysis IV**, *in which "I dressed very conservatively but stuffed a large red bath towel in the side of my mouth until my cheeks bulged to about twice their normal size, letting the rest of it hang down my front, and riding the bus, subway, and Empire State Building elevator";* **Catalysis VI**, *"in which I attached helium-filled Mickey Mouse balloons from each of my ears, under my nose, to my two front teeth, and from thin strands of my hair, then walked through Central Park, the lobby of the Plaza Hotel, and rode the subway during morning rush hours";* **Catalysis III**, *"in which I painted some clothing with sticky white paint with a sign attached saying 'WET PAINT', then went shopping at Macy's for some gloves and sunglasses";* **Catalysis V**, *"in which I recorded loud belches made at five-minute intervals, then concealed the tape recorder on myself and replayed it all full volume while reading, doing research, and taking out some books and records at the Donnell Library";* **Catalysis VII**, *"in which I went to the Metropolitan Museum's* **Before Cortes** *show, while chewing large wads of bubble gum, blowing large bubbles and allowing the gum to adhere to my face . . . [and] filling a leather purse with catsup, then adding wallet, comb, keys, etc; opening and digging out change for bus or subway, a comb for my hair in the ladies' room at Macy's, a mirror to check my face on the bus, etc; coating my hands with rubber cement, then browsing at a newspaper stand . . . ." And so on.*

PIPER: I hold monologues with myself, and whenever anyone passes near me, within hearing distance, I try to direct the monologue toward them without changing the presentation or the content of what I'm saying. Usually, when I know that someone is approaching me, I find that I'm psychologically preparing myself for their approach. I'm turning around to meet them, and I have a whole presentation for their benefit, because they are there, and I'm aware of them. I'm trying *not* to do that. I'm not sure whether or not I'm involving myself in a contradiction. On the one hand, I want to register my awareness of someone else's existence, of someone approaching me and intruding into my sense of self, but I don't want to present myself artificially in any way. I want to try to incorporate them into my own consciousness.

QUESTION: Do you look at them?

PIPER: Yes. That's another thing: I've been trying to work with. When I started doing this kind of work I found I was really having trouble looking people in the eye while I was doing it; it was very hairy. I looked odd and grotesque, and somehow just confronting them head-on was very difficult. It makes me cringe every time I do it, but I'm trying to approach them in a different way.

QUESTION: This is much subtler than the things you were doing last year. Are you still in that context?

PIPER: Yes. These came out of them. Not formally, but through the kinds of experiences that I was having when I was doing these things. I feel that I went through some really heavy personality changes as a result of them.

QUESTION: Just to be able to do them at all, in the first place . . .

PIPER: Well, a lot of things happened. I seem to have gotten more aware of the boundaries of my personality, and how much I intrude myself upon other people's realities by introducing this kind of image, this facade, and a lot of things happen to me psychologically. Initially, it was really hard to look people in the eye. I simply couldn't overcome the sense that if I was going to keep my own composure and maintain my own identity, it was just impossible. I would have to pretend that they weren't there, even though I needed them. Then something really weird happened; it doesn't happen all the time. Something I really like. It is almost as if I manage to make contact in spite of how I look, in spite of what I'm doing. There was a piece I did last summer that was part of the work I was doing before. I had on very large knit clothes and I got a lot of Mickey Mouse balloons, which have three shapes, with the two ears. I stuffed them into the clothes, so I was not only very obese, but I was also bulging out all over; it was very strange. I was on the subway and the balloons were breaking and people were getting very hostile because I was taking up a lot of space, and it just occurred to me to ask someone what time it was. So I did, and they answered me in a perfectly normal voice. This was very enlightening. I decided that was a worthwhile thing to go after. Somehow transcending the differences I was presenting to them by making that kind of contact . . .

QUESTION: How often do you do it?

PIPER: Maybe two or three times a week in different kinds of situations; wherever I find myself. I haven't started cataloging the kinds of reactions I have gotten . . . The scary thing about it for me is that there is something about doing this that involves you in a kind of universal solipsism. When you start realizing that you can do things like that, that you are capable of incorporating all those different things into your realm of experience, there comes a point where you can't be sure whether what you are seeing is of your own making, or whether it is objectively true.

QUESTION: Because you begin to have almost too much power over the situation?

PIPER: Yes. You know you are in control, that you are a force acting on things, and it distorts your perception. The question is whether there is *anything* left to external devices or chance. How are people when you're not there? It gets into a whole philosophical question. I found that at times it's exhilarating, too. It is a heady thing, which has to do with power, obviously . . .

QUESTION: What do you think it has to do with being a woman? Or being black? It's a very aggressive thing. Do you think you're getting out some of your aggressions about how women are treated? Is it related to that at all?

PIPER: Well, not in terms of intention. As far as the work goes, I feel it is completely apolitical. But I do think that the work is a product of me as an individual, and the fact that I am a woman surely has a lot to do with it. You know, here I am, or was, "violating my body"; I was making it public. I was turning myself into an object.

QUESTION: But an object that wasn't attractive, the way it was supposed to be; instead it was repellent, as if you were fighting back.

PIPER: In retrospect, all these things seem valid, even though they weren't considerations when I did the pieces.
One thing I don't do, is say: "I'm doing a piece", because somehow that puts me back into the situation I am trying to avoid. It immediately establishes an audience separation – "Now we will perform" – that destroys the whole thing. As soon as you say, this is a piece, or an experiment, or guerrilla theatre – that makes everything all right, just as set up and expected as if you were sitting in front of a stage. The audience situation and the whole art context makes it impossible to do anything.

QUESTION: Don't you feel that this is kind of infinite? That you have to cut it off someplace so that it *is* a piece, and not life? If you're making art, you have to have a limit.

PIPER: I really don't know. For quite a while I felt absolutely unanchored in terms of what I was doing. I'm not sure I can describe that. Now I feel certain of what I'm doing because it is necessary for me to do it, but I do not feel terribly certain as to what my frame of reference is. It seems that since I've stopped using gallery space, and stopped announcing the pieces, I've stopped using art frameworks. There is very little that separates what I'm doing from quirky personal activity. Except I've been thinking a lot about the fact that I relate what I'm doing to people. Occasionally, I meet somebody I know while I'm doing a piece, and it seems okay to me, because it affirms what I'm doing as art. That gives me some kind of anchor. But when I just tell people what I'm doing, I don't think it has the same effect. What it does is reaffirm my own identity as an artist to me. If you ask me what I'm doing, I'll tell you I'm doing this, rather than saying, well, you know, I'm not doing any work lately, but I've been doing some really weird things in the street. I subscribe to the idea that art reflects the society to a certain extent, and I feel as though a lot of the work I'm doing is being done because I am a paradigm of what the society is.

Part IV:
Contemporary Challenges to Representations
African-American Women Playwrights

FOUR BAD SISTERS (1998)

Eugene Nesmith

The four artists you will encounter in this section are rare and defiant. All have created new and challenging work, and by their contributions to African-American dramatic literature and performance practices have altered the contours of the creations of all future artists. Part of a tradition of African-American women writers and performers, they have defiantly broken with that tradition by daring to break new ground doing and speaking the unspeakable. They attack their subjects with fierce passion and midnight magic, creating words and images that reveal bitter truths we would rather not know, all the while breathing life into dying souls.

Adrienne Kennedy is a modernist writer of the avant-garde who combines myths, symbols, historical figures, and racial images to create autobiographical plays that penetrate the soul and the psyche. The best place to start to understand her work would be with her fascinating and unusual memoir, *People Who Led to My Plays* (1987), in which she presents a series of fragments and images bearing upon the course of her life journey. The snapshot of Kennedy as a little girl on the cover alone seems to say so much about her particular take as an artist. Born in 1931 in Pittsburgh into a middle-class family, raised in Cleveland, she received a good education, one that included considerable exposure to music and art. However, she was always uncertain about her identity and where she belonged. In her plays, she blends surrealism and expressionism with poetic dialogue to create complex, haunting characters in crisis, who are searching for their identity and their place in the world.

An observer of life, Kennedy asks not what, but why? A product of her time and her environment, she nevertheless defies tradition and authority. Her style reveals that she views herself not as part of any particular tradition, but as an artist who is searching for the inner truth that will define her. Thus, the world and the self are not constructed only by language, but also by images. What makes her work so powerful is not only how she uses images and language but how she forces us to contend with and see things that we would rather not see. Not interested in telling us a nice linear story, she wants to reveal the unspoken, the unconscious, and the dreams. Her world is one of psychological torture, pain, death, agony and struggling toward individual wholeness based on freedom of choice via self-expression.

As can be seen in her essay "A Growth of Images" (Chapter 19, in this part of this book), the dramatist Kennedy is unique not only because of her resistance to the tradition of realism and naturalism, but as a woman and an artist of African descent she has gone beyond writing about race in relation to racism. Not only does she challenge the construction and the limitations of the notion of race, but she grapples with larger issues such as gender, identity, psychology, time, and space. She is also keenly aware of the impact of popular culture on her world view. Although inspired by other writers, it was her ability to listen and to see the world from her own vantage point that has led to her particular style, creating a unique form for others to build upon.

Robbie McCauley's art is about allowing a space for dialogue between different groups. Following in the footsteps of Kennedy, she uses her work to explore her past and the history and oppression of African Americans in this country. In her interview with Vicki Patraka excerpted here (Chapter 20, "Obsessing in Public"), she confirms that childhood memories, history, racism, music, tradition, and rituals are important sources for her. Mining the same vein as Kennedy, McCauley's work is politically and socially oriented, and it is designed to raise the consciousness of its viewer. Following the interview with Vicki Patraka is McCauley's play *Sally's Rape* which uses direct address to bring the historical events of rape and slavery into the present, while forcing the audience to face their own complicity in the unjust treatment of people of color. By so doing, one is led to meditate on present injustices. As in the entire body of McCauley's work, the endeavor is to break down barriers, and to bring communities closer together. This involves connecting history to the realities of the present moment, which requires excavating the shame and guilt whites have about slavery, as well as confronting blacks with their feelings of continuing to blame whites for whatever opportunities they have been denied because of slavery. As the play begins, the two characters playing themselves converse about the play. It is immediately revealed that these two people know one another, and are in the process of getting to know one another better. They talk about themselves, their respective histories and families. By the sixth line of the play, it is stated that the play is about Robbie and that Jeannie is in it because she was put there by Robbie. Her history is intertwined with Robbie's as these two characters serve as archetypes for the larger history of race relations in the USA. Their dialogue is a dialogue on the construction of a national identity.

In the section of the play in which the audience is invited to participate, Robbie assures them that she is in control, and gives them explicit instructions about what is expected. She divides the audience into three groups and asks them to respond. By so doing, she is invoking the African-American oral tradition of call and response. The audience must question their feelings about the historical situation of the rape of Robbie's great-great-grandmother, in addition to the general ignorance of whites about African-American history. The image of her grandmother's rape came to McCauley in a dream. Thus once again, the recollection of a dream is an important element in the creation of the theatrical event. By conflating Sally's rape with her dreams, McCauley makes the past and the present into one. The re-creation of a slave auction with McCauley standing naked on the auction block situates the audience as the slave buyers. Both Kennedy and McCauley use autobiographical material as a foundation for their work, to create politically charged art with a narrative constructed of layered non-linear fragments, personal moments, aspects of African-American history designed to challenge traditional values and systems of beliefs. Unlike Kennedy, McCauley works as an actor and a director. She has established herself over the past twenty years as one of a few African-American performance artists who consistently does cutting-edge work, and in this regard she has extended upon Kennedy's lead.

Both Anna Deavere Smith and McCauley have in common that they are solo performers creating art from real-life experience. Although Smith's work is quite different than Kennedy's or McCauley's, the common thread that binds them, aside from the preoccupation with issues of race and gender, is that they all started out being marginalized artists in theatre, but have managed to create a space for their voices to be heard. Smith started her *On the Road* series in 1982 when she was directing Adrienne Kennedy's *A Movie Star Has to Star in Black and White* at Carnegie–Mellon University because her students had difficulties developing characters. Her performances of the stories of people she has interviewed over the years have made a major impact on the theatrical scene. Her two most recent shows, *Fires in the Mirror: Crown Heights Brooklyn and Other Identities* and *Twilight: Los Angeles, 1992* had superior runs both off-Broadway and on Broadway.

In his essay "Acting as Incorporation", Richard Schechner persuasively argues that Smith does what she does as an actress by virtue of "incorporating" the individuals she presents on stage. "To incorporate means to be possessed by", Schechner writes, "to open oneself up thoroughly and deeply to another being". Nonetheless, on those occasions when I have seen Smith perform, she has not gotten close to being possessed. On the contrary, her acting style is presentational: it was clear that this was someone who was imitating the speech patterns and gestures of whatever person she was enacting at the time. If you know or have seen the behavior of some of these people, her exaggerated presentation becomes all the more evident and provocative. Smith reveals in "The Word Becomes You", an interview by Carol Martin, that in her performance of these individuals she presents the person as they present themselves to the world rather than as the actor becoming the character. She also says in this article that she attempts to heighten the sense of inclusion for everybody by using the pronouns "us" and "we". Yet, as a constructed piece of art, the creator cannot abdicate the position of ultimate authority.

Smith's gift is her ability to present the characters as if she were only the vessel for their embodiment. Her success hinges on the fact that she has the ability to make an audience feel that she is objective and that she can be fair in telling both sides of a story that is charged with racial and emotional conflict. However, because her work has been so well received by the dominant culture, I always leave her performances thinking about what it means in terms of power relations. She documents selected individuals who are constructed on a descriptive performative net of past events. It is her choice whom she interviews. Smith went into the Crown Heights project, suggests the interview with her, very clear about the kinds of people she wanted to meet and how to find them. As it turned out, a pivotal character, the "bad boy", was not one of the people that she had planned to interview. Yet after her encounter with him, she felt as though she needed to include him. It was because the particular way he used language was important to her. Like Kennedy and McCauley she is concerned about being accessible. In her recreation of the "bad boy", race and class boundaries are transgressed as the audience is allowed to see different worlds that are side by side, but still worlds apart.

Suzan-Lori Parks is also continuing to build on Kennedy's avant-gardist precedent. However, in some ways her work is much more experimental than Kennedy's, or even McCauley's or Smith's. Parks' work creates a history that is not specifically about race but more about historiography. Her use of poetic language, non-traditional characters, and extraordinary images, creates work of a dense structure that is often impenetrable for an audience. Like Bertolt Brecht, her primary concern is not with an emotional identification with the characters presented on stage, but rather with bringing to our consciousness a critical awareness of larger structural dynamics that are operating and impacting upon the lives of the masses. Often present in her work are concerns about how individuals are perceived by the outside world, as well as dealing with the inner and outer lives of her characters.

For a fairly young experimental writer, Parks has been phenomenally successful. Nevertheless, a pioneer such as Kennedy has yet to receive the recognition she deserves. For many years Kennedy's work has been absent from the stage of most professional theatre companies in America. It is to the credit of the Signature Theatre, which devotes an entire season to a single playwright, that Kennedy was the recipient of this honor during their 1995–6 New York season. Aside from Parks' talent, her success is also built upon the contribution of those writers who preceded her, and these three writers, Kennedy, McCauley and Smith, have played a major role in paving the road for her success.

The America Play, one of Parks' later works, is an excellent example of her style: how she plays with language, her construction of characters and multiple themes, how she plays with representation and images, and how she uses repetition to create a variation on a theme in the manner of a jazz composition. Parks' focus in *The America Play* is on history, but not with history as we are used to thinking about history. In the interview by Steven Drukman, Parks explains that she starts from the fabricated absence of black people. "It's the hole idea", she says. Parks contests this fabricated absence, this construction of history that has left out contributions made by people of color, as well as a construction of history which presents Europeans as superior. Parks also wants to play with and entertain her audience, at the same time that she is making them think serious thoughts.

The work of these four writers is challenging, breaking new ground, and moving us beyond naturalism. By consistently testing the landscape of accepted theatrical practices, these four bad sisters refuse to be categorized or silenced as they lead us toward the twenty-first century.

BIBLIOGRAPHY

Kennedy, Adrienne, *In One Act*, Minneapolis, Minnesota, University of Minnesota Press, 1987.

————, *People Who Led to My Plays*, New York, Knopf, 1987.

McCauley, Robbie, "Thoughts on My Career, *The Other Weapon*, and Other Projects", *Performance and Cultural Politics*, ed. Elin Diamond, New York, Routledge, 1996.

Richards, Sandra I., "Caught in the Act of Social Definition: On the Road with Anna Deavere Smith", *Acting Out: Feminist Performances*, ed. Lynda Hart and Peggy Phelan, Ann Arbor, Michigan, University of Michigan Press, 1993.

Solomon, Alisa, "Signifying on the Signifyin': The Plays of Suzan-Lori Parks", *Theatre*, Summer/Fall 1990, 73–80.

A GROWTH OF IMAGES (1997)

Adrienne Kennedy

Autobiographical work is the only thing that interests me, apparently because that is what I do best. I write about my family. In many ways I would like to break out of that, but I don't know how to break out of it. In fact I would really like to write more about the people who were before my own immediate family, like my grandparents and their family. I have two children, but I've never been able to write about them.

I feel overwhelmed by family problems and family realities. I see my writing as being an outlet for inner, psychological confusion and questions stemming from childhood. I don't know any other way. It's really figuring out the "why" of things – that is, if that is even possible. I'm not sure you can figure out the "why" of anything anymore.

You try to struggle with the material that is lodged in your unconscious, and try to bring it to the conscious level. You try to remain as honest about that as possible, without fear. I don't believe you intentionally set out to write the things you write. For instance, I would like to write mystery stories like Agatha Christie, or much lighter things which are far less tortuous, but I feel you must be honest by letting the material come to the surface. And just accept it.

It's not necessarily that easy, because I think your intellect is always working against you to censor. You must just let the material come out and not be frightened about it and not censor it. Just trust yourself and do not have an opinion of your previous work. One must always fight against that imitation of oneself.

My writing, therefore, really requires a certain amount of time-lapse between the event and the written product. I do keep a journal and have always kept some type of written diary, but I have never been happy with that. Diaries and journals always seem so time-consuming. You can only spend so many hours a day writing about yourself or your world. I trust those periods when I'm not writing constantly. I believe in long periods of resting, not working against yourself by forcing yourself to write when you don't want to. I believe in being relaxed but not in letting things lie dormant for a long time or in between times.

Work does, however, play a very big part in my life. I do write and then go back and work on it some more. Most important, it's really a lot of hard work. I think about things for many years and keep loads of notebooks, with images, dreams, ideas I've jotted down. I see my writing as a growth of images. I think all my plays come out of dreams I had two or three years before; I played around with the images for a long period of time to try to get to the most powerful dreams.

As an example, *A Rat's Mass* was based on a dream I had once when I was on a train. I was very frightened, doing something I had never done before. I was on a train going from Paris to Rome, and I was going to try to live in Rome for a few months. I was with my seven-year-old son. It was a very difficult thing for me to do because I'm not really that adventurous. I had never tried to do something like this. In a way, I just wanted to turn around and go back. I had this dream in which I was being pursued by red, bloodied rats. It was a very powerful dream, and when I woke up the train had stopped in the Alps. It was at night. I had never felt that way. It was a crucial night in my life. So, I was just haunted by that image for years, about being pursued by these big, red rats.

Then I try to take these images and try to find what the sources for them are. All this is unconscious, all this takes a long time. I'm not in that much control of it. In the case of *A Rat's Mass*, there was a connection to my brother. At that time my brother was in an automobile accident, from which he subsequently died. This evoked an almost unreal memory of when we were children and we used to play in the attic, and there used to be a closet in the floor of the attic. I didn't like to go up there by myself because I would imagine that there would be something in that closet.

In *Cities in Bezique*, the character of Clara Passmore was a composite of my aunt and my mother and, of course, myself. Clara was very much my aunt's life. She was this girl who grew up in a small Georgia town. She was quite brilliant. Her father was white. She came to live with us when I was in high school. They wanted her to go to school in Cleveland because they figured she was so smart. This was many, many years ago – more than twenty-five years ago she got her Masters at Teacher's College at Columbia. She teaches English somewhere in the South now. I used to listen to her talk a lot. She was very hysterical. I haven't seen her for many years now, but what struck me as a child – as a young person, not necessarily as a child – was how she used to talk, how she didn't belong anywhere. She's very much a basis to that girl in *The Owl Answers*, and my mother also, in a different way, talks about things like that.

Yes, those two people did have a very big influence on me; they both are very articulate and, in different ways, both are very pretty. Somehow, it always struck me, unconsciously, what a tragedy that these very pretty women seemed so tormented. So of course I used them as a model.

I was always interested in English literature and I've traveled in England. There's always been a fascination with Queen Victoria. It always seemed to amaze me that one person could have a whole era named after them. I find the obsession with royalty fascinating. Not only

Queen Victoria, but other great historical literary figures such as Patrice Lamumba and, it's obvious, Jesus Christ. Well, I took these people, which became a pattern in *The Owl Answers*, and then used them to represent different points of view – metaphors really.

Obviously there was always great confusion in my own mind of where I belonged, if anywhere. It's not such a preoccupation now, since I see myself as a writer I don't worry about the rest of it anymore.

I first had my plays done in the early 1960s and, as a result, I'm really a product of that time when *Zoo Story* and *American Dream* were the models of success. I studied with Edward Albee at one point, just after I had written *Funny House of a Negro*. I would never have even gone for the one-act, except for the fact that everyone was going to see *Zoo Story* and because I was not happy with any of the three-acts I had written up to that point. I couldn't seem to sustain the power and still can't seem to write really long, huge works.

I admire Tennessee Williams and Garcia Lorca, and I struggled for a long time to write plays – as typified by *Funny House* – in which the person is in conflict with their inner forces, with the conflicting sides to their personality, which I found to be my own particular, greatest conflict. I am a relatively quiet person who just mulls over all these things and, in a sense, it was an attempt to articulate that – your inner conflicts. I had worked for a long time before I did *Funny House* on having people in a room with conflicts. I was very much in awe of Tennessee Williams at the time and so I imitated him. Somehow it just didn't work. It didn't have any power. I just didn't believe it when I read it. Starting with *Funny House*, I finally came up with this one character, Sarah, who, rather than talk to her father or mother, talked with these people she created about her problems. It's very easy for me to fall into fantasy.

Most people seem to feel that *Funny House of a Negro* is still my most powerful play. Of course I find that depressing, seeing that I wrote that over 16 years ago. But *Funny House* was a build-up of an idea I had been working on for over five years. Finally that idea just suddenly exploded. The subsequent plays were ideas that I had been trying to work on in my twenties, but then they just suddenly came at the same time, because all those plays were written quite close together. They all came out eleven months to a year from the time *Funny House* came out. All those plays are a product of ideas I've been working on from the time I was twenty-five to thirty. I was struggling with those ideas for a long time. Once I found a way to express them in *Funny House*, I think that was when I found a technique. I employed that technique for the rest.

Transcribed and edited by Lisa Lehman from a recorded interview

OBSESSING IN PUBLIC

An Interview with Robbie McCauley[1] (1993)

Vicki Patraka

"IS WE FREE YET?"
Family Stories and Serial
Collaborations

PATRAKA: Candy stores figure in two of your performance pieces – the candy store where a white store owner in a black neighborhood falsely accuses you of shoplifting, and the candy store deep in a white neighborhood that you walk into to buy strawberry bubble-gum. It made me think about the way you encase history in childhood events.

McCAULEY: The store was a magical place for me as a kid, where you go in and buy things, especially sweet things. I have store references in a lot of pieces. I hadn't thought of it as a category, except that I know it's the place where events that had to do with white people happened. It was that other world. The incidents that I talk about are the troublesome ones, but the other side of that store thing was the magic of the things up on the shelves. There's one story I have about Mr Reddick's store in Columbus, Georgia. He couldn't read and write and my sister and I considered him "trash". But he had the store, and we felt connected to that. My grandmother would send us with a note and my sister and I had to read it to him. I even taught his daughter Martha Fay how to read, but when we got to be ten, we didn't play together anymore.

PATRAKA: Suddenly you had to behave in a particular way.

McCAULEY: That store had to do with class and caste issues in a working class neighborhood in the South – the segregation was more internal than external. White people simply lived on the *other side* of the street and the store was right there, and we knew we had "more class" than they did, but there were certain boundaries you didn't cross that had to do with white as privilege, caste.

PATRAKA: For a child, buying candy would be a way to move into the public arena. There's a powerful place in your performing, after you've been accused of stealing and have come home, where you're crying and pushing out the pain of that story . . . When do you move your body most in performance?

McCAULEY: The lighter moments are when I move most, when I'm trying to release and dance it out. The part that you mention about the pain and hurt over these incidents, I don't like to do. I have to go through those. I wish I were a dancer and could dance on the pain. But I feel more like a clown than a tragedian. Like that song I perform, "The Oppressor Tango", with the line "The oppressor is smarter than we thought", a funny song with a tragic element to it, which forms the moment of release after the gas station story. Dancing "The Oppressor Tango" means to look oppression in the face and dance. And doing that is movement: to face the oppressive elements, to understand and move through them *is* change. It's where an artist is useful because the audience can share that kind of release.

PATRAKA: Lisa Kennedy described [*Kennedy 1990*] the 1990 version of *Sally's Rape* performed at BACA [*New York*] as an exorcism. Does that really fit with what you were just describing?

McCAULEY: That's too easy. It's fine if it's an exorcism for an audience member, but I see it more as an opening for movement, as creating a kind of groundwork for dialog. The idea of releasing for its own sake means that you then don't move anywhere. I prefer when people say, "You made me think; I disagreed with you, but I was moved to think".

PATRAKA: Being moved to think is different from a traditional kind of catharsis where the experience is over.

McCAULEY: Yes. I think the mind and the body have to work together in order to create the movement of political theatre. When I say movement, I mean going from something blocked and unclear to something open and clearer so that we can move to change things. That's what my art is about. It's not political in the sense that right after the show we're going to march to the capital. But it is something for a regular audience to *use*, rather than simply having an evening in the theatre.

PATRAKA: Something for the audience to use to start thinking about particular issues that have somehow become unspeakable, invisible?

McCAULEY: Yes. To help them to think and speak about those things that are blocked. It's more for individuals within communities than for a mass movement kind of thing. People are going to react in different ways, but I hope they don't go backwards. I like the concept of speaking the unspeakable.

PATRAKA: I write about the Holocaust, and sometimes I write about sexual abuse to women and children, and I always have a problem with storing that content on my body. There's a disco and a blues club in Toledo and I do go and dance, but it's difficult to get it off once you've moved into the weight of that kind of pain.

McCAULEY: That's part of what I'm addressing, the idea that the oppression stays on you unless you dialog about it. Dancing is, of course, a way to speak, but not if there's no dialog, not if nothing comes back. I could go on just rapping and singing by myself in a show, but I try to open it so that the audience is involved if by no more than eating with me or, as in *Sally's Rape* [*1994*], by giving them moments to talk. I know it's very controlled, but it still allows me to create an event for the audience to come into around this oppression. I also want them to identify with me. I don't want to scream and yell at the oppressor. I consider the audience as with me, I'm not against the audience, so "they" are always those who are not in the room. Even if they are in the room, I want them for the moment to identify with me. One of the good jokes about *Sally's Rape* is that Jeannie Hutchins and I had a long talk about whether or not she was playing "the stupid white girl". And it's not that, it's the two of us enjoying the dialog about my stuff. But it's not one of those equal-time things, not like "this is about the white view and the black view", but that we're joined in it being my view, my personal view, so it's not even all black people.

PATRAKA: And part of what *Sally's Rape* is about is making people in the audience who are carrying that history – who don't feel like they are – making them aware of what they are carrying with them.

McCAULEY: I'm carrying shame, and many others are carrying guilt. And those two are distortions of information and of the material that we are living with. When the material of our past turns into shame and guilt, we stop talking about it, and it gets bigger and bigger and more distorted.

PATRAKA: And one of the things you say is that guilt is really a covering emotion for pain.

McCAULEY: And shame is a real feeling but it's often mixed up with blame. It's like any rape victim who walks around feeling like she's at fault and is therefore ashamed.

PATRAKA: There seems to me to be two kinds of invisibility. There's white people not seeing black people, making them invisible, but there's also the room of white men who are invisible to themselves because they are the norm. So part of the power of whiteness is its invisibility.

McCAULEY: You know, there have always been more nonwhite people in the world. Except that now this fact is more visible because we are smarter about the demographics. And that brings up the question, what are *we* going to do about it? One thing I like about Julie Dash's film *Daughters of the Dust* [*1991*], is that she tells a story and we're all in it, all have our parts in it and can therefore see ourselves. When the story is told this way, the blame and guilt and responsibility are all part of it. Otherwise, if we've behaved as separate parts disconnected from each other, we don't get the connections between us that lead to the ability to change things that aren't working.

PATRAKA: I recently saw an autobiographical and political performance piece and there was almost a kind of nostalgia because of the absence of references to contemporary events, something beautiful in the piece that almost closed it off. In your pieces you have a number of key, what I might call "signature stories", that belong to your life and history, and that you move around, recycle, from one piece to another. But the larger context isn't the narrative of that personal history, it is the political perspective that you have on that personal history, on events that are happening in the past and events that are shaped by them now. It's your vision, and the stories are part of it, but the stories aren't the narrative that you're creating. Does that make sense?

McCAULEY: Put that in the interview. Because people are always asking me about stories, and I say I'm not a storyteller, although I understand the worth of stories. But I'm not interested in telling the old stories. I think the worth of them is pleasure, nostalgia, and connection and those are good things. Again, what I liked about Julie Dash's work was that it was not a period piece: it was set at a time, used a time and gave us information about that time. History of the past is simply folklore. History has to be connected to the realities of the present.

PATRAKA: I'm reminded of a question that runs insistently through so much of your work, "Is we free yet?", and how you push audiences to think about it in terms of understanding its implications in 1992.

McCAULEY: Yes. And if I do any of this work again, I want to find a way to move the audience to have to say, "Is we free? Massa, is we free?"

PATRAKA: And one of the things that your work makes clear continually is that history is a text that changes all the time, that you're the interpreter of it, and that you're arranging it in a number of different ways from music, to slides, to voice, and to the multiple voices I especially love in *Indian Blood* [*1987*], where you have a number of different personae on video. We need to emphasize that difference in your work between the larger story you're telling and the individual very powerful stories, such as your father and the car and the gas station, and the time that your grandfather's car breaks down, and the Uncle Buck stories.

McCAULEY: I recently heard another black woman tell a gas station story, a travel story with her family. So these *are* signature stories, but they're also stories that have the universality of the father driving the car with the family in it. And it's also a black family story. One thing that most black people of that era recognize is that we had to drive at night, because if you drove in the day you were too visible and could get in trouble. There was something so dangerous about my father walking out there being bold in the daytime.

PATRAKA: I remember when I was a kid growing up in East New York, and we'd be driving through black neighborhoods, and my mother would say "Lock Your Doors". And that's real hard-wired, that "Lock Your Doors".

McCAULEY: It's that bit of message and its effect I try to get to when I'm working with or on white people in these community histories that I'm doing. To get you to find the racism in your lives. Most of the white people I'm working with are "the good guys". *The Buffalo Project* [*1990*] people wouldn't accept cross-burners in their families, except that when the stories came out, there were the little things that resonate in your psyche, like "Lock your doors from the horde, from the danger".

PATRAKA: And that fear is irrational, you can hardly control it.

McCAULEY: Now there is a psychological syndrome, fear of young black males. It's become a psychological syndrome disconnected from all the real reasons that anybody should be afraid of danger. Of course, you're stupid to get into a subway car late at night with a bunch of guys who look tough, but it is a syndrome when you see a bunch of young black males and go nuts. That's how those guys got shot by Bernard Goetz, which was why I put him in my performance as a metaphor. It's the white man, the Goetzian type – my father was what the Goetzian white man feared. It's a white syndrome to have that terror of black people that's out of control.

PATRAKA: I remember a moment in *Sally's Rape* where you say to your audience, "Don't worry, I'm in control". What are you telling them when you say that?

McCAULEY: I might have felt then as if they're going to think I'm crazy, going to lose control. I don't want them to think that. I want them to know that I'm under control. There's a perception that black people getting too close to rage is dangerous. It's one of the big fears in this country. I think people have been sold the metaphor of how bad black is and that's associated with all those other negative images that are unspeakably dangerous – you know, black is dark, black is violent, black is anger, black is our deepest, darkest . . . And I set myself up as the messenger who is black. I'm not neutral and therefore, at that moment, you saw me saying "Don't worry . . . ". Some people may find that patronizing, but I think many need it.

PATRAKA: Let me see if this works with what you're saying. When you perform the part about Sally being raped, there is tremendous anger and pain, and also, visually, the tremendous physical vulnerability of standing there naked on the auction block. Do you think your own physical vulnerability is part of the reason the audience can hear the anger without being so scared that they shut down?

McCAULEY: I did that because I had to. I got an impulse, I dreamed the taking off of the clothes and the feeling, "Do you see this now? Now can you see me, who I really am, and that this is essential to who I am?" I know that here is where the artist and the person meet. I know that it is a strong moment because I'm so vulnerable and in performance vulnerability is strength. And I wanted to find a way to make the point as strongly as possible that the real rape – and this is not to diminish anybody's individual experience of rape – was that we couldn't even begin to have a rape crisis center: "There is no rape crisis center on a plantation". That kind of rape changed who we were as a people and that was not our choice. We didn't choose to make ourselves as a result of that rape, we had to improvise ourselves.

PATRAKA: I was glad to have the opportunity to see the improvised beginnings of the current piece, *Persimmon Peel* [*1992*], in the 1990 tape of Laurie Carlos and you performing at La Mama. The special rapport and trust between you is both physical and in the improvised dialog. In a sense you and Laurie are not only performing the "Star Spangled Banner" and trying to reconceive it, to invent new words for new concepts, you are also performing your friendship and intimacy with each other. Is it just the shape of *Teenytown* [*1988*][2] and its different purpose that makes that rapport less palpable?

McCAULEY: Yes, you are comparing two different things. The dialog among the three of us, Jessica Hagedorn, Laurie Carlos, and me, can have the same flavor. What you didn't see is the rapport amongst us performed in other contexts. *Teenytown* was our content piece, *the* show with all the elements in it, and we did it as a theatrical piece, so there was very little organized improvisation in it. In a more recent work called *The Food Show* [*1992*], our dialog has that same kind of improvisatory flavor. It's because we know who we are individually that we can have that kind of play between us.

PATRAKA: So it has to do with the quality of an improvised piece as compared to the quality of a piece that's deliberately planned and episodic, made out of various individual pieces you've written and then worked into a structure containing arias, duets, trios?

McCAULEY: Right. *Teenytown* was more structured than any of our other performances together.

PATRAKA: Robert Hurwitt labeled *Teenytown* "in-your-face comedy".[3] What is in our faces in *Teenytown*?

McCAULEY: The subject matter. And the subject matter is that there are three different nonwhite women from three different places – one of us is from a colonized country and the other two from different parts of the USA, one South, one North – and the three of us are connected and we state that connection in performance. *Teenytown* is a microcosm of the connection that nonwhite people today have all over the world. While the separations amongst us are useful to the oppressor, the connections are those that *we* understand and make and can, in that sense, put up in your face.

PATRAKA: And there's a kind of cross-cultural dialog happening among you.

McCAULEY: We share similar experiences we had in different cultures of US racist oppression – me in the apartheid South, Laurie in the unofficial apartheid North, and Jessica in the colonized Philippines.

PATRAKA: Another element performed in *Teenytown* is how ugly racial, ethnic, and sexual stereotypes are still circulating despite our conscious rejection of them, that they've filtered into our unconscious – especially the ones in those cartoons you show.

McCAULEY: Yes. Stereotypes have a lot of information. They tell a lot about both the perpetrator and the object of the stereotype. For instance, the minstrel comedy shows how easy it is for all of us to laugh at stereotypes of nonwhite people, how easily disrespect becomes internalized.

PATRAKA: There's a part in *My Father and the Wars* [*1985*] I think, where your grandfather says that the men in the family respect themselves a lot and because of that they're going to end up on the chain-gang.

McCAULEY: He says, "That's why I'm taking you boys out of the South, because you're strong, mannish boys. Stay down here and you'll end up on the chain-gang". I'm sure that lesson struck deep in them.

PATRAKA: When we talked earlier I mentioned your generosity in the way that you do *Sally's Rape*, and you said, "I'm not being generous, that's a particular strategy". Maybe we need to mark this strategizing more for this interview.

McCAULEY: Well, in this work I continually explain what I'm doing as part of the form. And I'm not trying to push people away. It's the ritual aspect, the joining that's important. Even though I often exaggerate difference, I make it possible to explore what I'm doing with the audience's participation.

PATRAKA: In one performance tape of *Sally's Rape* you bring on the table/auction block again and Jeannie stands on it this time and you say to her, "Take off your clothes", and she can't do it, or she chooses not to. I've thought a lot about that: it suggests that you can't necessarily inhabit somebody else's history, or that you won't take the same kind of risks showing it if it's not your history. I try to imagine, if I were a performer, the circumstances under which I would take off my clothes. And the only circumstances I could come up with, where my body would be an instrument for history, is if I were to stand there as a person, as a woman, in the Holocaust. Tied to a situation I claim as my own history, I could do it and I would have to do it.

McCAULEY: That's it. She didn't have to do it. As a performer she could have chosen to do it. Or I could have asked her to do it as the director–creator of the piece, and she would have done it. But we decided in dialog with some other women artists that it would be stronger to show that she didn't have to do it. I think the point reads better that way.

PATRAKA: She also tells the audience, before you get up there, "Come on, you have to help her" by chanting "Bid 'em in" while you're on the auction block. Does the helping mean participating and so acknowledging complicity or connection to these events?

McCAULEY: It means sharing the ritual. I'm not on exhibition, I'm doing it as part of a ritual and so it's like helping the drummer by dancing. Jeannie is the interlocutor at that moment, so it's up to her to get the people to participate.

PATRAKA: It's a very different kind of collision, having her in front of you leading the audience with you up there, than the first time I saw the piece, at our Women and Theatre Program conference [*1989, New York University*], where there is no Jeannie figure yet.

McCAULEY: That was really hard because I was alone. Dialog is always better. When I'm touring by myself and do excerpts from *My Father and the Wars*, I make sure I am in dialog with the audience somehow, at least a kind of social dialog. And I always have food, use it in *My Father and the Wars* when I'm traveling alone as a way to connect with the audience, so I don't feel so alone up there. But part of it is also that I get hungry during a show, and want to eat, and we were taught that you can't eat in front of anybody without offering.

PATRAKA: When you talk about private schools for black children in *Sally's Rape*, you make very clear that those schools were about reading and writing and knowledge, but that you also learned to walk, keeping your hips in, being slightly provocative. Would you want to change the part of it that relates to how women should behave?

McCAULEY: I have a line in *Sally's Rape* that says, "Sometimes I think we did it for the sake of itself alone". That's about upward mobility, but it's also about survival. This piece is about class, but more about the complicated issue of survival for black people and how it relates to class. I mean, you'd get knocked upside the head if you said or did the wrong thing, because it could be misinterpreted, and then the whole family would be in trouble. That's an irrational, though rational, fear that black people in the South . . . if you looked wrong, had the wrong expression on your face . . .

PATRAKA: It reminds me of how abused children become careful readers of people, responsive to the slightest shift in their behavior and mood, all of which are actually unpredictable. And you're suggesting that the situation of racism is full of unpredictable violence, and one has to make up a code of behavior, of having papers, of giving the right signals to ward off the danger when ultimately . . .

McCAULEY: . . . there's nothing you can do.

PATRAKA: And when your father responds in the gas station, it's a kind of performance he does based on his personal power that makes the other person participate in a kind of negotiation between them.

McCAULEY: *My Father and the Wars* and *Indian Blood* are about men from a special point of view. I mean, it's from the daughter's perspective. I have no large analysis of what it must feel like for African-American men to be in struggle all day, every day. But I imagine it's pretty overwhelming, which is why feminism is different for us. In the piece I say, "I know he fought their wars. And they defined manhood for him. And don't anybody tell me you know what it is. I know men tend to go in circles and women can think straight ahead, but I will not let my arrogance about blood and the moon obscure my perceptions of the government".

PATRAKA: C. Carr wrote that *My Father and the Wars* testifies to the everyday wars that don't make the evening news.[4] What are some of the wars that you include in this piece?

McCAULEY: The survival from moment to moment of the men. The man who is trying to be a man, whatever the value of that is, whatever the value of a man being able to take care of and protect his family. Whatever its value, it becomes a life-and-death struggle every day that is particular to black men. That's what I saw with my father. He could have been killed at the gas station, all that guy had to do was pick up a phone and signal to somebody. It was literally the strength of my father's bearing that made it come out like that. And my father had trouble all over the place in terms of his inability to maintain his strength and power as time went on.

PATRAKA: In *Indian Blood* and *My Father and the Wars*, you talk about the appeal for black men of the visible symbols of authority, such as the uniform. Also, you talk about their intense patriotism, partly simply as a commitment to the country, but partly as a kind of strategy to create racism as un-American.

McCAULEY: Yes, and for my father and grandfather to use patriotism for survival is understandable. I also want to show that it is *my* story that puts it in perspective. Someone challenged me for telling my grandfather's story through my own contradictions, and I thought, "He doesn't have a story, *I* have a story". And so at the end of the piece I say, "Somebody said, is it fair to stir your fathers in their graves?" – and I say, "I'm not sure they are resting there", because I think it's up to me to state the contradictions. They were such patriots they couldn't deal with contradictions about, for example, hurting other people of color.

PATRAKA: One of the most powerful lines in *Indian Blood* is "We are exiles and yet we are at home". Is that one of the "resolvable contradictions" you mention in *Teenytown*?

McCAULEY: It's who we are. I mean some people call it schizophrenia or ambivalence, but I think that our ability to live with the history, with both the reality of being in exile and being home, is what makes us strong.

PATRAKA: Africans are the people who didn't immigrate voluntarily, who were dragged to this country and died in the process. What Julie Dash does in *Daughters of the Dust* is reconfigure black people on that island as immigrants coming voluntarily to America. At the same time she includes much on the history of slavery right beside this voluntary journey.

McCAULEY: That's why they had that long leaving. "You can't go nowhere unless you know who you are, girl" – that's what they would tell me. There's the line I have in *Teenytown*, "You tell what we know down here, girl. If you got to go, girl, you tell what we know down here, girl". That means carry it in you. Or, as I say in *Sally's Rape*, "These young ones with the alligators act like they weren't born with no memory". To deny your history is to disconnect yourself from the planet.

PATRAKA: What does it mean to be a witness to that history, because I think that's one of the things that you're performing?

McCAULEY: I'm being a witness by choosing to remember. What's important about the witnessing is that the audience is doing it with

Plate 19: In *Indian Blood* at The Kitchen, 1987, Robbie McCauley speaks about her obsession with connecting with her ancestors, even if it means telling the "untellable stories." Photo by Vivian Selbo.

me. One of the problems with modern industrial society is the disconnection from that constant witnessing of the past, of where we came from, of being with the stories, and so that's my work.

PATRAKA: And what the audience is witnessing is not simply "your history", it's not about I-came-to-a-performance-to-watch-black-people's-history, but it's their history as well.

McCAULEY: Yes, and it's not folklore, it's not something they're outside of.

PATRAKA: Therefore the performance is a ritual?

McCAULEY: Yes, because it's not like "us and them" or "me and them". I invite them to participate and the ritual happens differently each time. Your part in it may be to listen, but that is certainly a participatory listening that I'm asking you to do because you're in it.

"TELLING IT" AND "GIVING RANGE TO THE TELLER"
Performance Strategies

PATRAKA: When you talk about witnessing, one of the things that interests me is the shift in how video is used from *My Father and the Wars* to *Indian Blood*. In *My Father and the Wars*, when you're speaking on one of the videos, the "live" you, may watch it in silence or may speak in unison [with] what's on the tape. In *Indian Blood*, you made a decision to shape very definite personae, such as the school teacher, who are clearly different personae from the live one performing onstage. Does this create a kind of multiplicity of witnesses?

McCAULEY: Yes, and it also gives more range to the teller. Part of it is a range of characters and emotions, theatrical elements. But the visual part has to do with the television set as comforting to an audience these days. One person talking, going on and on, can be too much or just tiresome, so in *Indian Blood* the use of various elements helps give variety and texture.

[. . .]

PATRAKA: One of the things that you told me was that *Nicaragua in Perspective* served as a transition from the Sedition Ensemble pieces to what you call your "personal biography work". What made you decide to concentrate on personal biography work?

McCAULEY: Well, I think the story gets told better. I was also moved from my ancestors to do that. I was dogging the government so much in my work that I heard my father tell me to tell it. "Well tell it", he said in a dream. And I didn't know what he was talking about until I just started writing. *My Father and the Wars* came out of that message. I do have dreams where my ancestors talk to me. I don't even understand it, but I do accept it, because it happens, but I have no rational discourse about it.

PATRAKA: And part of that is to tell the unofficial history and make it a history that is shared among people.

McCAULEY: When my father said "tell it", it was the part of him that I connected to as a child, the part that was special between me and him, where he knew that I had something to say to the world. He used to tell me to write down things so I wouldn't forget them. So I started with notebooks. He was always telling me how to act, was very authoritative in that way, but he and I used to sit up late at night and he would drink his bourbon and I would drink cocoa and eat cheese and sardines and he would always end up telling me, "Well just tell it; if that's what you think, just tell it". And I never remembered that until his voice came to me in the dream and said "Tell it". And I'd been just running around, sprouting all this anti-imperialist text like what was coming out in the Sedition Ensemble work. But my own voice wasn't there, my own story wasn't there. As a performer, I always knew the power of that voice, I just didn't know how to get there and when my father spoke to me, suddenly the connections came. The first image was him dressed as a soldier or sailor: "Seems like my father was always in somebody's army, navy, air force, national guard".

PATRAKA: So telling your story is partly telling his story. You're telling a story of race and gender about the men in your family in these pieces. You say in one of these pieces, in response to people who have told you your rage is at mothers, "No, my rage is at the government".

McCAULEY: I tend not to identify with my mother in my work. I tend to identify with my father and see my mother as a co-conspirator with authoritarian values. But I know better now. And that's what I mean by "My rage is at the government", not at my mother. My mother understood survival.

PATRAKA: And like many women who feel that they don't have very much power, she was often conservative.

McCAULEY: Of course she ends up the most radical as time goes on. I think for women, the survival of their children and themselves is number one. And they're not dumb about their compromising choices for survival. Men can miss a lot of things, because they can leave. Once they get the kids out of the way, if they live long enough, women tend to get more and more radical.

PATRAKA: One of the things Lucy Lippard quotes you as saying, in her book *Mixed Blessings: New Art in a Multicultural America*, is that "music is the art that has *functioned* for my culture. The music comes out of the pain of being chained to the ship. Amiri Baraka's play *Slave Ship* is the image of everything about our lives in the US symbolized on that ship. Pain, being bound. The one thing that wasn't physically bound was the voice. The scream turned into music. Although I'm not trained as a musician, blues and jazz inform all of my work. The idea that one can hurt and turn it into something beautiful is the way I use the pain".[5] And so, music is partly about pain, music is about voice.

McCAULEY: Not only the music, but most of the talking in my pieces is orchestrated. This comes out of a long tradition of black performance culture. During the 1960s black poetry – which I ought to name as an influence on my work – was directly connected to jazz. You also see it in the old minstrels, which is what *Teenytown* is based on. There's certain drum beats, certain kinds of takes or approaches, and certain kinds of transitional rhythms that come from the old black musical minstrel shows. My mother talked about the black medicine shows that came to towns in the South. It had a horn and a dressed-up woman and it came out to sell snake oil. She started off by saying, "Some folks try to act like they don't remember the medicine show".

"BURNING LIBRARIES" AND "UP-SOUTH"
Memory and Geography

PATRAKA: Let's talk about people in their forties or so. One of the things that's not true for generations after us is we knew, intimately, lots of people the bulk of whose history was in the first part of the century.

McCAULEY: It's a real difference. And it's a desperate call for those of us who remember. People in Mississippi who were in my mother's generation, are now old people. And they say "the libraries are burning down" – that's what they call themselves – "so you better get it because the libraries are burning down". Their line is "come and talk to us, because we're getting out of here". And part of my work is performing those libraries.

PATRAKA: What does it mean when you label your performance "obsessing in public?"

McCAULEY: My obsession is with connection and continuity. "The confessions are a mourning for the lost connections", the telling of the untellable stories. For instance, my grandfather being up there at the border, standing watch, having to shoot Indians who come across from Canada, was a devastating image to me, and I would rather not know it. But if I connect with my ancestors, I have to tell it.

PATRAKA: Somebody described the purpose of *Indian Blood* as an act of atonement, is that accurate?

MCCAULEY: (*laughter*) You can't escape religion in all this. Atonement, though, sounds like a finish, like you have confessed and been forgiven. My work is more an opening than a closing, more like "if I show you mine, then you can show me yours", and we can move together with our imperfections, with our wounds. In the US we often use folklore, patriotism, and mythology to try to make us all "all right", but art gives us the right to make the wounds part of the beauty.

PATRAKA: And those contradictions are painful.

MCCAULEY: Yes.

PATRAKA: People live with them. For me, being a Holocaust scholar, being Jewish, having a certain kind of politics, means my feelings about Israel are going to be a contradiction, incredibly ambivalent, and not politically correct.

MCCAULEY: Alisa Solomon said that she was reminded by *Indian Blood* of the Israelis.[6] And there is a connection because we are survivors. I think that the survivors of the Holocaust have unspeakable stories about it, and those are the kinds of things I wish could come up. In terms of my own work, I call it admitting things that we can choose to tell or not about ourselves. For instance, we say, "Black people are not racists", and it's according to how you define the word. Since white supremacy has become a more accurate term for systematic racism, I prefer it. But I wonder, even in the old definition of racism, if my grandfather was not a racist, because he had the power at that border in his hands.

PATRAKA: Brecht said a guinea-pig in a laboratory does not learn, through being experimented on, to become a doctor. Oppression is a stain, it does things to you, and it doesn't necessarily make you good or noble.

MCCAULEY: There is something both cynical and genocidal about not having good education for black people, because the more we know, the more able we are to survive what's being put on us. I think *we* need to deal with the fact that we sold slaves. The question of who bought them we deal with very well. It helps to have dialog about these things. To add to Brecht, to be enslaved and then to be free and watch each other stumble around, that's not enough. We can continue to survive by watching, learning, improvising and making it work. That is what I take from my culture and put into performance art.

PATRAKA: How do you position people to read the body in your performances in a different way than they read it in the everyday?

McCAULEY: One thing is for them to see me entering and exiting. I mark this with theatrical strategies that employ changes of lights, media, rhythms of speech and movement, and various kinds of music. I want the audience to see whoever I am as the instrument, I want them to see me as the instrument, and that it's a moment in theatre, that's all it is.

PATRAKA: A sense of entrance and exit also operates thematically in your work: on the road, in the car, going to the candy store – shifting spaces is especially dangerous. Shifting into any kind of unknown territory, especially if it's white, is about potential danger.

McCAULEY: I think it's true for us all, but the danger of entering a strange space is intensified because of racism, where you enter a space wherein you must have the right bearing or you die.

PATRAKA: I've noticed you play with notions of geography in performance and how the context for this is the history of racism. Two examples I think of right away are first, the terror of being sold off "way down further South", which you image as a deadly and terrifying journey. But second, there's the other thing you say, "There is no North. North is a state of mind, everything is up-South". So there's down-South and up-South.

McCAULEY: The "so further South" is a contextual image. When I did my piece in Mississippi, I started with "in Georgia, they used to say Mississippi, like something was worse than Georgia". For me and others, the textures are clear in terms of place. Up North during slavery time was free, the up-South image instead of North came later in our culture because we realized racist attitudes were deeply embedded in both places. There's also the geography of the ocean that reflects its history. In *Teenytown*, I have that piece called "Sharks". I actually heard the story that "there is a place in the mid-Atlantic where the sharks still go, still remember the blood where thousands of us were thrown overboard mid passage". And that image helped me understand my overwhelming feelings of fear about the water, to be able to approach the water, because the spirits are there, present and clear.

[. . .]

"THE STRUGGLE AS THE AESTHETIC"
Defining the Work

PATRAKA: Let me suggest a way of grouping your work into four categories and see how you like it. I'd put the early work, done with Sedition and so on, and also *Nicaragua*, in one group; I'd put *Sally's Rape, Indian Blood*, and *My Father and the Wars* together as a continuing serial performance of family stories; I'd put the collaborations with Thought Music in another and think of them as a kind of continuing performance; and another group would be the site-specific projects that involve community interviews and shaping a piece in response to them. Does that make sense?

McCAULEY: Sure. Everything that's happened in the last almost 15 years has been the cycle that you're talking about: from Sedition through to the community work, the issues are the same: bearing witness to racism, really, that's what I do.

PATRAKA: Let's focus on some of your earliest theatre experience. Which lady did you play in *For Colored Girls . . . [by Ntozake Shange]*?

McCAULEY I played them all. I ended up playing the Lady in Red, but I went on as the understudy on Broadway for all of them. And the Adrienne Kennedy work was very important. I did *A Movie Star Has*

Plate 20: In a part of *My Father and the Wars* performed at The Kitchen in 1987, McCauley speaks about the everyday life-and-death struggle that is particular to black men. Photo by Marlis Momber.

to Star in Black and White at the Public. The first professional piece of theatre I did was *Cities in Bezique*. So now when I criticize the lack of vision in theatre, I still want to acknowledge that I got nurtured by the good stuff.

PATRAKA: You've acted the role of Joan Little in Ed Bullins' *Joanne!* and been in his play *The Taking of Miss Janie*. You've been in Joseph Chaikin's *The Winter Project* and a production of Shakespeare's *Coriolanus* at the Public Theatre. The list could go on. How is your acting experience related to your performance work?

McCAULEY: The acting roles and what they were connected to began to open up voices inside me, especially the roles of rebel, intellectual, angry black woman, all of that. The actor has to be connected to the subtext, and the subtext started to emerge, and that stimulated the emergence of my writing. So, my work comes directly from acting in that way.

Back to categories for a moment. They do give some sense of how to look at my work but I'd also like to talk about context itself as category. My work is the work of an actor, whatever I'm doing is connected to playing the actor's thoughts. There are descriptions of the craft of African-American acting. The National Black Theatre, I think, came up with certain personae or attitudes that are affecting our work. There is the militant, the radical, and the Negro or assimilator. What I try to do in my work is to break open even those categories, and out of that comes text and the form of the work. What I'm interested in comes through a system of work that is based in African-American traditions – I don't mean I've learned them systematically – but this is what I call on in myself. The contemporary avant-garde art world has been part of that, but I've found that it calls on the same kinds of things that I call on. For example, there is no collage art without an understanding of jazz, admitted or not.

So when I talk about my work, I like to talk about the sources that are African-American, so that it's clear. . . . I'm glad to hear that you teach *Slave Ship* by Amiri Baraka because I think that it is the main source in black culture for all that I'm talking about. His work is based in the idea that the aesthetic *is* the activism itself, the involvement in the struggle. And his work is an ongoing, changing, inspiring presence. When the struggle is the aesthetic, then criticizing particular pieces of work becomes irrelevant. I'm trying to say this simply: I am not struggling to get a piece done, I am struggling to help get us through to a more equitable society.

PATRAKA: And one of the reasons you call your performances "works in progress" is because you are constantly shifting the work in response to audiences?

McCAULEY: Yes, but this is also a play on that word progress. Because it

also means a work in *progress*, in people moving forward. So the working in progress is also the labor of struggle that shapes the performance.

PATRAKA: I think those groups I came up with were from the point of view of you as a writer: particular kinds of collaboration with jazz musician and writer Ed Montgomery; pieces that were solely written by you; pieces that were conceived in a particular community to be shaped by you; and collaborations with other women of color.

McCAULEY: Just bringing up how to talk about the work is important, because *we* must define our work. Otherwise people will do it for us. Suddenly we start playing out these definitions rather than going back to our own sources. In one way, the point of the kind of work we do is understanding how *we* define it. It's something that has to be understood from a non-white supremacist perspective – that our work is complicated and broad, that it has specific sources and is universal.

PATRAKA: And you're saying that while you do work on an avant-garde performance circuit, that's not what you want to define you. Unlike a postmodern conception, you see yourself as working from a black tradition that you acknowledge and that isn't separated off between modern and post-, but that you are fracturing and expanding in certain ways.

McCAULEY: In my view tradition and ritual are misunderstood. Tradition tends to be thought of as something "back there" that is romantic and has little to do with contemporary politics, and ritual is conceived as closed off and exactly repeatable. Yet in the way I understand it, the way people I work with and the black folks I admire understand it, tradition and ritual are expanding constantly. That's why I think the black classical music and/or jazz metaphor is the right one for black art.

PATRAKA: You've performed at La Mama, at The Kitchen, at Franklin Furnace, at The Painted Bride, at many major performance venues. How did you get there?

McCAULEY: Well, the performance art world in New York had been closed to people of color except for tokens. When I got in, I was surprised to find so few of us there, so what I like that has happened once one of us does perform is that we open the doors for more of us. We turn each other on, we write a grant [*together*]. The whole grant world was unconsciously white, though they wanted to do the right thing. But in the performance world they thought they *were* doing the right thing, and they suddenly looked around and went, "Oh! Look at us!" So, how did I get there? Lucy Lippard.

PATRAKA: She is an amazing figure, isn't she?

McCAULEY: Who has done a great deal in terms of making our work known on a broader scale. Lucy Lippard, who I didn't know at the time, was one of only two people in the audience with three of us onstage deciding to do the show anyway. It was the first time we did a collage of elements from *My Father and the Wars* and *Indian Blood*. We did the whole thing – me, Ed Montgomery, and Bob Carroll (who died a few years ago, and was an important source for me in performance). In fact there were four of us, because I had my daughter Jessie in my arms, onstage with me. It was 1981 because Jessie was just born, and she was great, she just went on through it. And Lucy asked me if I'd heard of Franklin Furnace. And I hadn't. And she told me how to write a grant [*application*] for them, and I did, and that's the first place I did *My Father and the Wars*.

PATRAKA: The story has a certain power to it about what people can do when they take responsibility. In "Variations On Negation and the Heresy of Black Feminist Creativity", Michele Wallace writes that "in more politically articulate fields, such as film, theatre and TV news commentary, black feminist creativity is routinely gagged and 'disappeared.' " [7] How do you combat this?

McCAULEY: You keep doing the work. I mean, like my story about Lucy, we could have gone home that night instead of performing. Use as much energy as you can to keep going as long as you can. You can use a little bit of that old work-ethic stuff but *for yourself*. And what we do as black women is to support each other. I have nurturance from women, especially black women. We call on each other. We don't disappear from each other, we can not disappear to each other. When you feel like you're being disappeared, the thing is not to dwell on it. What you must dwell on is keeping your nurturance, your sources. You die out there by yourself.

PATRAKA: I'm interested in those moments of refuge in *Indian Blood* and *My Father and the Wars* where you perform the ritual of going to the garden. That's interesting in the context of Alice Walker's essay, "In Search of Our Mothers' Gardens", because although in some ways in your work you don't spend much time in your mother's garden, you are saying that in the present other black women are that kind of source of creativity, a kind of contemporary garden.

McCAULEY: That garden is not necessarily a garden of plants. For me that garden is my aloneness, and it's very private, and always been an important place for me. I mean I make it up. I think it came from a story of my mother's though. My mother didn't want to stay in Columbus, in Georgia, with her sisters, she wanted to get away. I was the one who got away from my own family, while my mother became a very traditional wife. But she told me that when she was a little girl she went to visit an aunt in Macon, Georgia, who the family wasn't

Plate 21: Slide projections are often used as backdrops in McCauley's productions. Pictured is McCauley in a section of *My Father and the Wars* performed at The Kitchen in 1987. Photo by Marlis Momber.

even that close to. But every once in a while the children could just go off for a visit because the house was full of kids, and she volunteered to go. And the way she told it was in a voice of wonder and delight, "And she had a garden, and there were little rocks in the garden, and I just played all day in that garden by myself". And when my mother told me that story I realized that it was a part of me that was connected to my mother, though as her daughter it was always a problem for me because she had such a privacy about her. But when she told me that story I realized that she and I both had that same need for privacy.

"WRITING ON MY FEET"
Performing the Body, Constructing the Audience

PATRAKA: How do you go about writing one of your performance pieces?

McCAULEY: What I want to write about comes first. I write on my feet. I dance and move around, I sit down and I talk to myself, do scenes. I do it until I feel like writing. I become the audience, I become the story, I ask myself what happens next? That opens up a process. My pieces often come out of mournings I have within me and I know for a long time I'm going to write about them.

PATRAKA: What you're telling me especially makes sense for a performance artist: first, that the writing comes out of experiences that are inscribed in your body, through your own past. And second that you're moving through them physically, and making performance through that moving. So there isn't a space where you have a script, words, separate from your body: the body and the words you perform come together.

McCAULEY: Yes. And that is the reason I have a hard time talking about it; I want it to sound rational because it is perfectly rational. And when I do work in other communities, for me even the taped interviews have a physicality to them. And some of my dialogs are snips of conversation, since so much of my writing is based in live sources. I think most writers have these thoughts that come through the body.

PATRAKA: Part of what you've just described are pieces that follow your own personal history. What comes out of the body is only viewed as irrational when you don't consider the social construction of the body and the way in which the body is mapped by history.

McCAULEY: It's getting harder for me to keep the memories of the process of how a piece came to me in my body. I used to be able to do that really easily, work out of it in performance, but everything is getting slower with age. So I'm trying to find other ways of writing than that process, while keeping that source.

PATRAKA: I'm thinking about the topic of nudity in performance and women. Karen Finley's nudity has become a kind of signature, and one expects her to be nude at some point in her work. One does not expect that in yours; there is only one piece in which you disrobe. One woman I talked with after seeing Finley's *We Keep Our Victims Ready* [*1992*] in Ann Arbor was unhappy about Finley's nudity, because she hated to see a woman's body displayed in front of men and wanted an all-female audience instead. I tried to think about that, and about the way in which a performer's body is her instrument in a way that it isn't, for example, when an actress is nude as part of someone else's script. The control is yours when you're performing as Robbie McCauley and not as an actress. Even if you are enacting objectification, that's precisely the point, and the power of that body belongs to you when you enact it. Because saying the female body can never be shown is almost acceding to a sense of powerlessness. There's a kind of ownership of that body in performance that's made very clear in your work.

McCAULEY: Right. And Karen Finley is on the list of people who have affected my work – for her boldness, which is one way we make our point. The idea for *Sally's Rape* came years ago, but I'm not sure I would have been able to do it without Karen opening up that area to make women comfortable with using our bodies for our own point within our own context. She's bold, she's satirical, and she's made an opening for me to step in there and do that strong moment in *Sally's Rape*.

PATRAKA: I want to congratulate you on winning the Obie in 1992 for the best new American play for *Sally's Rape*.

McCAULEY: It was especially important and exciting that the award was for being a writer. In a sense, I still feel like "a performer on paper". But it's great to have that recognition from people that my work is a play or has the same stature as one.

PATRAKA: There are moments when your voice is soft, and moments when it's loud and intense. When do you raise your voice in performance?

McCAULEY: It has to do with rage. In *Sally's Rape* I try to pull my voice back in, I personalize that moment. It is about the rage that I have embraced, that is necessary, that is healing, and I release it out of a personal need to do so, but I don't want it to push people away, so I find out in the process of making a performance where it comes, and then I plan the places for its release.

PATRAKA: When I saw Finley's *We Keep Our Victims Ready*, people almost felt Finley wasn't angry enough and they were hostile to the idea that she was attempting to create community with her audience. It's as if we have a kind of resistance to the 1960s, whether we lived through them or not, that translates into a kind of resentment that someone may want to create community.

McCAULEY: What you just described is part of our conditioning to resist communion. What I've been trying to do is pay attention to that resistance, to feel audiences pushing themselves away and find ways to connect. What some performers are doing when they attack the audience is keeping the audience alienated, which isn't my major strategy. And some people don't want to be brought in. It's like going to church, when you come for one thing and get another. And if you're not open to it, you resist it. I mean, the relationship between theatre and the church is direct in terms of community. You come and engage in a ritual and either it's very stoic and rigid, or it's very inclusive, and you either give yourself to the ritual or not.

PATRAKA: I'm always curious about the kind of audience who prides itself on a certain knowledgeability and resistance to being moved. You know, they understand the "trick" of it, they understand the strategies of it, almost past the point where it can be effective.

McCAULEY: For those reasons, I think the most challenging audiences are in New York. And yet I learn from that to try to get through to them and learn from their looking for the seduction, looking for those things that I'm using to involve them. To me that's a challenge, not an insoluble problem.

PATRAKA: Would you like to have the opportunity to perform for more black audiences?

McCAULEY: The best performance of *Sally's Rape* Jeannie and I did was at Crossroads Theater, a black theatre in New Jersey. The audience really enacted the role of group number three, whose function was to comment. They also did the slave ritual, the auction block ritual, with relish. They knew what playing an auctioneer meant. This was part of the Crossroads Genesis project, and at the panel afterward we were told, "Thank you for bringing us into the dialog, we really appreciated it". That certainly disproved the idea that black audiences don't want performance, are not ready for it, want something safe and familiar. The problem is that the business of theatre, *because* it is business, is conservative. And so black theatres have had to be conservative. Now black performers are beginning to be more innovative in performance, such as at Crossroads where people like Sydné Mahone, who does so many wonderful things there, is responding to this fact. Black theatres need to keep doing that.

THE MISSISSIPPI PROJECT
Community Collaborations

PATRAKA: Tell me about the current projects in Mississippi.

McCAULEY: *The Mississippi Project* [1992] is part of a three-project series being produced by the Arts Company, by Marie Cieri. What I'm doing in Mississippi is part of a larger project of interviewing people in various places about historical events related to civil rights. The first part, in Mississippi, is mainly about voting rights. The second part takes place in Boston and will be about the 1970s busing in Boston, and the third project will be about police brutality. We're considering Watts, Los Angeles, and Chicago as the city.

Part of *The Mississippi Project* is called *Mississippi Freedom*, named for the Mississippi Freedom Democratic party that Fanny Lou Hamer was connected to. I knew Fanny Lou Hamer's story because at the time it was unfolding I watched it with my head pasted to the TV. I wanted to explore the voting rights struggle and the personal stories about it, and, among the actors, dialog about the voting rights struggle now. The process was the same as *The Buffalo Project*; I found a good group of actors in Jackson, Mississippi, both black and white, who traveled throughout the state, collecting the witnesses and their texts. There's a theatre company in Mississippi called Potpourri, led by a woman named Sameerah Muhammad. She was instrumental in helping me find the actors.

The other project was done at the Rural Organizing and Cultural Center in Lexington, Mississippi. I taught and directed teenagers in a storytelling piece that came out of the stories on Civil Rights they had already collected. In the process of making it, adults came and sat in – the aim was to make it an intergenerational story group. The teenagers performed it at Tougaloo College and a busload of community people came to see it. What we did was to revitalize the telling aspect of the culture, and help make that happen again – not the telling of the old stories but the work with dialog about them in the present.

PATRAKA: I'm going to ask you a very unpleasant question, that I don't necessarily agree with, but I'll ask nonetheless. I heard someone saying that the audience for theatre and performance, especially political theatre, never really expands, and so what you are really doing . . .

McCAULEY: . . . is preaching to the converted. I think that criticism is a cop-out. First of all, how much do the converted know? And things resonate, ripple out. This is not to say that you do not work constantly for audience development; we need to grapple with finding ways to expand audiences. But we don't need to put that problem in the way of doing the work, making our work clear and beautiful for our audiences. The whole issue is just a block.

PATRAKA: Do you think that it's also a way of underestimating our own potential power and effect, the way the Right never underestimates it?

McCAULEY: That's what I mean. The oppressor is smarter than we think about our power. It's debilitating to have them with the power to develop audiences, and not us, but I think to understand our possibilities now is essential.

"LIVING IN AMERICA"
Final Questions

PATRAKA: Is there anything else that I haven't asked you that I should have? In this hour number six? (*laughter*)

McCAULEY: Oh, sure, there's four more hours. (*laughter*) Did I mention Marxism? Marxism informs my sense of history, which is probably the least original statement I could make. I worried about using it until I realized it was the rigidity in Marxism that always bothered me. Russia is, of course, a horrible example of communism – for me, one of the repeating images of Russia is of those *same men* you see in all of Western culture, that same bunch of big, well-endowed, powerful-looking white men. This was not the picture of communism I had imagined studying Marx and his explanation of history. I'm interested in the way that using Marxism explains materially why things have happened and in using it creatively.

PATRAKA: One thing you're trying to do, then, is portray a range of the factors that relate to oppression at once – class, gender, and race.

McCAULEY: Yes, and the specific ways that they're related. When we are not given the time and space in which to understand how these connect, and how it's possible to change, it's useful for the systematic oppressors. It's useful that we work too hard. A line in my song "Nuclear Meltdown" goes: "Living in America is so hard, you get so tired, it's too hard to change". And it's useful for them that we're fatalistic and stuck, for us to think "that's the way white people are, that's the way black people are, that's the way men and women are, you can't change it".

PATRAKA: So the dialogs you create demystify things. And show the relations and connections between them.

McCAULEY: Yes, that racism is not natural or innate, or genetic . . . . I'm thinking about race being at the bottom of it all. And that racism is also material. Even now, thinking about art, we feel that even if we are given the credit as sources, what happens to us materially? In the music world, it's admitted that the Beatles wouldn't be the Beatles without the blues singers who ended up with a few cents in their pockets. The admittance of that brings up some overwhelming changes that white people would have to go through in order to make things right.

PATRAKA: Instead, there are silences about situations that get worse and worse.

McCAULEY: And so we are in this spiral that is worsening. I think the feelings of our own past mistakes, past misunderstandings, are so scary that we keep the denial and reaction going on. My feeling is that denial is the worst response possible and that we have internalized it. Under that is the material reality, the question "How do we get out of here?" Instead of facing it, we get the idea of black people in particular as "the bad guy" in order to lock this denial (and us) up – that's what's going on in this country now.

PATRAKA: What do you mean "as the bad guy"?

McCAULEY: As the welfare mother, the young black male, the intellectual who keeps on speaking about this stuff, rather than just assimilate, who can then be dismissed.

PATRAKA: As opposed to say, the older woman who takes care of your house, and loves your children, and gives you her caring?

MCCAULEY: She's considered human. What I feel hopeful about in all of this is the ability to keep trying to understand it and work on it.

PATRAKA: If for some terrible reason, and I'm not even sure I want to pose this kind of question, you were to wink out tomorrow, what would you most want to be remembered for in terms of your performance work?

MCCAULEY: I can never answer that in the moment, it's too hard . . . . I want people to have their own memories, that's what I want. If I can inspire people to connect with and value, use their own memories, that would mean something important.

NOTES

1. I wish to thank Mary Callahan Boone, my research assistant, for her valuable help in preparing this interview. Her labor was funded by a Graduate Research Assistant Award from Bowling Green State University, 1992.
2. See McCauley, Carlos and Hagedorn 1990 for a printed text of *Teenytown*.
3. Hurwitt 1990.
4. Carr 1986.
5. Lippard 1990:90.
6. Solomon 1987:115.
7. Wallace 1989:69.

BIBLIOGRAPHY

Carr, C., "The Unofficial Story", *The Village Voice*, 18 November 1986:93.

Hurwitt, Robert, "*Teenytown*: In-your-face comedy", *San Francisco Examiner*, 12 October 1990.

Kennedy, Lisa, "Cameos", *The Village Voice*, 30 January 1990:100.

Lippard, Lucy R., *Mixed Blessings: New Art in a Multicultural America*, New York: Pantheon, 1990.

McCauley, Robbie, Laurie Carlos, and Jessica Hagedorn, *Teenytown*. In *Out From Under: Texts by Women Performance Artists*, edited by Lenora Champagne, 89–117. New York: Theatre Communications Group, 1990.

Solomon, Alisa, "True Confessions", *The Village Voice*, 8 December 1987:115.

Wallace, Michele, "Variations On Negation and the Heresy of Black Feminist Creativity", *Heresies* 6, no.4 (#24), 1989:69–75.

SALLY'S RAPE (1994)

Robbie McCauley

PLAYWRIGHT'S NOTE

I wrote *Sally's Rape* in 1989 out of certain personal, socio-economic, and historical issues that push at me. It is now commonly accepted that slavery in the United States was a great shame for all concerned. The deeply rooted presence of black women at the core of this shameful history resonates both consciously and unconsciously in the way some of us perceive ourselves and the way others perceive us still. A performance theatre piece consisting of dialogue with a white woman and people in the audience, the script was inspired by my effort to find a passageway in the performance through my often blind rage over these issues.

Performance artist Jeannie Hutchins collaborated with me on the improvisations in the piece as we played it throughout the country as a work in progress. I reworked the script, mainly concerned with creating a way to write – to weave in – the improvisational aspects for publication in Sydné Mahone's 1994 anthology, *Moon Marked & Touched by Sun: Plays by African-American Women* (New York: Theatre Communications Group).

Robbie McCauley
December 1997

PLAYERS

ROBBIE, the one who plays the people in her and who tells all she wants to tell. She is an actor who sings and dances. She is black.
JEANNIE, the one who plays the roles she's given and who sometimes erupts. She is a dancer who sings and acts. She is white.
AUDIENCE, those who are there, who witness and talk back.

A bench up right. A piano up left. A large, sturdy square table up center and two chairs. All are set at angles. Rocks are lying about the space. General lighting. Audience enters, sits.

Prologue
Talking About What It Is About

(*Robbie and Jeannie enter with cups of tea on saucers. They walk to a space down left in conversation between themselves, aware of Audience. Easy talk.*)

ROBBIE: Somebody said it was about cups.

JEANNIE: Somebody else said it was about language.

ROBBIE: What do you think it's about?

JEANNIE: Well, that one person said it was about you and me. And I know it's not about me, but it's about you and I'm in it.

ROBBIE: It's my story, and you're in it because I put you in it.

JEANNIE: Fair enough.

ROBBIE: It *is* about cups.

JEANNIE: It's about getting culture.

ROBBIE: Cup says culture.

JEANNIE: Comportment.

ROBBIE: Commonality. Well actually, where I come from, cups and saucers were like. . . . We had to learn about these things. I mean we went from jars to cups and saucers . . . nothing in between. I once went to a class in tea pouring. . . . It was Japanese, but it was about containment . . . proper . . . deportment.

JEANNIE: Doing the . . . proper . . .

ROBBIE AND JEANNIE: . . . right . . . thing.

ROBBIE: Like my Aunt Nell said: If you do the wrong thing, you could get your ass killed, so it was more like a matter of life and death.

JEANNIE: You know, we had cups and saucers. I even think we had six that matched. But mostly we used mugs.

ROBBIE: Mugs?

JEANNIE: Because they hold a little more, and they have a bigger bottom, so they don't tip. The only disadvantage of a mug is after you use a spoon you have to just kind of put it on the table, and it leaves a little mark.

ROBBIE: I think sometimes we did this for the sake of itself. Cups and saucers. Charm school. White gloves.

JEANNIE: But that's South, too. I mean, that's southern stuff. The one girl that was like that I knew . . . she had gone to charm school, she was being groomed to be a Southern Belle. She had monogrammed sweaters. She went to charm school one summer in junior high, and she learned to walk like this . . . (*does the walk*) with a book on her head. And we all tried.

ROBBIE: We didn't worry about books on our heads. We already had this *up* thing. I guess that was the African in us before I even knew it. But we (*walking, Jeannie following*) had to contain our hips. To keep tucked up. Slightly seductive but not too much . . . (*at the bench*) and when you sit . . . you know this part.

JEANNIE: Yeah, you touch the front of the seat with the back of the calf, and then you descend without bending at the waist.

(*They sit together; Jeannie crosses her legs*)

ROBBIE: Now you can – no! (*hits Jeannie's knee away*) Don't do that. (*Jeannie corrects*) *Now* you can drink your tea. (*they sip simultaneously*) My Aunt Nell would have *died* if she saw you –

JEANNIE: – cross my legs like that.

ROBBIE: That's it. Put your feet just so, or slightly cross at the ankle.

JEANNIE: Why was that?

1

Confessing About Family and Religion and Work in Progress

ROBBIE: Almost everybody in my mother's family was half white. But that wasn't nothing but some rape. These confessions are like a mourning for the lost connections.

(*Robbie starts singing and Jeannie joins in.*)

ROBBIE AND JEANNIE:

> "I'm going there to meet my mother
> I'm going there no more to roam
> I'm just a-going over Jordan
> I'm just a-going over home . . ."

(*Robbie continues humming like in church*)

JEANNIE: That was the only thing that would make it worth going to church for me, to sing those songs. But I didn't really have a religion, so that's why I invented one. When I was about seven, I invented a religion, and it was all about rocks, and trees and leaves, and nature and so forth, everything that I knew. And I tried to convert my best friend, Eileen, who was Catholic. It ended up just being mine.

ROBBIE: I envy that. To have a religion that you find where you are was something I couldn't even conceive of until Africa. Before that, of course, it was the big white god up there. . . . If oppression is at the core, if there must be one at the top and others on the bottom . . . the struggle will always be . . . . (*gesture of pushing and straining*) You know, I mean, the way I dealt with religion was to be a Marxist . . .

JEANNIE AND ROBBIE: . . . another . . . big white god . . .

JEANNIE: What was it your Aunt Nell said when you said you were a Marxist?

ROBBIE: "Well, at least you're *sumpthin'*." If this . . . (*same gesture*) kind of struggle, if oppression, is at the core, then this work will never end. It's work in progress . . .

JEANNIE: Well, if you can dialogue, you can get rid of some of that.

ROBBIE: Well, *if* you can weed it out. *If* it's about something else, then –

JEANNIE: *Then* it's a work in progress . . .

ROBBIE: . . . a dialogue . . .

JEANNIE: Otherwise, there is no progress.

ROBBIE AND JEANNIE: (*to audience, alternating the lines between them*) And we can't have a dialogue by ourselves. So you're in it. Don't worry, I won't jump in your face or down your throat. We'll feed you. (*they pass out cookies and apples, improvising about "fishes and loaves" and about how food eases tension, may help you talk*) We'll use hand signals, lead like camp directors, divide you into groups. One . . . (*one of them points out sections of the audience*) Two . . . Three. Well, it doesn't matter what section you're in, it just matters who you are, and you can change your opinion as time goes on.

Group One will be the agreeable ones. When we signal like this, (*two fingers up*) you say "That's right!", "Yes indeed" or "I'm telling you". Any short sentence of agreement. Let's practice. (*they lead responses with Group One*) Good . . . !

Group Two will be the bass line. You just go "uh huh", "umm humm", or "yeah, yeah". Here's your signal . . . (*one finger pointed out*) Let's try it. (*Group Two practices with sounds*) Very nice.

(*talking fast*) Group Three is the dialogue group, people who have something to add, to disagree with, who like to talk.

ROBBIE: Don't worry, I'm in control. Your signal is two hands out flat like this. . . . Dialogue?

JEANNIE: Let's practice with something from the context of the piece. Lights!

(*Lights on Robbie and Jeannie in two house aisles; stage black*)

2
Stating the Context

ROBBIE: I believe white is a condition that anyone can take in. It causes one to feel superior in order to be okay.

(*They signal to Groups. Groups respond. In this improvisation with the audience, when Robbie feels someone makes a strong point, agreeable to her or not, she impulsively stomps her feet.*
   Stage lights up, aisle lights off. Jeannie moves among rocks.)

(*walking in 6/8 time*) It's about my great-great-grandmother Sally who was a young woman with children when official slavery ended. And she's in me. She was house but *field*.
   My Aunt Jessie who died at the age of ninety-three –

JEANNIE: Ninety-six.

ROBBIE: She always put her age back. She said we was bad off in Harris County 'cause the white folks wasn't doing too good, and we were brought up to believe that, that our well-being depended on white people being well-off. You know how families can raise you with counterrevolutionary ideas in order to survive.

(*They call for audience response. Robbie waves off dialogue.*)

We don't hafta discuss *that*.

(*Jeannie moves among the rocks. Robbie continues in 6/8 rhythm.*)

It wasn't *fine* like the gone-with-the-wind-type house-nigger mythology. Sally did the housework and the cooking, and she tended to Mistress when some really fine white folks come to visit. They say that day might not a been really rich white folks anyhow. They say Sally had them chillun by the master like that was supposed to a been something. They say Massa was mean and nasty. You know how white folks gets when they ain't doin' good. Word was freedom was coming, everybody know what happen on that day freedom come when we follow Uncle Buck – I believe that was his name –

JEANNIE: Yeah, Uncle Buck.

ROBBIE: – up to the Massa porch. (*sudden anger*) But back up in *heah* 'fore freedom they say po' citter white folks was buying us ignorant! No telling what woulda happen! (*she pauses*)

3
Trying to Transform

ROBBIE: (*upset, she moves over left*) I I I become others inside me, standing at the bus stop with my socks rolled down screaming things I shoulda said, "Just because people are crazy don't mean they can't think straight!" Hollering periodically at white men "YOU RAPED ME! GODDAMN MOTHER-FUKA! YOU RAPED ME!" (*reaching out, gathering air*) Sometimes I'll gather and push away the wall of vibrations that make walls between us . . . (*throws air to Jeannie*) Black

JEANNIE: (*catching, molding the bunch of air*) Black

ROBBIE: Women

JEANNIE: Women

ROBBIE: Get

JEANNIE: Get

ROBBIE AND JEANNIE: Bitter.

JEANNIE: Black women get bitter. Scared somebody gonna look at them run and search for the wind, look at them go to the bottom of the pain and sadness, looking for breezes. You know how black folks gets when they ain't doing good.

ROBBIE: It's a journey of chains.

JEANNIE: I latched on, crawled in like a spider clinging to the walls, looking for light in tunnels of despair. I wanted to go deeper, darker, never to remember the empty days. I wanted to be . . . Billie Holiday.

ROBBIE: I wanted to be Rosa Luxemburg!

JEANNIE: Rosa Luxemburg?

ROBBIE: Poland.

JEANNIE: That's so idealistic.

ROBBIE: (*aside*) So was Billie Holiday.

JEANNIE: (*responding to aside*) I didn't have to know that to want to be her.

ROBBIE: (*does dance kicks*) Poland. She like Poland. Communism wasn't even a word back then. The main deity in Poland is a Black Madonna. In Eastern Europe women were more revered, more venerated.

JEANNIE: Do you have proof? Who told you that?

ROBBIE: A woman from Eastern Europe.

JEANNIE: Well, a woman from Turkey told me there was no racism in Turkey.

ROBBIE: Well, from her point of view, there probably wasn't.

JEANNIE: Why are you so understanding, so generous toward people in another part of the world?

ROBBIE: I was listening to a woman who had pride in her ancestors and that turned me on.

JEANNIE: That's very nice.

ROBBIE: Socialism goes way back. Way back women gathered in groups to pick. And Africa. Let's do 1964.

(*Light change: a pool of light center. They stand in it. Other areas dim.*)

ROBBIE: In 1964 at the library job a US history major who'd graduated from Smith College said –

JEANNIE: I never knew white men did anything with colored women on plantations.

ROBBIE: I said, "It was rape". Her eyes turned red. She choked on her sandwich and quit the job.

JEANNIE: (*pointing at each audience group in turn*) Was the Smith College graduate denying . . . ? lying . . . ? or dumb? (*audience response*) Yeah she was dumb. I keep telling you that.

(*They cross past each other. Light change.*)

ROBBIE: Why do I feel like crying . . . because she went to Smith College. . . . I think of the dumb educated bourgeois thing in me . . .

JEANNIE: You have this thing that an Ivy League education could prevent her dumbness about that, and there's nothing that can prevent that.

ROBBIE: Right, I do have a thing that an Ivy League education oughta prevent that. I mean, look, okay. I wanted to go to Barnard, and they didn't let me in . . . a rejection letter . . .

JEANNIE: And you're bitter.

ROBBIE: Bitterness about Barnard I admit. But when I'm sitting around my grandmother's breakfast table, and she's telling me something that this woman who went to Smith College didn't know, a US history major –

JEANNIE: (*overlap*) Well, aren't you more fortunate then, that you learned so much more through your grandmother?

ROBBIE: The point is that Smith College, all those colleges, are places that people should go to learn things that help the world. All right? And if she went there and studied US history and comes out sounding dumb about what went on during slavery time, I don't understand. I can't give her no credit for just being dumb. I mean my grandmother would also teach us that. . . . You know, we lived in a neighborhood back then down south that had black people and white people, back when they had signs that said *white* and *colored* to separate bathrooms and stuff. Well, back then there were white people who lived down the street from us because that was where they had to live. And we played together till we were about ten. After ten back then we couldn't speak to each other. Even back then my grandmother taught us that white people were not genetically evil or anything, they were just dumb, and when they learned something, they would be smarter about us . . .

(*Jeannie starts to do folk-dance steps in 3/4 time. Robbie joins in.*)

. . . and we could get together and change the world.

JEANNIE: Rosa Luxemburg had no patience for bourgeois women who didn't work. She called them –

ROBBIE: Co-consumptive.

JEANNIE: More parasitic than the parasites. She was a small, powerful woman.

ROBBIE: Zaftig.

JEANNIE: When she talked, people listened. I believe she would have marched with us.

ROBBIE AND JEANNIE: (*they stop dancing*) She was murdered by men who would later be Nazis.

ROBBIE: (*turning, kicking, squatting*) Dancing in half circles. Trying to connect. She was internationalist – so far ahead of her time – we haven't begun to get there yet.

JEANNIE: (*overlap*) – as opposed to nationalist.

ROBBIE: (*still dancing*) In Pennsylvania a town with the Black Madonna and the little brown Jesus. A Polish town. In Eastern Europe way back . . . women more venerated . . .

JEANNIE: There's one in Texas too. I sent you the postcard. The shrine to Our Lady of Czestochowa.

ROBBIE: Not long ago in Poland a pilgrimage to her.

JEANNIE: But you've never explained why in Poland there'd be a black Madonna.

(*pause*)

ROBBIE: Socialism goes way back.

JEANNIE: But a burned statue or anything, there's no explanation for it?

ROBBIE: Way back, way back! Women gathered in groups to pick and hunt.

JEANNIE: Did they really hunt? That's unsubstantiated.

(*pause*)

ROBBIE: (*stops dancing*) Of *course* they hunted. And of course it's unsubstantiated. And Africa.

JEANNIE: Old memories. Ancient stuff. We all come from one African woman. Dancing in circles, pushing walls. I was underneath him in the dirt too – he doesn't want to hear this, he thinks he civilized the world! I sold slaves when I worked at the Welfare Department. Did you put them on the ship?

(*Jeannie puts her hands on Robbie's hair. Pause. Robbie lifts them off.*)

4
Moment in the Chairs

(*They set up the two chairs. Light changes: One bright circle, other areas dark. They sit in the light, face each other, hold hands and move their arms to and fro, as if giving and receiving dialogue.*
   They improvise on why they are angry with each other. The differences go deep. Jeannie thinks Robbie can see through her to something she can't admit. She thinks their idealism is similar. Robbie thinks admitting the differences in their histories is more important. Jeannie is concerned that she can't win. They try to reveal something to each other as if they are alone and honest about their differences. The following is an example of the dialogue that has resulted in performance.)

JEANNIE: Your hands are like ice.

ROBBIE: What upsets me is language. I can't win in your language.

JEANNIE: You're going to win anyway. What upsets me is there's an underlying implication that you're gonna unmask me. That you're gonna get underneath something and pull it out. That you can see it and I can't.

ROBBIE: What do you think it is? I mean, it's better if you say it.

JEANNIE: Some kind of delusion, self-deception.

ROBBIE: About what? I mean, what's the content of it?

JEANNIE: About my idealism. I have some idea of ... humanism, something that we share, more important than our differences. Of greater. . . . Of greater value.

ROBBIE: Let me see if I can use the language to say what I feel about your idealism. I think it covers over something in your history that makes your idealism still a whim. It angers me that even though your ancestors might have been slaves – because they did have white slaves ... only made black slavery mandatory for economic reasons, so they could catch us when we ran away – that history has given you the ability to forget your shame about being oppressed by being ignorant, mean or idealistic ... which makes it dangerous for me. (*stands*)

JEANNIE: I have the same thing about education you were talking about.

Plate 22: Robbie McCauley and Jeannie Hutchins in McCauley's play *Sally's Rape*, directed by Demetria Royals in the performance-based documentary feature film, *Conjure Women* (1995). Photo by Ann Limongello. © Diamond/Royals Production/ Rebekah Films.

I mean I believed that through education, if I could change my thinking, that anything would be possible. And it just sounds so stupid.

(*Robbie may use this moment to say something more to audience. Jeannie takes chairs away, joins Robbie facing audience. Beat. They go stand in front of bench, pick up cups and drink tea.*)

5
Sally's Rape

ROBBIE:

> Do you think Thomas
> took his Sally to European tea rooms?
> And what did she wear?
> And what do you think Mrs J. thought?

ROBBIE AND JEANNIE: That musta been some business, huh?

(*They take their cups to piano. Jeannie first sings with Robbie, then becomes Mrs J. and does the dance of the frail white lady.*)

ROBBIE (*plays piano and sings*):

> Grandma Sally had two children
> by the master. One of 'em
> was my Grandma Alice, my mother's
> grandmother, where my mother got her name.

(*Robbie continues to play. Mrs J. speaks, conscious of the music.*)

JEANNIE:

> In the woods . . .
> I immediately become Harriet
> in the woods.
> Swamps are my memory.

ROBBIE (*coaching*): Shoot.

JEANNIE:

> Shoot, how you gonna be scared of freedom?
> Some teachers don't know nothing.

ROBBIE: Once.

JEANNIE:

> Once somebody I almost married
> said I was too scared of dogs.
> I said I'm scared of slavery.
> I wanted to be . . . darker . . . deeper.

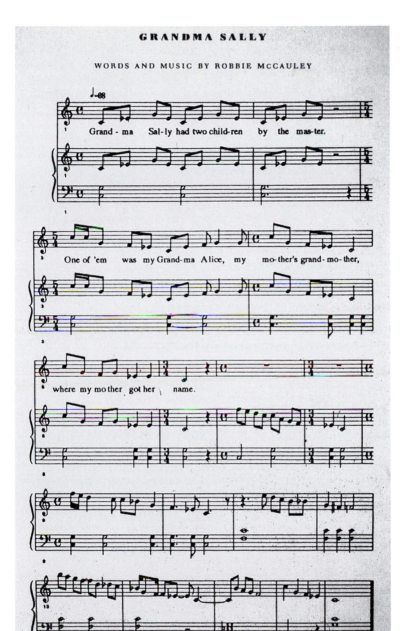

Figure 5: "Grandma Sally", from the play *Sally's Rape*: words and music by Robbie McCauley.

> These are dreams but the wounds remain
> and there are no meetings of ourselves
> at these crossroads.

(*Lights change. The auction block. Jeannie moves bench center to be the auction block, but then improvises with Robbie, deciding to move big table there instead. Jeannie takes bench down left. Robbie steps onto auction block, takes off her sack dress, drops it on the block. She is naked. Jeannie starts to chant, "Bid 'em in", coaxing the audience, taking time to thank them for joining in. It should be a moment of communion.*)

ROBBIE:

> On the auction block. With my socks rolled down,
> I take off my sack dress. Mistress? Come on.
> This is what they brought us here for.
> On the auction block. They put their hands all down our bodies
> to sell you, for folks to measure you, smeltcha . . .
> They say in Ecuador where 40% of the population is African,
> that Jesuits heaped us into huts by the hundreds
> and listened while we bred.

JEANNIE: That's what they brought us here for.

(*Auction block light is blue. Jeannie circles down near audience, leading the chant, and back to dim light up right.*)

ROBBIE: (*still naked*) Aunt Jessie said that's how they got their manhood on the plantations. They'd come down to the quarters and do it to us and the chickens.
A TIGHTNESS BETWEEN HER THIGHS. WHEN IT LETS GO SHE SCREAMS WITH TERROR. AND THEN TIGHTENS AGAIN. WHY DOES SHE KEEP COMING TO ME IN THESE NIGHTMARES? THEY SAY SALLY WAS TOUGH. BOUGHT A HOUSE AFTER SLAVERY TIME. TAUGHT HER DAUGHTERS TO BE LADIES. ASKED THE WHITE MAN, HOW MUCH WAS THE HOUSE ON 23RD STREET. HE TOLD HER AND LAUGHED. LIVING IN ONE OF THE RED HOUSES, PAYING BY THE MONTH, TOOK IN WASHING, CLEANED UP THEIR HOUSES FOR MONEY. SHE ALWAYS SAID FOR MONEY. TOOK $750 TO THE BANK, WHICH IS WHERE THE COLORED HAD TO GO TO GET THE PAPER FOR PROPERTY. SAID SHE DID ALL THAT AND NONE OF US EVER HAD TO BE WHORES.

(*Jeannie ends chant, signaling with her hands like a conductor. Robbie asks the light board operator to bring up the lights as she picks up the sack dress and holds it in front of her.*)

(*to audience*) I wanted to do this – stand naked in public on the auction block. I thought somehow it could help free us from *this*. (*refers to her naked body*) Any old socialist knows, one can't be free till all are free.

(*Lights back to auction-block blue. Robbie curls down onto block.*)

In the dream I. I am Sally being (*an involuntary sound of pain*) b'ah. Bein' bein' I . . . I being bound down I didn't I didn't wanna be in the dream, bound down in the dream I am I am Sally being done it to I am down on the groundbeing done it to bound down didn't wanna be bound down on the ground. In the dream I am Sally down on the groundbeing done it to. In the dream I am Sally being done it to bound down on the ground.

(*Jeannie moves auction block back, places chairs down right and crosses past Robbie to bench. Robbie, carrying dress, goes to Jeannie's light.*)

6

In a Rape Crisis Center

ROBBIE: (*putting on dress*) Before they changed the Bill of Rights/ Constitution/Articles of Confederation – whatever it was for white men before they changed it – it said they all had a right to land, cattle, Negroes, and other livestock . . . pigs . . . dogs . . .

JEANNIE: (*curled up on bench*)

> To be raped is not to scream
> but to whimper and lock and never to remember
> but feel the closing in the thighs
> between the legs locking up everything
> biting lips, the teeth bleed.

ROBBIE:

> On the plantation you hafta stay tough and tight
> no matter how many times they come down there.
> Sally stayed down there with us in the quarters
> and at night they pulled us out in the dirt.

(*Jeannie crosses to chairs, stands. Robbie crosses to bench, sits.*)

Wasn't nothing to it. You just stay tight till they finish. Sally worked in the house, but she stayed down in the quarters with us. He took Sally out on the ground.

JEANNIE: In a rape crisis center, your wounds are fresh. They can put warm cloths on you, tell you it's not your fault.

ROBBIE:

> Wadn't nuthin' to it. The others watched.
> Sometimes they did it too.

(Pause. She crosses and stands down left of Jeannie.)

> They say Sally had
> dem chillun by the massa like it was supposed
> to a been something. Shit, Thomas' Sally was just as
> much a slave as our grandma and it was just as much a rape.
> One Sally's rape by the massa no gooder n'an n'othern.

JEANNIE: All anyone would have to do is keep you warm.

ROBBIE: After slaverytime, say Sally married Gilford, a black man, and they had two boys. And nobody, not even them two chillun she had by the massa – which is what everybody called 'em like that was supposed to a been something – nobody ever blamed Sally for calling them two *boys* her real chillun.

JEANNIE: There's no reason to feel that cold all the time.

ROBBIE: COLD. VERY COLD. VERY VERY VERY COLD.

JEANNIE: Someone would give you a cup of tea. Hot chocolate. Warm milk.

ROBBIE: These new ones with the alligators act like they wadn't born with no memory. I don't know what all went on underneath those houses of women and silent men.

JEANNIE: Herb tea.

ROBBIE: You . . . let the cabs roll by . . . let shit roll off your back . . . *stay* . . . ain't no rape crisis center on the plantation.

JEANNIE: Then what do you do about it?

7

Talking About Different Schools, and How to Do

(Pause. Robbie crosses over to chairs. They both sit.)

ROBBIE: My Ma Willie and my Aunt Jessie had a school. It was called – well, their school, I don't remember what it was called. But they had gone to Mr Pierce's school. Now, Mr Pierce's father or grandfather was –

JEANNIE: I think it was his grandfather.

ROBBIE: But Mr Pierce himself had taught my grandmother and them, so it must have been his father who had been a slave and had worked in the big house and looked in and learned how the white folks do. So his son had a school called Mr Pierce's School where the girls, and I reckon some of the boys, went to learn how to do. Now when my Ma

Willie and Aunt Jessie opened their school it wasn't just for how to do. It was for reading, writing, and numbers, and Aunt –

JEANNIE: Tell them about the motto.

ROBBIE: Jeannie likes this. Back then they said, "Each one teach one". And that's how the learning was transmitted. My Aunt Jessie could name the capital and the river it was on of every state in the United States.

JEANNIE: Alphabetically.

ROBBIE: Alphabetically. One of the first words they learned was *garage*. It was a new word back then. Garage – a building in which you place an automobile.

JEANNIE: What about rhetoric?

ROBBIE: Oh yes, they learned rhetoric. My mother said rhetoric was learning to tell the truth over and over.

JEANNIE: You know we had classes in a garage too. But I think they were opposite. The whole idea was wild abandon. This was about a year before I invented the religion. But the whole thing was nature. My teacher had a long red ponytail and a drum under her arm, and we'd go running across the room. We were about six years old, all girls. Some forest . . . some beast . . . some storm . . . you know the whole thing – wild, free, running!

(*Robbie runs across the space and back.*)

Yeah, we were freer than that.

ROBBIE: (*in her own world*)

> What difference it a been, it a been by the master?
> They all come down there. They all do it to you.
> And do it to the chickens too.
> What difference it a been?

JEANNIE: What do you do about it? See, this section to me is where everything is clear. The difference in weight. I say the word "free", and what do you think of? A feather, or a butterfly. You say the word "free", it's totally different. It's light . . . substantial, flimsy . . . weighty . . .

ROBBIE: Come, let's do this.

(*Robbie and Jeannie get the auction block.*)

JEANNIE: I thought we weren't going to do this. It's so . . . art.

ROBBIE: Get up there. (*to light board operator*) Put the auction block lights on, please. (*to Jeannie*) Take off your dress. (*to audience*) Let's do it for her, please. . . . Bid 'em in. Bid 'em in.

(*Jeannie takes down one strap.*)

(*to Jeannie*) Do you have something to say? (*Jeannie shakes her head "no"*) That's something right there.

(*Jeannie gets down and moves block back.*)

8
The Language Lesson

(*Robbie holds Jeannie by her shoulders from behind.*)

ROBBIE: Everybody know how on the day freedom come, we followed Uncle Buck up to the massa porch. And Uncle Buck said,

JEANNIE: Massa is we free?

ROBBIE: And that white man took out his shotgun, and said "Yeah, nigger, you free" and shot Uncle Buck dead.

JEANNIE: Massa is we free?

ROBBIE: Shot Uncle Buck dead.

JEANNIE: Massa is we free?

ROBBIE: Say it again.

JEANIE: Is we free?

ROBBIE: (*to audience*) They say Massa was mean and nasty. He was all dressed up, and the ladies too, and they all came back to the kitchen. And one of the uncles took the blame for stealing the bucket of fatback and greens that Sally was gon' bring down to the quarters for us. And they made him eat the whole bucket of fatback and greens, until he commenced to rolling on the floor and passing gas, and they laughed and laughed . . . and the ladies too.

JEANNIE: Is that it?

ROBBIE: (*aside*) They say that day might not a been really rich white folks anyhow. (*to audience*) On the day the really rich white folks came, they dressed up Sally and one of the uncles like staff, like house staff, so Massa and them would seem richer than they were and so we'd seem more profitable. They were figna sell us! Figna sell us further down south Georgia! If the war hadn't a come, no telling what woulda happened. (*pause*) I reckon we'd a never been here to tell y'all this.

(*They call for audience response. Robbie waves off dialogue. Jeannie sits on bench.*)

JEANNIE: But you were already in south Georgia. How much further down could you go?

ROBBIE: (*sits next to Jeannie*) They say Sally had them children by the master to save us. How come they thought she had a choice? Survival is luck. Or unlucky.

(*They improvise. The following is an example of the dialogue that has resulted in performance.*)

You wanna try the language lesson?

JEANNIE: Okay. . . . They was from south o' Albany way down Seminole or Decatur.

ROBBIE: That's sort of –

JEANNIE: Jimmy Carter.

ROBBIE: Sort of a bad imitation of a white southerner.

JEANNIE: I'm not trying . . .

ROBBIE: As I've said before, try to know, like actors do, what you're talking about.

JEANNIE: Further south?

ROBBIE: Where slaves were sent, couldn't get back from, way away from their loved ones. It resonated dread. See it, know it, feel the dread when you say where that place was. (*doing it*) They's from souf a Allbeny way down Semino o' De kaytuh.

JEANNIE: They's from south o' Al bany way down Semino o' Decatur.

ROBBIE: Better. When we learned the English language, we had to learn the English culture. I only learned later that iambic pentameter was street language . . . like rap . . . "To be or not to be, that is the question". Deep ambivalence. I could play Hamlet.

JEANNIE: If they let you.

ROBBIE: If I wanted to.

(*They sit quiet. Lights out. Applause.*)

Epilogue
Leaving the Audience Talking

(*Lights up. Jeannie and Robbie get their cups of tea.*)

JEANNIE: There's a part we sort of want to do to involve the audience, but we get more involved . . .

ROBBIE: It has to do with talking to people, even if you already know 'em, and especially if you don't, how a lot of people in different cultures greet each other, I know some Native American cultures do: "Who are you and who are your people?" And where I come from, African-American folk be like, "Who children you?"

JEANNIE: So our idea was that you were going to turn to somebody else and find out something.

ROBBIE: Which you can do.

(*Robbie and Jeannie walk off.*)

ANNA DEAVERE SMITH

Acting as Incorporation (1993)

Richard Schechner

A woman faces the camera, her voice nasal and New York. Roz Malamud speaks with the kind of accent that sounds "Jewish". "I wish I could [. . .] go on television. I wanna scream to the whole world. [. . .] I don't love my neighbors, I don't know my black neighbors". A few minutes later television time, Carmel Cato, from the same Crown Heights, Brooklyn, neighborhood as Malamud, but a world away, his voice roundly "black" in its tones, talks through tears about how a car slammed into his daughter, Angela, and his seven-year-old son, Gavin, killing him. "Angela she was on the ground but she was trying to move. Gavin was still. They was trying to pound him. I was trying to explain it was my kid!"

These two people – plus many others: men and women, professors and street people, blacks, Jews, rabbis, reverends, lawyers, professors, and politicians – are enacted by Anna Deavere Smith, an African-American performer of immense abilities. My concern here will not be with the events in Brooklyn in 1991 and 1992, nor with the "black–white race thing" that continues to torture America, but with Smith's artwork. I want to investigate how Smith does what she does in *Fires in the Mirror*.

In conventional acting a performer develops a character by reading a play text written before rehearsals begin, improvising situations based on the dramatic situation depicted in the play, and slowly coming to understand the external social situation and the internal emotional state of the character – Hamlet, Hedda Gabler, whoever. The character is a complex fiction created collectively by the actor, the playwright, the director, the scenographer, the costumer, and the musician. The whole team works together to create onstage a believable, if temporary, social world.

Smith works differently. She does not "act" the people you see and listen to in *Fires in the Mirror*. She "incorporates" them. Her way of working is less like that of a conventional Euro-American actor and more like that of African, Native American, and Asian ritualists. Smith works by means of deep mimesis, a process opposite to that of "pretend". To incorporate means to be possessed by, to open oneself up thoroughly and deeply to another being. Smith composed *Fires in the Mirror* as a ritual shaman might investigate and heal a diseased or possessed patient. Like a ritualist, Smith consulted the people most closely involved, opening to their intimacy, spending lots of time with them face-to-face. Using both the most contemporary techniques of tape recording and the oldest technique of close looking and listening, Smith went far beyond "interviewing" the participants in the Crown Heights drama. Her text was not a pre-existing literary drama but other human beings. Smith composed *Fires in the Mirror* by confronting in person those most deeply involved – both the famous and the ordinary.

Meeting people face-to-face made it possible for Smith to move like them, sound like them, and allow what they were to enter her own body. This is a dangerous process, a form of shamanism. Some shamans exorcise demons by transforming themselves into the various beings – good, bad, dangerous, benign, helpful, destructive. The events of August 1991 revealed that Crown Heights was possessed: by anger, racism, fear, and much misunderstanding. The deaths of Gavin Cato and Yankel Rosenbaum stirred up hatreds. And yet, even in their rage, fear, confusion, and partisanship, people of every persuasion and at every level of education and sophistication opened up to Smith. Why?

Because she — like a great shaman — earned the respect of those she talked with by giving them her respect, her focused attention. People are sensitive to such deep listening. Even as a fine painter looks with a penetrating vision, so Smith looks and listens with uncanny empathy. Empathy goes beyond sympathy. Empathy is the ability to allow the other in, to feel what the other is feeling. Smith absorbs the gestures, the tone of voice, the look, the intensity, the moment-by-moment details of a conversation.

But in so doing, she does not destroy the others or parody them. Nor does she lose herself. A shaman who loses herself cannot help others to attain understanding. As spectators we are not fooled into thinking we are really seeing Al Sharpton, Angela Davis, Norman Rosenbaum, or any of the others. Smith's shamanic invocation is her ability to bring into existence the wondrous "doubling" that marks great performances. This doubling is the simultaneous presence of performer and performed. Because of this doubling Smith's audiences – consciously perhaps, unconsciously certainly – learn to "let the other in", to accomplish in their own way what Smith so masterfully achieves.

THE WORD BECOMES YOU

An Interview with Anne Deavere Smith (1993)

Carol Martin

Anna Deavere Smith's *Fires in the Mirror: Crown Heights Brooklyn and Other Identities* is a series of portraits of people enmeshed in the Crown Heights riots where Jews and blacks were so violently pitted against one another, in Brooklyn, August 1991. The riots were provoked when Gavin Cato, a black child, was hit and killed by a Lubavitch rebbe's motorcade. By the end of that day Yankel Rosenbaum, a young Jewish scholar from Australia, was murdered in retaliation. The piece was first performed at the Public Theatre in the late spring and summer of 1992, with Christopher Ashley as director. *Fires in the Mirror* was then mediated for television broadcast by PBS's "American Playhouse", directed by George C. Wolfe. The TV adaptation first aired in April 1993.

In the stage version Smith performed barefoot in a white shirt and black pants. Sitting in an armchair, or at a desk, donning a yarmulke, or a cap of African Kente cloth, or a spangled sweater, Smith brought her 29 subjects to the stage to speak *their own* lines. That there were unresolvable contradictions in the multiple versions of truth Smith portrayed did not diminish the conviction of each character that what they said was true.

Smith's apparently hypernaturalistic mimesis – in which she replicates not only the words of different individuals but their bodily style as well – is deceiving. Derived from a method more documentary than "artistic" in the usual sense, Smith's performance can easily be understood as a feat of technical virtuosity. Brilliantly portrayed characters, however, are not enough to generate the enormous critical success of a work about a very turbulent set of events. The authority of one group over another, of one individual over others, is undermined by the presence of Smith as the person through whom so many voices travel.

Smith gives these people the chance to speak as if to each other – in much the same way a "spirit doctor" brings ancestors or other spirits in contact with the living – in the presence of the community of the audience. It is this fictional and yet actual convergence of presences that gives Smith's work its power. Angela Davis, Nzotake Shange, Letty

Cottin Pogrebin, Rabbi Shea Hecht, Reverend Al Sharpton, and others, known and unknown, speak together. They speak together across race, history, theory, and differences in their own words through Smith's conjuring performative language. Their "presence" and words mark the absence and silence of the two people around whom the drama revolves, Gavin Cato and Yankel Rosenbaum.

Fires in the Mirror is part of a series of performances titled *On the Road: A Search for American Character*. Smith began working on this series in 1979 by walking up to people on the street and saying "I know an actor who looks like you. If you'll give me an hour of your time, I'll invite you to see yourself performed" (1992:18). Early in her work Smith's focus shifted from individuals to groups of individuals at gatherings, conferences, or as members of a community.

Some of the work has been commissioned and performed for specific conferences, while other pieces were developed for theatre audiences. Often the title of the work reveals the theme: *Building Bridges Not Walls* (1985); *Gender Bending: On the Road Princeton University* (1989); *On Black Identity and Black Theatre* (1990); *From the Outside Looking In* (1990). Smith's desire is to "capture the personality of a place by attempting to embody its varied population and varied points of view in one person – myself" (Smith 1992:18).

I spoke with Smith in August 1992 after seeing *Fires in the Mirror* at the Public Theatre.

MARTIN: How did you become interested in Crown Heights?

SMITH: George Wolfe had asked me to participate in a festival of performance artists called "New Voices of Color" last December [*1991 at the Public Theatre*]. The thought of coming to New York and doing *On the Road* was pretty overwhelming.

Then, on August 19th Crown Heights happened. I put it in the back of my mind. When I went to the Bunting Institute at Harvard in September I still didn't know if the festival was going to happen. It wasn't until the day Anita Hill began to testify that I got a call from the theatre formally inviting me to the festival. I didn't have a commission so there was no money to build anything big. I thought I would do a show that I'd already done before and just put a couple of things about New York in it. I asked the Public Theatre for four days in a hotel and a round-trip air ticket. In those four days I had to get everything. I only performed it twice but it went very well so they decided to think of it for a run.

What was personally compelling about Crown Heights was that it was a community with very graphic differences. Everyone wears their beliefs on their bodies – their costumes. You can't pass. Crown Heights is no melting pot and I really respect that.

MARTIN: You were already dealing with issues of race, identity, and difference.

SMITH: Yes.

MARTIN: So Crown Heights was really a graphic way for you to . . .

SMITH: Explore.

MARTIN: How did you make your contacts?

SMITH: I usually get a few contacts from the newspaper and then try to make my way into any institution, to somebody in authority. In this case, I went to various people in the mayor's office and asked them for ideas for people to interview. People lead to more people. Eventually, I know very specifically what kind of person I want to meet so I know what kind of person to try to find.

MARTIN: Did people in the community get to know your presence?

SMITH: I wasn't there long enough. I did all the interviews in about eight days.

MARTIN: The two anonymous young black men were very interesting and very important. How did you find them?

SMITH: That was lucky. There were few women in the piece. In the "Crown Heights" section there was only one. One of my goals when I came back to New York in the spring was to do a few more interviews with women. I found one young woman who was a friend of Henry Rice. I went to interview her. She runs – it's so sad – a center in the Ebbets Field apartment houses, but it's just an empty dark room with a few chairs. A radio was playing in the background. It's no place for her [Kim] to be making activities.

    I went to interview Kim around eight o'clock at night and two boys were just sitting there. They inched their way into the interview. I didn't invite them in. They just, you know, invited themselves. The second one, the "bad boy", really did not even come into the group. The one who talked about justice was "Anonymous #1". He came right into Kim's interview and sat down with his friend. His friend said nothing the entire time but the "bad boy" [Anonymous #2] just lurked in the dark corner watching. When we discussed Limerick Nelson, the 16-year-old accused of killing Yankel Rosenbaum, the "bad boy" started talking. None of these kids believe that Limerick did it. They told me they know who it is but they won't tell. So then he [the "bad boy"] spoke up. I loved what he said and I just loved how he talked.

MARTIN: There is a sense in the performance that when you interview blacks they acknowledge you as a member of their community. There's no sense, however, when you're interviewing the Jews that they looked at you as a member of the black community.

of emotions and histories. I connect this approach to feminist ideas about open-ended narratives, about the refusal of ultimate authority – even though there's an authority operating.

SMITH: I think you're right. But the honest truth would be that I've always been like this. Since I was a girl my creative life has been about trying to find a way of being me in my work. I felt very oppressed by the formal structures of theatre, the first one being the role of an acting teacher in a classroom. When I became the acting teacher, there was this expectation that I was going to be this authority who resolved everything and came up with the answers.

The through-line always made me feel bad in teaching, reading, and trying to write plays. It was something inherently I, Anna, was trying to express. Period. If anything opened me intellectually it was when I was trying to write about acting in order to find out why I had trouble with the Stanislavsky technique. I came across a graph of the objectives of the Stanislavsky technique. Super objective. Little objective. It was straight lines with arrows. Quite soon after that I was reading a book about African philosophical systems and saw a picture of a wheel that had all these little spokes with arrows pointing towards the center. I knew then that I wanted to try to find a way of thinking or a structure that was more like that.

As you know, the black church is not only about speaking to one God. The whole thing is supposed to be an occasion to evoke a spirit. This was one of the things that lead me to thinking in more circular ways and resisting the through-line.

MARTIN: You don't really understand feminism?

SMITH: It's not that I don't understand feminism. I try to understand things but I'm also an empathetic and intuitive person.

Why don't you offer some words and I'll see if I feel like they fit. I understand that feminism is . . . is about us, finding our place and finding our language.

MARTIN: Yes, but it's also given women a means to read texts, life, power relations, and interactions. Feminism is implicated in ways of seeing, believing, and feeling as well as intellectual life. Intellectual life is divorced from other senses. The lack of closure in *Fires in the Mirror* worked so well because it kept expanding the complexities of the communities and giving us an opportunity to acknowledge that truth, in both the divine and mundane sense, is difficult to discern. Acknowledging this difficulty is a humbling experience that also contains the possibility of acknowledging difference.

Your performing style, not the obvious – that you play both men and women – but the way that you present and characterize people through language and at the same time remain present as Anna also seems informed by feminist ideas. You're not invisible nor do you step aside in a Brechtian way and comment on those you are presenting. You're visible and yet so are all those other people. This palimpsest creates a density and authority in individual characters and, at the same time, calls into question the absoluteness of our differences.

Sometimes we see you obliquely when someone refers to the process of being interviewed. You've formed this difficult material in a very emotional and human way. It must take some struggle, to get to that place, to make those decisions.

SMITH: My grandfather told me that if you say a word often enough, it becomes you. I was very interested before I developed this project in how manipulating words has a spiritual power.

I can learn to know who somebody is, not from what they tell me, but from *how* they tell me. This will make an impression on my body and eventually on my psyche. Not that I would understand it but I would feel it. My goal would be to – these kinds of words are funny and probably, in print they sound even worse – become possessed, so to speak, of the person. I don't set out to do anything as intellectual as what you're talking about.

MARTIN: My observations are from the outside.

SMITH: I know that this is there. I've emphasized to my students that acting is becoming the other. To acknowledge the other, you have to acknowledge yourself.

It's not psychological realism. I don't want to own the character and endow the character with my own experience. It's the opposite of that. What has to exist, in order to try to allow the other to be, is separation between the actor's self and the other.

What I'm ultimately interested in is the struggle. The struggle that the speaker has when he or she speaks to me, the struggle that he or she has to sift through language to come through. Somewhere I'm probably also leaving myself room as a performer to struggle and come through. Richard Schechner talks about this much better than I when he talks about "not me" and "not not me".

MARTIN: Yes, but in the case of *Fires in the Mirror* we know several of the people from the media. There is the media image of people like the Lubavitchers and Al Sharpton. Familiar representatives of different communities are brought onstage through you and this is somehow less fictional than documentary footage or journalistic accounts of the same people.

How did you decide to give Carmel Cato the last word? I thought it was right and emotionally difficult at the end of the piece.

SMITH: In December, he did not have the last word. The Crown Heights section ended with him, but I had more stuff. JoAnne [*Akalaitis*] said

"When the father speaks the show is over".

When I left that interview, I knew that I'd met a remarkable man. I have never heard anybody journey in a language across so many realms of experience. From the facts of a personal experience, to his own belief system and his own sensitivity – his power – to the circumstances of his birth. When I first developed *On the Road*, and was learning how to do this, I would ask people for an hour interview and I would talk to them. I'd tell them we could talk about anything. I was looking specifically, not for what they said but for these places where they would struggle with language and come through. I talked to a linguist about it and she gave me three questions I could ask that would guarantee this would happen.

MARTIN: What were the questions?

SMITH: One of them was: What were the circumstances of your birth? So I end this show with how I began my own exploration. He [*Carmel Cato*] answers that question. I didn't ask him. I didn't ask him.

MARTIN: You didn't ask him!

SMITH: No! He just said it. I interviewed him on the street at night. We were standing on the street and this man was talking about knowing his kid was going to die before he dies. Then he says he's a man, a special person. I thought he was going to say, "I'm a man, a black man". But he said "I was born with my foot" [*feet first*]. The very beginning of my project was that question so, in a way, for me, it would have to be the end.

MARTIN: You've spoken about integration being a nostalgic idea. Where are we now? There's no operative paradigm – not multicultural or intercultural. What do you think about us now?

SMITH: I'm very excited because I think we're going to find something better. I think a lot of people feel very betrayed by integration because it didn't work.

MARTIN: Did people really try it?

SMITH: Some people gave their lives, some people died for it. Died. I would never say that people didn't try. It's only going to be a few people who are willing to sacrifice their lives for the experiment.

There are people who are willing to change the course of their lives for the experiment. At Bellagio [*a 1991 conference on intercultural performance*[1]] there was this language about negotiating boundaries and difference that I hadn't heard before. I've been wondering how to find the tools for thinking about difference as a very active negotiation rather than an image of all of us holding hands. There are too many contradictions, problems, and lies in American society about the melting pot. You're invited to jump into the hot stew but

Plate 24: Upon the advice of JoAnne Akalaitis, Smith chose to end *Fires in the Mirror* with the powerful monologue of Carmel Cato, the father of the accident victim Gavin Cato. This performance was at the Joseph Papp Public Theatre, New York, in 1992. Photo by William Gibson/Martha Swope Studios.

you're not wanted. That's the case for black people, even with seemingly well-meaning, well-minded people who would benefit from my presence and the presence of others like me. We're not wanted.

It's going to be hard.

Motion is what I'm interested in right now. People who talk about motion, who use the word move. In my show I've become interested in which characters can move in the space and which ones can't.

Angela [*Davis*] walks. Richard Green walks. Sharpton moves his chair. Whatever we think about Sharpton's limitations, he's in motion.

You know, we normally think of passing as something that you do. You pass up, right? If you're a light-skinned black, you pass up. You never pass down. Guillermo Gómez-Peña talks about passing as going back and forth between borders. This is very exciting to me. It brings back images of the underground railroad . . .

MARTIN: Seems impossible. I taught public speaking at City College [*City University of New York*] at 138th Street for a year. My experience there was very different. Just taking the subway was a demonstration of inequities. The white and Asian students got off at Columbia, the rest of us got off two stops later and walked through a park of drug dealers. In that situation, I was a minority among minorities [*a white person among mostly black and Hispanic students*] in a very heated atmosphere. It was during the time of the clash between Leonard Jeffries and Michael Levin.[2] I had to bridge the gap being a white woman speaking to a class of 25 mostly black and Hispanic men.

SMITH: Oh my God!

MARTIN: I could never pass in any sense of the word. I had to be who I was or they would surely feel I was disingenuous. I had to allow them to see my vulnerability. The class was a public-speaking class and one of the required speeches was a commemorative speech. Many of these young men used this as an opportunity to talk about their lives and the people who inspired them and helped them survive – mothers, uncles, clergy. A few even cried during their speeches. There was always this silence after each of them spoke. I knew they were witnessing one another in ways they never had before. Many of them found a way to talk about the reality of their lives to one another and to me. They were able to be supportive *and* critical of one another's work. The dynamic was about each of us being who we were, not about passing. I was teaching them about how to use language to present themselves – a calculated performance of self that would help them gain entry. Ultimately, I wasn't wanted. The Speech Department wanted me and so did my students but there was a feeling on campus that only black and Hispanic professors belonged there. Anyway . . .

SMITH: In terms of passing up and passing down, it's probably harder for a white person to pass in, if we think of the social structure as black on the bottom and white on the top. There's less structure for you to pass than for those black males. For them there is a structure. They could go to jail on the way but there is a structure. It may be corrupt but there are steps for going up. Very few and mysterious steps but they are there.

It's just like in speech. It's easier to make a rising inflection and it's much harder to do a downward build because you have to work with gravity a different way.

MARTIN: What we are talking about is a concern with language and what language reveals and . . .

SMITH: That was the birth of the project ten years ago.

MARTIN: Language?

SMITH: My major fascination in the world.

MARTIN: You do quote Shakespeare a lot.

SMITH: If it hadn't been for Shakespeare, I wouldn't be where I am because it was my Shakespeare teacher who got to me. In the first class we had to take any 14 lines of Shakespeare and say it over and over again to see what happened. So I picked, of all things, Queen Margaret in *Richard III*:

> From forth the kennel of thy womb hath crept
> A hellhound that doth hunt us all to death.
> That dog that had his teeth before his eyes
> To worry lambs and lap their gentle blood,
> That foul defacer of God's handiwork,
> That excellent grand tyrant of the earth
> That reigns in galled eyes of weeping souls,
> Thy womb let loose to chase us to our graves
>
> (*Richard III*, 4.4.47–54)

Right? I knew nothing; it was my first acting class ever and I had some kind of a transcendental experience. I was terrified, I was mystified. For the next three years, as I trained seriously, I never had an experience like that again. Ever. I kept wanting to have it so I kept exploring what language was.

I remembered what my grandfather told me because it's one of those experiences that is so peculiar you have try to explain it to somebody. What happened to me? Was I crazy? What was it? It sounds really interesting but nobody can name it, so it's your quest.

MARTIN: No more psychological realism?

SMITH: The opposite. Psychological realism is about – this is a real over-simplification of Stanislavsky – saying: Here's Leonard Jeffries. You have to play Leonard Jeffries now. Let's look at Leonard. Let's look at his circumstances. Let's look at your circumstances. How are you two alike? How can you draw from your own experience? Contrary to that, I say this is what Leonard Jeffries said. Don't even write it down. Put on your headphones, repeat what he said. That's all. That's it.

MARTIN: And what happens as you repeat what he said?

SMITH: When dealing with somebody as powerful as Leonard Jeffries with such a fascination with details, I almost didn't have to memorize him. He made a psychic impression, it just went, FOOM! You and I could talk at great length or go into a studio and work on Leonard Jeffries. We'd have a good time figuring out his psychological realities, we'd get a blast, right?

MARTIN: Maybe.

SMITH: That's not the point. The point is simply to repeat it until I begin to feel it and what I begin to feel is his song and that helps me remember more about his body. For example, I remembered he sat up but it wasn't until well into rehearsal that my body began to remember, not me, my body began to remember. He had a way of lifting his soft palate or something. I can't see it because it's happening inside. But the way it played itself out in early per-formances is that I would yawn, you know, 'cause he yawned at a sort of inappropriate moment [*yawns*]. I've realized now what is going on. My body begins to do the things that he probably must do inside while he's speaking. I begin to feel that I'm becoming more like him.

MARTIN: What you're saying in *Fires in the Mirror* is that differences between people are very complicated and maybe unresolvable as well as interesting and wonderful. When you perform, however, you give over to each person in a very deep way and become them.

SMITH: In spite of myself. Many of the characters have chiselled away at the gate that's between them and Anna. That's the part that's very fascinating, challenging, difficult, painful. Psychological technique is built on metaphors for a reason. I believe it's quite organic. You listen to some of the characters and you begin to identify with them. Because I'm saying the stuff over and over again every night, part of me is becoming them through repetition – by doing the performance of themselves that they do.

I become the "them" that they present to the world. For all of us, the performance of ourselves has very much to do with the self of ourselves. That's what we're articulating in language and in flesh –

something we feel inside as we develop an identity.

These words are knocking at my door and they're saying, "parts of Anna, come out".

MARTIN: Where is the spectator in all this?

SMITH: I don't know. I'm just talking about my process. I hope that the words are knocking at their door too.

MARTIN: How much did you edit the interviews? You may have an hour of material but you obviously can't give each person an hour of time.

SMITH: I try to find a section that I don't have to interrupt. The performance is much more difficult if I've created chaos in their frame of thought. I'd rather have a section in which their psychological through-line is reflected in language. Everybody does it. I just wait. I think the longest section is seven minutes.

MARTIN: What were the other two questions that the linguist advised you to ask?

SMITH: Have you ever come close to death? and, Have you ever been accused of something that you didn't do?

Plate 25: In her play *Twilight: Los Angeles, 1992*, here performed at the Mark Taper Forum in May 1993, Smith performed the Los Angeles segment of her *On the Road* series by dramatizing the conflicts of a community resisting the popular myth of an American melting pot. Photo by Jay Thompson.

MARTIN: Did you use those in any interview?

SMITH: That was way back when I was inventing this in the early 1980s. Now I'm working with events. I'm just trying to get the story.

MARTIN: The deaths of Gavin Cato and Yankel Rosenbaum created an event but in a certain sense they're not the subject of your piece.

SMITH: That's the real reason I ended with Mr Cato. Around Thanksgiving [*in late autumn*] I read an article in the *Voice* called "Toilet Diplomacy". It was all about the big figures in the [*Crown Heights*] story. I didn't know why I was so sad, and over a series of days I realized I was so sad because the more I read, the more Gavin Cato's name was disappearing.

Only the first rabbi in my show refers to Angela Cato [*Gavin's sister, who was also struck by the car*]. That the father's first line is, "In the meanwhile" – in the meanwhile, 90 minutes ago, we started talking. In the meanwhile, Angela was on the ground and she was trying to move. This little girl was in a body cast for months. The neighbors were still concerned about Gavin. I thought it would be powerful to have the audience forget about Gavin. I'm sure many people leave the theatre and still don't know anything about Angela. She's only mentioned twice.

There's a way in which the larger powers obliterate the smaller powers even when those smaller powers are the very reason for our gathering. It's like parents giving their kid a birthday party and getting drunk.

MARTIN: Is there such a thing as an American character, as the subtitle of *On the Road* suggests?

SMITH: I'm looking for it. I think different people are shaping it. I suppose what I should do is try to collaborate with David Hammonds [*an installation artist*] or somebody like that.

MARTIN: In the US there was the myth of the American character formed on the frontier. This myth was destroyed by industrialization, massive immigration at the beginning of this century, and the resulting urbanization. Now the question seems to be, what experience constitutes being an American?

Are we specialists in diversity? When one goes to Europe it's apparent that there's very little conversation or language about diversity, about difference – even where there needs to be.

SMITH: We could be specialists. That's what's exciting. We could become specialists if we could get up off of our hate and our elitism. Some of the people who have the best equipment for helping to do this are such snobs and the system makes people who have the ability into snobs.

I know from interviewing people who are experts that they have a lot of armor. I guess they have to get it to survive. Some of the people who have a real facility for language get very snobby about the very language they own. To talk about passing again – I think we need to pass language back and forth across borders.

There is great resistance to including less articulated ideas. All this does is force words on us that have nothing to do with our experience. I know I don't have the language to argue with the people who have the key and have the privilege.

MARTIN: Having the language is one thing. Having the presence of mind or the ability to keep one's emotional nerve is also necessary. One has to be able to say, "Hey, wait a second, this is not quite right or what it should be".

SMITH: This is why the "bad boy" is so fascinating. When he talked to me I knew he did not have very many words. I knew he wasn't telling the complete truth because he knows, he thinks he knows, who killed Yankel Rosenbaum. He performed for me, looked me straight in the eye with very kind eyes – talking to me as though I were stupid. Not like condescending stupid, not like that. More like "this sister doesn't understand so I'm going to help the sister get it". He wasn't arrogant but more like the kindest person talking to Sophia [*Martin's five-year-old daughter*]. I loved that. I am the sister who don't get it and he was nice enough to tell me the way it is. With his repetition of words he sang it to me. That's what's compelling.

MARTIN: What about his final line: "That's between me and my creator".

SMITH: He's saying: "I have to have my dignity. I know who did it and I'm not telling you". He doesn't appropriate his own culture.

ANONYMOUS BOY #2

from Anna Deavere Smith's *Fires in the Mirror: Crown Heights Brooklyn and Other Identities*

A stark recreation room. Anonymous Boy #2 is wearing a black jacket over his clothes. He has a gold tooth. He has some dreadlocks, and a very odd-shaped multicolored hat. He is soft spoken, and has a direct gaze. He seems to be very patient with his explanation.

BAD BOY: That sixteen year old
didn't murder that Jew
For one thing
He played baseball
Right?
He was a athalete

Right?
A bad boy
does
bad things
is
does bad things
only a bad boy could stabbed a man
somebody who
does those type a things
A atha lete
sees people
is interested in
stretchin
excercisin
goin to his football games
or his baseball games
He's not interested
in stabbin
people
so
it's not on his mind
to stab
to just jump into somethin
that he has no idea about
and kill a man
Somebody who's groomed in badness
or did badness before
stabbed the man
Because I used to be a atha lete
and I used to be a bad boy
and when I was a atha lete
I was a atha lete
all I thought about was atha lete
I'm not gonna jeoparsize my athleticism
or my career to do the things
that bad people do
And when I became a bad boy
I'm not a atha lete no more
I'm a bad boy
and I'm groomin myself in things that is bad
you understand so
He's a athalete
he's not a bad boy
It's a big difference
Like

> mostly the black youth in Crown Heights have two things
>   to do
> either DJ or a bad boy right
> You either
> DJ be a MC
> rapper
> or Jamaican rapper
> ragamuffin
> or you be a bad boy
> you sell drugs and rob people
> What do you do
> I sell drugs
> what do you do
> I rap
> That's how it is in Crown Heights
> I been living in Crown Heights most a my life
> I know for a fact that that youth
> didn't kill that that that that Jew
> that's between me and my creator

NOTES

1. Under the auspices of the Rockefeller Foundation, Richard Schechner, working with a steering committee that included Peggy Phelan, Jean Franco, Folabo Ajayi, Judith Mitoma, and Tomas Ybarra-Frausto, convened a conference on "intercultural performance" that met at the Bellagio Conference Center from 17 to 22 February 1991 – at the height of the Gulf War. Participants in the conference included Eugenio Barba, Barbara Kirshenblatt-Gimblett, Guillermo Gómez-Peña, Sanjukta Panigrahi, Trinh T. Minh-ha, William Sun, Gayatri Chakravorty Spivak, Michael Taussig, Yamaguchi Masao, Drew Taylor, and Smith.
2. A heated black/white, Jewish/black conflict roiled New York's City University in the early 1990s. Professor Leonard Jeffries made a public speech disparaging Jews and accusing Jews of controlling and manipulating the media; Professor Michael Levin voiced the opinion that blacks were not mentally the equal of whites. After a particularly inflammatory speech in Albany (July 1991), Jeffries was replaced as chair of the Black Studies Department. He sued, claiming his First Amendment rights were denied him. In May 1993, he won his case in federal court.

REFERENCE

Smith, Anna Deavere (1992) *Playbill 92* (no. 7):18. Program for *Fires in the Mirror: Crown Heights Brooklyn and Other Identities.*

DOO-A-DIDDLY-DIT-DIT

An Interview with Suzan-Lori Parks and Liz Diamond (1995)

Steven Drukman

> A continuous present is a continuous present.
> **Gertrude Stein** (1990 [1926])

The first time I read a Suzan-Lori Parks play I flashed to Wittgenstein, not Gertrude Stein. There seemed to me to be a utilitarian focus to Parks' words – a surgical intensity – that belied her play's surface impression of hypnotic languor. Surely this is what Wittgenstein meant when he spoke of language games, I thought, and the contingencies of various meanings in languages' various contexts, words having uses and not mere dictionary definitions,[1] family resemblances of certain words, and so on. Wittgenstein believed that the philosopher's task was to bring words back from their metaphysical usage to their everyday usage, and Parks' drama seems to play between the boundaries of both. There is a momentum in Parks' musicality, an aim in mind, a propulsion. But unlike surgical instruments, Parks' words do not seem sharp somehow, but blunt and easy: "meaning", it seemed, would come to the reader after the fourth downbeat, or maybe the fifth, head nodding, foot tapping. I couldn't conceive of actually seeing these dramas staged in the theatre; when, I wondered, would I get to close my eyes and listen?

Language does have an "unearthing" function – à la Wittgenstein – in Parks' dramas, most explicitly in *The America Play* (1994). "He digged the hole and the hole held him", Parks writes in a footnote to the play, as "History" itself is excavated from the "great hole of history". If it's taken for granted in our so-called postmodern condition that history is a narrative about the events of the past, then *The America Play* is, on one level, an example of a staging of that idea. But the play goes further: aware of the uses made of language, Parks suggests that – even if objective truth and knowledge are impossible – there are some discourses that are more powerful than others. This notion shows up in the detritus scattered throughout the great hole of history: the Lincoln-head pennies, the false beards, the stovepipe hats. All these historical fetishes (or "tshatschkes", as Parks likes to call them)[2] are themselves "put to use" in what director Liz Diamond and Parks call a "rep and rev" strategy. In *The America Play*, they are, in fact, the by-products of the repetitions and revisions of history itself. Following Jeffrey Mehlman, who noted in his *Revolution and Repetition* (rev and rep?) the "absurdity [of] the history of a grotesque repetition",[3] Parks one-ups Marx: *The America Play* shows that historical events and personages happen first as tragedy, second as farce, and thereafter as Theatre of the Absurd.

Although Parks is clearly not, strictly speaking, an "absurdist", there is something like the myth of Tantalus (if not Sisyphus) going on when one is being swept away in her drama.[4] The "rep and rev" strategy keeps the spectator/reader ever-vigilant, looking for something missed in the last repetition while scrutinizing the upcoming revision. Closure seems just on the horizon . . . where it remains. This narrative tease is then coupled with Parks' semiology: a conflation of usually discrete elements of the drama (such as character, line of dialog, stage action) into one package. The spectator is hyper-aware of language, yet follows the traces of that language toward a narrative conclusion that never comes. It's like Gertrude Stein, if Gertrude Stein liked to dangle carrots.

This is why I like to think of Parks' words as useful, or "use-full": there's the melding of utilitarian words-as-tools with words packed full of suggestion and musicality. But what seems like such theoretical sophistication comes naturally to Parks, as she explains at the beginning of this interview in her discussion of "meaning". This ease with language adds lilt and up-front aplomb to her drama, still unmatched in the contemporary theatre.

Jazz is a useful (that word again) way of thinking about the theatrical collaborations of Parks and Diamond. Of course, Diamond has already mentioned this in discussing Parks' "rep and rev" strategy, but there's the complicated racial inflection of jazz that is relevant as well. As we discussed in the interview, Parks' drama is both about and NOT about the "black experience"; it is concerned with the stories her figures tell to inhabit their experience as they speak their way into history. In the telling, identities (including, but not limited to, racial) are performed, reinhabited, reimprinted . . . but never for the first time. Jazz, as a genre, has always had both strains in its forming, reforming, and informing. Thelonious Monk, even as he played "white" standards, wanted to forge a music that couldn't be appropriated by white folks, to "create something they can't steal because they can't play it".[5]

Jazz is also analogous to Parks' peculiar use of puns. Just as tenor saxophone masters Dexter Gordon and Sonny Rollins were so fond of "quotation" in their solos – momentarily weaving strands of the corniest white chestnuts into their free-blowing sessions – the "Foundling" Father repeats and revises the assassination of Lincoln in *The America Play*. (Of course, the "foundling" father is itself a fully packed pun,

Father means "x" and if you figure out what that means, what he stands for, then that will enable you to figure out the play. People are welcome to understand the production in any way they choose, but I see that process as completely unhelpful. So I don't understand your notion of "giving up meaning". I mean, I don't understand that whole idea of meaning anyway, so I don't think we're giving up anything, I think we're, together, giving meanings.

DRUKMAN: Well, *Foundling Father* is a good example because one meaning is "founding father". Another meaning is "foundling" father, i.e., a father who is an orphan is a foundling. And that's just on the level of language, that's just the words. Already with one pun you've put into motion this idea of an origin-less father of our country's history! Then there's Liz's task: you have a person standing there as the foundling father, but he's only standing in as the foundling father, he's not really saying he *is* the foundling father. So all those different meanings sort of coexist, and they all sort of sprout from this one word.

PARKS: Right. But, I don't think you can do a play and not have that happen because the word is always there for me, and the guy would be there, so I don't think we'd be giving up "meaning". I guess what I'm saying is that I don't go in the direction saying, "this is what this means, this is a metaphor for . . . " whatever. If I watch the production, I don't see that I've given up something, or lost something. Because I don't have that in mind, I don't lose anything.

DRUKMAN: But do you see the text that you write as something that has full "meaning" on the page? I ask this because your plays are both more literary, a better read than most plays, and yet, they're also like scores for a play, that can only be fully realized in a live performance. So, speaking about meaning now, can meaning be apprehended from just reading your plays?

PARKS: Sure, I think there are meanings there. I mean, there's more if you do it, you know? I think there's meaning just in reading the play, and there's more meaning because it's a play and it's performed.

DIAMOND: When we first sit down and read the play together and talk about it, I don't ask what something "means". I'll often ask Suzan-Lori if she had an image in her head, if she sees it in a certain way, what the relationship of the figure is to the whole. I, as director, do concern myself very much with meanings, but I resist the temptation to impose one meaning on an event, a moment, a figure in the play. What I hope is happening in the course of the production is that the field of meanings that the play makes possible – the multitude of readings that a figure known as the Foundling Father and the Fo'/ Faux/Foe Father will generate – are offered up by the particular way

Plate 26: In Parks' *The America Play*, the Foundling Father (Reggie Montgomery) allows frustrated African Americans to reenact Lincoln's assassination. From the 1993 Yale Repertory Theatre production, directed by Liz Diamond. In addition to Montgomery, the photo features Tyrone Mitchell Henderson. Photo by T. Charles Erickson.

that figure's been cast, moves, speaks, etc.; that there will be a kind of wavelike effect so that one possible reading will be in the next instant contradicted by another and that all kinds of reverberating and clashing ideas will come up because that's very much the nature of this poetry.

I do not agree with those directors who claim not to interpret the text when they direct. I think that one is always an interpreter if by interpreter we mean reader. All I'm offering the world is my own very partial perspective on this amazingly rich play that will have many, many, many, many other lives. But the act of reading is an interpretive act, and one has to be prepared to defend one's point of view at any step along the way. That's what makes directing an exciting and powerful enterprise. And there are stronger and weaker readings of the same text and if I were to judge a strong or weak reading of a play, the sort of play that Suzan-Lori writes, it would have to do with the ability of the production to set up those resonating waves of meaning, which I think the play does so magnificently.

PARKS: I'd rather talk about the "reading" of my plays than the "meaning". Every time I talk about meaning to people it sounds like they're trying to substitute something else for what I've written. I've had so many interviews where someone would say, "So what does it mean? What does The Foundling Father mean? What are you trying to say?" And I'd say, "Well, it's a guy and it's his life. I'm trying to show you guys what this guy's doing". "Yeah, but what does it mean?" That's basically saying, "You're being obscure and why don't you tell us what you want, what you really mean", thinking the writer has some sort of agenda that hides somewhere behind or underneath the text or behind the production somewhere.

Well, one meaning or reading is the fact that there are all black people in the play. And that's something I feel very strongly about, but it's not about just that. But then it's "Oh, so the play's about black-on-black violence". That's what I mean about meaning. It's like, oh shit, that's the little limit we get. (*laughs*)

DRUKMAN: Houston Baker says that African Americans are ultimately always theorists or theoretical because "primary to their survival was the work of consciousness, of a nonmaterial counterintelligence";[12] I'm suggesting, as you're suggesting, that critics are resistant to seeing you as a formally innovative writer, a theoretical writer. You always have to be writing about, as you just said, "black-on-black violence", or something like that.

PARKS: Right.

DRUKMAN: I'm not quite sure why that is, what this resistance is of critics to seeing you as a formalist, or as formally experimental.

PARKS: I can't figure it. I think it has something to do with what we allow ourselves – we, meaning the world, black people included – what we allow black people to do and one of them is not theory, despite what you just quoted. You can get away with it if you are in an academic setting, and they're beginning to get away with it in the visual arts. Or if you're Houston Baker, whose work is fabulous. In theatre it's still . . . theatre's like the lag behind . . .

DRUKMAN: As usual . . .

PARKS: Yeah, so it's going to be the last thing to come around, after visual arts, after music. In theatre we still have more simplistic forms of representation that are still held up as examples of the best kind of theatre that black people can involve themselves in. (*laughing*) It's just a long road, a long dumb road.

DIAMOND: Just jumping back for a second to this question of this thorny word "meaning", and also sort of the secondary problematic term of "interpretation": I think one of the reasons we struggle with it so much in this postmodern period is that the notion of a "meaning" lying at the heart of a work – immanent and waiting to be unlocked – has been blown out of the water by theorists and artists themselves. Meaning is now understood to be a highly contingent artifact of the process of reading as opposed to something that exists in the text. And I think that most theatre people who want to talk about meaning, still refer to a one-to-one interpretation as a translation: this means that, x means y, whatever. There's gotta be a more flexible, plastic way of thinking about "meaning" that allows it to be as contingent, permeable, ever-changing as possible in the theatre.

PARKS: Or just stick to the play. Instead of saying, "What does that mean?" which is already a sentence that is outside of the play, ask you to fill in some blanks: it means this – that's an equation that's outside of the play. Stick to the play. So, let's see: you got a black guy onstage running around looking like Abraham Lincoln. If that's not enough for people to stick in their heads and go, "Hmmmm". Or, hey, you know, he talks in the third person, well that makes me think of . . . he's not comfortable with himself, he's alienated, he's left his family, he's living in a hole . . . If that's not enough already! But see, instead of digging there, they say, "What does it mean?" which is a sentence that is outside of the play and already you're not talking about our play anymore. You want me to say something like "black-on-black violence". That is an answer to that kind of question, something that you saw on the news (people love that, you know); or, the "So your father left your family" someone said to me once!

DRUKMAN: It's pretty "demeaning", isn't it?

PARKS: (*laughing*) Good one.

DIAMOND: Sure, or you see black people picking up a gun, fake or not, and shooting a black man who's wearing a blond beard and, you know . . .

PARKS: Yeah, yeah.

DRUKMAN: You're anticipating my questions so well . . .

PARKS: We have ESP.

DRUKMAN: You've said somewhere else that you want your plays to be dense, leaden, which makes me think of . . .

PARKS: I swear, don't put that in this interview! I cannot remember saying that and Liz keeps telling me I said it once but I'll be damned . . . (*laughing*) I hate that!

DRUKMAN: Well, I'm wondering . . .

PARKS: (*laughing*) It's like I want my cookies to be leaden, you know . . .

DRUKMAN: Well, I was going to ask if you think audiences are too dense. I mean, you require a lot of audiences.

PARKS: Yes! Well, sure. I think they are a bit. They only want something simple.

DRUKMAN: Well, I wonder if we're so used to seeing mimetic art on television and film, that psychological realism just made us lazy . . .

PARKS: Right, right.

DIAMOND: Well, this is where this whole rage about people taking your words and twisting them into something else drives you crazy: that "lead" comment . . .

PARKS: I must have said it, like maybe six or seven years ago . . .

DIAMOND: Exactly.

PARKS: I cannot remember saying it . . . Plutonium! Plutonium is what, in my new, enlightened state, I would say . . .

DIAMOND: Right, right.

PARKS: That makes much more sense. Plutonium moves, it has a great half-life, it's deadly.

DIAMOND: Yeah.

PARKS: If it gets inside you, it can kill you. That's it. Lead is like something else . . . you think of cookies.

DIAMOND: No, but it's still a good quote, (*to Parks*) not because you want to torture people, because you want your plays to be lead, i.e., dense, i.e., unreadable, impenetrable. What I remember our conversation having to do with, which I thought was really powerful at the time and was why it was an idea I got excited about, was Suzan-Lori saying to me precisely that she wanted her plays strong enough to stand up to millions and millions of readings. (*to Parks*) That's what you were on about.

PARKS: That's still the wrong word to use, let me tell you. I was not as good with words as I am now. Because lead is the wrong word! Lead is impenetrable . . .

DIAMOND: And it's inert. Too inert.

PARKS: Yes. Plutonium is alive. Lead is dead.

DRUKMAN: So may I use this if I include all this? (*laughter*)

PARKS: Why not? Go for it. It's your interview.

DIAMOND: But your question was about . . .

DRUKMAN: If audiences are too dense.

PARKS: If audiences are too . . . plutonic!

DRUKMAN: I was wondering if audiences are lazy.

PARKS: Yeah, probably. I think so. I mean, I can be . . .

DRUKMAN: I have a hard time believing you're lazy.

PARKS: Well, I'm lazy in certain areas. You just don't catch me when I'm being lazy. It's like a muscle – you don't exercise it and . . . I just wrote a recommendation for somebody and I wrote "You may think theatre is alive and well and that all these 'special interest groups' are getting their work done and winning the big prizes, but actually it's a pretty pitiful place because it's a place of easy answers and easy questions and those are the kinds of works that are being lauded". Easy question, easy answer, x=y, the meaning – go back to that word. (I can't think of another word to use; we'll kill this whole word.) But it shows in the form of new theatre.

I heard a reading of a play a couple of months ago, it was all about, you know, someone kind of bursting out of their shell and going and changing the world. And it had some exciting ideas. The playwright obviously thought: "Wow, I'm gonna say all this stuff!" But the structure of the play was a three-act play, you know, with little scenes and a beginning, middle, and end and I thought, "Jesus fucking Christ!" In no other art form would that be acceptable, you know what I mean? Nowhere else! People laugh at us in the theatre, other artists. And they should maybe. Yeah, we're lazy. I think we've all got big bellies.

DIAMOND: The theatre has one foot firmly in the mud of popular entertainment, you know – snake swallowers and flame throwers and conversations, about what it means. The problem that arises is when they don't trust their own experience of it enough to go on a journey of exploration with themselves and their friends about what they've seen or what they've read. But really, you can watch *The America Play*, you can look at that glistening black coal dust on the floor and look at those old columns all smeared with filth, you know, and look at Lucy wandering around and listening, listening, listening for echoes of her husband and you can talk about those images for days and trust that the ideas that come up in you about those images are valid. Talking about those images – outside of the theatre – is part of theatre.

DRUKMAN: See, as long as we have audiences that are not allowed that experience by artistic directors who keep these plays out of the theatres and just want the "belch factor", audiences don't trust themselves to take that journey.

PARKS: That's true. I know my plays aren't for everybody.

DRUKMAN: Let's talk about history . . . Toni Morrison said in *Playing in the Dark* that what she calls American Africanism are the ways in which the Africanist presence or persona is constructed in the United States by literature, and the imaginative uses that this fabricated presence has served. Now it seems that when you make a stage figure or character, you start from that point, from the fabricated presence. In other words, you assume that the figure is a historical construction.

PARKS: From the fabricated . . .

DRUKMAN: From the fabricated presence.

PARKS: From the fabricated absence, actually. It's a fabricated absence. That's where I start from. And that's where The Foundling Father came from. It's the hole idea.

DRUKMAN: So the figures are holes?

PARKS: Well, yes and no, they come from holes, it's the fabricated absence. It's the story that you're told that goes, "Once upon a time you weren't here". (*laughter*) You weren't here and you didn't do shit! And it's that, that fabricated absence.

DRUKMAN: So, like, the hole is the hole in Lincoln's head, the great hole in history, the holes in the gums of Aretha Saxton. These are all absences, holes . . .

PARKS: Or abscesses!

DIAMOND: There's a gap . . . in *Greeks* [the first part of *Imperceptible Mutabilities*, 1989] there's a gap . . .

PARKS: Right, right. "Overlap's uh gap", it says.

DRUKMAN: And to me, that's "theatre" in your plays. The recirculation of meaning, the holes versus the closure of the photograph and the chronicle of another history by people who told the story.

PARKS: Right, right. And whoever told the story, I mean, black people told stories and still do . . . it's not just "evil white people out there". They're two different stories but the same story, really.

DRUKMAN: I think of jazz as an analog for the way you write, because, like you said, there are two stories. When I think of my favorite jazz standards, there's John Coltrane playing "My Favorite Things", Miles Davis playing "Bye Blackbird", and Charlie Parker playing "Laura" – black musicians playing white standards, as written by whites. But then, also in jazz, there's a completely different language – John Coltrane playing "Naima", Miles Davis playing "So What?", Charlie Parker playing "Night in Tunisia", and it seems that both those discourses are in your plays and that might be what people miss, that there are two stories that you're accounting for.

PARKS: That's a good point. There's the standard and then there's the . . .

DRUKMAN: The rep of the standard.

PARKS: Right. It's like "blubblubblub" or "She be doo be waaah doo wah" – that's a great line from *Death of the Last Black Man . . .* but what does that "mean"? You know, I've actually made a little dictionary – foreign words and phrases.

DRUKMAN: You actually made the dictionary?

PARKS: It's coming out in the spring (*laughs*), in the new book of my plays.

DRUKMAN: Really?

PARKS: Yeah, but I put a little thing in the book, "Foreign Words and Phrases" and how to interpret the words, the pronunciation guide . . . we'll take care of all those people . . .

DRUKMAN: Your invented glossary . . .

DIAMOND: The "gloss"-ary! (*laughter*)

DRUKMAN: The gloss.

PARKS: That's right, the gloss. No, they're words from the play that are, like, THEP (*makes inhaling noise*): I say how to do it and what it means . . . no, not what it "means", why it's there . . . like "doo-a-diddly-dit-dit" . . . that one means "yes". Actually, that's more like, "yeah!" or, sometimes, "yeah?" (*laughter*) That's about it.

DRUKMAN: See, that's what boggles me, Liz, how . . . when I read one of these plays, I don't . . . I feel like I wouldn't know how to stage it, but of course, I'm reading the play on my couch. Maybe if I had people listening, you know, or listening to people saying it, then "THEP" or whatever would become very clear and I would just suddenly know in the performance how it's supposed to be and then *what* it means because I know *how* it's said.

PARKS: But it's also about how we read, you know. We should read aloud. Definitely. Any book, not just a play. I think I write to be read aloud.

DRUKMAN: What about all the hyphens and ellipses? How do you know how to stage the "dash-dash-dash"? For example, the Lucy/Brazil scene when they're playing the location game and there'd be two dashes, and the next time there'd be four dashes . . .

DIAMOND: Well, that's just learning how to read the play as a musical score, determining that every single thing on the page is there for a reason. Again, it's like reading it formally, the way you would try to decode a map or the way you would read a poem. I think that periods and commas and semicolons and dashes and the distance between the heading and a line of text and the way it is written on a page are all full of rich clues for the director. I think what's fun is to experiment with it in rehearsal and Suzan-Lori and I will listen to it and we'll try having four dashes be one length of time and then we'll realize, well, you know, we've got eight coming up, we'd better shrink that. You just develop a sense of structure, a rhythmic structure.

There's clearly a difference between a moment when a writer has not given a character anything to say and that character's name doesn't even appear on the page and when that character's name appears on the page, has been given space, and says nothing. Something's happening there! That character is not speaking but is taking up space on the page and is taking up time on the page and must take up space and time similarly on the stage. Discovering exactly what the rhythmic shape of that space should be is what makes rehearsal so much fun, because you're just discovering what those musical, aural dynamics are, that are going to make it . . . pop. And you can't do that – you can't even do that reading out loud – you can only do that when everybody is up on their feet and their bodies are moving in space and you've got somebody 15 feet away from somebody else. It's fascinating with these plays to see that.

DRUKMAN: Do you think when you stage Suzan-Lori's plays that they change more or less during the course of the run? Do you feel like you need to "set the score" and so they actually change less in the course of the run or, because there are so many textual clues, the performances change even more throughout a run?

DIAMOND: Boy. I don't know how to answer that. When I did "Open House" in *Imperceptible Mutabilities*, I knew very much I wanted

Aretha's bed to be just floating in space and I wanted it to be spinning around and I wanted her to be wrenched from the bed and I wanted those pliers over her head . . . the shape of the play felt like it had to be a really wild hallucinogenic, sort-of-nightmarish event. And I knew there was something about the stately rhythm of the sound of the text in *Greeks* that made it feel – and the name itself, *Greeks* – that made it seem that there needed to be a very strong choric quality to the family, and that the family somehow needed to have a military bearing. That was something that came from the rhythm of the way they spoke to each other.

And in *The America Play*, you're given this amazing opportunity to have George Washington's wooden teeth on stage, it's completely irresistible. Staging these plays has to do with taking the text absolutely at its word. I mean, literally. It's finding stage directions embedded in the writing that is an enormous part of my task and it's through that process that the actors start to discover the code by discovering that (unlike traditional "psychological" American acting training) *there is no code outside of what's on the page*. It's kind of an old-fashioned idea, really. This is what we're supposed to do when we direct or work on Shakespeare. But it's amazing how little American acting training prepares them for that kind of exploration of action in language! I guess that's what you mean when you say "performative".

My big breakthrough on *Death of the Last Black Man* was realizing that the so-called choruses took up more space on the page than the tableaux. There's the "meaning" . . . perform that!

DRUKMAN: Another thing I want to talk about is intertexuality. I've noticed that there's a lot of Beckett filtering through your plays. This might just be my own personal rep and rev reading. But, for example, in *Devotees* [1992], Lilly reminds me of a sort of *Endgame* character, maybe it's just the wheelchair . . .

PARKS: (*laughing*) I can't remember! She's an old mother, right?

DRUKMAN: Right. There's something about the two of them that's like Hamm and Clov . . . she's an old mother . . .

PARKS: Right. Okay, I'll accept that.

DRUKMAN: But certainly in *The America Play* . . . Now, the Beckett I got from *Devotees* is in the text, but in *The America Play* it's in Liz's staging. There's something, somehow, Godot-like about it. I've never seen *Devotees*.

PARKS: Neither have I.

DRUKMAN: And also, the hole sort of reminded me of the mound in *Happy Days*, sort of the inverse of that. I'm just wondering if Beckett's one of the biggest . . .

PARKS: He's an influence, but he's no bigger than Adrienne Kennedy. They both make me think of things. Faulkner, too, actually . . . Beckett's not, for me, as big as Faulkner. To think of, "Wow, that's a writer I thoroughly love" . . . I mean, Beckett, yeah I think he's great and all that, but Faulkner's the writer that I think is my favorite.

DRUKMAN: What about other intertextual quotes from your plays? "Prunes and prisms" comes from Joyce, right?

PARKS: Joyce, yeah. That's from, what's it from?

DRUKMAN: *Ulysses.*

PARKS: *Ulysses*, right. It's just, like, I was reading along and I went, "Wow! what a great line".

DRUKMAN: But you're not gesturing towards *Ulysses* . . .

PARKS: No, no, but there is something . . . I'm fascinated with what they are allowed to do, I guess. What Joyce was allowed to do or what Joyce allowed himself to do, what Beckett allowed himself to do, what Faulkner allowed himself to do, Woolf . . . What they got away with . . . Doin' "diddly did did the drop" comes out of that tradition of doing whatever you want (*laughter*) and saying, "Here it is! You Mr or Ms critic, you guys go away and think about it and exercise your brains and come up with something thrilling!"

DRUKMAN: There's a lot of humor there, I think. But you've said somewhere that you've gotten a lot of humor from Liz.

PARKS: Yeah. I've become more socially acceptable since hanging out with Liz. (*laughter*) It's true. When she met me, I was really, really weird. Now I'm only a little weird . . . Liz has an incredible sense of humor and (*to Diamond*) I've really learned from hanging around and working with you, 'cause my humor is so perverted . . .

DIAMOND: You're pretty funny yourself . . .

PARKS: Mine's like, twisted, and Liz's is like, the kind of humor you can say in front of people, so we can get away with saying things like, "the great hole" and "prenuptial excitement", and stuff that's unseemly. There are so many dirty jokes in *The America Play*. And Liz points them out to me, even though I've written them, I guess . . .

DIAMOND: Well, I maintain that it's there. I think the play is a riot. I mean, it's completely heartbreaking, but I think it's unbelievably funny and I think when he reminisces about his honeymoon and says, "We'd stand on the lip of that hole" . . .

DRUKMAN: Most audiences miss the dirty joke there?

PARKS: Yeah.

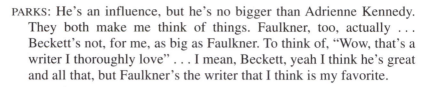

DIAMOND: And I think the idea of a woman listening for her husband's echo with an ear trumpet is brilliant and heartbreaking and extremely funny. For me, again, it helped to be literal, so I started thinking about the echoes *qua* echoes, as stuff she was picking up. I liked thinking about the stuff that was coming into the hole. The Great Hole of History. It's like a wastebasket – there's gonna be crap that collects. And then, who are these people wearing these crazy outfits doing these shards from *Our American Cousin*?[13]

PARKS: I mean, humor's a great way of getting to the deep shit, isn't it? Humor is a very effective way of saying something that you probably could never say ordinarily. And, you know, we do it everyday. I say all kinds of bizarre things with a little laugh, or as a joke.

DRUKMAN: What are you working on now?

PARKS: I'm working on a film. I am. I just finished the first draft of it. It's due this week.

DRUKMAN: What is it?

PARKS: It's . . .

DIAMOND: . . . top secret! Top secret stuff!

PARKS: It's my first feature-length film and it's with Spike Lee, and the other night Liz and her husband, Ralph, helped me . . .

DIAMOND: . . . figure out what it meant! (*laughter*)

PARKS: It's the first time I actually sat down and said – because films are written in a completely different way – you need this plot point and those things to happen at certain times, and you need to say, "So what does this mean to you guys? Okay, that's a good reading of that, I'll put that in the pressure cooker and make it produce popcorn on page 96".

DRUKMAN: And what about you, Liz?

DIAMOND: I'm working on a children's musical, by Mac Wellman, called "Tiger, Tiger, Tiger" and we're going to do it out at Sundance and Michael Roth is composing the music.

DRUKMAN: And your newest play, *Venus*? I couldn't find . . .

PARKS: Because it's not written.

DRUKMAN: It's not written yet?

PARKS: I mean, it's written, but I have to write some more. It's the new play . . . it's um . . . I'm even worse talking about plays before they're done. It's a play about love and fame and . . . and . . . somebody's ass. (*laughter*) No, it's a play about this woman called the Venus Hottentot who had a big butt and exhibited it in the nineteenth century.

DRUKMAN: Do you mean . . . she really did?

PARKS: Yeah, yeah. And she had a large butt.

DIAMOND: And a large following.

PARKS: And a larger following. (*laughter*)

DIAMOND: Her rear end was only exceeded by the . . . size of her audience. (*laughter*)

PARKS: That's right. Like me, maybe, some day.

NOTES

1. See Hallett 1967.
2. Parks as quoted in Pearce 1994:26.
3. Mehlman 1977:14.
4. As I have written elsewhere (1994:191) Parks' plays are almost unbearably tantalizing, because meaning, it seems, is always just around the bend.
5. See Ross 1989.
6. Robinson 1994:191.
7. Solomon 1990:80.
8. See Pearce 1992:39.
9. Adorno 1967:126.
10. *Ibid*.
11. See Stein 1990.
12. Baker 1993.
13. *Our American Cousin* was the popular nineteenth-century American comedy by Tom Taylor. It was made famous by Laura Keene's production, which starred Joseph Jefferson and E.A. Sothern, and by the fact that it was in performance at Ford's Theatre in Washington, DC when Abraham Lincoln was assassinated.

BIBLIOGRAPHY

Adorno, Theodor, "Perennial Fashion – Jazz" in *Prisms*, Cambridge Massachusetts: MIT Press, 1967.

Baker, Houston, Jr, *Black Studies, Rap and the Academy*, Chicago: University of Chicago Press, 1993.

Drukman, Steven, "*The America Play*", *Women and Performance* 13, 7:1, 1994.

Hallett, Garth, *Wittgenstein's Definition of Meaning and Use*, New York: Fordham University Press, 1967.

Plate 27: (*opposite*) In the 1990 Yale Repertory Theatre production of Suzan-Lori Parks' *The Death of the Last Black Man in the Whole Entire World*, the Black Man with Watermelon (Leon Addison Brown) comforts the Black Woman with Fried Drumstick (Fanni Green). Directed by Liz Diamond. Photo by Gerry Goodstein.

Mehlman, Jeffrey, *Revolution and Repetition: Marx/Hugo/Balzac*, Berkeley: University of California Press, 1977.

Pearce, Michele, "Liz Diamond", *American Theatre*, May 1992:38–40.

———. "Alien Nation: An Interview with the Playwright [Suzan-Lori Parks]", *American Theatre*, March 1994:26.

Robinson, Marc, *The Other American Drama*, New York: Cambridge University Press, 1994.

Ross, Andrew, *No Respect: Intellectuals and Popular Culture*, New York: Routledge, 1989.

Solomon, Alisa, "Signifying on the Signifyin': The Plays of Suzan-Lori Parks", *Theatre*, Summer/Fall 1990:73-80.

Stein, Gertrude, "Composition as Explanation (1926)" in *Selected Writings of Gertrude Stein*, Carl Van Vechten, ed., New York: Vintage, 1990.

PRODUCTION HISTORY
LIZ DIAMOND

1985   *Fizzles* by Samuel Beckett: adaptation by Ryan Cutrona and Liz Diamond, at P.S. 122, New York City

1987   *The Hypothesis* by Robert Pinget, at La MaMa Etc., New York City

1988   *The Dispute* by Pierre Marivaux, at New Theatre of Brooklyn, New York

1989   *The Cézanne Syndrome* by Normand Canac-Marquis, at Soho Rep, New York City
Imperceptible Mutabilities in the Third Kingdom by Suzan-Lori Parks, at BACA Downtown, Brooklyn, New York
Hamlet's Ghosts Perform Hamlet by Charles Borkhuis, at Home for Contemporary Theatre, New York City
Sizwe Banzi Is Dead and *The Island* by Athol Fugard, John Kani, and Winston Ntshona, at Portland Stage Company, Portland, Maine

1990   *A Man's a Man* by Bertolt Brecht, at Portland Stage Company, Portland, Maine

1991   *Imperceptible Mutabilities in the Third Kingdom* by Suzan-Lori Parks, at New City Theatre, Seattle, Washington State
The Good Person of Sichuan by Bertolt Brecht, at Julliard, New York City

1992   *The Death of the Last Black Man in the Whole Entire World* by Suzan-Lori Parks, at Yale Repertory Theatre, New Haven, Connecticut
Dream of a Common Language by Heather McDonald, at The Women's Project, New York City

Julius Caesar by William Shakespeare, at Seattle Repertory Theatre, Seattle, Washington State
1993   *Saint Joan of the Stockyards* by Bertolt Brecht, at Yale Repertory Theatre, New Haven, Connecticut
1994   *The America Play* by Suzan-Lori Parks, at Yale Repertory Theatre, New Haven, Connecticut, and New York Shakespeare Festival, New York City
School for Wives by Molière, at Yale Repertory Theatre, New Haven, Connecticut
Antigone in New York by Janusz Glowacki, at Yale Repertory Theatre, New Haven, Connecticut
Le Bourgeois Avant Garde by Charles Ludlam, at Yale Repertory Theatre, New Haven, Connecticut

SUZAN-LORI PARKS

1987   *Betting on the Dust Commander*, at The Gas Station, New York City
Fishes, read at the International Women Playwrights Festival
The Sinner's Place, produced at the New Play Festival
1989   *Imperceptible Mutabilities in the Third Kingdom*, at BACA Downtown, Brooklyn, New York (directed by Liz Diamond)
1990   *Betting on the Dust Commander*, at Company One, Hartford, Connecticut
The Death of the Last Black Man in the Whole Entire World, at BACA Downtown, Brooklyn, New York (directed by Liz Diamond)
Anemone Me (film), produced by Apparatus Productions
Pickling (radio play), produced by New American Radio
1991   *Imperceptible Mutabilities in the Third Kingdom*, at New City Theatre, Seattle, Washington State (directed by Liz Diamond)
Betting on the Dust Commander, at The Working Theatre, New York City
1992   *The Death of the Last Black Man in the Whole Entire World,* at Yale Repertory Theatre, New Haven, Connecticut (directed by Liz Diamond)
Devotees in the Garden of Love, commissioned by the Humana Festival, Actors Theatre of Louisville, Kentucky
Alive from Off Center (video)
The Third Kingdom (radio play), produced by New American Radio
Locomotive (radio play), produced by New American Radio
1994   *The America Play*, commissioned by Theatre for a New Audience, New York City
————, developed by the Arena Stage,Washington, DC, and Dallas Theatre Center, Dallas, Texas

————, produced at Yale Repertory Theatre, New Haven, Connecticut, and New York Shakespeare Festival, New York City (directed by Liz Diamond)

1995   *Venus*, commissioned by the Women's Project, New York City and performed at the New York Shakespeare Festival/Public Theatre (directed by Richard Foreman)

THE AMERICA PLAY (1994)

Suzan-Lori Parks

THE ROLES

Act One:

> The Foundling Father, as Abraham Lincoln
> A variety of Visitors

Act Two:

> Lucy
> Brazil
> The Foundling Father, as Abraham Lincoln
> 2 Actors

The Visitors in Act One are played by the 2 Actors who assume the roles in the passages from *Our American Cousin* in Act Two.

PLACE

A great hole. In the middle of nowhere. The hole is an exact replica of The Great Hole of History.

SYNOPSIS OF ACTS AND SCENES

Act One: Lincoln Act

Act Two: The Hall of Wonders

> A. Big Bang
> B. Echo
> C. Archeology
> D. Echo
> E. Spadework
> F. Echo
> G. The Great Beyond

Brackets in the text indicate optional cuts for production.

In the beginning, all the world was *America*.
John Locke

Act One: Lincoln Act

(*A great hole. In the middle of nowhere. The hole is an exact replica of the Great Hole of History.*)

THE FOUNDLING FATHER AS ABRAHAM LINCOLN: "To stop too fearful and too faint to go".[1]

(*rest*)

"He digged the hole and the whole held him".

(*rest*)

"I cannot dig, to beg I am ashamed".[2]

(*rest*)

"He went to the theatre but home went she".[3]

(*rest*)

Goatee. Goatee. What he sported when he died. Its not my favorite.

(*rest*)

"He digged the hole and the whole held him". Huh.

(*rest*)

There was once a man who was told that he bore a strong resemblance to Abraham Lincoln. He was tall and thinly built just like the Great Man. His legs were the longer part just like the Great Mans legs. His hands and feet were large as the Great Mans were large. The Lesser Known had several beards which he carried around in a box. The beards were his although he himself had not grown them on his face but since he'd secretly bought the hairs from his barber and arranged their beard shapes and since the procurement and upkeep of his beards took so much work he figured that the beards were completely his. Were as authentic as he was, so to speak. His beard box was of cherry wood and lined with purple velvet. He had the initials "A.L." tooled in gold on the lid.

(*rest*)

While the Great Mans livelihood kept him in Big Town the Lesser Knowns work kept him in Small Town. The Great Man by trade was a President. The Lesser Known was a Digger by trade. From a family of Diggers. Digged graves. He was known in Small Town to dig his graves quickly and neatly. This brought him a steady business.

(*rest*)

A wink to Mr Lincolns pasteboard cutout. (*winks at Lincoln's pasteboard cutout*)

(*rest*)

It would be helpful to our story if when the Great Man died in death he were to meet the Lesser Known. It would be helpful to our story if, say, the Lesser Known were summoned to Big Town by the Great Mans wife: "*Emergency* oh, *Emergency*, please put the Great Man in the ground"[4] (they say the Great Mans wife was given to hysterics: one young son dead others sickly: even the Great Man couldnt save them: a war on then off and surrendered to: "Play Dixie I always liked that song"[5]: the brother against the brother: a new nation all conceived and ready to be hatched: the Great Man takes to guffawing guffawing at thin jokes in bad plays: "You sockdologizing old mantrap!"[6] haw haw haw because he wants so very badly to laugh at something and one moment guffawing and the next moment the Great Man is gunned down. In his rocker. "Useless Useless".[7] And there were bills to pay.) "*Emergency*, oh *Emergency* please put the Great Man in the ground".

(*rest*)

It is said that the Great Mans wife did call out and it is said that the Lesser Known would [sneak away from his digging and stand behind a tree where he couldnt be seen or get up and] leave his wife and child after the blessing had been said and [the meat carved during the distribution of the vegetables it is said that he would leave his wife and his child and] standing in the kitchen or sometimes out in the yard [between the right angles of the house] stand out there where he couldnt be seen standing with his ear cocked. "*Emergency*, oh *Emergency*, please put the Great Man in the ground".

(*rest*)

It would help if she had called out and if he had been summoned been given a ticket all bought and paid for and boarded a train in his look-alike black frock coat bought on time and already exhausted. Ridiculous. If he had been summoned. [Been summoned between the meat and the vegetables and boarded a train to Big Town where he would line up and gawk at the Great Mans corpse along with the rest of them.] But none of this was meant to be.

(*rest*)

A nod to the bust of Mr Lincoln. (*nods to the bust of Lincoln*) But none of this was meant to be. For the Great Man had been murdered long before the Lesser Known had been born. Howuhboutthat. [So that any calling that had been done he couldnt hear, any summoning he had hoped for he couldnt answer but somehow not even unheard and unanswered because he hadnt even been there] although you should note that he talked about the murder and the mourning that followed as if he'd been called away on business at the time and because of the business had missed it. Living regretting he hadnt arrived sooner. Being told from birth practically that he and the Great Man were dead ringers, more or less, and knowing that he, if he had been in the slightest vicinity back then, would have had at least a chance at the great honor of digging the Great Mans grave.

(*rest*)

This beard I wear for the holidays. I got shoes to match. Rarely wear em together. Its a little *much*.

(*rest*)

[His son named in a fit of meanspirit after the bad joke about fancy nuts and old mens toes his son looked like a nobody. Not Mr Lincoln or the father or the mother either for that matter although the father had assumed the superiority of his own blood and hadnt really expected the mother to exert any influence.]

(*rest*)

Sunday. Always slow on Sunday. I'll get thuh shoes. Youll see. A wink to Mr Lincolns pasteboard cutout. (*winks at Lincoln's cutout*)

(*rest*)

Everyone who has ever walked the earth has a shape around which their entire lives and their posterity shapes itself. The Great Man had his log cabin into which he was born, the distance between the cabin and Big Town multiplied by the half-life, the staying power of his words and image, being the true measurement of the Great Mans stature. The Lesser Known had a favorite hole. A chasm, really. Not a hole he had digged but one he'd visited. Long before the son was born. When he and his Lucy were newly wedded. Lucy kept secrets for the dead. And they figured what with his digging and her Confidence work they could build a mourning business. The son would be a weeper. Such a long time uhgo. So long uhgo. When he and his Lucy were newly wedded and looking for some postnuptial excitement: A Big Hole. A theme park. With historical parades. The size of the hole itself was enough to impress any Digger but it was the Historicity of the place the order and beauty of the pageants which marched by them the Greats on parade in front of them. From the sidelines he'd be calling "Ohwayohwhyohwayoh" and "Hello" and waving and saluting. The Hole and its Historicity and the part he played in it all gave a shape to the life and posterity of the Lesser Known that he could never shake.

(*rest*)

Here they are. I wont put them on. I'll just hold them up. See. Too much. Told ya. Much much later when the Lesser Known had made a name for himself he began to record his own movements. He hoped he'd be of interest to posterity. As in the Great Mans footsteps.

(*rest*)

Traveling home again from the honeymoon at the Big Hole riding the train with his Lucy: wife beside him the Reconstructed Historicities he has witnessed continue to march before him in his minds eye as they had at the Hole. Cannons wicks were lit and the rockets did blare and the enemy was slain and lay stretched out and smoldering for dead and rose up again to take their bows. On the way home again the histories paraded again on past him although it wasnt on past him at all it wasnt something he could expect but again like Lincolns life not "on past" but *past. Behind him.* Like an echo in his head.

(*rest*)

When he got home again he began to hear the summoning. At first they thought it only an echo. Memories sometimes stuck like that and he and his Lucy had both seen visions. But after a while it only called to him. And it became louder not softer but louder louder as if he were moving toward it.

(*rest*)

This is my fancy beard. Yellow. Mr Lincolns hair was dark so I dont wear it much. If you deviate too much they wont get their pleasure. Thats my experience. Some inconsistencies are perpetuatable because theyre good for business. But not the yellow beard. Its just my fancy. Ev-ery once and a while. Of course, his hair was dark.

(*rest*)

The Lesser Known left his wife and child and went out West finally. [Between the meat and the vegetables. A monumentous journey. Enduring all the elements. Without a friend in the world. And the beasts of the forest took him in. He got there and he got his plot he staked his claim he tried his hand at his own Big Hole.] As it had been back East everywhere out West he went people remarked on his likeness to Lincoln. How, in a limited sort of way, taking into account of course his natural God-given limitations, how he was identical to the Great Man in gait and manner how his legs were long and torso short. The Lesser Known had by this time taken to wearing a false wart on his cheek in remembrance of the Great Mans wart. When the Westerners noted his wart they pronounced the 2 men in virtual twinship.

(*rest*)

Goatee. Huh. Goatee.

(*rest*)

"He digged the Hole and the Whole held him".

(*rest*)

"I cannot dig, to beg I am ashamed".

(*rest*)

The Lesser Known had under his belt a few of the Great Mans words and after a day of digging, in the evenings, would stand in his hole reciting. But the Lesser Known was a curiosity at best. None of those who spoke of his virtual twinship with greatness would actually pay money to watch him be that greatness. One day he tacked up posters inviting them to come and throw old food at him while he spoke. This was a moderate success. People began to save their old food "for Mr Lincoln" they said. He took to traveling playing small towns. Made money. And when someone remarked that he played Lincoln so well that he ought to be shot, it was as if the Great Mans footsteps had been suddenly revealed:

(*rest*)

The Lesser Known returned to his hole and, instead of speeching, his act would now consist of a single chair, a rocker, in a dark box. The public was invited to pay a penny, choose from the selection of provided pistols, enter the darkened box and "Shoot Mr Lincoln". The Lesser Known became famous overnight.

(*A Man, as John Wilkes Booth, enters. He takes a gun and "stands in position": at the left side of the Foundling Father, as Abraham Lincoln, pointing the gun at the Foundling Father's head*)

A MAN: Ready.

THE FOUNDLING FATHER: Haw Haw Haw Haw

(*rest*)

HAW HAW HAW HAW

(*Booth shoots. Lincoln "slumps in his chair". Booth jumps*)

A MAN: (*theatrically*) "Thus to the tyrants!"[8]

(*rest*)

Hhhh. (*exits*)

THE FOUNDLING FATHER: Most of them do that, thuh "Thus to the tyrants!"

– what they say the killer said. "Thus to the tyrants!" The killer was also heard to say "The South is avenged!"[9] Sometimes they yell that.

(*A Man, the same man as before, enters again, again as John Wilkes Booth. He takes a gun and "stands in position": at the left side of the Foundling Father, as Abraham Lincoln, pointing the gun at the Foundling Father's head*)

A MAN: Ready.

THE FOUNDLING FATHER: Haw Haw Haw Haw

(*rest*)

HAW HAW HAW HAW

(*Booth shoots. Lincoln "slumps in his chair". Booth jumps*)

A MAN: (*theatrically*) "The South is avenged!"

(*rest*)

Hhhh.

(*rest*)

Thank you.

THE FOUNDLING FATHER: Pleasures mine.

A MAN: Till next week.

THE FOUNDLING FATHER: Till next week.

(*A Man exits*)

THE FOUNDLING FATHER: Comes once a week that one. Always chooses the Derringer although we've got several styles he always chooses the Derringer. Always "The tyrants" and then "The South avenged". The ones who choose the Derringer are the ones for History. He's one for History. As it Used to Be. Never wavers. No frills. By the book. Nothing excessive.

(*rest*)

A nod to Mr Lincolns bust. (*nods to Lincoln's bust*)

(*rest*)

I'll wear this one. He sported this style in the early war years. Years of uncertainty. When he didnt know if the war was right when it could be said he didnt always know which side he was on not because he was a stupid man but because it was sometimes not 2 different sides at all but one great side surging toward something beyond either Northern or Southern. A beard of uncertainty. The Lesser Known meanwhile living his life long after all this had happened and not knowing much about it until he was much older [(as a boy "The Civil War" was an afterschool game and his folks didnt mention the Great Mans murder for fear of frightening him)] knew only that he was a dead ringer in a family of Diggers and that he wanted to grow and have others think of him and remove their hats and touch their hearts and look up into the heavens and say something about the freeing of the slaves. That is, he wanted to make a great impression as he understood Mr Lincoln to have made.

(*rest*)

And so in his youth the Lesser Known familiarized himself with all aspects of the Great Mans existence. What interested the Lesser Known most was the murder and what was most captivating about the murder was the 20 feet –

(*A Woman, as Booth, enters*)

A WOMAN: Excuse me.

THE FOUNDLING FATHER: Not at all.

(*A Woman, as Booth, "stands in position"*)

THE FOUNDLING FATHER Haw Haw Haw Haw

(*rest*)

HAW HAW HAW HAW

(*Booth shoots. Lincoln "slumps in his chair". Booth jumps*)

A WOMAN: "Strike the tent".[10] (*exits*)

THE FOUNDLING FATHER: What interested the Lesser Known most about the Great Mans murder was the 20 feet which separated the presidents box from the stage. In the presidents box sat the president his wife and their 2 friends. On the stage that night was *Our American Cousin* starring Miss Laura Keene. The plot of this play is of little consequence to our story. Suffice it to say that it was thinly comedic and somewhere in the 3rd Act a man holds a gun to his head – something about despair –

(*rest*)

Ladies and Gentlemen: *Our American Cousin* –

(*B Woman, as Booth, enters. She "stands in position"*)

B WOMAN: Go ahead.

THE FOUNDLING FATHER: Haw Haw Haw Haw

(*rest*)

Plate 28: In Suzan-Lori Parks' *The America Play*, an African-American woman (Adriane Lenox) startles the Foundling Father (Reggie Montgomery) with her vocalized stress. From the 1993 Yale Repertory Theatre production, directed by Liz Diamond. Photo by T. Charles Erickson.

HAW HAW HAW HAW

(*Booth shoots. Lincoln "slumps in his chair". Booth jumps*)

B WOMAN: (*rest*) LIES!

(*rest*)

L I I I I I I I I I I I I I I I I I I I I I I I I I I I I E S!

(*rest*)

L I I I I I I I I I I I I I I I I I I I A R R R R R R R R R R R R R R S!

(*rest*)

Lies.

(*Rest. Exits. Reenters. Steps downstage. Rest*)

L I E S!

(*rest*)

L I I I I I I I I I I I I I I I I I I I I I I I I I I I I I E S!

(*rest*)

L I I I I I I I I I I I I I I I I I I I A R R R R R R R R R R R R R R S!

(*rest*)

Lies.

(*Rest. Exits.*)

THE FOUNDLING FATHER: (*rest*) I think I'll wear the yellow one. Variety. Works like uh tonic.

(*rest*)

Some inaccuracies are good for business. Take the stovepipe hat! Never really worn indoors but people dont like their Lincoln hatless.

(*rest*)

Mr Lincoln my apologies. (*nods to the bust and winks to the cutout*)

(*rest*)

[Blonde. Not bad if you like a stretch. Hmmm. Let us pretend for a moment that our beloved Mr Lincoln was a blonde. "The sun on his fair hair looked like the sun itself ".[11] – . Now. What interested our Mr Lesser Known most was those feet between where the Great *Blonde* Man sat, in his rocker, the stage, the time it took the murderer to cross that expanse, and how the murderer crossed it. He jumped. Broke his leg in the jumping. It was said that the Great Mans wife then began to scream. (She was given to hysterics several years afterward in fact declared insane did you know she ran around Big Town poor desperate for money trying to sell her clothing? On that sad night she begged her servant: "Bring in Taddy, Father will speak to Taddy".[12] But Father died instead unconscious. And she went mad from grief. Off her rocker. Mad Mary claims she hears her dead men. Summoning. The older son, Robert, he locked her up: "*Emergency*, oh, *Emergency* please put the Great Man in the ground".)

(Enter B Man, as Booth. He "stands in position")

THE FOUNDLING FATHER: Haw Haw Haw Haw

(rest)

HAW HAW HAW HAW

(Booth shoots. Lincoln "slumps in his chair". Booth jumps)

B MAN: "Now he belongs to the ages".[13]

(rest)

Blonde?

THE FOUNDLING FATHER: (I only talk with the regulars.)

B MAN: He wasnt blonde. *(exits)*

THE FOUNDLING FATHER: A slight deafness in this ear other than that there are no side effects.

(rest)

Hhh. Clean-shaven for a while. The face needs air. Clean-shaven as in his youth. When he met his Mary. – . Hhh. Blonde.

(rest)

6 feet under is a long way to go. Imagine. When the Lesser Known left to find his way out West he figured he had dug over 7 hundred and 23 graves. 7 hundred and 23. Excluding his Big Hole. Excluding the hundreds of shallow holes he later digs the hundreds of shallow holes he'll use to bury his faux-historical knickknacks when he finally quits this business. Not including those. 7 hundred and 23 graves.

(C Man and C Woman enter)

C MAN: You allow 2 at once?

THE FOUNDLING FATHER

(rest)

C WOMAN: We're just married. You know: newlyweds. We hope you dont mind. Us both at once.

THE FOUNDLING FATHER

(rest)

C MAN: We're just married.

C WOMAN: Newlyweds.

THE FOUNDLING FATHER

(rest)
(rest)

(They "stand in position". Both hold one gun)

C MAN AND C WOMAN: Shoot.

THE FOUNDLING FATHER: Haw Haw Haw Haw

(rest)

    HAW HAW HAW HAW

(rest)
(rest)

    HAW HAW HAW HAW

(They shoot. Lincoln "slumps in his chair". They jump)

C MAN: Go on.

C WOMAN: *(theatrically)* "Theyve killed the president!"[14]

(Rest. They exit)

THE FOUNDLING FATHER: Theyll have children and theyll bring their children here. A slight deafness in this ear other than that there are no side effects. Little ringing in the ears. Slight deafness. I cant complain.

(rest)

The passage of time. The crossing of space. [The Lesser Known recorded his every movement.] He'd hoped he'd be of interest in his posterity. [Once again riding in the Great Mans footsteps.] A nod to the presidents bust. *(nods)*

(rest)
(rest)

The Great Man lived in the past that is was an inhabitant of time immemorial and the Lesser Known out West alive a resident of the present. And the Great Mans deeds had transpired during the life of the Great Man somewhere in past-land that is somewhere "back there" and all this while the Lesser Known digging his holes bearing the burden of his resemblance all the while trying somehow to equal the Great Man in stature, word and deed going forward with his lesser life trying somehow to follow in the Great Mans footsteps footsteps that were of course behind him. The Lesser Known trying somehow to catch up to the Great Man all this while and maybe running too fast in the wrong direction. Which is to say that maybe the Great Man had to catch him. Hhhh. Ridiculous.

(*rest*)

Full fringe. The way he appears on the money.

(*rest*)

A wink to Mr Lincolns pasteboard cutout. A nod to Mr Lincolns bust.

(*Rest. Time passes. Rest*)

When someone remarked that he played Lincoln so well that he ought to be shot it was as if the Great Mans footsteps had been suddenly revealed: instead of making speeches his act would now consist of a single chair, a rocker, in a dark box. The public was cordially invited to pay a penny, choose from a selection of provided pistols enter the darkened box and "Shoot Mr Lincoln". The Lesser Known became famous overnight.

(*A Man, as John Wilkes Booth, enters. He takes a gun and "stands in position": at the left side of the Foundling Father, as Abraham Lincoln, pointing the gun at the Foundling Father's head*)

THE FOUNDLING FATHER: Mmm. Like clockwork.

A MAN: Ready.

THE FOUNDLING FATHER: Haw Haw Haw Haw

(*rest*)

HAW HAW HAW HAW

(*Booth shoots. Lincoln "slumps in his chair". Booth jumps*)

A MAN: (*theatrically*) "Thus to the tyrants!"

(*rest*)

Hhhh.

LINCOLN

BOOTH

LINCOLN

BOOTH

LINCOLN

BOOTH

LINCOLN

BOOTH

LINCOLN

(*Booth jumps*)

A MAN: (*theatrically*) "The South is avenged!"

(*rest*)

Hhhh.

(*rest*)

Thank you.

THE FOUNDLING FATHER: Pleasures mine.

A MAN: Next week then. (*exits*)

THE FOUNDLING FATHER: Little ringing in the ears. Slight deafness.

(*rest*)

Little ringing in the ears.

(*rest*)

A wink to the Great Mans cutout. A nod to the Great Mans bust. (*winks and nods*) Once again striding in the Great Mans footsteps. Riding on in. Riding to the rescue the way they do. They both had such long legs. Such big feet. And the Greater Man had such a lead although of course somehow still "back there". If the Lesser Known had slowed down stopped moving completely gone in reverse died maybe the Greater Man could have caught up. Woulda had a chance. Woulda sneaked up behind him the Greater Man would have sneaked up behind the Lesser Known unbeknownst and wrestled him to the ground. Stabbed him in the back. In revenge. "Thus to the tyrants!" Shot him maybe. The Lesser Known forgets who he is and just crumples. His bones cannot be found. The Greater Man continues on.

(*rest*)

"*Emergency*, oh *Emergency*, please put the Great Man in the ground".

(*rest*)

Only a little ringing in the ears. Thats all. Slight deafness.

(*rest*)

Huh. Whatdoyou say I wear the blonde.

(*rest*)
(*A gunshot echoes. Softly. And echoes*)

Act Two: The Hall of Wonders

(*A gunshot echoes. Loudly. And echoes.*)
(*They are in a great hole. In the middle of nowhere. The hole is an exact replica of The Great Hole of History.*)
(*A gunshot echoes. Loudly. And echoes. Lucy with ear trumpet circulates. Brazil digs.*)

A. BIG BANG

LUCY: Hear that?

BRAZIL: Zit him?

LUCY: No.

BRAZIL: Oh.

(*A gunshot echoes. Loudly. And echoes*)

LUCY: Hear?

BRAZIL: Zit him?!

LUCY: Nope. Ssuhecho.

BRAZIL: Ssuhecho.

LUCY: Uh echo uh huhn. Of gunplay. Once upon uh time somebody had uh little gunplay and now thuh gun goes on playing: *KER-BANG!* KERBANG-Kerbang-kerbang-(kerbang)-((kerbang)).

BRAZIL: Thuh echoes.

(*rest*)
(*rest*)

LUCY: Youre stopped.

BRAZIL: Mmlistenin.

LUCY: Dig on, Brazil. Cant stop diggin till you dig up somethin. Your Daddy was uh Digger.

BRAZIL: Uh huhnnn.

LUCY

BRAZIL

(*A gunshot echoes. Loudly. And echoes. Rest. A gunshot echoes. Loudly. And echoes. Rest*)

[LUCY: Itssalways been important in my line to distinguish. Tuh know thuh difference. Not like your Fathuh. Your Fathuh became confused.

His lonely death and lack of proper burial is our embarrassment. Go on: dig. Now me I need tuh know thuh real thing from thuh echo. Thuh truth from thuh hearsay.

(*rest*)

Bram Price for example. His dear ones and relations told me his dying words but Bram Price hisself of course told me something quite different.

BRAZIL: I wept forim.

LUCY: Whispered his true secrets to me and to me uhlone.

BRAZIL: Then he died.

LUCY: Then he died.

(*rest*)

Thuh things he told me I will never tell. Mr Bram Price. Huh.

(*rest*)

Dig on.

BRAZIL

LUCY

BRAZIL

LUCY: Little Bram Price Junior.

BRAZIL: Thuh fat one?

LUCY: Burned my eardrums. Just like his Dad did.

BRAZIL: I wailed forim.

LUCY: Ten days dead wept over and buried and that boy comes back. Not him though. His echo. Sits down tuh dinner and eats up everybodys food just like he did when he was livin.

(*rest*)
(*rest*)

Little Bram Junior. Burned my eardrums. Miz Penny Price his mother. Thuh things she told me I will never tell.

(*rest*)

You remember her.

BRAZIL: Wore red velvet in August.

LUCY: When her 2 Brams passed she sold herself, son.

BRAZIL: O.

LUCY: Also lost her mind. – . She finally went. Like your Fathuh went, perhaps. Foul play.

BRAZIL: I gnashed for her.

LUCY: You did.

BRAZIL: Couldnt choose between wailin or gnashin. Weepin sobbin or moanin. Went for gnashing. More to it. Gnashed for her and hers like I have never gnashed. I woulda tore at my coat but thats extra. Chipped uh tooth. One in thuh front.

LUCY: You did your job son.

BRAZIL: I did my job.

LUCY: Confidence. Huh. Thuh things she told me I will never tell. Miz Penny Price. Miz Penny Price.

(*rest*)

Youre stopped.

BRAZIL: Mmlistenin.

LUCY: Dig on, Brazil.

BRAZIL

LUCY

BRAZIL: We arent from these parts.

LUCY: No. We're not.

BRAZIL: Daddy iduhnt either.

LUCY: Your Daddy iduhnt either.

(*rest*)

Dig on, son. – . Cant stop diggin till you dig up somethin. You dig that something up you brush that something off you give that something uh designated place. Its own place. Along with thuh other discoveries. In thuh Hall of Wonders. Uh place in the Hall of Wonders right uhlong with thuh rest of thuh Wonders hear?

BRAZIL: Uh huhn.

(*rest*)

LUCY: Bram Price Senior, son. Bram Price Senior was not thuh man he claimed tuh be. Huh. Nope. Was not thuh man he claimed tuh be atall. You ever see him in his stocking feet? Or barefoot? Course not. I guessed before he told me. He told me then he died. He told me and I havent told no one. I'm uh good Confidence. As Confidences go. Huh. One of thuh best. As Confidence, mmonly contracted tuh keep quiet 12 years. After 12 years nobody cares. For 19 years I have kept his secret. In my bosom.

(*rest*)

He wore lifts in his shoes, son.

BRAZIL: Lifts?

LUCY: Lifts. Made him seem taller than he was.

BRAZIL: Bram Price Senior?

LUCY: Bram Price Senior wore lifts in his shoes yes he did, Brazil. I tell you just as he told me with his last breaths on his dying bed: "Lifts". Thats all he said. Then he died. I put thuh puzzle pieces in place. I put thuh puzzle pieces in place. Couldnt tell no one though. Not even your Pa. "Lifts". I never told no one son. For 19 years I have kept Brams secret in my bosom. Youre thuh first tuh know. Hhh! Dig on. Dig on.

BRAZIL: Dig on.

LUCY

BRAZIL

LUCY

(*A gunshot echoes. Loudly. And echoes*)

BRAZIL: (*rest*) Ff Pa was here weud find his bones.

LUCY: Not always.

BRAZIL: Thereud be his bones and thereud be thuh Wonders surrounding his bones.

LUCY: Ive heard of different.

BRAZIL: Thereud be thuh Wonders surrounding his bones and thereud be his Whispers.

LUCY: Maybe.

BRAZIL: Ffhe sspast like they say he'd of parlayed to uh Confidence his last words and dying wishes. His secrets and his dreams.

LUCY: Thats how we pass back East. They could pass different out here.

BRAZIL: We got Daddys ways Daddyssgot ours. When theres no Confidence available we just dribble thuh words out. In uh whisper.

LUCY: Sometimes.

BRAZIL: Thuh Confidencell gather up thuh whispers when she arrives.

LUCY: Youre uh prize, Brazil. Uh prize.]

BRAZIL

LUCY

BRAZIL

LUCY

BRAZIL

LUCY

BRAZIL: You hear him then? His whispers?

LUCY: Not exactly.

BRAZIL: He wuduhnt here then.

LUCY: He was here.

BRAZIL: Ffyou dont hear his whispers he wuduhnt here.

LUCY: Whispers dont always come up right away. Takes time sometimes. Whispers could travel different out West than they do back East. Maybe slower. Maybe. Whispers are secrets and often shy. We aint seen your Pa in 30 years. That could be part of it. We also could be experiencing some sort of interference. Or some sort of technical difficulty. Ssard tuh tell.

(*rest*)

So much to live for.

BRAZIL: So much to live for.

LUCY: Look on thuh bright side.

BRAZIL: Look on thuh bright side. Look on thuh bright side. Look onnnnn thuhhhh briiiiiiiight siiiiiiiiide!!!!

LUCY: DIIIIIIIIIIIG!

BRAZIL: Dig.

LUCY

BRAZIL

LUCY: Helloooo! – . Hellooooo!

BRAZIL

LUCY

BRAZIL: [We're from out East. We're not from these parts.

(*rest*)

My foe-father, her husband, my Daddy, her mate, her man, my Pa come out here. Out West.

(*rest*)

Come out here all uhlone. Cleared thuh path tamed thuh wilderness dug this whole Hole with his own 2 hands and et cetera.

(*rest*)

Left his family behind. Back East. His Lucy and his child. He waved "Goodbye". Left us tuh carry on. I was only 5.

(*rest*)

My Daddy was uh Digger. Shes whatcha call uh Confidence. I did thuh weepin and thuh moanin.

(*rest*)

His lonely death and lack of proper burial is our embarrassment.

(*rest*)

Diggin was his livelihood but fakin was his callin. Ssonly natural heud come out here and combine thuh 2. Back East he was always diggin. He was uh natural. Could dig uh hole for uh body that passed like no one else. Digged em quick and they looked good too. This Hole here – this large one – sshis biggest venture to date. So says hearsay.

(*rest*)

Uh exact replica of thuh Great Hole of History!

LUCY: Sshhhhhht.

BRAZIL: (*rest*) Thuh original ssback East. He and Lucy they honeymooned there. At thuh original Great Hole. Its uh popular spot. He and Her would sit on thuh lip and watch everybody who was ever anybody parade on by. Daily parades! Just like thuh Tee Vee. Mr George Washington, for example, thuh Fathuh of our Country hisself, would rise up from thuh dead and walk uhround and cross thuh Delaware and say stuff!! Right before their very eyes!!!!

LUCY: Son?

BRAZIL: Huh?

LUCY: That iduhnt how it went.

BRAZIL: Oh.

LUCY: Thuh Mr Washington me and your Daddy seen was uh lookuhlike of thuh Mr Washington of history-fame, son.

BRAZIL: Oh.

LUCY: Thuh original Mr Washingtonssbeen long dead.

BRAZIL: O.

LUCY: That Hole back East was uh theme park son. Keep your story to scale.

BRAZIL: K.

(*rest*)

Him and Her would sit by thuh lip uhlong with thuh others all in uh row cameras clickin and theyud look down into that Hole and see – ooooo – you name it. Ever-y-day you could look down that Hole and see – ooooo you name it. Amerigo Vespucci hisself made regular appearances. Marcus Garvey. Ferdinand and Isabella. Mary Queen of thuh Scots! Tarzan King of thuh Apes! Washington Jefferson Harding and Millard Fillmore. Mistufer Columbus even. Oh they saw all thuh greats. Parading daily in thuh Great Hole of History.

(*rest*)

My Fathuh did thuh living and thuh dead. Small-town and big-time. Mr Lincoln was of course his favorite.

(*rest*)

Not only Mr Lincoln but Mr Lincolns last show. His last deeds. His last laughs.

(*rest*)

Being uh Digger of some renown Daddy comes out here tuh build uh like attraction. So says hearsay. Figures theres people out here who'll enjoy amusements such as them amusements. He and Her enjoyed. We're all citizens of one country afterall.

(*rest*)

Mmrestin.

(*A gunshot echoes. Loudly. And echoes*)

BRAZIL: Woooo! (*drops dead*)

LUCY: Youre fakin Mr Brazil.

BRAZIL: Uh uhnnn.

LUCY: Tryin tuh get you some benefits.

BRAZIL: Uh uhnnnnnnnn.

LUCY: I know me uh faker when I see one. Your Father was uh faker.

Huh. One of thuh best. There wuduhnt nobody your Fathuh couldnt do. Did thuh living and thuh dead. Small-town and big-time. Made-up and historical. Fakin was your Daddys callin but diggin was his livelihood. Oh, back East he was always diggin. Was uh natural. Could dig uh hole for uh body that passed like no one else. Digged em quick and they looked good too. You dont remember of course you dont.

BRAZIL: I was only 5.

LUCY: You were only 5. When your Fathuh spoke he'd quote thuh Greats. Mister George Washington. Thuh Misters Roosevelt. Mister Millard Fillmore. Huh. All thuh greats. You dont remember of course you dont.

BRAZIL: I was only 5 –.

LUCY: – only 5. Mr Lincoln was of course your Fathuhs favorite. Wuz. Huh. Wuz. Huh. Heresay says he's past. Your Daddy. Digged this hole then he died. So says hearsay.

(*rest*)

Dig, Brazil.

BRAZIL: My paw –

LUCY: Ssonly natural that heud come out here tuh dig out one of his own. He loved that Great Hole so. He'd stand at thuh lip of that Great Hole: "OHWAYOHWHYOHWAYOH!"

BRAZIL: "OHWAYOHWHYOHWAYOH!"

LUCY: "OHWAYOHWHYOHWAYOH!" You know: hole talk. Ohway-ohwhyohwayoh, just tuh get their attention, then: "Hellooo!" He'd shout down to em. Theyd call back "Helllllooooo!" and wave. He loved that Great Hole so. Came out here. Digged this lookuhlike.

BRAZIL: Then he died?

LUCY: Then he died. Your Daddy died right here. Huh. Oh, he was uh faker. Uh greaaaaat biiiiig faker too. He was your Fathuh. Thats thuh connection. You take after him.

BRAZIL: I do?

LUCY: Sure. Put your paw back where it belongs. Go on – back on its stump. – . Poke it on out of your sleeve son. There you go. I'll draw uh X for you. See? Heresuh X. Huh. Dig here.

(*rest*)

DIG!

BRAZIL

LUCY

BRAZIL

LUCY: Woah! Woah!

BRAZIL: Whatchaheard?!

LUCY: No tellin, son. Cant say.

(*Brazil digs. Lucy circulates*)

BRAZIL: (*Rest. Rest*) On thuh day he claimed to be the 100th anniversary of the founding of our country the Father took the Son out into the yard. The Father threw himself down in front of the Son and bit into the dirt with his teeth. His eyes leaked. "This is how youll make your mark, Son" the Father said. The Son was only 2 then. "This is the Wail", the Father said. "There's money init", the Father said. The Son was only 2 then. Quiet. On what he claimed was the 101st anniversary the Father showed the Son "the Weep" "the Sob" and "the Moan". How to stand just so what to do with the hands and feet (to capitalize on what we in the business call "the Mourning Moment"). Formal stances the Fatherd picked up at the History Hole. The Son studied night and day. By candlelight. No one could best him. The money came pouring in. On the 102nd anniversary[15] the Son was 5 and the Father taught him "the Gnash". The day after that the Father left for out West. To seek his fortune. In the middle of dinnertime. The Son was eating his peas.

LUCY

BRAZIL

LUCY

BRAZIL

LUCY: Hellooooo! Hellooooo!

(*rest*)

BRAZIL

LUCY

BRAZIL: HO! (*unearths something*)

LUCY: Whatcha got?

BRAZIL: Uh Wonder!

LUCY: Uh Wonder!

BRAZIL: Uh Wonder: Ho!

LUCY: Dust it off and put it over with thuh rest of thuh Wonders.

BRAZIL: Uh bust.

LUCY: Whose?

BRAZIL: Says "A. Lincoln". A. Lincolns bust. – . Abraham Lincolns bust!!!

LUCY: Howuhboutthat!

(*rest*)
(*rest*)

    Woah! Woah!

BRAZIL: Whatchaheard?

LUCY: Uh – . Cant say.

BRAZIL: Whatchaheard?!!

LUCY: SSShhhhhhhhhhhhhhhhhht!

(*rest*)

    dig!

B. ECHO

THE FOUNDLING FATHER: Ladies and Gentlemen: *Our American Cousin*, Act III, scene 5:

MR TRENCHARD: Have you found it?

MISS KEENE: I find no trace of it. (*discovering*) What is this?!

MR TRENCHARD: This is the place where father kept all the old deeds.

MISS KEENE: Oh my poor muddled brain! What can this mean?!

MR TRENCHARD: (*with difficulty*) I cannot survive the downfall of my house but choose instead to end my life with a pistol to my head!

(*applause*)

THE FOUNDLING FATHER: OHWAYOHWHYOHWAYOH!

(*rest*)
(*rest*)

    Hellloooooooo!

(*rest*)

Hellloooooooo!

(*Rest. Waves*)

C. ARCHEOLOGY

BRAZIL: You hear im?

LUCY: Echo of thuh first sort: thuh sound. (E.g. thuh gunplay.)

(*rest*)

> Echo of thuh 2nd sort: thuh words. Type A: thuh words from thuh dead. Category: Unrelated.

(*rest*)

> Echo of thuh 2nd sort, Type B: words less fortunate: thuh Disembodied Voice. Also known as "Thuh Whispers". Category: Related. Like your Fathuhs.

(*rest*)

> Echo of thuh 3rd sort: thuh body itself.

(*rest*)

BRAZIL: You hear im.

LUCY: Cant say. Cant say, son.

BRAZIL: My faux-father. Thuh one who comed out here before us. Thuh one who left us behind. Tuh come out here all uhlone. Tuh do his bit. All them who comed before us – my Daddy. He's one of them.

LUCY

(*rest*)
(*rest*)

BRAZIL: He's one of them. All of them who comed before us – my Daddy.

(*rest*)

> I'd say thuh creation of thuh world must uh been just like thuh clearing off of this plot. Just like him diggin his Hole. I'd say. Must uh been just as dug up. And unfair.

(*rest*)

> Peoples (or thuh what-was), just had tuh hit thuh road. In thuh beginning there was one of those voids here and then "bang" and then *voilà*! And here we is.

(*rest*)

> But where did those voids that was here before *we* was here go off to? Hmmm. In thuh beginning there were some of them voids here and then: KERBANG-KERBLAMMO! And now it all belongs tuh us.

LUCY

(*rest*)
(*rest*)

BRAZIL: This Hole is our inheritance of sorts. My Daddy died and left it to me and Her. And when She goes, Shes gonna give it all to me!!

LUCY: Dig, son.

BRAZIL: I'd rather dust and polish. (*puts something on*)

LUCY: Dust and polish then. – . You dont got tuh put on that tuh do it.

BRAZIL: It helps. Uh Hehm. *Uh Hehm.* WELCOME WELCOME WELCOME TUH THUH HALL OF –

LUCY: Sssht.

BRAZIL

LUCY

BRAZIL

LUCY

BRAZIL

LUCY

BRAZIL

LUCY

BRAZIL: (welcome welcome welcome to thuh hall. of. wonnndersss: To our right A Jewel Box made of cherry wood, lined in velvet, letters "A. L." carved in gold on thuh lid: the jewels have long escaped. Over here one of Mr Washingtons bones, right pointer so they say; here is his likeness and here: his wooden teeth. Yes, uh top and bottom pair of nibblers: nibblers, lookin for uh meal. Nibblin. I iduhnt your lunch. Quit nibblin. Quit that nibblin you. Quit that nibblin you nibblers you nibblin nibblers you.)

LUCY: Keep it tuh scale.

BRAZIL: (Over here our newest Wonder: uh bust of Mr Lincoln carved of marble lookin like he looked in life. Right heress thuh bit from thuh mouth of thuh mount on which some great Someone rode tuh thuh rescue. This is all thats left. Uh glass tradin bead – one of thuh first. Here are thuh lick-ed boots. Here, uh dried scrap of whales blubber. Uh petrified scrap of uh great blubberer, servin to remind us that once this land was covered with sea. And blubberers were Kings. In this area here are several documents: peace pacts, writs, bills of sale, treaties, notices, handbills and circulars, freein papers, summonses, declarations of war, addresses, title deeds, obits, long lists of dids. And thuh medals: for bravery and honesty; for trustworthiness and for standing straight; for standing tall; for standing still. For advancing and retreating. For makin do. For skills in whittlin, for skills in painting and drawing, for uh knowledge of sewin, of handicrafts and building things, for leather tannin, blacksmithery, lacemakin, horseback riding, swimmin, croquet and badminton. Community Service. For cookin and for cleanin. For bowin and scrapin, Uh medal for fakin? Huh. This could uh been his. Zsis his? This is his! This is his!!!

LUCY: Keep it tuh scale, Brazil.

BRAZIL: This could be his!

LUCY: May well be.

BRAZIL: (*rest*) Whaddyahear?

LUCY: Bits and pieces.

BRAZIL: This could be his.

LUCY: Could well be.

BRAZIL: (*rest. rest*) waaaaaahhhhhhhhHHHHHHHHHHHHHH! HUH HEE HUH HEE HUH HEE HUH.

LUCY: There there, Brazil. Dont weep.

BRAZIL: WAHHHHHHHHHHH! – imissim – WAHHHHHHHHHHHH!

LUCY: It is an honor to be of his line. He cleared this plot for us. He was uh Digger.

BRAZIL: Huh huh huh. Uh Digger.

LUCY: Mr Lincoln was his favorite.

BRAZIL: I was only 5.

LUCY: He dug this whole Hole.

BRAZIL: Sssnuch. This whole Hole.

LUCY: This whole Hole.

(*rest*)

BRAZIL

LUCY

BRAZIL

LUCY

BRAZIL

LUCY:

>I couldnt never deny him nothin.
>I gived intuh him on everything.
>Thuh moon. Thuh stars.
>Thuh bees knees. Thuh cats pyjamas.

(*rest*)

BRAZIL

LUCY

BRAZIL: Anything?

LUCY: Stories too horrible tuh mention.

BRAZIL: His stories?

LUCY: Nope.

(*rest*)

BRAZIL

LUCY

BRAZIL

LUCY

BRAZIL: Mama Lucy?

LUCY: Whut.

BRAZIL: – Imissim – .

LUCY: Hhh. ((dig.))

D. ECHO

THE FOUNDLING FATHER: Ladies and Gentlemen: *Our American Cousin*, Act III, scene 2:

MR TRENCHARD: You crave affection, *you* do. Now I've no fortune, but I'm biling over with affections, which I'm ready to pour out to all of you, like apple sass over roast pork.

AUGUSTA: Sir, your American talk do woo me.

THE FOUNDLING FATHER: (*as Mrs Mount*) Mr Trenchard, you will please recollect you are addressing my daughter and in my presence.

MR TRENCHARD: Yes, I'm offering her my heart and hand just as she wants them, with nothing in 'em.

THE FOUNDLING FATHER: (*as Mrs Mount*) Augusta dear, to your room.

AUGUSTA: Yes, Ma, the nasty beast.

THE FOUNDLING FATHER: (*as Mrs Mount*) I am aware, Mr Trenchard, that you are not used to the manners of good society, and that, alone, will excuse the impertinence of which you have been guilty.

MR TRENCHARD: Don't know the manners of good society, eh? Wal, I guess I know enough to turn you inside out, old gal – you sockdologizing old man-trap.

(*Laughter. Applause*)

THE FOUNDLING FATHER: Thanks. Thanks so much. Snyder has always been a very special very favorite town uh mine. Thank you thank you so very much. Loverly loverly evening loverly tuh be here loverly tuh be here with you with all of you thank you very much.

(*rest*)

Uh Hehm. I *only* do thuh greats.

(*rest*)

A crowd pleaser: 4score and 7 years ago our fathers brought forth upon this continent a new nation conceived in Liberty and dedicated to the proposition that all men are created equal!

(*applause*)

Observe!: Indiana? Indianapolis. Louisiana? Baton Rouge. Concord? New Hampshire. Pierre? South Dakota. Honolulu? Hawaii. Springfield? Illinois. Frankfort? Kentucky. Lincoln? Nebraska. Ha! Lickety split!

(*applause*)

And now, the centerpiece of the evening!!

(*rest*)

Uh Hehm. The Death of Lincoln!: – . The watching of the play, the laughter, the smiles of Lincoln and Mary Todd, the slipping of Booth into the presidential box unseen, the freeing of the slaves, the pulling of the trigger, the bullets piercing above the left ear, the bullets entrance into the great head, the bullets lodging behind the great right eye, the slumping of Lincoln, the leaping onto the stage of Booth, the screaming of Todd, the screaming of Todd, the screaming of Keene, the leaping onto the stage of Booth; the screaming of Todd, the screaming of Keene, the shouting of Booth "Thus to the tyrants!", the death of Lincoln! – And the silence of the nation.

(*rest*)

> Yes. – . The year was way back when. The place: our nations capitol. 4score, back in the olden days, and Mr Lincolns great head. The the-a-ter was "Fords". The wife "Mary Todd". Thuh freeing of the slaves and thuh great black hole that thuh fatal bullet bored. And how that great head was bleedin. Thuh body stretched crossways acrosst thuh bed. Thuh last words. Thuh last breaths. And how thuh nation mourned.

(*applause*)

E. SPADEWORK

LUCY: Thats uh hard nut tuh crack uh hard nut tuh crack indeed.

BRAZIL: Alaska – ?

LUCY: Thats uh hard nut tuh crack. Thats uh hard nut tuh crack indeed. – . Huh. Juneau.

BRAZIL: Good!

LUCY: Go uhgain.

BRAZIL: – . Texas?

LUCY: – . Austin. Wyoming?

BRAZIL: – . – . Cheyenne. Florida?

LUCY: Tallahassee.

(*rest*)

> Ohio.

BRAZIL: Oh. Uh. Well: Columbus. Louisiana?

LUCY: Baton Rouge. Arkansas.

BRAZIL: Little Rock. Jackson.

LUCY: Mississippi. Spell it.

BRAZIL: M-i-s-s-i-s-s-i-p-p-i!

LUCY: Huh. Youre good. Montgomery.

BRAZIL: Alabama.

LUCY: Topeka.

BRAZIL: Kansas?

LUCY: Kansas.

BRAZIL: Boise, Idaho?

LUCY: Boise, Idaho.

BRAZIL: Huh. Nebraska.

LUCY: Nebraska. Lincoln.

(*rest*)

Thuh year was way back when. Thuh place: our nations capitol.

(*rest*)

Your Fathuh couldnt get that story out of his head: Mr Lincolns great head. And thuh hole thuh fatal bullet bored. How that great head was bleedin. Thuh body stretched crossways acrosst thuh bed. Thuh last words. Thuh last breaths. And how thuh nation mourned. Huh. Changed your Fathuhs life.

(*rest*)

Couldnt get that story out of his head. Whuduhnt my favorite page from thuh book of Mr Lincolns life, me myself now I prefer thuh part where he gets married to Mary Todd and she begins to lose her mind (and then of course where he frees all thuh slaves) but shoot, he couldnt get that story out of his head. Hhh. Changed his life.

(*rest*)

BRAZIL: (wahhhhhhhh –)

LUCY: There there, Brazil.

BRAZIL: (wahhhhhh –)

LUCY: Dont weep. Got somethin for ya.

BRAZIL: (o)?

LUCY: Spade. – . Dont scrunch up your face like that, son. go on. Take it.

BRAZIL: Spade?

LUCY: Spade. He woulda wanted you tuh have it.

BRAZIL: Daddys diggin spade? Ssnnuch.

LUCY: I swannee you look more and more and more and more like him ever-y day.

BRAZIL: His chin?

LUCY: You got his chin.

BRAZIL: His lips?

LUCY: You got his lips.

BRAZIL: His teeths?

LUCY: Top and bottom. In his youth. He had some. Just like yours. His frock coat. Was just like that. He had hisself uh stovepipe hat which you lack. His medals – yours are for weepin his of course were for diggin.

BRAZIL: And I got his spade.

LUCY: And now you got his spade.

BRAZIL: We could say I'm his spittin image.

LUCY: We could say that.

BRAZIL: We could say I just may follow in thuh footsteps of my foe-father.

LUCY: We could say that.

BRAZIL: Look on thuh bright side!

LUCY: Look on thuh bright side!

BRAZIL: So much tuh live for!

LUCY: So much tuh live for! Sweet land of – ! Sweet land of – ?

BRAZIL: Of liberty!

LUCY: Of liberty! Thats it thats it and "*Woah*!" Lets say I hear his words!

BRAZIL: And you could say?

LUCY: And I could say.

BRAZIL: Lets say you hear his words!

LUCY: *Woah*!

BRAZIL: Whatwouldhesay?!

LUCY: He'd say: "Hello". He'd say. – . "Hope you like your spade".

BRAZIL: Tell him I do.

LUCY: He'd say: "My how youve grown!" He'd say: "Hows your weepin?" He'd say: – Ha! He's running through his states and capitals! Licketysplit!

BRAZIL: Howuhboutthat!

LUCY: He'd say: "Uh house divided cannot stand!" He'd say: "4score and 7 years uhgoh". Say: "Of thuh people by thuh people and for thuh people". Say: "Malice toward none and charity toward all". Say: "Cheat some of thuh people some of thuh time". He'd say: (and this is only to be spoken between you and me and him –)

BRAZIL: K.

LUCY: Lean in. Ssfor our ears and our ears uhlone.

(*rest*)

BRAZIL: O.

LUCY: Howuhboutthat. And here he comes. Striding on in striding on in and he surveys thuh situation. And he nods tuh what we found cause he knows his Wonders. And he smiles. And he tells us of his doins all these years. And he does his Mr Lincoln for us. Uh great page from thuh great mans great life! And you n me llsmile, cause then, we'll know, more or less, exactly where he is.

(*rest*)

BRAZIL: Lucy? Where is he?

LUCY: Lincoln?

BRAZIL: Papa.

LUCY: Close by, I guess. Huh. Dig.

(*Brazil digs. Times passes*)

Youre uh Digger. Youre uh Digger. Your Daddy was uh Digger and so are you.

BRAZIL: Ho!

LUCY: I couldnt never deny him nothin.

BRAZIL: Wonder: Ho! Wonder: Ho!

LUCY: I gived intuh him on everything.

BRAZIL: Ssuhtrumpet.

LUCY: Gived intuh him on everything.

BRAZIL: Ssuhtrumpet, Lucy.

LUCY: Howboutthat.

BRAZIL: Try it out.

LUCY: How uh-bout that.

BRAZIL: Anythin?

LUCY: Cant say, son. Cant say.

(*rest*)

I couldnt never deny him nothin.
I gived intuh him on everything.
Thuh moon. Thuh stars.

BRAZIL: Ho!

LUCY: Thuh bees knees. Thuh cats pyjamas.

BRAZIL: Wonder: Ho! Wonder: Ho!

(*rest*)

Howuhboutthat: Uh bag of pennies. Money, Lucy.

LUCY: Howuhboutthat.

(*rest*)

Thuh bees knees.
Thuh cats pyjamas.
Thuh best cuts of mean.
My baby teeth.

BRAZIL: Wonder: Ho! Wonder: HO!

LUCY:

Thuh apron from uhround my waist.
Thuh hair from off my head.

BRAZIL: Huh. Yellow fur.

LUCY: My mores and my folkways.

BRAZIL: Oh. Uh beard. Howuhboutthat.

(*rest*)

LUCY: WOAH. WOAH!

BRAZIL: Whatchaheard?

LUCY

(*rest*)
(*rest*)

BRAZIL: Whatchaheard?!

LUCY: You dont wanna know.

BRAZIL

LUCY

BRAZIL

LUCY

BRAZIL: Wonder: Ho! Wonder: HO! WONDER: HO!

LUCY:

Thuh apron from uhround my waist.
Thuh hair from off my head.

BRAZIL: Huh: uh Tee-Vee.

LUCY: Huh.

BRAZIL: I'll hold ontooit for uh minit.

(*rest*)

LUCY:
> Thuh apron from uhround my waist.
> Thuh hair from off my head.
> My mores and my folkways.
> My rock and my foundation.

BRAZIL

LUCY

BRAZIL

LUCY: My re-memberies – you know – thuh stuff out of my head.

(*The TV comes on. The Foundling Father's face appears*)

BRAZIL: (ho! ho! wonder: ho!)

LUCY:
> My spare buttons in their envelopes.
> Thuh leftovers from all my unmade meals.
> Thuh letter R.
> Thuh key of G.

BRAZIL: (ho! ho! wonder: ho!)

LUCY:
> All my good jokes. All my jokes that fell flat.
> Thuh way I walked, cause you liked it so much.
> All my winnin dance steps.
> My teeth when yours runned out.
> My smile.

BRAZIL: (ho! ho! wonder: ho!)

LUCY: Sssssht.

(*rest*)

> Well. Its him.

F. ECHO

(*A gunshot echoes. Loudly. And echoes.*)

G. THE GREAT BEYOND

(Lucy and Brazil watch the TV: a replay of "The Lincoln Act". The Foundling Father has returned. His coffin awaits him.)

LUCY: Howuhboutthat!

BRAZIL: They just gunned him down uhgain.

LUCY: Howuhboutthat.

BRAZIL: He's dead but not really.

LUCY: Howuhboutthat.

BRAZIL: Only fakin. Only fakin. See? Hesupuhgain.

LUCY: What-izzysayin?

BRAZIL: Sound duhnt work.

LUCY: Zat right.

(rest)

THE FOUNDLING FATHER: I believe this is the place where I do the Gettysburg Address, I believe.

BRAZIL

THE FOUNDLING FATHER

LUCY

BRAZIL: Woah!

LUCY: Howuhboutthat.

BRAZIL: Huh. Well.

(rest)

  Huh. Zit him?

LUCY: Its him.

BRAZIL: He's dead?

LUCY: He's dead.

BRAZIL: Howuhboutthat.

(rest)

  Shit.

LUCY

BRAZIL

LUCY

BRAZIL: Mail the in-vites?

LUCY: I did.

BRAZIL: Think theyll come?

LUCY: I do. There are hundreds upon thousands who knew of your Daddy, glorified his reputation, and would like to pay their respects.

THE FOUNDLING FATHER: Howuhboutthat.

BRAZIL: Howuhboutthat!

LUCY: Turn that off, son.

(*rest*)

You gonna get in now or later?

THE FOUNDLING FATHER: I'd like tuh wait uhwhile.

LUCY: Youd like tuh wait uhwhile.

BRAZIL: Mmgonna gnash for you. You know: teeth in thuh dirt, hands like this, then jump up rip my clothes up, you know, you know go all out.

THE FOUNDLING FATHER: Howuhboutthat. Open casket or closed?

LUCY: – . Closed.

(*rest*)

Turn that off, son.

BRAZIL: K.

THE FOUNDLING FATHER: Hug me.

BRAZIL: Not yet.

THE FOUNDLING FATHER: You?

LUCY: Gimmieuhminute.

(*A gunshot echoes. Loudly. And echoes.*)

LUCY

BRAZIL

THE FOUNDLING FATHER

LUCY

BRAZIL

THE FOUNDLING FATHER

LUCY: That gunplay. Wierdiduhntit. Comes. And goze.

(*They ready his coffin. He inspects it*)

At thuh Great Hole where we honeymooned – son, at thuh Original Great Hole, you could see thuh whole world without goin too far. You could look intuh that Hole and see your entire life pass before you. Not your own life but someones life from history, you know, [someone who'd done somethin of note, got theirselves known somehow, uh President or] somebody who killed somebody important, uh face on uh postal stamp, you know, someone from History. *Like* you, but *not* you. You know: *Known.*

THE FOUNDLING FATHER: "*Emergency*, oh, *Emergency*, please put the Great Man in the ground".

LUCY: Go on. Get in. Try it out. Ssnot so bad. See? Sstight, but private. Bought on time but we'll manage. And you got enough height for your hat.

(*rest*)

THE FOUNDLING FATHER: Hug me.

LUCY: Not yet.

THE FOUNDLING FATHER: You?

BRAZIL: Gimmieuhminute.

(*rest*)

LUCY: He loved that Great Hole so. Came out here. Digged this lookuhlike.

BRAZIL: Then he died?

LUCY: Then he died.

THE FOUNDLING FATHER

BRAZIL

LUCY

THE FOUNDLING FATHER

BRAZIL

LUCY

THE FOUNDLING FATHER: A monumentous occasion. I'd like to say a few words from the grave. Maybe a little conversation: Such a long story. Uhhem. I quit the business. And buried all my things. I dropped anchor: Bottomless. Your turn.

Plate 29: The Foundling Father (Reggie Montgomery) in Parks' *The America Play* exhibits his likeness to Abraham Lincoln. From the 1993 staging at Yale Repertory Theatre, directed by Liz Diamond. Photo by T. Charles Erickson.

LUCY

BRAZIL

THE FOUNDLING FATHER

LUCY: (*rest*) Do your Lincoln for im.

THE FOUNDLING FATHER: Yeah?

LUCY: He was only 5.

THE FOUNDLING FATHER: Only 5. *Uh Hehm.* So very loverly to be here so very very loverly to be here the town of – Wonderville has always been a special favorite of mine always has been a very very special favorite of mine. Now, I *only* do thuh greats. Uh hehm: I was born in a log cabin of humble parentage. But I picked up uh few things. Uh Hehm: 4score and 7 years ago our fathers – ah you know thuh rest. Lets see now. Yes. Uh house divided cannot stand! You can fool some of thuh people some of thuh time! Of thuh people by thuh people and for thuh people! Malice toward none and charity toward all! Ha! The Death of Lincoln! (Highlights): Haw Haw Haw Haw

(*rest*)

HAW HAW HAW HAW

(*A gunshot echoes. Loudly. And echoes. The Foundling Father "slumps in his chair"*)

THE FOUNDLING FATHER

LUCY

BRAZIL

LUCY

THE FOUNDLING FATHER

BRAZIL: [Izzy dead?

LUCY: Mmlistenin.

BRAZIL: Anything?

LUCY: Nothin.

BRAZIL: (*rest*) As a child it was her luck tuh be in thuh same room with her Uncle when he died. Her family wanted to know what he had said. What his last words had been. Theyre hadnt been any. Only screaming. Or, you know, breath. Didnt have uh shape to it. Her family thought she was holding on to thuh words. For safekeeping. And they proclaimed thuh girl uh Confidence. At the age of 8. Sworn tuh secrecy. She picked up thuh tricks of thuh trade as she went uhlong.]

(*rest*)

Should I gnash now?

LUCY: Better save it for thuh guests. I guess.

(*rest*)

Well. Dust and polish, son. I'll circulate.

BRAZIL: Welcome Welcome Welcome to thuh hall. Of. Wonders.

(*rest*)

To our right A Jewel Box of cherry wood, lined in velvet, letters "A.L." carved in gold on thuh lid. Over here one of Mr Washingtons bones and here: his wooden teeth. Over here: uh bust of Mr Lincoln carved of marble lookin like he looked in life. – More or less. And thuh medals: for bravery and honesty; for trustworthiness and for standing straight; for standing tall; for standing still. For advancing and retreating. For makin do. For skills in whittlin, for skills in painting and drawing, for uh knowledge of sewin, of handicrafts and building things, for leather tannin, blacksmithery, lacemakin, horseback riding, swimmin, croquet and badminton. Community Service. For cookin and for cleanin. For bowin and scrapin. Uh medal for fakin.

(*rest*)

To my right: our newest Wonder: One of thuh greats Hisself! Note: thuh body sitting propped upright in our great Hole. Note the large mouth opened wide. Note the top hat and frock coat, just like the greats. Note the death wound: thuh great black hole – thuh great black hole in thuh great head. – And how this great head is bleedin. – Note: thuh last words. – And thuh last breaths. – And how thuh nation mourns –

(*takes his leave*)

NOTES

1. An example of chiasmus, by Oliver Goldsmith, cited under "chiasmus" in *Webster's Ninth New Collegiate Dictionary* (Springfield, Massachusetts: Merriam-Webster, Inc., 1983) p. 232. Notes 2 and 3 also refer to examples of chiasmus.
2. *A Dictionary of Modern English Usage*, H.W. Fowler (New York: Oxford University Press, 1983) p. 86. The quotation is from the Gospel of Luke, 16:3.
3. *The New American Heritage Dictionary of the English Language*, William Morris, ed. (Boston: Houghton Mifflin Co., 1981) p. 232.
4. Possibly the words of Mary Todd Lincoln after the death of her husband.
5. At the end of the Civil War, President Lincoln told his troops to play "Dixie", the song of the South, in tribute to the Confederacy.
6. A very funny line from the play *Our American Cousin*. As the audience roared with laughter, Booth entered Lincoln's box and shot him dead.
7. The last words of President Lincoln's assassin, John Wilkes Booth.
8. Or "Sic semper tyrannis". Purportedly, Booth's words after he slew Lincoln and leapt from the presidential box to the stage of Ford's Theatre in Washington, D.C. on 14 April 1865, not only killing the President but also interrupting a performance of *Our American Cousin*, starring Miss Laura Keene.
9. Allegedly, Booth's words.

10. The last words of General Robert E. Lee, Commander of the Confederate Army.
11. From "The Sun", a composition by The Foundling Father, unpublished.
12. Mary Todd Lincoln, wanting her dying husband to speak to their son Tad, might have said this that night.
13. The words of Secretary of War, Edwin Stanton, as Lincoln died.
14. The words of Mary Todd, just after Lincoln was shot.
15. Hearsay.

INDEX